M000099471

SALONICA TERMINUS

Travels into the Balkan Nightmare

Fred A. Reed

Talonbooks
1996

Copyright © 1996 Fred A. Reed

Published with the assistance of the Canada Council.

Talonbooks
#104—3100 Production Way
Burnaby, British Columbia
Canada V5A 4R4

Typeset in Times and printed and bound in Canada by Hignell Printing Ltd.

First Printing: October 1996

Thanks to Princeton University Press for permission to quote from *Sabbatai Sevi, the Mystical Messiah 1626-1676* by Gershom Scholem, published under the Bollingen Series imprint, number XCII, in 1973; to Indiana University Press, for permission to quote from Hugh Poulton's *Who are the Macedonians*, 1995; to Farrar Strauss and Giroux, for permission to quote from Michael Ignatieff's *Blood and Belonging*, 1995; and to Kedros Publishers, Athens, for permission to reprint photographs from Elias Petropoulous' *Old Salonica*, 1980

No part of this book, covered by the copyright hereon, may be reproduced or used in any form or by any means—graphic, electronic or mechanical—without prior permission of the publisher, except for excerpts in a review. Any request for photocopying of any part of this book shall be directed in writing to CANCOPY (Canadian Copyright Licensing Agency), 6 Adelaide Street East, Suite 900, Toronto, Ontario, Canada, M5C 1H6, Tel.: (416) 868-1620; Fax: (416) 868-1621.

Canadian Cataloguing in Publication Data

Reed, Fred A., 1939—
Salonica Terminus

Includes bibliographical references.
ISBN 0-88922-368-8

1. Balkan Peninsula—Social conditions. 2. Balkan Peninsula—Politics and government—1989- I. Title.
HN613.5.R44 1996 949.61'039 C96-910508-8

Table of Contents

Acknowledgments

THIS BOOK would not have been possible without the contributions of many. To Sokol Kondi and to David Sherman, who read sections of the manuscript with a critical yet compassionate eye, my heartfelt thanks. I alone, however, assume responsibility for the book's errors, inevitable when the subject is as complex and multi-faceted as the Balkans.

In Montréal, André Patry and Melhem Moubarak were instrumental in setting me off on my journey, while David Homel led me, with a sure hand, into and through the antinomian precincts of Sabbatai Sevi. Gilles Gougeon, of Radio-Canada, was constant in his support, as was filmmaker Jean-Daniel Lafond. Jacques Bouchard's wise counsel and encyclopedic knowledge of Greece helped at several crucial moments. Dragenja Damjanovich's interest and enthusiasm for the project spurred me on.

A debt is due to Sandy Fainer, who helped me grasp the full complexity of the sad tale of the fall of Salonica's Jewish community. Thanks, too, to Nafsika Papanikolatou and her colleagues in the Greek human rights movement, to Dimitris Lithoxoou, and to Nikos Ziogas, for their advice and thoughtful comments; and to Dumitru Nastase who provided me with precious insight into the Vlach question.

In Thessaloniki, which was my Balkan *pied-à-terre* for three eventful months, Viki and Yannis Hassiotis opened many doors, including that of their home, to me. My gratitude as well to Professor Faidon Malingkoudis of the University of Thessaloniki, and to Xenia Kotzageorgi of the Institute of Balkan Studies, to Yanna Kambouridou, Frangiski Abatzopoulou and Lina Eligmitou, to Lela Salem, and to Fani Kazantzi and her family, to authors Elias Koutsoukos, Christos Zafiris, and Yorgos Skabardonis, to Fotis Kilipidis of the Vlach Brotherhood and to Nikos Karatzas, proprietor of Ianos Bookstore, all of whom gave generously and gracefully of their time and their knowledge.

Special thanks are due to the staff of the library of the Institute for Balkan Studies, to Traïanos Hatzidimitriou and Yannis Kourtis of *The Balkan Review*, to Albert Nar of the Salonica Jewish Community, to poet and historian Dinos Christianopoulos, to the ebullient Andonis Sourounis, who led me by the hand through the heart of his home town, and to Julie Blum for her tonic allergy to complacency in all its disguises.

My first, harrowing trip to Albania would not have been possible without the assistance of Dimitris Kokkinos, of the Greek Foundation for National Repatriation, and to the Foundation's staff in Athens and Ioannina. In Tirana, Sokol Kondi and Frok Cupi not only acted as guides, eyes and ears, but quickly became friends and confidants. The hospitality of Loreta and Ilir Cheftia was unforgettable in its generosity, while Kastriot Robo of the Albanian Foreign Ministry provided timely assistance.

In Macedonia, Ljupco Naumovski, founder of the Macedonia Information and Liaison Service, was of inestimable kindness and supreme utility. I would also like to express my gratitude to Dr. Tzvetan Grozdanov, and to several other individuals who cannot be named. Victoria Peti made my stay in Krushevo a memorable one. And no catalogue of Macedonian benefactors would be complete without Mary Dimitriou, the Macedonian connection in Toronto.

These acknowledgments would be incomplete without mention of Elias Petropoulos, indefatigable chronicler of Salonica and of the foibles of modern Greece. Sections of **Salonica Terminus** were previously published in a different form in *Le Devoir* and *La Presse*. A portion of the research and writing of this book was made possible thanks to the financial support of the Canada Council.

And finally, to Soula and Manolis Roussakis, whose lifelong friendship and encouragement made this book possible, my boundless gratitude. This book is for them.

ὄψις τε ἐμὴ καὶ γνώμη καὶ ἱστορίη

All I have said is the record of what I have seen, my own judgment and inquiry.

— *Herotodus II, 99*

FOREWORD

THIS IS A BOOK of Balkan stories. The kind of stories people tell about themselves and their neighbors. Some have the factual simplicity of tall tales; others, the tortuous and convoluted quality of verisimilitude. We should attend to the Balkans, they whisper to us, not only because the truths, lies and conflicts these stories embody may touch off another European war, but because they uncannily resemble the self-deception and illusion we take as the truth about ourselves.

With the city of Salonica as my point of departure and arrival I traveled through the southern Balkans—northern Greece, Albania, Kosova, Macedonia and Bulgaria—in the fall of 1994, and again in the spring of 1995. There I found a landscape thronged by figures bent beneath the weight of history; a human geography shaped by the claim and counterclaim of ethnic and religious identity, national consciousness, denial of the Other. Into and across this landscape have strode conquerors and tyrants, empires and federations, faiths and heresies. Some stayed; others moved on. All have left traces: sometimes indelible, sometimes as evanescent as mist. All are being swept away; all cling to the soil.

In the Balkans hope and illusion persist side by side with disillusion. Socialism has failed. Free market democracy, the late twentieth century mantra that everywhere flutters like Tibetan prayer flags in a stiff breeze, thrives in a realm ruled by post-communist confidence men, gangsters, foreign investors and international bankers.

THE GREECE I ENCOUNTERED when I stepped ashore in Piraeus in June, 1960, having been lured from my native California by the power of Nikos Kazantzakis, was a benign and peaceable kingdom. The scene could have been straight out of *Never on Sunday*. Wasn't that Melina Mercouri, leggy and lissome, swimming in the clear waters of the harbor, and Jules Dassin turning cartwheels in smoke-filled tavernas to the infectious rhythm of *bouzouki* music? It was a young man's dream: a place removed from history, fresh in its ancient newness, spontaneous, exuberant.

The scales of this and other amiable delusions slowly fell from my eyes as I learned the living tongue of the Greeks, and with it their culture and their modern history. The long process of voluntary cultural osmosis began. But there exists at the heart of every people an irreducible core which cannot be apprehended except by full surrender; by the dissolution of self, in the manner of the Sufi, in the intoxicating wine of the Beloved. Though I desired to sip deeply, I was unprepared to drain the cup.

Still, when I departed Greece for Canada three years later, I left behind a part of that self, but took with me a lucidity which distance strengthened. Postcard perfect Piraeus of 1960; Athens where the clouds were like white birds and the air after a rain was fragrant with the perfume of the soil; the island villages, cubist in their geometrical imperfection: all were vanishing, to be replaced by polluted water, urban sprawl and raw concrete. Once objects, the grizzled fishermen, the peasants, the proletarians, the leftist students had taken on human forms, individual and collective personalities, had become subjects. Friendship and enmity, class solidarity and fratricidal conflict, lust and jealousy, hunger and satiation, oppression and resistance lurched across the land like the disjointed figures in a *karaghiozis* shadow puppet play, life-size, compelling, threatening.

Greece had become "real," had acquired in my less innocent eyes what it had never lacked: a present. This present was more, however, than a space to be inhabited. I hungered to understand what had shaped it, and was determined to seek out its history by traveling not across the landscape, but by burrowing down into it. As I did so I began, metaphorically, to unearth relics. These relics could take the form of bones, of concealed images, of ruined buildings and dead cities. They could also take the shape of myths of primordial power.

The country was also, I came to realize over three decades of constant returning (interrupted only by the seven wretched years of the American-inspired military dictatorship) an imaginary construct. Greece's founding mythology, though ostensibly logical and linear, was more complex, tortuous and ramified than the genesis of the Olympian pantheon, more arbitrary and intense than the passions of the Homeric heroes and demi-gods. Reaching deep into the past, it had appropriated the social, intellectual and moral heritage of Athens, Sparta, ancient Macedon, Rome and Byzantium, reconciling the irreconcilable—Athenian democracy and Alexander the Great, pagan polytheism and Orthodox Christianity—as it went. In its representation of identity it suppressed dissenting myths, silenced counter-narratives, consigned subversive versions to oblivion, wiped away centuries. Ultimately the myth secreted the tyranny of the absolute: All who are not with us are against us; all who are not of us do not exist.

Myth sustained the nation in its darkest hours and nourished some of its greatest creative spirits. In symbiosis with European nationalism, creature of the Enlightenment, it transmuted itself into a powerful identity-producing mechanism, and, in the early years of the nineteenth century, laid the foundations for an exclusionary, expansionist state. Greece alone in all the Balkans was able to call on the historical sophistication that devolved to the self-affirmed heirs of ancient Athens and Byzantium. But it was soon to be challenged by its Romanian, Serbian and Bulgarian neighbors; later by the Albanians; latest of all by the Macedonians. All hastened to mobilize their own heroic traditions, their founding myths. A fury of national parthenogenesis—what Stefan Zweig calls the megalomania of the small—wracked the southeastern extremity of the continent. Legitimacies began to clash; identities to deny one another. Modernity, that undifferentiated catalyst, was available to all, who would use it in sharply differentiated ways.

THE BALKANS TODAY are the bastard child of the Ottoman Empire and Western imperialism. The name of the region derives from the Turkish word for mountain. It is, for the most part, a mass of rugged, irregular ranges which have exerted a determining influence on social, economic and political development. Until recently, the peninsula was administered not by nation states, but by two multinational empires, the Hapsburgs and the Ottomans. What set the Balkans apart from Western Europe was that the peoples who settled there had been able to preserve their identity down to the present. When, driven by the flood tide of nationalism which arose early in the nineteenth century and has yet to crest, the identity of one began to impinge on that of the other, the result was predictably disastrous.

Conventional wisdom tells us—as do expert analysts and mainstream journalists—that the latest Balkan catastrophe which began in the early 1990s with the collapse of Yugoslavia and the violent partition of Bosnia, was the work of a handful of ruthless, power-hungry regional demagogues wielding nationalism as the Grim Reaper wields his scythe. It was if the rational West could not bear to hear of blood enmity, of ancient hatreds and myths, those building stones of its own cultural identity. Yet my travels in the southern Balkans persuade me that the failure of Yugoslavia is not simply the gruesome work of Slobodan Milosevic or Franjo Tudjman, though it is that too. The agony of Bosnia, the Damoclean sword suspended above the head of Macedonia, the coming upheaval in Kosova, are not merely the poisoned heritage of Tito's Yugoslavia, though they are that too.

Tito's was the second attempt to construct, on the basis of the mutual consent of Serbs, Croats and Slovenes, a state of the South Slavs which also encompassed non-consenting Albanians. The first Yugoslavia was founded in 1918; its borders and the status of its minorities were legitimized by the peace of Versailles, Europe and America's poisoned gift to humanity, synthesis of Wilson's 14 Points and Great Power greed. It collapsed 20 years later amidst the debris of dictatorship as Nazi Germany thrust southeastward into the Balkans, setting up an independent fascist Croat state as it went, a development uncannily reflected in Christian Democratic Germany's hasty recognition of an independent Croatia in 1991. Events in Albania, occupied by fascist Italy, followed a similar course.

Nationalism, as much a creature of the Enlightenment as the world culture which now bids to replace it, had already been at work for decades, transmitted by the codification of national languages and the creation of national histories and pedigrees. Nationalism, and the passions it released, was also the sword wielded by the European powers—France, England, Austria-Hungary, Germany and Russia—in their mortal struggle against the Ottoman Empire, and in their expansionist drive to capture new markets. Had the Ottomans actively proselytized for Islam, had not Ottoman misrule provided it with the fertile ground of rancor and poverty, nationalism of such particular virulence might less likely have taken root in the Balkans. But they didn't, and it did.

There was more. Oil, the viscous black liquid that lights men's eyes and kindles their avarice, lay beyond the end station of the Berlin-Baghdad railway, across the shipping lanes that radiated from Salonica harbor, the great Balkan terminus. The once-feared empire whose capital spanned two continents stood as the great barrier blocking European access to the newly discovered petroleum resources of the Arabian peninsula and the Persian Gulf. There, the precious commodity which lay beneath the land was soon to be portioned out by men meeting in secret chambers: Mr. Sykes and Monsieur Picot.

The Ottomans represented yet another encumbrance: they were Muslims. Weak, corrupt Muslims to be sure, but bearers of a creed that posits a non-national model of social organization. Ottoman cities, in comparison with the mode prevailing in Europe, were havens of cosmopolitan tolerance. Places where people of all three monotheistic religions, and of a huge diversity of languages and ethnic attachments, coexisted in relative peace. These cities had names like Üsküb (Skopje), Sarajevo, and Selanik (Salonica).

As the empire withered, driven south and eastward by encroaching, oil-thirsty Europe and devoured from within by a virulent strain of Turkish nationalism, Sarajevo, Salonica and Skopje survived like islands on the land. Capital of tiny, fragile, landlocked and debt-ridden Macedonia, Skopje still preserves its national ambiguity and multiethnic harmony, but jagged fault lines run just beneath the surface. Sarajevo is a smoking ruin, the head of a corpse being systematically picked apart by the vultures of the international financial establishment.[1] Salonica, second city of two empires, once known as the Sepharade of the Balkans, had long ago been reduced, in a long spasm of exclusion and ethnic cleansing, to a unidimensional provincial capital.

The journeys through the Balkans which form the armature of this book begin and end in the city on Salonica Bay. There, I hypothesized, I would find keys to the calamity of Sarajevo and insight into the future of Skopje, perhaps even penetrate the secret of Macedonia. Acting on Edward Said's admonition, I did not accept the politics of identity as given, but attempted to "show how representations are constructed, for what purpose, and with what components."[2]

Salonica Terminus is itself a Balkan story, bypassing analysis for the random, chaotic fascination of events. It forsakes straight-line travel for the baroque pleasures of looping back, of retracing steps; eschews the linear view of history for a relativist perspective dictated not by the fickle fashion of a postmodernism, already disappearing into the rearview mirror with the speed of last year's advertising slogan, as outmoded as last year's digital prodigy, but by the very nature of its subject(s).

Perhaps more intensely than anywhere else, Truth and History, in the Balkans, are national considerations. In Greece, they are generated and reproduced by what a scholar, who asked that I not reveal his name, termed the "archeological Mafia," and by an academic establishment which maintains an incestuous relationship with the State. To cast doubt upon the approved version is to court danger. In Salonica and in Athens I received pointed advice, some good-natured, some hostile, about what might be appropriately written. Greek sensitivities are extreme, sensibilities easily bruised.

In Macedonia, the mechanism of identity formation was, under the Communists, if anything less subtle than that which had occurred in Greece. Today, despite the ostensible collapse of the *ancien régime*, the same academics propound the same analyses in the same rigorously disciplined congresses, as if nothing had changed. The continuum of historical doctrine has remained stubbornly unbroken.

Albania was the most extraordinary case. The doctrine of Albanicity, dovetailing with neo-Stalinist historical inevitability, had been elevated to the status of a religion. Enver Hoxha is long gone, but the aftertaste lingers on among intellectuals who proclaim their faith in his perverted legacy while denying him.

In Serbia, whose much-condemned, ill-understood woes cast a long shadow across the peninsula, the construction of a national self included myth, legend and the legendary obduracy of the Serbs themselves. Serbia, like its southern Balkan neighbors a latecomer to the intoxication of the national ideal, looked longingly to a glorious pre-Ottoman past. In the mid-fourteenth century, the great king Stefan Dusan had extended Serbian hegemony throughout the Balkans, barely failing to capture Salonica. Though Dusan's empire did not survive his reign, which ended with his death in 1355, it has never ceased to haunt—and inspire—Belgrade. Though Serbia falls beyond the scope of this book, I often found its presence impinging on the narrative, as it did on the perceptions of Greeks, Macedonians, Bulgarians and Albanians...and, of course, of the Kosovars.

IN A REGION where one man's national martyr is another's war criminal, where one country's founding myth is another's tale of woe and usurpation, what other refuge can the chronicler of human absurdity seek than compassionate relativism? If this account appears particularly critical toward Greece, there are reasons. My long, deep emotional attachment to the country reflects the interplay of love and hatred that are the hallmark of any relationship founded in passion. Greece, too, as self-defined heir to the Byzantines and depository of the legacy of Athens, wields a cultural power that its neighbors cannot easily equal.

Greece is, at the same time, a raw, new country whose creation and expansion partake of the same forces that would shape Serbia, Romania, Bulgaria, Albania and now, Macedonia. Yet it would deny to its minuscule northern neighbor the right to construct its own representation of itself. Insofar as it does this, it stands open to the accusation of historical injustice.

This, finally, is a book that does not deign to conceal its *parti pris*. Against the mighty, the specialists and the experts, the economic determinists who would strap life, in all its numinous richness, to the Procrustean bed of inevitability; against the arrogance of the nation-state masquerading as the agent of post-modern supra-nationalism; against the long-fanged world-culturalists who posit their ideology as the entire discursive field, secreting blood enmity and ethnic strife as they totter across the land, hands fluttering in mock innocence.

It speaks for the marginal, the despised, the concealed and the dissimulated; for the small countries (like Macedonia or Québec) who have inexplicably missed the cut-off date for national legitimacy as decreed by their overbearing neighbors or masters; for the minority languages that dare not speak their names; for the Vlachs, for the Kosovars, for the Macedonians of Greece, for the Gypsies everywhere.

It offers no solution, only the certainty that European nationalism has failed the Balkans as surely as communist "internationalism." Free market democracy, hailed as the panacea, is more likely to recreate a situation similar to that which prevailed in the closing years of the nineteenth century, and release old tensions, new dangers and the whisper of war.

The southern Balkans—the area encompassing Greece, Albania, Macedonia, Kosova and Bulgaria—possess a potential for conflict, and for disaster, which exceeds that of Bosnia. The *status quo* is unjust and unstable; economic disparities are on the rise, outside powers are locked in bitter commercial and political rivalry through their local proxies. Even the slightest shift in the ethnic imbalance could trigger hostilities involving the region's two heaviest armed potential belligerents, Greece and Turkey.

The process known as globalization, for all its claims, provides no inoculation against the lurking bacillus of national resurgence. Instead, it is likely to awaken local and regional particularisms, driven by the ideology of competition of which war is merely the continuation by other means. Not in the Balkans will the exquisite corpse of nationalism be easily laid to rest.

The Southern Balkans, 1996

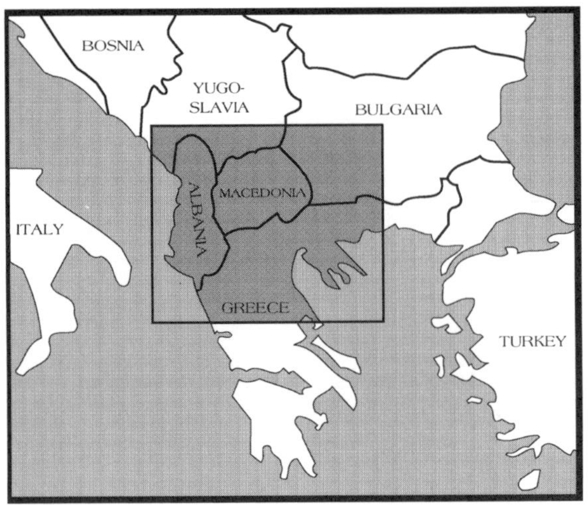

Chapter 1

CITY OF SHADOWS

DAWN IS BREAKING as the night train from Athens sways and rattles along the northern Aegean shore. Crouched around fires, knots of Albanian refugees look up as it rushes by. Suddenly my fellow passengers begin to rouse themselves, talking excitedly. My eyes follow their pointing fingers. On the northeastern horizon the lights of Salonica glisten, reflected on the still waters of the bay. Time seems to accelerate as the express picks up speed for the long, swooping curve into the place which is to be my home for three months. Forehead pressed against the cold glass of the window I watch the city awaken as the train glides through the rail yard, whistle hooting, then creaks to a stop in the station. Salonica terminus; end of the line. My long journey into the Balkans has begun, a journey of short distances which will lead me deep into history, and carry me across a landscape disfigured by the battle for land and identity.

FROM MY SECOND-FLOOR BALCONY I look on as life unfolds in the tiny square below. Waiters deliver cups of coffee to the season's last, hard-core outdoor customers at the Café Doré, older men in overcoats, their collars turned up against the wind as leaves from the plane tree flutter to the ground. Nearby, three drunks carefully spread rolls of corrugated cardboard before flopping down on the park benches to snooze in the sunlight. A cat stalks, then attacks and captures a butterfly. A blond-haired young woman dressed in tights and high-heeled boots paces back and forth impatiently, then stalks off. The buzz of small-displacement motorbikes runs like the obbligato of a million wasps over the bass roar of automobiles and buses. Or is the din I hear simply the concentrated conversation of the city, the distillation of one hundred thousand domestic quarrels and coffee-house altercations, market disputes and lapel-tugging street-corner encounters?

My neighborhood is a petrified forest of apartment buildings. Light rarely penetrates to street level, and on weekends when the municipal garbage collection crews are not at work—or during one of their frequent strikes—rubbish rapidly piles up on the sidewalk, drawing hungry cats, stray dogs, and at this proximity to the waterfront, harbor rats. At street level are night-clubs whose patrons are wont to block the narrow sidewalk with their motorcycles and affect an arrogant swagger, their narrowly post-pubescent lady friends a practiced pout.

There is, I learn after a few weeks of residence, a profound consistency about the place. Back in the days before the Café Doré and the apartment buildings, these few square blocks formed one of Salonica's toughest districts: a place where its *rebetiko* music milieu lived, performed, fought, occasionally prospered and more often went hungry over cheap wine in makeshift *tavernas*, or got high in hashish dens. Here was the "Koutsoura" ("the stumps") of a certain Mr. Delamangas, later to be immortalized in Vassilis Tsitsanis' late-'40s hit *Bakché Ciftliki.* In the song, named for a Turkish estate which flourished as a summer bathing spot back when the water was clear, Tsitsanis leads us on a musical excursion, self-referential before such things became fashionable post-modernist devices, through the high spots and the low-down dives of the Salonica shoreline underworld.

Come with me for a whirl
out to Bakché Ciftliki
My sweet little girl
from Thessaloniki...
Marigo you'll go crazy
when you hear Tsitsani

In Salonica not one, but several layers of the past lie poultice-like, so superposed, so interlocked, their lines of demarcation so blurred that they can hardly be distinguished. The shards of the ancient Macedonian, Roman and Byzantine city lie intermingled, at peace now, with the rubble and the ruin left by Venetians, Ottomans, Sephardic Jews, and Modern Greeks. What is true of historical artifact is true, too, of the mercurial substance of culture, the mist of memory. Adjacent to my neighborhood stood, at some point in its life, a Muslim cemetery of which not a trace remains. This was natural enough, considering its proximity to the White Tower, the main prison which then formed the south-easternmost apex of the city's walls. Over time the grave-yard fell into disuse, and by the late nineteenth century the shoreline around the Tower became the center of passenger and cargo traffic in the harbor, and home to the independent boatmen who plied their craft between the shore and the caïques and steamers anchored offshore. It was a place of constant din, where the cries of the waterfront mingled with the screams of tortured prisoners. With the boatmen came whores, hashish and liquor—the essential components of a mariner's shore leave. And when the boatmen disappeared with the construction of a modern harbor, the whorehouses and hashish dens stayed on as incubators of *rebetiko*, hybrid offspring of Turkish and Byzantine musical traditions that expresses, far better than any Greek author with the possible exception of Nikos Kazantzakis, the country's divided soul.

Tsitsanis, its master, made his home in these mean streets for 17 years, a spectator to the upheavals which wracked Salonica during and after World War II: Nazi occupation, the deportation of the Jews, liberation by the Communist-led guerrillas, civil war and political repression. *Rebetiko* music was far too subtle to allow itself to become immersed in the contentious political particularities of the moment, though; to speak, as the Greeks elegantly put it, of rope in the house of the hanged. It told, instead, the quotidian stories of people caught in the meat-grinder of social and economic stress; sang of the flight of misery from reality; celebrated the mundane and the commonplace, the carnal and the banal—the better to transfigure them. The more abyssal the sadness evoked, the greater the cathartic effect obtained. Divine intercession of art. "Cloudy Sunday", Tsitsanis' four-minute masterpiece of the *rebetiko* repertoire (and unofficial national anthem of Greece), exudes urban melancholy compounded by the emptiness of that day of the week when, alone, we must endure the company of ourselves:

Cloudy Sunday, how much you're like my heart
Always clouds, nothing but clouds
Holy Jesus, Mother of God...

Rebetiko music, now squirreled away in tiny basement clubs in Athens where it has been reduced to a diversion for aging purists is still alive and well in Salonica. At the head of my street is a hole-in-the-wall restaurant which serves the neighborhood's auto mechanics at noon before metamorphosing each night into a place where students and mature couples from what used to be called the working class can rub elbows, quaff cheap resinated wine, and order their favorite songs as they nibble from plates of grilled sausage, spicy meat-balls or lemony joints of roast lamb.

The house act is a guitar-bouzouki (a long-necked relative of the mandolin) duo which performs from a stage consisting of two straw-bottomed chairs shoved up against the wall next to the toilet door. No amplification is necessary in these cramped, resonant confines where tolerance of good-natured intimacy, a forgiving ear and winey nostalgia are the sole criteria for enjoyment. Kostas, the bouzouki player, makes up in enthusiasm what he lacks in pitch, and his enthusiasm is as substantial as it is contagious. But his sideman Theodoris, the guitarist, plays like a man battling for the fundamental values of rhythm and intonation against all but hopeless odds, speeding up or slowing down in an effort to keep pace with his surging, impetuous partner.

Late one midday Theodoris and I strike up an acquaintance. I'm wolfing down a portion of spaghetti in the restaurant after my daily labors in the library of the Institute for Balkan Studies while he and the proprietor discuss arrangements for the evening's program. Indiscreetly I join the conversation (indiscretion in conversation is the rule in Greece where the most intimate details of your life are soon the stuff of well-meaning banter, clicking tongues and empathetic 'po po po's'), my eyes straying to the guitar case resting, resonant with potential, on the table next to mine. His business completed, Theodoris snaps open the case, pulls out his instrument and asks me what I would like to hear. Luxury of an autumn afternoon with no pressing engagements; with no engagements whatsoever. Play me Tsitsanis' "Beautiful Salonica"...

You are the pride of my heart
Thessaloniki my beauty, my sweet;
I may live with Athens, that beguiler
But it's you I sing for every night...

ACROSS THE SQUARE, glaring into my living room, stands the White Tower: the massive, enigmatic cylindrical structure that is the emblem of Salonica. At dawn the sun's first soft rays give it contour and depth. At noon it stands out in stark, almost one-dimensional relief against the sea and sky. On clear days when the biting north wind the Salonicians call the *Vardari* whistles down from the Balkans you can see it against the distant peak of Mount Olympus whence the old Gods, driven away by the monotheists, have fled to take up their stations as constellations in the night sky.

And at night, brightly lit by floodlights which obscure those faint constellations, it squats, stocky and self-assured and immovable, as opaque and inscrutable as the history of this darkly ancient town that smells still of the raw concrete that encases memory in an impenetrable shroud. But no matter how thick the concrete, that which it seeks to confine contrives to seep free, to ooze osmotically into the soil and the air.

The White Tower is to Salonica what the Acropolis is to Athens: a concentrated presence that does triple duty as identity, trade mark, and symbol. Like the Acropolis, it is every bit as ambiguous. Perhaps even—as talisman and expression of that most highly prized of contemporary values now that righteous indignation has become risible—ironic. Athenians in their millions file daily beneath the sharply etched rock crowned by the Parthenon, in the inescapable, overbearing shadow of one luminous moment of civilization far greater than their own could ever be. And, height of indignity, the emblem of a civilization since appropriated by the West in its inclusive frenzy to define itself against an Oriental Other of which modern Greece unwillingly partakes.

Here in Salonica, the White Tower functioned for almost five centuries not simply as symbol, but as the thing itself: the palpable material presence of that Other, the Ottoman Empire. But the Ottomans, who ruled the city with what cultivated misconception holds to have been the distillation of tyranny, also—inevitably—infused modern Greece with a repressed Oriental self, a hidden "soul" whose denial, concealment and effacement is the unifying thread of official modern Greek historiography as it attempts to fashion for itself, *ex nihilo*, a Western identity. For without such an identity, runs contemporary conventional wisdom, there can be no modernity and thus no existence.

The White Tower, say what historians call the sources, was probably built by the Venetians during their brief tour of duty as Salonica's last Christian masters, before the Turks under Murad II, took the city for good in 1430. Its brutal yet sophisticated stone construction and crenellated battlements resemble nothing else: not the remains of the Byzantine walls nor the surviving Islamic monuments which possess none of its brooding power. Some say that when Sultan Soleiman I, "the Magnificent," undertook repairs in the mid-sixteenth century, his skilled masons left an inscription which read "Tower of the Lion," probably in reference to the lion of St. Mark, emblem of the Serenissima Repubblica, which up until then had marked the structure.[3]

During the early years of the Turkish regime the tower housed the Janissaries, the elite corps which forcibly recruited its members in early adolescence from among the non-Muslim population. But at the beginning of the eighteenth century it was transformed into a prison, and rapidly became known as the "Tower of Blood," for the tortures and executions which were practiced there. Late in the nineteenth century, on the order of Sultan Abdulhamid II, but at the behest of the Western Powers, it was whitewashed, renamed the White Tower, and relieved of its carceral functions. Irony, did you say? Abdulhamid, the "Red Sultan" whose reputation for brutality went hand in hand with an equally firm resolve to shake up, nay, Westernize, the semi-moribund Empire, ended his reign in ignominy, a prisoner in Salonica, the city he was determined to reconstruct as a window to Europe, the city which was to provide clear proof of Ottoman Turkey's will and capacity to haul itself into the modern world. It would do this by providing optimum conditions for foreign investment and by guaranteeing human rights. Thus was accelerated a process which could only culminate in the Empire's destruction; a process that reform, instead of halting, hastened. If it signifies nothing else, the story of Salonica's White Tower points to the one and sovereign inevitability: the evanescence of the imperial project and the enduring presence of stones.

FIVE MINUTES' WALK ALONG THE CORNICHE from the White Tower lies Liberty Square, a negative landmark, a place no one visits, where no one strolls, where no one nurses a tiny cup of coffee through the afternoon, where no romantic assignation is ever set. Afflicted with a heroic name, it is the most anti-heroic of places. Liberty Square today is a downtown parking lot and an urban bus terminal, a vital urban space usurped, a place to be avoided, to rush by as quickly as possible, a place upon which the city has turned its back, its canopy of trees the only remnant of its former vocation. The effacement of the square that was once its heart, its window to the world during the turbulent years when Salonica was the metropolis of Ottoman-ruled Macedonia, is a function of an unavowed Modern Greek selective memory syndrome—a condition which dictates that all that does not mesh with the founding myth must be obscured, buried, eliminated, caused to vanish from public historical consciousness. The process need be neither violent nor even conscious, the square reminds us. How better to neutralize a powerfully symbolic space than to transform it into a parking lot, and disguise the act as a case of rogue urban renewal later to be sincerely regretted before "turning the page." Remove the cars, restore the tree-lined square to its original function? Be serious. In a city which once seriously entertained the notion of an immense subterranean parking garage beneath the corniche, one must not flirt with utopia. Automobiles invading public space, along with cigarettes whose smoke is forever being blown in your face, are essential components of modern Greek individuality.

King George with his succesor Constantine in front of the White Tower, 1912.
From *Old Salonica*, ©1980, Elias Petropoulos

Liberty Square, Salonica, before the fire of 1917.
From *Old Salonica*, ©1980, Elias Petropoulos

The greater the haste with which the architects of national identity—or of whatever new verity—seek to expunge discordant evidence from historical consciousness, to excise it from the living urban fabric, the greater the effort to reclaim that evidence must be. In Athens, the rupture with the past has been long consummated. The sole connection with the golden age remains a rhetorical one, preserved by a tissue of museums and green spaces protecting archeological sites of interest to tourists but ignored by the shop-keepers, civil servants, rentiers and businessmen who populate the city core. Salonica, a vital urban continuum for nearly 2,500 years and a relative latecomer to the leaden influence of national integration, remains fertile terrain for the unmediated archeology of memory.

Liberty Square is not a place to linger. Often I circumnavigate it, and always hastily, on my way to or from the west end of town. Today, lined with bank headquarters on one side, fast-food restaurants and travel agencies on the other, the square which lies hard by the elegant, despairingly silent maritime passenger terminal, owes its name not to some putative liberation of Greek Macedonia. The embarrassment, for Salonica's masters, is that the Greeks had very little to do with it, except as onlookers.

The name commemorates the short-lived experiment in Ottoman democracy known as the Young Turk revolution which flowered here; celebrates a string of upheavals that catapulted Salonica overnight into the forefront of history. For a millennium it had been the second city of an empire; fleetingly it became the first, though the Empire over which it briefly ruled was already in its death throes.

How majestic our hindsight as we dispose of events which, for the participants, were ripe with the chaos of hope and potentiality. July 24, 1908. From the balcony of the Club de Salonique, the Masonic Lodge overlooking what was then called Olympos Square, Enver Bey, leader of the uprising, proclaimed to a cheering crowd: "There are no longer Bulgars, Greeks, Rumanians, Jews, Mussulmans. We are all brothers beneath the same blue sky. We are all equal, we glory in being Ottoman."[4]

Enver's new constitutional order was to usher in an era of peace, freedom and democracy for the subject peoples of the Ottoman state. But its unavowed intent was to restore the tottering Empire itself. The constitutional order did exist for a few months, before turning, inevitably, into its opposite. Or perhaps, to speak the language of the long ago, far away dialectic, it had carried its negation within it all along.

The Young Turks were the natural ideological offspring of a political and social order which had become increasingly schizophrenic as it confronted the West's military, social and political superiority. A catastrophic series of military and political defeats were followed by first a subtle, then a violent, penetration of European nationalism into the Balkans. This opened the door to the creation of quasi-independent national states in Serbia and Greece by the end of the third decade of the nineteenth century. The once-immense multinational Ottoman Empire had begun to shrink. Worse yet for Istanbul, the fledgling states were little better than creatures of the Great Powers of Europe, who saw them as useful agents in their war of attrition against the Ottomans. Urgent action was needed to halt the slide. In 1839, Sultan Abdulmejid I launched a series of social, political and economic reforms known as the *Tanzimat*. For the pro-western forces of the Empire, the evidence was as inescapable as it was overwhelming: Turkey had to modernize or perish. Modernize it would. In the event, it was done in by the cure—a half-willing victim of the New World Order of the day.

The European Powers had dubbed the long, slow collapse of Turkey the Eastern Question. The term euphemistically concealed their aim: to dismantle and redistribute the Empire, particularly its far western and eastern extremities—Macedonia and Mesopotamia—among themselves. The only serious questions, those addressed in back-room negotiations and consigned to secret treaties, were "when?" and "who?" Political and economic divergence among the suitor/rapists gradually became more acute, coming to a peak in August, 1914. The process bore—are we remiss in noticing the forever unclothed emperor?—an uncanny resemblance to the haste with which the European powers and their American cousins now rush to divide the former Yugoslavia and the ex-USSR, fighting the battle for global culture and economic domination to the last Bosnian, Serb or Croat; the last Chechen, Ingush or Tadjik?

The remedy chosen touched off an accelerated decline. By introducing a foreign form of government, under foreign pressure, the *Tanzimat* threw the country wide open to foreign influence and interference. Foreigners had been given the right to own land in Turkey, and were acquiring positions of control in every branch of the economic and public life of the Empire. To domestic tyranny the men of the *Tanzimat* had added foreign exploitation.[5]

No reform, no homeopathic dose of "westernization," could stem the Ottoman decline. Markets were being globalized in the usual aggressive fashion. Throughout the nineteenth century, the continued erosion of Turkish military power coupled with the Empire's industrial inferiority combined to set the stage for a full-scale European economic invasion of the Balkans, foreshadowing the lines of battle that would score the peninsula during the First World War. This invasion would take place in Macedonia, core of Istanbul's European possessions, Salonica's economic hinterland and key to the prosperity—even the survival—of the regime.

The process was sped along by Turkey's violent suppression of embryonic Macedonian nationalism. The cruelty of the Ottoman forces had aroused Western public opinion, as malleable then as now, and brought foreign military observers to Macedonia. This combination of crowning indignity and mortal threat to the integrity of the Empire came to a head in early 1908 when Austro-Hungary, which had ruled Bosnia-Herzegovina as a protectorate since the fateful year of 1878, proclaimed its intention to link the Bosnian railway to the Macedonian system, the terminus of which was Salonica. Pan-Germanism was on the ascendancy; the Austro-Prussian *Drang nach Osten* was but a breath away from becoming reality and Istanbul, gateway to the oil fields of Iraq, was the ultimate prize. Russia, which dreamed of incorporating Tsargrad (as it called Istanbul)—and the Straits, with the promise of access to ice-free seas—into its own expanding Orthodox co-prosperity sphere, immediately responded by announcing construction of a Panslav railway line which would cross the Balkans from East to West, cutting off the Teutonic march to the southeast. The rush for railway expansion along the lines of force of Great Power strategy eerily prefigured the competing north-south and east-west highway and pipeline projects taking shape in the post-communist Balkans today.

Suddenly the port of Salonica had become the focus of conflicting, yet converging, imperial designs. In April, Edward VII and Tsar Nicholas II met at Revel, on the Baltic, where they put the finishing touches to an accord on the pacification program needed to carry out their railway construction program. The scheme was as brilliant as it was disastrous. The Great Powers, caught up in bitter economic competition, would cooperate peacefully to dispossess the Sick Man of Europe. The Turks, as a corollary, would cease to be masters in Macedonia.[6]

For the better part of two decades dissident intellectuals who had sought refuge in European capitals had been agitating for a the re-establishment of the constitutional order, which they saw as the only way to save the crumbling Turkish state. They called their movement the Committee for Union and Progress, establishing its headquarters in Paris, where they modeled it on the nationalist-revolutionary movements that flourished throughout Europe.

But the Young Turks' forced march to the balcony overlooking Liberty Square, and thence to Istanbul, only began in earnest when a clandestine group of officers of the Ottoman Third Army Corps in Macedonia—one of whose members was a Salonica native named Mustafa Kemal, later self-baptized as Atatürk, "father of the Turks"—merged with the Union and Progress organization in September 1907. The merger channeled the national humiliation felt by the idealist intellectuals into the day-to-day humiliation faced by the hard-bitten field commanders of the Ottoman army at the hands of overbearing foreign "observers." To this explosive cocktail was added a groundswell of discontent among the ranks of underpaid and underfed conscripts. The troops of the reformed Empire were now expected to behave like professional soldiers; no longer could pillage be accepted as the army's chief method of sustaining its men in the field.

In early 1908, insurrection spread like a viral contagion through the Macedonian garrisons of the Third Army Corps, along the very railway lines the Ottomans had built to enable them to transport troops into the hinterland. A full-fledged mutiny was in progress, sped along by the cricket song of the telegraph key and the rhythmic click of wheels on steel rails: the lines of communication had been turned against those who had built them. Emboldened, the mutineers came out into the open. They petitioned Salonica's European consulates to pressure Istanbul to restore the never-applied constitution. Sultan Adbulhamid scoffed. The revolt spread. By now the revolutionaries had established contact with the city's Bulgarian, Greek, Rumanian, Armenian and Albanian clandestine organizations. The Jews, Salonica's largest ethno-religious community, quickly organized a levy to propagate the good tidings throughout the Balkans, as far afield as Sofia and Bucharest.[7]

Now the sovereign played for time, attempting to forestall the inevitable with the "time dishonored" carrot and stick of bribery and repression. All failed. On July 24, 1908, Hussein Hilmi Pasha, Inspector General of European Turkey and a late convert to the revolutionary cause, proclaimed the Constitution.[8]

Liberty Square became the focal point of public festivities: Jews, Turks, Greeks, Bulgars, Albanians, Armenians and Levantines fraternized, wept tears of joy and cheered. Forgotten were the blood feuds and deadly rivalries which had transformed the surrounding countryside into a bewildering warren of no-go zones and battlefields. Orthodox popes, rabbis and Muslim imams embraced in public. Brass bands marched and countermarched along the quay, blaring the *Marseillaise*.

Down from the hills came the guerrilla band leaders: Bulgarian and Macedonian *comitajis*, Serbian *chetajis*, Greek *andartes*. Blood hatreds suddenly dissolved as yesterday's bandits mingled, hugging and kissing, in the cafés, and were photographed for posterity, their wild beards set off by the cartridge belts criss-crossed over their chests. Sandanski, comrade-in-arms of the martyred Gotse Delchev and one of the most feared of the Bulgaro-Macedonian anarchists/terrorists/freedom fighters, posed in the dignified dark suit of an incipient Father of his Country. The liberation of the subject peoples was at hand. Talk of the old dream of Balkan federation was in the air. Even the town's Free Masons, who had discretely lent their lodges to the revolutionaries, appeared in public beneath their banners, to the acclaim of a populace in a state of near-rapture. "Long live the Constitution! Long live the Army!" trumpeted souvenir postcards depicting a dashing, rapier-thin Enver Bey. "Liberty, equality, fraternity, justice!" roared the crowd in a Babel of tongues.

To the astonishment of Europe, Salonica overnight became the *de facto* capital of the Empire, issuing orders, appointing governors, instituting reforms, administering the widespread dominion. Delegations bearing messages of solidarity converged on the city from Greece and Serbia, from Austro-Hungary, from Romania and France. Citizens were suddenly free to speak their minds, to meet in public. The press flourished. But when a delegation from Bulgaria arrived several weeks later, it was welcomed by a shut-down of the city's coffee-houses and restaurants, including the most prestigious of them all, the Olympus. The Bulgarian government had just declared its intention to free itself of its status as an Ottoman protectorate, upsetting the fragile Balkan equilibrium. The proprietors of the closed establishments were Greek to a man.[9]

Meanwhile, strikes by workers acting in defense of their class interests had already begun in the heady first days of the revolution under the leadership of the Fédération socialiste, established by radicals who had accompanied the Bulgarian delegation. Salonica, in the first decade of the twentieth century, was not only the second port of the Empire after Izmir, it was Turkey's largest industrial center, its doorway to European industrial modernity. The propaganda and organizing efforts of the socialists, spurred on by a combative press, rapidly overflowed the small Bulgarian community and took root among the Jews, who formed the majority of the city's 25,000-strong proletariat, and the Turks. Dozens of strikes broke out, involving longshoremen, bank employees and tobacco workers.

Not only the Greeks, who were the third most numerous population group after the Jews and the Muslim Turks, stood aloof from the growing labor unrest. The Young Turk leadership, which had initially supported the workers, feared that the sudden outburst of industrial activity would scare away the European capitalists who were to revitalize the semi-moribund Empire and transform it into a model of free-market democracy. The situation became even more alarming—from the government's point of view—when the Fédération sought and was granted affiliation with the International Socialist Federation as sole representative of the Ottoman state.

For decades the ghost of the Fédération haunted the square. During the thirties it was the rallying point for workers' demonstrations organized by Greece's militant Communist party. One day in May, 1936, a cortege of strikers set out from Liberty Square led by pallbearers carrying the body of a young worker killed by police. By day's end ten more strikers had been shot down in the streets. Three months later, on the eve of a nationwide general strike, an army officer called Ioannis Metaxas had declared himself dictator and instituted a fascist regime named for the date—August 4—on which it was proclaimed.

As art stands for the primacy of experience in the world and against the re-engineering of the past, so Yannis Ritsos' "Epitaph" cast the tragic May events in poetic form, as a mother's lament over the body of her dead son. In the early sixties composer Mikis Theodorakis set Ritsos' poetry to music, adapting it to the austere, percussive cadences of the *rebetiko* style.

There you stood at your window
And your strong shoulders
Hid the sea, the streets below...

You were like a helmsman, my son,
and the neighborhood was your ship

On another day in May, Liberty Square claimed its last sacrificial victim. Grigoris Lambrakis, a left-wing member of parliament, was killed by a three-wheeled motorcycle in a street just two blocks away after leaving a political meeting. The "accidental" death was quickly proved to have been an assassination plotted by the country's highest political authorities, and carried out by the same kind of lumpen patriots who, in 1967, scuttled Greece's fragile democracy and set up the Junta. Today a bronze dove surrounded by upreaching, outstretched hands and identified only by the date—May 22, 1963—marks the place of the crime. While every other statue in Salonica bears a name, the Lambrakis memorial is anonymous. But the sculpture is never without fresh-cut flowers—red carnations, mostly—even on this raw winter evening, as the *Vardari*, sweeping dust and scraps of oily paper before it, rips down the streets like the scythe of some elemental grim reaper.

LIKE ALL REVOLUTIONARY MOVEMENTS, the Young Turks carried within them sharply contradictory objectives, both of which had been latent during the decades of opposition and exile. Those whom we might call liberals favored decentralization, and some degree of autonomy for the Empire's rich mosaic of religious, linguistic and national minorities. Their adversaries were dedicated to reinforcing the centralizing power of Istanbul, and to Turkish domination. Within less than a year, the Committee of Union and Progress had fallen under the control of the centralizers.[10]

In their objective, they enjoyed the support of their military allies, whose prime objective had always been to remove the corrupt, incompetent Abdulhamid, and to replace him with a government which would defend the Ottoman state, not liquidate it at discount prices to the Great Powers and their financial backers. The officers were indifferent to ideology. What concerned them was the survival of the institutions they and their fathers had served.[11]

As with all revolutions, seizing power was the easy part. The Young Turks' honeymoon was as fleeting as a mayfly's prime. On the home front, the Islamic Committee of Salonica accused the revolutionaries of atheism, echoing the views of the Caliphate in Istanbul. And as Enver, Talat and their associates slid deeper into the conceptual swamps of Pan-Turkism, the subject peoples of the Empire began to pick up the scent of mortal danger—not only to their prospects for building a multinational state in whose life they could participate as equals, but to their very existence. For what the Committee of Union and Progress had done was to steal a march on its Balkan tormentors. Its new, improved edition of the Ottoman state would apply the same Jacobin nation-state model as they had done, but on a much broader scale, and with all the force and coercive power it could muster. The subject peoples who had rallied to the Young Turk banner—the Armenians in particular—would pay a heavy price for their presumption.

In a speech to a secret conclave of the Salonica Committee of Union and Progress, in 1911, as reported by the acting British Consul in Monastir, Talat Bey declared: "We have made unsuccessful attempts to convert the Ghiaur [Christian Ottoman subjects] into a loyal Osmanli and all such efforts must inevitably fail, as long as the small independent states in the Balkan

Peninsula remain in a position to propagate ideas of Separatism among the inhabitants of Macedonia. There can therefore be no question of equality, until we have succeeded in our task of Ottomanizing the Empire..."[12]

International reaction to the events in Salonica was swift and, given the weakness of the Empire's new, untested, and unconsolidated rulers, crippling. Within four months Greece had declared Crete part of the Kingdom of the Hellenes; formerly docile Albania, long a source of dedicated Ottoman soldiers, was in turmoil; Tsar Ferdinand I had crowned himself ruler of an independent Bulgaria; farther north, Austria-Hungary had annexed Bosnia-Herzegovina. With Bosnia in Austrian hands, the frustrated, landlocked Serbs turned their attention south and westward, toward Macedonia and the ports of the Adriatic littoral, while at the same time plotting revenge against Vienna. Now, as the Ottoman collapse accelerated, national myths were being honed to a razor edge. And where myth became historical necessity, disaster was sure to follow.

Meanwhile, in Istanbul, traditionalist resistance came to a head with a bloody mutiny against the Young Turks by soldiers and theological students in April, 1909. Ten days later, the constitutionalist "Army of Action" from Salonica crushed the insurgents and on April 27, Abdulhamid, the man who had ruled an Empire that stretched from the Adriatic to the Persian Gulf, was officially deposed and sent into exile, replaced by his brother Mehmed Reshad. When his captors informed him of his destination, the "Red Sultan" is said to have fainted. It was to be Salonica.

THE VILLA ALLATINI stands, like a fairy-tale castle nestled in a grove of pines on the eastern outskirts of the city, surrounded by the usual suburban disorder of apartment blocks, gas stations and parking lots. The elegant three-story country estate, designed by architect Vitaliano Poselli for the Allatini family, one of Salonica's most powerful Jewish industrial and banking clans, is one of a handful of structures to have survived the leveling wrath of the developers.

Here Abdulhamid was dispatched. Along with five wives, several children and a retinue of servants, he lived under house arrest for three years, an object of curiosity for the citizens who, of an evening's spin in a horse-drawn buggy, might catch a glimpse of the mustachioed old Sultan, red fez atop his head, gazing from the second floor window of the Villa toward Salonica Bay.[13]

Abdulhamid's ultimate humiliation came two years later when his brother, now designated Mehmed V, visited Salonica to climax an imperial swing through what the Europeans now called Macedonia. "The population gave their beloved sovereign a reception worthy of the first Constitutional Sultan. Marvelous triumphal arches were erected wherever the monarch was to pass," rhapsodized journalist Sami Levi, compiler of a lavish photographic album commemorating the royal tour.[14]

The arches were erected by the city's principal religious groups—Jews, Muslims, Orthodox (Greek) and Bulgarian, its main industrial establishments which included fez and woolen fabric manufacturing, the Ottoman Tobacco Monopoly, the Light and Power Company, the railways, and the port, as well as several of its most prominent commercial firms: the Café Crystal in Liberty Square, the Splendid Palace Hotel on the quay, and the Au Louvre department store. One of them drew Levi's admiring attention:

"On the road leading to the city, at the entrance to Union Boulevard, soars an arch of truly monumental aspect. It has been erected by the Ottoman Industrial and Trading Company of Salonica [formerly the Allatini mill and brick works]. Here we behold, in an ingeniously conveyed contrast, the felicitous encounter of Moorish architecture with modern industry. For while the central section of the monument which forms the principal arch, stands against the sky with a silhouette suggestive of the Orient, it is flanked by two huge factory smokestacks creating a most pleasing effect. The harmony of contrasts achieved here, a harmony which a skeptic would have considered impossible, does honor to the architects. Upon the pediment, giving onto the sea-front, is a picture of the mill, on the other side is a picture of the brick works. Both are accompanied by illustrations of the machinery used in the two factories."[15]

The diligent Levi could not, of course, dare mention that the dethroned predecessor and elder brother of the beloved sovereign was an involuntary guest in the villa of the Allatini family, owners of those self-same mill and brick-works. For at the conclusion of the imperial visit, "on the following day, Sunday, in the morning, we had the honor of presenting to him a copy of this album. The Caliph deigned to leaf through our work, with which he was well pleased, and which caused him to bestow upon the publisher of the Journal de Salonique, Daout effendi Levy, an imperial gift consisting of a set of diamond cuff-links."[16]

The beloved sovereign was, alas, little more than a figurehead; proof that for all their martial bravado, the Young Turks—like all reformers—lacked both confidence and audacity. Their objective had never been to abolish the

Empire, but to rescue it. Instead of killing Abdulhamid, they held him as insurance. You never knew what might happen: revolutions are notoriously unpredictable. In the event, the hard-headed imperial dedication of Enver and Talat proved their undoing, and was soon to precipitate Salonica into another maelstrom. In Athens, Sofia and Belgrade the carving knives were being sharpened. London, Paris, Moscow and Vienna watched with ill-concealed glee as their general staffs drew up mobilization plans. If Macedonia was to be the meal, Salonica would be the *plat de résistance.*

FROM THE SUMMIT OF THE RUE MOUFFETARD, Salonica glimmers in the haze of time and distance, multifaceted, complex and exotic. My vantage point, like a *camera obscura* of the imagination, is the work room of Elias Petropoulos, a cubbyhole overlooking a tiny Parisian courtyard in the heart of the Cinquième Arrondissement. *Rebetiko* music spills, like plates being tossed in a taverna, from a tape machine wedged in among the books which line the walls from floor to ceiling, overflowing onto chairs and tables. Petropoulos can take credit for almost single-handedly resurrecting this once-scorned genre, turning his formidable talents as a researcher and popularizer to writing down the lyrics of virtually every *rebetiko* song ever sung. Published in a plump, richly illustrated album, Petropoulos' compendium set the prim and proper Athenian literary establishment on its ear, and went on to become a perennial best-seller.

Setting the Athenian establishment on its ear has been the cornerstone of Petropoulos' career. From his twenty year self-exile in Paris—"I'll never go back, never!" he rumbles, eyes flashing with benign malice—a steady stream of outrageous essays, provocative articles and exasperatingly accurate, often hilarious books has flowed from his prolific pen as celestial retsina might flow from the unquenchable barrels of some cosmic taverna. Subjects embraced astonish in their diversity: Greece's traditional bean soup, complete with a sophisticated etymological analysis of the various Balkanic and Eastern terms for the common yet extraordinary white kidney bean and its many local variants; the hilarious—and vituperatively condemned—"Good Thief's Handbook," which posits the world of second-story men and cat-burglars as a microcosmic metaphor for bourgeois society, with its own rigorous code of behavior and social norms. Academic convention and literary propriety intimidate Petropoulos not in the slightest. He has taken on, with Olympian equanimity, the Piraeus bird market; the ubiquitous kiosque/news-stand/mini-variety store called the *periptero*; and Greek homosexual slang. But despite the broad range of his work and the hidden sophistication of his method, his approach has always been dictated less by intellectual considerations, more by the roiling viscera. "I'm simply not interested in writing academic books which will be read only by other academics," he snorts.

Today, pushing seventy, Petropoulos has mellowed slightly. His bushy white beard seems less the avenging prophet's and more that of the veteran Parisian *intello*. His manner has become more expansive, perhaps even contemplative as he looks back with affection on the micro-history of his past. Petropoulos' anecdotes evoke a state of constant temporal flux as they weave back and forth across the decades. The years of absence have pried geographic particulars from his grasp, have liberated names and events from the constraints of linear chronology, but they have produced a limpid essence that has penetrated into every crevice and hollow of his consciousness. Nowhere does this subterranean wellspring of reminiscence flow closer to the surface than when the subject is Salonica in whose teeming streets he quickly learned, as a boy, to identify each national or religious group by its appearance and its speech. "To know who you were," he says, "you had to know who everyone else was."

Each could be recognized by the trades and occupations most of its members exercised, a legacy of Ottoman rule. Armenians monopolized the coffee trade; Albanians specialized as butchers; Serbs held the pastry franchise; Thracian Greeks sold milk and yogurt; porters and itinerant tobacco sellers were Jewish. Under the Turks, the Albanians, who enjoyed a reputation for indomitable toughness and devotion to their masters, had been employed as security guards. Their responsibilities included protecting private property, and accompanying children to and from school. Both duties they performed with gusto. Danger, primarily from pederasts as bold as they were numerous, was acute and constant. After the capture of Salonica by the Greeks, the armed guards vanished as the community gradually abandoned its particularities. But a few Albanians stayed on, hawking *baklava* made with stale bread crumbs instead of the traditional walnuts. As for the pederasts, he laughs, "We kids knew how to resist, and who to stay away from." Shoemaker's and tailor's shops were to be avoided; dry-goods merchants and boatmen given a wide berth.

In Old Salonica each of the main national groups—the Turks, the Greeks, the Jews—had their own fire brigade, which patrolled their respective communities every night, waiting for the cannon high atop the Citadel to sound the alarm. The brigades would likewise fight fires only among their own, he reminisces, slipping effortlessly across the decades. The Turkish firemen had direct connections with the underworld, and would demand payment before unrolling their hoses. In many cases, these brigades—who were little more than organized brigands—would demolish intact houses in order to reach the building in flames. The luckless owners could only avoid disaster at the hands of the fire fighters by paying a handsome on-the-spot ransom. The Jewish brigades, while less given to depredation than their Turkish comrades-in-arms, sang marching songs in Ladino, which featured obscene or insulting refrains in Greek. "Relations between the communities were not necessarily idyllic, even then," he says with a chuckle. "But that was Salonica. That was its wealth."

As befitted rulers and administrators, the Turks lived in isolation, their contact with the locals restricted to the barest minimum. The Ottoman system devolved considerable powers to the religious communities whose spiritual and relative administrative autonomy was protected by Islamic law. As rulers and mandatees of God, few learned Ladino, Greek, Bulgarian, Albanian, Armenian or any of the other tongues spoken in Salonica: those supplicants who wished to speak to the Pasha could bring their dragoman. The Turkish overlords would spend their days in idleness, passing time in the city's many coffee-houses, puffing on water pipes or sipping thick, syrupy coffee from demitasses, relates Petropoulos. "Back then, Salonica was famous for its plane trees, many of whose trunks were so thick that several men had to link arms to encircle them completely. In the summer, under these trees, the Turks would play backgammon. These same trees were also home to enormous bird populations, and it often happened that the backgammon players would be spattered by droppings. But they would keep right on playing, imperturbable, waiting until the foreign material was quite dry before brushing it carefully to the ground. They were the rulers, after all."

THE RULERS BEQUEATHED TO SALONICA—as they did to all of Greece—a legacy both cultural and material. Extirpating the Ottoman heritage has been one of the central tasks of the fabricators of Greek national consciousness. Proto-Hellenistic language purifiers sought to return Greek to the golden age of Periclean Athens by recreating a modern-day version of the ancient Attic dialect, expunging Turkish, Arabic and Italian words as they went. City planners conspired and acted to Europeanize the Balkan cities they inherited as Greece expanded northward.

The ethno-purist mythifiers were quick to batten onto the Hegelian doctrine of rectilinear progress, recasting it as a kind of Balkan manifest destiny from which, 100 years later, modern-day Greek scholars still seem unable to break free. "Ottoman rule in the Balkans had been identified not only as religious and political oppression" writes University of Thessaloniki professor Alexandra Yerolympou, "but also as economic and social stagnation," and describes its institutions as obsolete, "relying on juridical distinction of its subjects on the basis of religious affiliation."[17]

These judgments seem ironic when we compare the relative harmony in which dozens of ethnic groups coexisted within an Ottoman state where distinctions were made only along religious lines, to the region's bloody history of ethnic strife between and within tiny states organized on the Western nationalist principle. Or when we reflect on the fate of Salonica's once-flourishing Jewish community, now reduced by the triple-headed *deus ex machina* of fire, urban renewal and genocide, to a tiny, fearful remnant.

But to cast the earnest, well-meaning Greek urbanists as first the agents, then the apologists for the destruction of the old city would be to fall too easily into a perverse kind of inverted nationalism. In fact, the progress-doctrine of the nineteenth century had become the main force within the "medieval" Ottoman state as a whole, and had marshaled behind it the prestige and might of expanding colonial Europe. As the *Tanzimat* of 1839 signaled the political and social westernization of the Empire, so it also sounded the death knell of the medieval city with its dark, fetid, disease-breeding lanes. On imperial order, sections of the Byzantine ramparts which ringed Salonica were demolished. The harbor-side walls were removed in 1870, opening the city to the sea and strengthening its vocation as a crossroads of Balkan trade and the Empire's gateway to the West. A grid system was introduced, and the former rigid religious divisions were abolished as people of all religious groups were authorized to purchase property and build houses, offices, theaters and restaurants. Salonica, show-window of the Empire, was marching double-time toward its European destiny with the kind of inevitability the latter-day high-priests of Structural Adjustment could recognize, maybe even identify with. The spectacle was as pathetic as it was grandiose.

Istanbul itself had established the precedent. Where once the Empire's architects were commissioned by the Sultans to build mosques which gave material depth and contour to the Qur'anic dispensation, and in whose beauty the Sultans could accessorily bask, they now turned their talents to lavish sea-front palaces, state structures, and commercial buildings. In both the capital and in its second city the Empire proclaimed to all who could read the signs embodied in these new buildings that Islam, the cement which had held it together for six centuries, had turned frail and brittle, had become irrelevant.

PETROPOULOS SHOWS ME A SKETCH of the Salonica skyline in triptych: at the end of the nineteenth century; shortly after the Greek conquest during the First Balkan War of 1912; and today. The first panel shows a field of minarets, scattered like wild-flowers against a backdrop of hills; the second, rows of low-lying buildings minus the minarets against the same background; the third, a wall of high-rise apartments obliterating the background. The Ottomans' attempts to transform it into a modern European city reflected the confluence of political power, speculation and high desperation that characterized the Empire's last days. The project was short-lived: the change of masters amputated Salonica from the Macedonian hinterland, and rapidly reduced it to a bustling provincial town which would have to reinvent itself through the erasure of five centuries, a process some Greeks describe as "awakening from a long nightmare."

Thus Salonica's fleeting glory as the bridgehead of Ottoman modernity met its brutal end in early November, 1912, when the Greek army led by the Glücksbergs, *père et fils*—King George I and Crown Prince Constantine—entered the city in a driving rain. Symbolically, their route followed the Via Egnatia and beneath the triumphal arch of Galerius, in the footsteps of the legions of Rome and Byzantium. Popular acclaim was less than delirious; the occasion well short of triumphant. As the bandy-legged, unshaven, dark-skinned, mud-spattered infantrymen marched through the heart of the commercial district led by their mounted officers they encountered not happy throngs but indifference, locked shops and closed shutters. Small knots of enthusiastic Greeks looked on, of course, cheering and waving Greek flags. But the majority, the Jews, not only considered themselves loyal Ottoman citizens; they remembered how they had celebrated the victory of 1897, which had seen Turkish armies humiliate the Greeks and thrust far south into Greece. They remembered, too, that the Sultan had given them a new home more than four centuries before when a Christian monarch had expelled them from Spain. "The Greeks claim they liberated Salonica," snorts Petropoulos. "But exactly whom did they liberate?"

The putative liberators of Salonica may have had more on their minds than the release from bondage of their unredeemed brethren, for the city's Greek minority was relatively small. The first census carried out by the occupation authorities, in 1913, showed 61,439 Jews, 45,867 Turks, 39,956 Greeks, 6,263 Bulgars and nearly 5,000 of diverse other nationalities.[18] As interpretation of census figures in defense of national interests has provided much of the ammunition for Balkan bloodshed, extreme caution must be employed in their use. The most reliable rule of thumb is to consider all ethnic-based census reports as flawed and suspect. The problem is, that in this region, there are none other.

Greece, in the first three decades of the twentieth century, was in the throes of the *Megali Idea* (the" Great Idea") an aggressive strategy of national expansion designed to "restore" the Byzantine Empire and establish the capital of Greece in Constantinople. If this meant removing the infidel Turks, and blocking the equally exalted national aspirations of the Balkan states to the north, so be it. Athenian intellectuals dreamed of a Greece of "five seas and two continents," while Greek military intelligence officers disguised as consular officials subverted the previously law-abiding minority communities scattered throughout the faltering Ottoman state. As the greater subversion of Ottoman Turkey was the principal aim of the Great Powers, they found it useful to flatter Athens' megalomaniac aspirations, now letting the horse gallop ahead, now reining it in, to suit their own political and geostrategic designs.

King George was to pay the ultimate price for his ostentatious public support of Hellenic nationalism. Instead of retiring to the safety of the royal palace in the countryside near Athens, he chose to stay on in Salonica. The desire to calm increasingly vociferous anti-monarchical sentiments directed against the German-Danish royal family by the pro-British republican faction led by an ambitious Cretan politician called Eleftherios Venizelos may also have been a consideration. The King was wont to stroll unguarded through the streets, a living demonstration as much of his concern for the realm's newly acquired subjects as of his foolhardiness. On one such constitutional, in early March, 1913, he was shot and killed on a quiet street in the eastern suburbs by a lone gunman, a Greek. The alleged killer, a mental defective, was said to have killed himself—conveniently—shortly after his arrest.

Crown Prince Constantine, liberator of Salonica and victor over the Turks, quickly ascended the throne. Unlike his cautious, diplomatically-minded father, the blustering, headstrong but mental light-weight Constantine fancied himself as a Supreme Commander. He was also an ardent Germanophile, who affected the spiked Prussian helmet as he participated in military exercises with his friends of the imperial German general staff. No one had failed to notice that King George had enjoyed close relations with the Entente, one member of which, France, had trained and equipped the victorious Greek army. Greek historians, asserts Petropoulos, have handled the assassination with an uncustomary lack of curiosity. Though no links between the killer and the pro-German lobby in Greece have ever been established, the regicide poisoned Greek domestic and foreign politics for decades, pitting the pro-German royalist faction against the pro-British supporters of Venizelos.

Nowadays Greece is a republic, of course, though the playboy grandson of the King, former heir apparent Constantine Glücksberg, still flirts with posing as a national unifier for a populace increasingly disgruntled with the cupidity of elected politicians, a concept copied from dusty British and American Cold War manuals. In the modishly nondescript Euro-capital, Athens, royalty has vanished both as memory and concept. In parochial Salonica, however, both monarchs still linger on in statue form. George I, the father, slumbers in leafy, marbled obscurity, remembered in a bust set in a mini-park marking the spot where he was shot, surrounded today by the indifference of pizza parlors, ice-cream shops and green-grocers. But Constantine the son, he of martial mien, can be seen astride his war-horse on the southern flank of Vardar Square. It was not always, however, thus.

For years, the monarch's equestrian statue—Salonica's marble horseman which has inspired, as far as I know, no local Pushkin—was hidden shamefully away in an obscure square named for the pre-war fascist dictator Metaxas. But during what the Greeks now call "the miserable seven years" of the Junta, the statue was installed at the foot of the Via Egnatia where it stands today, torso facing due eastward toward Constantinople, ultimate goal of Greek national fantasy, head turned harborward, toward the red-light district.

GREECE WAS NOT ALONE, of course, in pursuing an expansionist national policy. Its Balkan neighbors were assiduously pressing their own claims to all, or a portion, of European Turkey, at the heart of which lay Macedonia. Bulgaria, which had been brief master of most of the territory following Istanbul's defeat in the 1877 Russo-Turkish war, had never abandoned its claim. Serbian extremists, stung by the Austrian occupation of Bosnia, founded an organization called "Black Hand" which was to provide exemplary leadership in the sacred struggle for Greater Serbia.

By early 1912, Austrian designs on the Balkans had become unmistakable. Serbia and Bulgaria, under Russian patronage, joined forces to block Austro-German expansion toward the Adriatic and the Aegean. A month later Greece and Bulgaria entered into a defensive alliance. The Russian scheme was a brilliant success. So brilliant that its creature, the Balkan League, soon began to act as though it had its own agenda. In the event, it did: the military defeat of Turkey and the partition of Macedonia.

In early October, Moscow and Vienna, those erstwhile adversaries, warned their Balkan protégés against precisely such a temptation. The warning came too late; the puppet had taken on a life of its own, had slipped its strings, and now acted independently of the puppet-master. Montenegro, the smallest of the allied states, declared war on Turkey. Serbia, Bulgaria and Greece followed suit. Forced to wage war on three fronts, the Ottomans hastily fell back towards Istanbul. The rapidity and completeness of the allied victories astonished their European patrons, and shattered what remained of Turkey's European dominions.[19]

For Greece, the Balkan campaign was sweet revenge for the humiliating defeat of 1897. The Greek forces bore north, sweeping away the Turkish army or surrounding and isolating its garrisons. Soon the road to Salonica, which lead through the marshy delta of the Vardar, lay open.

W. H. Crawford Price, a British journalist who could ill-conceal his sympathies for the doughty Hellenes, was an eyewitness to events in the Macedonian capital: "We were cut off from all communication with the outside world, and surrounded by hostile armies. At Yenidje there were Greeks, at Kuprili (Veles) Servians, at Strumnitza and Demi Hissar Bulgarians, while outside the range of the guns at Karaburun lay the Greek fleet, eager to rush in and seize its impotent prey. Provisions were at famine prices; wise housewives had laid in stores of flour; Consulates had made necessary arrangements for sheltering terrified subjects. Greeks were exultant but terrified; Jews downcast and fearful for their worldly possessions; Turks broken-spirited but stoical; Europeans indifferent but anxious."

"In the cold, muddied streets men wandered aimlessly hither and thither, discussing the eternal 'situation' in entire ignorance of fact or details."[20]

The citizens of Salonica, obsessed with the question of day-to-day survival, paid little heed to the Empire collapsing about them. Turkish refugees fleeing before the invading armies sought shelter in the city. The first arrivals were housed in mosques and schools, but their number soon exceeded available space. It was not until the evening of October 29 , 1912, when the German patrol boat "Lorelei" dropped anchor in the port that the Salonicians realized they would be losing their most illustrious guest, deposed Sultan Adbulhamid. Within a few hours the recluse of the Villa Allatini and his retinue had been transferred to the warship, which promptly steamed off toward Istanbul. The last thing the crumbling Young Turk regime could afford was the loss of the erstwhile "Red Sultan," its prize hostage and nemesis. He died in 1918, a lonely pariah, in the capital on the Bosphorus, a few months before the final defeat which sealed the fate of the Empire.

Meanwhile, the military situation continued to deteriorate. Greek forces were now within striking distance, and a Bulgarian army was rushing south toward Salonica in a forced march. The garrison could not withstand a siege; the Turks decided to capitulate. On November 8, Hassan Tahsin Pasha, the Ottoman commander, accepted terms which had been handed him the previous day. That evening, the indefatigable Crawford Price proceeded to the Konak, the government house: "I found Nazim Pasha, the Governor General, sitting on a divan with his legs curled up under him, calmly writing his last letter as Vali of Salonica. His nation had lost its reputation; Islam had been driven out from Macedonia, and he had lost his post; but he nevertheless sat there serene and apparently unaffected by the tremendous history in the making around him."[21]

Thus, with a whimper, ended 482 years of Turkish rule. The government house they built still stands. Its creaking wood floors no longer echo with the shuffling of Ottoman functionaries' slippered feet, but every morning supplicants arrive, congregating around sub-ministerial doorways, petitions and letters of recommendation in hand. Fine Persian rugs cover the floor of the Minister's office, not unlike those the Greeks found when they seized the Konak the following day.

A new, official victory parade was organized three days later after the occupation authorities had ordered all homes and shops to fly Greek flags. In the interim, the symbol makers had been hard at work. The capture of Salonica was decreed to have taken place on Saint Demetrius' day, October 26, a date calculated to make the hearts of the Greek citizens beat faster. Had not Salonica's Byzantine warrior patron, astride his red stallion, intervened miraculously in the past to save the metropolis? But in 1912, the old calendar was still in force in the Orthodox Church. Saint Demetrius' day had been celebrated two weeks before.

The occupiers took rapid action to change the face of Old Salonica. The process of Hellenization was relentless, thoroughgoing and even violent. Its first victims were, of course, the Turks. The city was quickly stripped of the primary symbol of its former identity. Virtually all of Salonica's 60 minarets were destroyed during the first five years of the Greek occupation, explains Petropoulos. The Greek military waged its own *kulturkampf.* Aided by Prime Minister Venizelos' much-loathed Cretan gendarmes, it obliterated signs in French and Spanish. Mosques were transformed into churches, as shown in post-cards of the day, guarded by armed Greek soldiers to discourage the Muslim faithful from attending to their religious duties. One minaret was left standing, at the Hortac Effendi mosque, the late-Roman circular structure known as the Rotonda. The municipal authorities attempted to destroy it too, on the pretext of imminent collapse, Petropoulos relates. "But minarets have a bad habit of not falling, even in the most powerful earthquakes. They're built to sway, not break."

For Salonica, the crucial question was that of Bulgaria's claim to the city. A few hours after the Greek forces had marched into the city along the coast road from the west, a Bulgarian army detachment had entered from the north. They immediately seized the former mosque of Saint Sofia, now reverted to an Orthodox cathedral, set up their military headquarters just across the street, and organized their own victory parade, complete with brass band.

"The Greeks found themselves preoccupied," wrote Crawford Price, "with the serious complications presented by the disconcerting behavior of the Bulgarians. They had become the unwilling hosts of ten instead of two battalions of allied troops; several public buildings and one of the largest mosques had been commandeered by the Bulgars; General Theodoroff had hastened to inform the King and the whole world that the Bulgarians had conquered the town. Moreover, Sandanski's 'komitadjis' had entered the citadel."[22]

The victorious allies—armed, trained and abetted by their Great Power sponsors—had all but succeeded in ousting the Turks from Europe. Now dissension grew in their ranks as among robbers arguing over the division of the spoils. To complicate matters further, the Great Powers were insisting that an autonomous Albanian state be created from the wreckage of European Turkey, which meant that the Serbs would have to give over to the new state some territory they had conquered. To turmoil was added opaque complexity.

In an atmosphere of claim and counter claim, Greece and Serbia concluded a secret alliance against their erstwhile ally Bulgaria. At this point the Bulgarians made yet another of the fatal blunders which have plagued the country's foreign policy. In late June, 1913, they attacked the Greek and Serbian lines in Macedonia. The move was intended as a political demonstration the aim of which was to provoke Russian mediation. But the Serbians and the Greeks replied to the Bulgarian "demonstration" with an energetic counter-demonstration of their own: they declared war. Once again Balkan peasants were handed rifles, given a fistful of bread and onions, and sent off to fertilize the Sacred Soil of the Nation with their blood, torn flesh and crushed bones. As they may yet do again if the secret Balkan deals we can assume are being made today are acted upon.

In Salonica, the Greeks swung into action immediately. The Bulgarian army had established small garrisons in half a dozen quarters of the town, and around each the Greeks had placed strong detachments of troops, thus rendering escape impossible, writes Crawford Price. "Against the principal Bulgarian stronghold...the Greeks showered bullets from the houses opposite, while from quick-firing guns posted on top of the famous White Tower, a murderous leaden hail swept up the street at given intervals.[23]

The Second Balkan War was short, intense and bloody. And though it was militarily decisive, it created an even greater political impasse than the one which had caused it. Surrounded, under attack from all sides, Bulgaria could offer no serious resistance to the coalition of Greek, Serbian, Rumanian and Ottoman forces. On August 10 peace was signed by the Balkan states at Bucharest. Greece was awarded Salonica. Bulgaria not only lost the city, but its territorial gains in Macedonia as well. Greater Bulgaria overnight became an irredentist's folly. The Bucharest treaty solved nothing: Bulgaria refused to accept the settlement; Serbia still chafed at Austria's occupation of Bosnia. The stage was set for the Third Round, which was to begin one year later, when Archduke Francis Ferdinand visited Sarajevo on June 28, 1914, St. Vitus' day, anniversary of the battle of Kosovo Polje, in 1389.

A HISTORIAN HAS APTLY DESCRIBED the Balkan crisis as causing "the spark that set off the fatal blast in the powder keg of Europe."[24] Salonica, which had been the apple of discord throughout the long agony of the Ottoman Empire, remained a ring-side spectator to the hostilities as Greece declared neutrality at the beginning of the First World War. This ill-suited the Entente powers, which attempted to entice Athens to enter the war on their side with promises of territory in Asia Minor in return for concessions to Bulgaria in Macedonia, thus laying the groundwork for another disaster. Venizelos, Great Statesman on the make, rose to the bait like a hungry carp. But the court and its pro-German friends in the armed forces favored the Central Powers and refused to take any action which might offend the Kaiser. Stalemate ensued.

A small French-British expeditionary force was promptly dispatched to Salonica under the pretext of honoring the Entente's treaty obligations to Serbia. The allies landed in October, 1915, at Karaburun, a promontory east of the city not far from Batche Ciftlik, and thus began a *de facto* military occupation/blockade which was to last until Greece finally agreed to join the war against the Central Powers.

Once more the cafés of Liberty Square hummed with the cosmopolitan confusion of tongues as French and English vied with Greek and Italian. Ladino, too, was never far out of earshot. The polylingual brothels of Vardar Square did ravishing business. For lack of military diversion, Generalissimo Paul Sarrail, the aging supreme commander of the allied forces, spent most of his time organizing glittering soirées the main attraction of which was his young and voluptuous bride, prompting French Prime Minister Clémenceau to remark that Sarrail had two fronts to defend.[25]

Into the morass of a city surrealistically aloof from combat while caught up in swirling, intertwining currents of intrigue, sailed a modern-day Argonaut-in-reverse. Alberto Savinio, younger brother of painter Giorgio De Chirico, had set out from Taranto aboard the troop-ship Savoia, a member of the Italian contingent of the Entente forces. Their final destination was Salonica.

> *We arrive at our goal. The sun rises above Mount Athos. I look to the left: from the middle of a boiling ridge of clouds the white wedge of Olympus opens out. Jove sleeps up there amidst the snow and the cries of lice infested eagles: ex-god, with thundering eyebrows who clasps Ganymede in his arms, tender little sacerdote of mystic pederasty. And look down there, another world: it's Salonica, which I nickname 'the disquieting city'..."* [26]

Savinio's vision of the Orient as represented by Salonica may have been a response to the Grecophile proclivities of his more gifted elder brother, an orientalizing counter-vision, a proto-Nietzschean parody or the congenital envy-tinged scorn we reserve for those who are almost identical to us. Something of each, probably. Savinio is nothing if not the ambiguous counterweight to the classicist de Chirico, who assimilated and later metaphorically depicted the mechanisms (including those of the engineer and the earth measurer) by which Europe had managed to appropriate ancient Greece while conjuring up a "Greece" of the imagination on the site of a former Byzantine outpost and Ottoman province. To call our visitor jaundiced would be to understate the matter:

> *I've even had to give up the little bourgeois diversion of reading the newspapers. I don't have the courage to barter away half my pay for one of those smart, hybrid multilingual sheets that tell me 'Luna di Moisè Molho and Guida Bejà Matarasso are fiancés' or 'Maison Saporta met en vent des articles militaires à prix très réduits...' Then there's the night life: 'The White Tower' and the little shack called the 'Variétés' where a Corinthian songwriter sings 'The Lover's*

> *Deaf' in the Neapolitan dialect... Oh, my far away friends, I have dreams, so many dreams (...)*
>
> *August. Half of Salonica burns in a single night. A bit of relief from the mattress of monotony. But the fire's put out and my relief with it.* [27]

What had succeeded only in stirring the semi-catatonic Savinio from his lethargy was, for Salonica, a monstrous convergence of disaster and opportunity: the Great Fire of August 5, 1917. Kindled in a tiny shack just north of Saint Demetrius Street, and fanned by hot winds, the blaze quickly engulfed the wood-framed constructions that made up most of Salonica's central district. Under orders from General Sarrail, the French forces bombarded the city to stop the fire from spreading, thereby encouraging its ravages. By the time it hand finally burnt itself out, 72,000 people were homeless, and more than 4,000 buildings had been destroyed. Gone were the cosmopolitan cafés and the great sea-front hotels, the department stores and hundreds of small craftsmen's shops. More tragically, the fire obliterated the infrastructure of the Jewish community, its synagogues and schools; most of the buildings lost had been owned by Jews. All that had given the city its distinctive flavor now lay in smoldering ruins.

The Venizelos government, which had begun as an anti-monarchist military rebellion in Salonica the preceding year, promptly expropriated the burned-out area, and appointed an international commission chaired by Ernest Hébrard, a French city-planner serving in the Army of the Orient, to supervise the transformation from a Jewish-Ottoman city to a Helleno-European one. Hébrard, who was later to gain higher distinction for his remake of French colonial Hanoi, devised a uniform architectural style, opened wide boulevards and diagonal transverse avenues in the manner of Baron Hausmann. The memory of the city was to be embodied—embalmed, better—in "noble" buildings harking back to the Roman and Byzantine past.[28] The plan, needless to say, expressed the prevailing ideology of the day: modern Greece as the reincarnation of Byzantine imperial glory, somehow combined with the democratic heritage of the Athenian Golden Age and seasoned with a liberal pinch of Alexander the Great. What the fire had not obliterated, Hébrard's plan would. The remaining vestiges of the Ottoman Empire, and the muscle and sinew of the Jewish community which for four centuries had given Salonica its inimitable character and its life, were swept away.

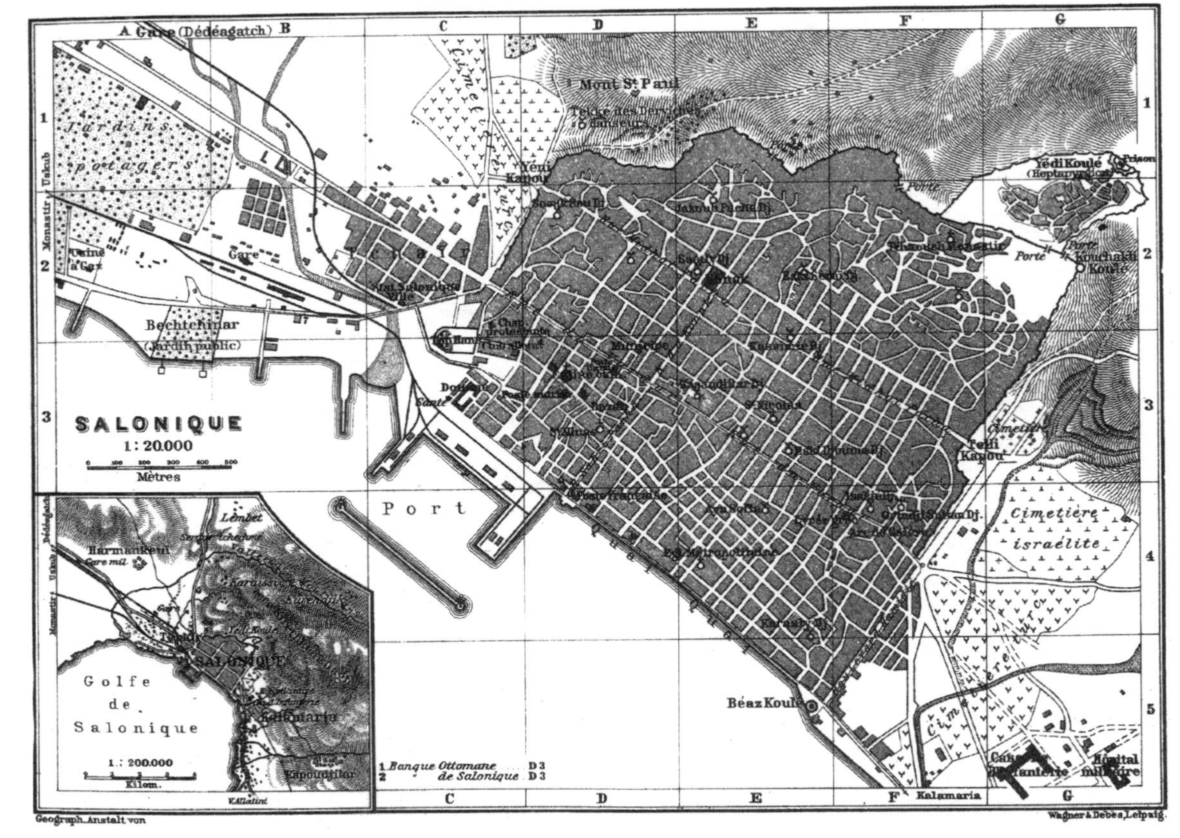

Map of Salonica from Karl Baedeker's guide (1914). From *Old Salonica*, ©1980, Elias Petropoulos

CHAPTER 2

SAINTS AND ZEALOTS

THE SALONICA SEA FRONT functions simultaneously as the city's focus and as a powerful dilatory organ which concentrates in one energy-charged space a succession of coffee-shops, bars, sweet emporiums, amusement parks, ice-cream parlors, pop-corn and toasted nut wagons, self-propelled sandwich outlets, strolling balloon and souvenir hawkers. When the weather is fine, the broad promenade is thronged with well-dressed peripatetic philosophers of a certain age who gesticulate more energetically than they walk, with youthful joggers, bicyclists, with groups of townspeople simply enjoying the cool, damp air; gulls, pigeons, and further offshore, cormorants. There is something romantic, even erotic—metaphorically at least—about this boundary zone where the city meets the sea, where the hot concrete and asphalt meld into the enveloping liquid embrace of the waters.

Further east, the paved promenade gives way to a narrow, weed-grown sidewalk; the perspective of Salonica Bay to a succession of water-sport installations, marinas and boat clubs, and then, to rows of psarotavernas where, later in the evening, the good burghers will repair for a meal of mussels stuffed with rice, fried baby squid, grilled shrimp and tangy cabbage salads laced with hot pepper, washed down with *raki* or dry white wine from the vineyards of the Halkidiki peninsula, in the shadow of Mount Athos.

It is here, along the sweeping arc of the sea-front that I found myself strolling briskly, of a cloudy evening in early April. A moist southerly breeze was blowing, but not strongly enough to ripple the foul smelling, viscous water lapping against the quay. Freighters, their bows and sterns aglow, rode low at anchor, silhouetted against the darkening sky.

My destination that April evening was the home of Tolis Kazantzis, the man who for me personified Salonica. In the spring of 1994, the face of the city, while unchanged, had become subtly unrecognizable. I was on my way to present my condolences to his widow, for Kazantzis had died on Christmas day, 1991, from acute internal bleeding brought on by chronic liver disease, his death precipitated by an exhausting series of public lectures in Athens on—what else?—Salonica's literary heritage and tradition. This was my first trip back to the city he loved so ardently; the city he, unlike many locally-born authors, refused to abandon for the blandishments and the notoriety of the Athenian literary whirl.

Mirror—and sculptor—of Salonica's identity, its literary tradition springs from a devotion to the particular: to the sweep of the water-line separating sea from land, to the forested hills that ring the town, to the fragility and violence of its history, and to the ephemeral yet enduring nature of its Greekness. Few writers captured these particulars better than Kazantzis, and no one defended them more pugnaciously, researched them more exhaustively, wrote of them with greater insight, affection and sharp-edged irony:

> *When the wind blows from the south clouds fill the sky. Then, for a few hours, the wind will stop before the rain begins or the Vardari picks up. Whenever the south wind stills, a choking stench rises up from the water. Half the town or more, as far as Koulé-Café and Tsinari, reeks like an open cesspool. But in spite of the thick cloud cover, there are moments when the sun glints through.*
>
> *On just such an afternoon you may find yourself sitting in a deserted coffee-house at the corner of Apostle Paul and Saint Demetrius streets, just across from the Turkish consulate and Kemal's house, and the waiter will come up to you. "Tripe soup and coffee don't really taste good unless they stink a bit," he'll say, to head off the observation you were about to make about the half-washed cup.*
>
> *Still, up from the water rose the stench and me, I was fresh out of observations. Just as I was in no mood to share my thoughts with the shoeshine boy who, as he had buffed my shoes earlier, grumbled on about how prices were going up. I don't know about you, but I've had it up to here with concierges and the people who run the sidewalk kiosks Now the shoeshine boys are trying to find out what's on our minds? What else were we supposed to tell these "specialists" so they could figure out what we were thinking? Subjecting our political beliefs to a kind of urinalysis, that's what it was. So much for concierges and kiosk proprietors and, nowadays, shoeshine boys...*
>
> —**Tolis Kazantis**, *Η Παρέλαση. Ενηλικίωση*, 1988

Our last meeting had taken place in Salonica a few months prior to his death. I was passing through the city on a reporting expedition to eastern Thrace, the home of Greece's Turkish minority. In a smoke-filled cafe—not literary cliché but inescapable reality, for in winter Greek cafes are, by definition, smoke-filled—Kazantzis regaled me with a rapid-fire succession of stories mixed with hair-raising inside information about infiltration of the minority community in Thrace by the Turkish secret police. This he had gleaned from a distant relative who worked for the Greek intelligence service while ostensibly teaching in a high-school attended by Turkish minority students. But all I could see were his burning, sunken eyes, his drawn face, the furious intensity of his gestures as he fired up one cigarette after another, all the while assuring me with the pride of perversity that he was under strict doctor's orders not to smoke. The Tolis Kazantzis I knew did not, I was certain, consciously seek death. But the man sitting across from me seemed to have accepted, in his innermost soul, that death was hard upon him, seemed to have decided to hasten its coming. The cutting force of his hands with their abrupt movements, and the fervid brilliance of his eyes spoke it though he did not.

In mourning, her black hair brushed austerely back, Kazantzis' widow Fani greets me at the door and shows me in. Her eyes have the grief-charged depth of the lamenting Holy Mother in a Byzantine icon but her strong hands are composed, calm. In a halting but firm voice she describes his last days, sparing little detail. I suppose this is what I've come to hear: the account of how an avoidable death became inevitable. And if his death was avoidable—if he had only stopped smoking, stopped drinking—why had Tolis Kazantzis defied good counsel? I wondered as I listened.

Perhaps to every man there comes a moment when it becomes clear that life cannot continue. Then he must carry out the bidding of a mysterious voice deep within him. Tolis Kazantzis had done that voice's bidding. His wife, children and friends buried him in the snow and biting cold on Christmas day, in the heart of the brief Salonica winter. That same day the lead item on the Athens television news featured homeless animals.

A FLOCK OF DIGNITARIES FLUTTERS to and fro outside the Basilica of Saint Demetrius, the glint of Greek full-dress military uniforms vivid against the phalanx of Orthodox clergymen in their black robes, cylindrical hats and full beards. From lamp-posts, flags and bunting in the national colors droop limply in the windless dusk. Police vans have blocked traffic on the street in front of the basilica, home and stronghold of Salonica's patron saint. Around the entrances squadrons of officers, walkie-talkies in hand, hover alertly, as if expecting a riot to break out at any moment. Any large gathering of Greeks generates a charge of excitement, a human magnetic field that crackles like static electricity in an overheated, dry room. But neither a civil servants' strike nor a student demonstration—public manifestations which attract anarchist violence as over-ripe fruit draws wasps—is in prospect. The evening's emanations are peaceful ones.

Inside the Basilica the dignitaries and the faithful have congregated to welcome a miraculous icon of the Holy Virgin transported for the occasion by Greek naval vessel from the island of Patmos to commemorate the feast of Saint Demetrius, holy martyr, warrior, and protector of the city. I select a vantage point near one of the side doors from which I can observe the worshippers as they shoulder their way into the church. Many are well-dressed young people and prosperous householders; several are exquisitely groomed women of the kind that turn heads on Tzimiski Street, the city's main shopping thoroughfare. The response of the multitude signifies this: faith has not yet been narrowed to a dark corridor inhabited by the old, the poor and the uneducated. Like a subterranean current it flows through public—and private—life, rising to the surface on the great festivals and saints' days, converging in seamless symbiosis with secular power. A blend of liturgical chanting, incense and pious intensity seems to radiate from the Basilica on this warm, humid evening. Was this the elusive sense of the sacred, a notion now floating in semi-respectability on the fringes of Western public discourse, an unavowed inversion of the world cult of the Golden Calf? Would I come upon a link, no matter how tenuous, no matter how deeply embedded in the interstices of collective memory, between the veneration of Saint Demetrius, the Orthodox Church as Authority and Hierarchy, and the resurgent, aggressive nationalism of the Greek state, very much on display this evening? That was another tale, one of the tales I had come to Salonica to hear told. Naively, as I was to discover.

Next morning, at the offices of the Metropolis, the Salonica Archdiocese, my pursuit of the tale began. Perhaps the better to ensure a near organic link between those heavenly Siamese twins of nationalism and religion, the offices are situated just around the corner from the Museum of the Macedonian Struggle. Only a few paces separate these two supposedly anachronistic but cantankerous survivors amidst the maelstrom of free-market glitz that would represent the city's contemporary identity, yet fools no one.

Despite the sanctimonious atmosphere, the place exudes a bureaucratic mustiness as unmistakable as its precise composition is complex: a faintly acrid odor of sweat and oft-worn clothes, rancid floor wax, mothballs, stale cigarette smoke and the cloying scent of false piety. The plastic flowers, crimson carpets and gilt-tipped furniture set up a jarring counterpoint to the expeditiously authoritative, pursed-lipped air of the bearded holy fathers I encounter as they scurry up and down their corridors, heads thrust forward like foraging ravens. Of course, Saint Demetrius' Day is just around the corner and the offices are busy. Still, would it be possible to speak with someone about him, I enquire of a young pope working at a computer in a room labeled 'Public Inquiries.' "Office number one or number four," he snaps back without lifting his head. "Knock and go right in."

I knock at the door of office number one and enter. At the far end of the room the secretary, a ruddy-faced pope ensconced behind a huge desk over which looms a huger potted plant, stops me with a highly inhospitable outstretched palm of the hand (in Greece the palm is usually only shown in anger; when this happens the gesture, known as the *moudza*, becomes an insult grievous enough to provoke a fight.) I elect to ignore the affront and retreat apologetically. Seeking my fortune at office number four, I peer around the frame of the open door. "What do you want?" rasps a slightly lesser presence, whom I've disturbed in the midst of a series of calls from the six telephones I manage to count on his desk. With obsequious wringing of hands I explain my case in the manner of a humble petitioner. I am favored with a reply. "Come to the Basilica this evening. You can meet professor Papadopoulos of the Theological School," he hisses. "After five." A phone—which one?—rings loudly. The audience is over.

On my way out, a painting displayed prominently in the hallway catches my eye. Done in the neo-Byzantine style affected by a certain nativist school, it depicts Salonica's religious and intellectual heritage against the background of a cityscape painted in the perspectiveless manner of a religious icon, the size of the figures depicted determined not by their nearness or distance in vanishing-point perspective but by their hieratical importance. Philip of Macedon and his illustrious son Alexander occupy the left quadrant; in the upper right-hand corner are the smaller figures of Aristotle and Democritus, identified in the stylized orthography of the Byzantine alphabet; more prominent is Saint Paul, who introduced the doctrine of Christ to the city's ever-skeptical Jews. At the center of the composition, set against a view of the Salonica International Exposition and the White Tower, are Saint Demetrius himself, the city's youthful warrior patron, and Saint Gregory Palamas, mortal foe of those fourteenth century radicals the Zealots, and one of the more controversial figures in late Byzantine Orthodoxy. At the top of the painting, overlooking city and port, are Jesus Christ and His Holy Mother, the Panaghia. Mother and Son loom almost as large as Alexander. Almost, but not quite.

In its methodical, triumphant subversion of Rome, Christianity rejected, then attempted to obliterate the Olympian pantheon of ancient Hellas, replacing the fractious, randy, unpredictable cohort of gods and heroes with an austere and omnipotent Father as whose viceroy the Emperor would rule. It also looked with extreme suspicion on ancient Greek science, art and philosophy, with its emphasis on the autonomy of the human spirit. Later, however, a shift took place. Latter-day icon-makers, following the lead of the Church itself, appropriated portions of the pagan heritage and incorporated them *holus bolus* into theologically incoherent but intellectually provoking—dare I say charming?—images depicting the ancient Athenian philosophers as forerunners of Christianity. As for Alexander, who died in the Orient shortly after declaring himself a Persian God, the process of co-option is so opaque as to defy explanation, notwithstanding the syncretic theories so dear to the hearts of religious scholars. Still, *Megalexandros* (as Greeks familiarly call the semi-barbarous world conqueror whom they claim as their own), that mainstay of folk song and legend, could hardly be absent from the pantheon. For without him the Greek claim to Macedonia would flounder and sink. And we are, lest it ever be forgotten, in Macedonia.

That evening, slightly after five o'clock, I make my way toward the Basilica office through a dense crowd of worshippers lined up to kiss the miraculous icon. There, a lone white-bearded pope is leafing furiously through a tattered telephone directory. I clear my throat, cough respectfully. He looks up. "What is it?" he barks. "Can't you see I'm busy?" Courtesy toward foreigner visitors was once tantamount to sacred law in Greece. That was before tourism. I'm looking for the professor, I explain, attempting to make my voice as humble as possible. Wasted effort. Waving the phone book in my direction, he shouts: "Out there, behind the altar. Now leave me alone!" I exit hastily. The priests may well represent the order of the sacred realm to the uncomprehending faithful; but these robed functionaries are more like the frocked equivalent of their secular colleagues, the men with the reptilian stares, hunched backs and tobacco-stained fingers who have encrusted the outlet pipes of the Greek state like exponentially expanding zebra mussels, and whose acutely self-protective mentality and nepotistic ardor has infected every cranny of public life.

Working my way cautiously through a scrum of clergymen jostling for position, for surely nothing enhances prestige and career prospects quite like an appearance inside the Holy of Holies alongside the archbishop, I approach the side-door to the altar. Providentially, a monk who is possibly even an anchorite, perhaps even, given his courtesy, a latter-day stylite, volunteers to seek out the professor for me. Three minutes later he emerges, accompanied by a man wearing a conservative dark suit. Professor Papadopoulos, I presume. I introduce myself, and we set an appointment. Byzantine chanting, sweet and melodious and cloying like warm, overripe peaches, echoes through the Basilica.

The next day, Saint Demetrius' eve, dawns fresh and bright. Salonica's protector has interceded to procure optimum weather conditions. This is the day when the Saint's icon departs the Basilica for its triumphant march through the city streets escorted by detachments of Greek soldiers in full battle dress, bayonets fixed to their rifles, followed by sailors, and elite commandos in camouflage suits. As an Air Force brass band strikes up a slow march, the bells of Saint Demetrius' burst into exited tolling. The effect is deeper than merely auditory. It sets the viscera ajar. Clouds of incense waft across the plaza, dissolving in bright sunlight, as the icon and its escort of high clergy emerge from the west portal. From the balconies of the surrounding apartment blocks the neighbors look on; a little boy waves a Greek flag from side to side. Now the parade forms up on Saint Demetrius street, headed by the brass band which is blaring out a dirge-like processional that sounds more German than Orthodox. Not the least contradiction of the day's festivities is that modern Greece's martial musical tradition was founded by the Bavarian—and Catholic—princes who were imported to rule the country after the European powers had decided to rescue the floundering 1821 mutiny against the Ottoman state.

The parade offers something for everyone, prefiguring the full-scale public ceremonies of the next two days. Groups of school children in starched uniforms march past, followed by monks and nuns carrying lighted candles, pre-adolescent girls in traditional regional costumes of the kind now only encountered in amateur regional folk-dance ensembles, and grizzled men representing Macedonian fighters in their full dress of black kilts and cross-buttoned vests. Then comes the clergy, arrayed in the fullest splendor of its festive crimson and gold vestments, moving with the majesty of its station, while close behind it, propped atop a Jeep-drawn caisson, follows the holy icon, followed by the silver-plated box containing the saint's remains. The Metropolitan himself, Panteleimon II, surrounded by the mayor, the prefect and the minister of Macedonia and Thrace, brings up the rear, beard flowing luxuriantly as, with his shepherd's gold cross, he blesses the flock lining the shady side of the street.

"WHEN THE CHRISTIANS BUILT CHURCHES on the sites of pagan sanctuaries, incorporating the old capitals and columns in their naves," writes Roberto Calasso[29], they were, like Heracles and the Nemean lion, killing the monster to incorporate it in themselves, taking its place. Such is the career of Saint Demetrius, a resurrection in Christian garb of the cult of the Cabiri, Salonica's semi-divine protectors in pagan times. These Cabiri—a non-Greek word, notes Robert Graves, thus of non-Greek origin—were the servants of Persephone, bringer of destruction, with whom Zeus had secretly begotten his son Zagreus. They were lesser deities, worshipped in grottos and caves, whose initiates wore pointed hats of the kind affected by the wily Odysseus. Their cult, which may have arisen in the islands of the northern Aegean, spread to the mainland in Thrace and Macedonia, sending down deep roots in the city founded by King Cassander when he took the sister of Alexander the Great, Thessaloniki, for his wife in 316 B.C., naming it after her. There, they became the patrons of navigators, miners and metal workers, and were worshipped as staunch defenders of the city. Not without cause. Had not these same holy ancestral gods turned back the great Gothic attack on Salonica in 268 A.D?[30]

When the Romans came, incorporating Macedonia into the Empire after the battle of Pydna in 168 B.C., they established public baths on the site of the Basilica where an earlier temple to the cthonic Cabiri may well have stood. In these baths, four hundred years later at the beginning of the fourth century, a certain Demetrius, Roman citizen and minor official, was slain by order of the Roman Emperor Galerius. Demetrius had been arrested several days earlier for participating in an illegal gatherings of a subversive group, the Christians. Then, in a gladiatorial combat in the arena the Emperor's favorite, Lyaeus, had been killed by a Christian called Nestor who had been blessed, the Roman police soon learned, by the imprisoned Demetrius who now stood exposed as ringleader of a plot. Aggrieved at the death of his protégé and humiliated by the victory of the subversives—a victory which had pleased the crowd in the arena too much for the emperor's taste—the emperor ordered the two upstarts killed by spear in the baths. That night, a handful of Christians buried their martyrs where they had perished.

A few years later Galerius, implacable tormentor of Christians, proclaimed a policy of religious tolerance which was later endorsed by his successor Constantine. A small church was built atop the grave site, which incorporated into its foundations a grotto from which—shades of the Cabiri—miracle-working myrrh would flow, an unquenchable source of lubrication for the legend. More than one century later, in the middle of the fifth century, a certain Leontius, prefect of Illyricum, is said to have ordered a great basilica to be constructed in the same place, in gratitude for having been cured of a grave illness through the miraculous intervention of the saint.[31] Today's Basilica, which is built upon the shell of the building almost totally destroyed in the great fire of 1917, conserves only fragmentary remains of its vast armature of pictorial decoration. The mosaics, survivals from the earliest structure, illustrate scenes from the life of the Saint himself, clad in a white tunic, often alongside local notables. None depict him in the attitude which, in the later icons by which he is best known, personifies him as Salonica's protector: the stern-faced horseman slaying an enemy with his lance. It was in this incarnation that he would despatch the putative foes of Hellenic Christendom with grim-eyed satisfaction, and preserve the city from barbarian depredations.

One of the few surviving frescoes curiously illustrates the saint not at all, but the triumphal entry of Byzantine Emperor Justinian II , surnamed "He of the Cut-off Nose," into Salonica after his defeat of an invading Bulgarian army in 688. That the arbitrary and impulsive Justinian collaborated with the Bulgars to regain his throne in 705 and wrought terrible vengeance on the adversaries who had earlier truncated his nose and ears is beside the point. The fresco symbolizes, claim its modern Greek explicators, less the triumph of Justinian II, an embarrassingly violent tyrant by any other name, than that of Hellenism over those traditional race enemies, the Slavs, all with the divinely inspired assistance of Saint Demetrius.[32] Thus is a wildly sanguinary Emperor retroactively press-ganged into the service of national-religious mysticism. That Justinian II and the other rulers of Byzantium would have considered themselves less as legatees of Hellenism than of Imperial Roman power seems, by comparison, a trifling consideration.

On the great feast day devoted to its namesake a powerful current of devotion ripples through the Basilica, invisible yet palpable, like the unseen forces—the hand and the eye of God—which seize and guide the hand of the iconographer. In the bright sunlight on the sidewalk outside the church I encounter art historian Haralambos Bakirdzis, a professor at the University of Thessaloniki. After I explain what has brought me to Salonica, and to Saint Demetrius' on this day, professor Bakirdzis invites me into the shady interior of the church, showing me through the plaza portal as though welcoming me into his own home. Reasonably enough, for the saint's house, in the hearts of Salonica's devout Greek citizens, has always been the ultimate refuge, and the saint, the protector of the communal hearth and miraculous talisman when outside forces threatened.

"The rationalism of the West makes it hard for you to understand Byzantium," Bakirdzis says with a self-assured smile as we move down the high, colonnaded nave, now hazy with a fragrant cloud of incense. I want to ask him why, if Byzantium so confounds the rational, do the fabulators of modern Greek identity insist that it be seen as an integral part of the unbroken cultural continuum leading from the ancient Athenian heritage of democracy, philosophical inquiry and, yes, rationality, to the present day. But at that precise instant, as if on cue, the holy icon sweeps into the church, its round of the city completed. The air has grown hot from the crush of bodies and the thousands of flames from the votive candles which candle-lighters clad in blue coveralls snatch away and discard as soon as they are lighted to make way for the next.

The existence of Saint Demetrius, explains the professor as we settle into two of the high-backed pews that line the side walls of the Basilica, is truer than any reality. "He cannot be grasped by rational means, and if you try to do so, you will be making a big mistake. You see," he whispers, leaning toward me, "the icon truly is Saint Demetrius, as well as being his depiction." In vain I search for a hint of irony in his words: I find none.

Like every Orthodox church, which not only replicates by visual means the heavenly order, beginning with Christ Pantocrator high in the dome, and descending through concentric rings of the Holy Family, the Archangels, the saints and the holy martyrs, the Basilica physically contains and embodies that order as well. "The Byzantine esthetic is based on replication," he explains. "Not on the search for originality. How else can you explain its remarkable life-span? There was no such thing as 'intellectual property' in Byzantium; the orthodox tradition is one of anonymity; the great icon painters never signed their works—those who did were influenced by the West." As the icon pushes its way through the crowd and up the central aisle, the hymn of Saint Demetrius rings out, and professor Bakirdzis sings along in a mellifluous tenor voice. When the silver-plated casket containing the saint's remains wheels into view, he turns to me, perhaps a touch archly: "That's for you rationalists. We don't need it."

Now his holiness Pantaleimon, the Metropolitan of Salonica, mounts his pulpit: "Saint Demetrius will defend his city against all those who covet it, against all those who plot to destroy it. He will support us in our great struggle to protect our identity as Greeks and as Macedonians," he thunders, ever responsive to the political imperatives of the hour, and the great church reverberates. To climax his homily, jarringly yet refreshingly coherent in its incoherence, the Metropolitan leads the congregation in singing the Greek national anthem, a stirring hymn to secular freedom written by the early nineteenth century poet Dionysios Solomos, a free-thinking bard from whose oeuvre religion is famously absent. Here, in the temple of timeless non-rationalism (for none of the three great monotheistic religions can be accurately described as irrational; only romantic nationalism, the ill-begotten offspring of their union with the Enlightenment, can make such a claim, and it too is a false claim) echoes the incandescent voice of the doctrine of secularity and of the emergent nation-state—"Hail, hail Liberty!"—against a background of imperial, supranational, divine dispensation which simultaneously symbolizes and embodies the true and only heaven.

The Metropolitan's sermon, in its barely concealed clash of symbols, invests the painting I'd encountered at Dioscean headquarters a few days earlier with sudden rhetorical depth. Greece, like the cityscape of Salonica, can be depicted in neo-Byzantine style, as a paradox: a full-fledged member of the European Union in which putatively non-rational Orthodoxy is the official religion, a religion so powerfully established, so deeply rooted in popular consciousness, that in the colloquial idiom "Christian" is taken to mean Greek. Furthermore, the Church enjoys promiscuous familiarity with the corridors of secular power, particularly in the aftermath of the collapse of "real socialism" in the Balkans and the powerful upsurge of national and religious sentiment that has flowed (or been pumped) in to fill the void.

Communism in Bulgaria and ex-Yugoslavia, not to mention tiny Albania, stifled religion and suffocated national impulses beneath a cloak of ersatz internationalism. In Greece, however, the Orthodox Church acted not only as handmaiden of state repression during the bitter civil war, but gave fervent blessing to the seven-year "Greek Christian" regime of the colonels. Had it bargained away its soul, or was it simply acting in its own, historic interests? More to the point, how had these historic interests become one with the modern Greek state?

Modern Greece, the creation of Western Europe in its war of attrition against the Grand Turk, has been a curious hybrid from birth. A Europeanized intelligentsia insisted that the new state be organized on the Jacobin model, leaving little room for religion, much less a state church. But its revolutionary thrust had been blunted by the Congress of Vienna, in 1814-1815, which enshrined the regime of hereditary monarchies and decreed the restoration of the pre-1789 status quo. The Greek uprising against the Ottoman state which broke out in 1821 only to be almost obliterated by the victorious Peloponesean campaign of Ibrahim Pasha in 1824, was rescued *in extremis* when a French-British-Russian fleet destroyed the Turkish armada at Navarino. The European victors, not the tattered and beaten Greek insurgents, would set the terms for the new state's existence.

Hardly a democracy on the exalted Athenian model, the new country was ruled by the youthful Prince Otho of Bavaria, overseen by a Regency Council established by the protecting powers. One of the first initiatives of the tiny, poverty-stricken, debt-ridden state was to have the Church of Greece declared independent from the Ecumenical Patriarch of Constantinople, the rock of faith upon which Orthodox religious identity had endured and thrived throughout the four hundred years of Ottoman rule. Where the Church of Constantinople ministered to the spiritual needs of a huge, multi-lingual and pluri-national flock spread across the Balkans and the Middle East, the newly founded Church of Greece was, from the beginning, the prisoner of the autocratic, Bavarian-ruled Greek state. The breakaway, which was denounced by the Patriarchate, touched off violent reactions among the religious conservatives who hewed to the strict traditions of Orthodoxy. Canonical communion between Constantinople and Athens was restored in 1850, but by then the Church of Greece had been totally converted to the secular values of nationalism, and transformed into an arm of the state, becoming the spearhead of the aggressive, irredentist ideology which has dominated Greece ever since.[33] The greater tragedy lay in the gradual conversion of the supra-national Patriarchate, under the influence of Athens, into an agent of Hellenization. From there, it was a slippery slide into the morass of national-religious identity. The Serbs, the Bulgarians, and ultimately the Macedonians insisted on asserting their own national-spiritual autonomy from Constantinople. The stage was set for the fragmentation of the Balkans along the historic and cultural fault-lines, what Thierry Hentsch calls the "imaginary frontiers" whose bloody fissures, zigzagging through Bosnia, Kosova and Albania, gape open still.

Late that evening I return to Saint Demetrius', drawn by the market atmosphere. More than a simple religious feast, the Saint's day marked the end of the trading and agriculture season throughout the southern Balkans. Salonica itself had been, for centuries, the site of a market fair which drew merchants from as far away as Serbia, Italy and Asia Minor, an event which lives on, some claim, in its latest reincarnation, the Salonica International Trade Fair. On the broad portico in front of the church, ill-shaven, dark-skinned men with strange accents sell tiny Greek flags and balloons; stooped old women in tattered black dresses beg in the shadows, repeatedly invoking the grace of God, the Saint and of thee, most merciful passer-by. Mercifully, the passers-by drop coins into her gnarled hand. Saint Demetrius' at night is redolent with beeswax and incense; for an instant I catch a whiff of rosewater, as if to underline the underlying community of devotion which, like the dark sea depths of the Mediterranean, unites Christianity with Islam, the invisible former inhabitant of this space.

PROFESSOR PAPADOPOULOS IS PRIMED for our meeting, a meeting for which I contrive to be precisely on time at nine o'clock one crisp morning. I've barely managed to sit down in his office in the Theology Faculty of the University of Thessaloniki before he plies me with books on—what else?—Saint Demetrius. No other saint in Orthodoxy has generated such a rich and extensive literature. All its religious tendencies claim him as their own, he volunteers. Even the quietists—the Hesychastes—a shadowy movement of fourteenth century mystics who fought a bitter and ultimately victorious battle against the ideas of the Western European renaissance. But, I insist, I want to know the professor's own views on the saint's identity; is he truly present in the icon, as professor Bakirdzis claimed the day before, or is the representation a symbolic one. Yes, yes, he reassures me, there is an identity of the two, the saint and his icon, in the sense that the icon leads you directly to the worship of the sacred. Professor Papadopoulos' true interest is less the icon, more its hidden—and, he would argue, truer—essence. "Only when the Son of God becomes human," he assures me, can He be depicted in His visible dimension. The icon, he explains, provides the agency.

Once the leap of faith has been made, worship through icons or the remains of saints provides solutions to the problems of life, he asserts. "Makes sense, doesn't it?" he says, looking at me from under bushy, arched eyebrows. "We venerate the images of the saints because they express man's material nature which in turn is created by God." By now the professor is in full flight, and I'm nodding and muttering uh-huh as my pen scratches furiously across the pages of my note-book. "Science can only deal with what is materially existent. But religion deals with the immaterial. Studying religious objects like icons leads us to knowledge of God. But this is not science. You know, the work of Orthodox icon painters is a form of prayer; the painter is preserving the spirit in the work. Without faith, it's impossible to depict the sacred, impossible to touch it."

Professor Papadopoulos' formula is both reassuring and troubling. The theoretical principal may be, from the theological point of view, unassailable. But when we come to an examination of cases, it is not always clear what exactly is the spirit preserved in the work and how it is apprehended by the faithful who look upon it. In the icon I have in mind, the one which best embodies the faith of the Salonicians, their protector Saint Demetrius, astride his rearing stallion, plunges a lance into the thorax of a bearded man who twists on the ground, teeth gnashing in finely drawn and exquisite agony.

Who is the bearded man that he should have so infuriated the saintly martyr? Greeks and Bulgarians both agree: the victim is a Bulgar. What they do not agree upon how he should be named.

In 1207 the Tsar of the Bulgars, Kalojan—John the Good—laid siege to Salonica, then a Frankish duchy. Those were dark days for Byzantium. Popish schismatics—the drunkards, master pillagers and freebooters who called themselves the Fourth Crusade—fresh from their conquest of Constantinople in 1204, defiled the throne and carved up the Byzantine dominions. Kalojan, his pride piqued at having been brushed aside like a vassal by the Latin conquerors, entered into a *contre nature* alliance with the Greeks. Restoring the offended glory of Orthodoxy may indeed have been the Tsar's prime motivation. More probably, he longed to wear the crown of the Basilieus and had aimed for the main chance: establishment of a Bulgarian empire at Constantinople.[34]

Short-lived and tenuous, the alliance crested with the battle of Adrianople, where the Greco-Bulgar armies under Kalojan routed the Crusaders. Soon thereafter the alliance collapsed, and the Tsar turned vengefully on his erstwhile comrades-in-arms, who had meanwhile thrown in their lot with the Greek-speaking Empire of Nicea, in Asia Minor. He took to styling himself Romaioctonos, the "Roman Slayer." In none too subtle a manner the nickname scornfully reminded the Byzantines that they would pay one day for the exploits of Basil II, known as Bulgaroctonos, the "Bulgar Slayer." As for the Greeks, they called him—inimitably—Skyloïoannes, "John-the-Dog."

Despite the population's lack of enthusiasm for their current overlords, the Franks, the siege of Salonica dragged on, and as it did, the Tsar's patience began to wane. Kalojan, relates a chronicler called Stavrakios, impudently implored Saint Demetrius to deliver the city to him, for which he would cause a great monastery to be built. Long converted to Orthodoxy, the Bulgars had come to venerate Saint Demetrius as ardently as they longed for his city. Were they to capture Salonica, the mounted saint would be theirs, blessing their military virtues and dreams of empire. Providentially, however, Kalojan was murdered in his tent by a rival. For the Greeks the Tsar's death had clearly been the work of the saint himself, determined to protect his city from the Bulgars. Saint Demetrius, not a rival, had entered Kalojan's tent and dispatched the presumptuous monarch while he slept.[35]

One can understand the frustration of the Bulgars—and their intense desire to lay hands on the icon which was, lest we forget, simultaneously the saint himself. Demetrius alone, so it seemed, had blocked their path when in the early years of the seventh century they swept into the southern Balkans from the steppes of Central Asia in the footsteps of their Hunnish predecessors, determined to build an empire of their own. All they lacked was a respectable capital city. Byzantine Emperor Heraclius, engrossed in plans for his campaign against the Sassanids in Persia, could not come to their aid. The people of Salonica were abandoned to their own devices. Repeatedly, relate the Miracles of Saint Demetrius, the monkish compilation of his life and posthumous achievements, the saint sallied forth from the citadel resplendent in his white tunic to rescue Salonica and repulse the besiegers. But while the Bulgars and other marauding Slavs never succeeded in establishing a toe-hold within the city, later waves of invaders—Franks, Venetians and Turks—displayed a curious immunity to the saintly proscription.

The Slavs' failure to capture Salonica came to haunt them, and sowed the seeds of Great Bulgarian and Great Serbian designs on the city. But hypersensitivity to their presence still rules Greek historiography, and occupies the conceptual core of the country's reaction to the existence of a Slav-speaking Macedonian national minority within the country's boundaries, and to the creation of a state called Macedonia on its northern border.

BY THE FOLLOWING DAY Salonica's defender has vanished, retreated into the gilded unidimensionality of his icon, no longer the horseman who appears on the ramparts to rally the troops, repulse the barbarian Slavs and save the city in its hour of need. A more contemporary warrior deity—national security—which brooks no uncertainty, no theological disputation, has usurped his place as the Greek armed forces stage their annual march-past of military preparedness to mark another, more recent anniversary: the rejection of fascist Italy's 1940 ultimatum by the equally fascist Greek government of the day. The ensuing war, brief and bitter, was the country's last victorious encounter on the battlefield against an external foe. When Hitler dispatched Panzer divisions and SS units in overwhelming strength to rescue his hapless Italian ally, the Greek forces, their morale sapped by pro-Nazi commanders, were forced to surrender.

After a late and raucous night with writers Yorgos Skabardonis and Christos Zafiris, men whose passionate avocation is the micro-history of their home town, I was in no mind for an early wake-up call. But a roar shook me from sleep and to my feet at the crack of dawn. Dashing to my front window, the one which overlooks the White Tower, I saw phalanxes of tanks and armored personnel carriers careening full bore down the corniche in the pre-dawn mist. "Doesn't bother us a bit, as long as they only come out on national holidays," a friend joked later. "But if you hear that sound on a normal work day, it just might be a *coup d'État*." A reminder that Greece, for all its democratic patina, has spent much of its brief national life as a succession of military dictatorships, the last of which collapsed ignominiously in 1974.

Several hours later the same fire-snorting dragons come roaring back along the same broad boulevard—slower this time, but with the same belly-churning roar—escorting folklore groups in regional costume, ranks of school children, the Salonica police and fire brigade, and detachments of military cadets, soldiers, sailors and commandos, while Mirages and F-16s scream overhead at low altitude. Then come the same brass bands which had performed in the Saint Demetrius' day parade, this time belting out jaunty military marches. The musicians are true to counter-type: plump flutists, thin men stooped under fat tubas, and a French horn player with artsy flowing auburn hair.

After the parade, the citizens in their tens of thousands stroll homeward along the corniche in brilliant late-October sunlight, past an impromptu sea-front bazaar staffed by men and women of dark complexion shouting the quintessentially Balkanic "*ande ande*" ("hurry hurry," or "step right up") as they hawk bargain glassware; cheap socks and underwear; peanuts, pistachios, roasted chickpeas and sunflower seeds; souvlaki and ice-cream; miracle spot removing fluids and soda pop which may well be the same stuff in different bottles.

On the eve of the long holiday weekend it was unlikely that many Salonicians had Saint Demetrius on their minds as they rose at dusk from their late-afternoon siesta, sipped a long, lingering coffee, then fanned out toward the *tavernas* that line the seashore or dot the walled precincts of the upper town, and thence to the city's throbbing, smoky night-clubs, discotheques and strip joints. Everyone knows danger is remote. The display of military might which had rumbled past the reviewing stand earlier in the day has been, after all, enough to give pause to Greece's Balkan opponents. More than enough to dissuade any cheap regional reincarnation of Saddam Hussein. Tirana and Skopje and Ankara, watch yourselves, was the parade's underlying message, a judicious admixture of barely sublimated aggressivity and confidence. Perhaps overconfidence.

Greece's tug-of-war with Europe—with the world at large—over the name and symbols of the Former Yugoslav Republic of Macedonia has revealed a deep-seated emotional sub-stratum which, once activated, is creating a dynamic all its own. The universe, in the southern Balkans, is not unfolding as it should, and although the smoke and blood and misery of Bosnia are well over the horizon, the re-emergence of powerful national and religious currents is now a fact throughout the region. Greek youth—who this very evening will be thronging the night clubs and the pinball parlors—have grown plump and indolent, addicted to motorcycles and a diet of cigarettes, fast-food and late nights spiced with random hooliganism. They would make a poor match for the tough, wiry, hungry mountaineers or shanty-town dwellers of Albania or Turkey, should push ever come to shove. Once again the Salonicians may have to summon Saint Demetrius to defend the city.

ANOTHER FINE NOVEMBER DAY I SET OUT on a whirlwind tour of Salonica's Byzantine and post-Byzantine churches, attaching myself to a group of fresh-faced and earnest Princeton University graduate students. Their professor, Slobodan Curcic, a Serbian Byzantinologist has graciously permitted me to tag along. Distances are short and the walking is easy as we hasten from one impromptu lecture hall to the next through the city's compact central core where the remains of its Roman, Byzantine and Ottoman past are concealed. There is not a moment to spare for wandering down a winding lane, for turning right when we should turn left: time is of the essence. Professor Curcic has drawn up a militarily precise schedule of on-the-spot lessons to be given by local art historians and archeologists, each designed to tease a deeply concealed meaning from these historic relics, like garlic snails to be extracted from their shells with a combination of sharp forks and strong wrists.

Our first stop is Panaghia Halkeon—Our Lady of the Brass Founders—named for the craftsmen whose workshops have been located in the area for more than two millennia. The tiny church lies below street level just off the Via Egnatia, Salonica's historic main thoroughfare. Founded in the eleventh century, the church is built entirely of fired brick and mortar, materials of extraordinary plasticity and endurance. But beneath the building, we learn, lies a vaulted sub-structure: perhaps catacombs dating from the Roman period, perhaps even a Cabirian shrine from post-Alexandrian days when the cult, dear to metal workers, thrived here. The void below ground has caused the church to settle, explain the specialists. Even as we speak ultra-sound mapping techniques, they claim proudly, are being used to chart these spaces. Technology is expected to shed new light on the subterranean mysteries and allow the church to be stabilized.

Previous attempts to clean the exquisite frescoes that coat the inside surfaces of the dome and walls have, however, a rather more cautionary tale to tell. Experts of a previous generation used an abrasive powder to cut through the grime of centuries, scouring the delicate paintings and forever altering their intense colors. Will the perspicacity of today's experts, technically competent men and women who seem quite unmoved by the holy precincts in which they wield their disincarnate technique, prove to be substantially greater? Their exemplary discipline may have blinded them to the dimension of faith without which these monuments are little more than predictable compositions, the mere sum of their physical components. Sophisticated though soulless constructs of brick, mortar, wood, mosaic and pigment. Don't, whispers an inner voice. Do not attempt to open the vaults, do not listen to the seductive ping-pinging of the ultra-sound sensors. Leave the concave inner spaces to the sacred mysteries which may inhabit them still, but which will surely flee if exposed to the cruel light of scientific inquiry, to the polluted air of the late twentieth century. For though we may have abandoned the gods—the Cabiri and the saints—they may not have irrevocably abandoned us.

Time to move on, says professor Curcic, glancing at his watch. The group rushes off breathlessly, notebook pages flapping, toward Aghioi Apostoli—The Church of the Holy Apostles—all that remains of the late Byzantine monastic complex abutting the city's western ramparts. Ranks of brooding, peeling apartment blocks, their balconies hung with laundry, leer down at the church, whose once ample courtyard now opens only onto the weed-grown remnants of the cyclopean walls. That such a space has endured is nothing short of miraculous. What little of the Byzantine city survived the great fire of 1917 was all but obliterated by the construction boom of the mid '20s, when hundreds of thousands of destitute refugees from Asia Minor sought shelter and work, transforming the remains of the Jewish-Ottoman city of Selanik into Salonica, "poor mother" of the ingathering of the Greeks, metropolis of the scorned and the downtrodden, a seed-bed for communist agitation. The *coup de grace* was administered by the second boom, which was touched off by the Colonels' junta. Architecturally, Salonica is their legacy: an anarchic gimcrack hodge-podge of concrete, speed and acquisitiveness which surpasses in its caricatural excess even the matrix from which it sprang.

As it was a monastic property, the Holy Apostles' was one of Salonica's wealthiest churches. For this reason its frescoes and mosaics—for both techniques were used in this graceful building erected in the waning years of the Byzantine Empire—bear the scars of time and human depredation, the worst of which came at the hands of fellow Christians: Catholics, schismatics, barbarians. In 1185, marauding Normans from Sicily sacked Salonica. A detailed account of events by Eusthathios, the Archbishop who witnessed its capture, survives in the form of a funeral oration for the sufferings of the city brimming with indignation at the abandonment of the defenseless citizenry by the Byzantine military who had been sent to rescue them in their hour of need.

> *...now the city, after our opponents had burst into it, was subjected to the usual ravages of war. Our own men...fled without turning round, with no exceptions except for a few who could be counted easily. (...) The barbarians, having filled the whole city, beginning with the eastern gates, now mowed down our men and heaped up those sheaves in many stacks to make the fodder beloved of Hades... no house could be found in which mercy was shown to the inhabitants.* [36]

The Normans, who Greek historians of today liken to the Nazi occupiers of 1941-1944, stripped the icons and wall paintings of the Holy Apostles' of their gold leaf and melted it down as booty before departing. The great mosaics were added later, on the eve of the Turkish conquest when, under the Paleologue dynasty, religious art reached new summits of expressiveness. In their fluid, harmonious interplay of form and color, the works resemble those of the anonymous masters who created the masterworks of the Monastery of Chora, in Constantinople, the pinnacle of late-Byzantine iconography.

The Holy Apostles', like most of Salonica's main churches, was transformed into a mosque by the conquering Ottomans who, it is said, methodically pock-marked fresco-bearing surfaces to prepare them for a coating of new plaster which would hide the religiously offensive images. Or so the resident byzantinologist suggests, although it was common enough Byzantine practice for church frescos to be plastered over to provide a fresh surface for an improved version of the religious scenes depicted, to make room for a portrait of the church's benefactor, or to display its patron saint in a more flattering or martial light. Providentially, the church's mosaics, while superficially damaged, are intact. They are breathtaking.

The Ottomans must have been, in the eyes of Salonica's pious Orthodox population, a reincarnation of the iconoclasts, the image-smashers they had despised. The city of Saint Demetrius owed its reputation as Protector of the True Faith to its staunch opposition to the Iconoclast movement that swept the Empire in the late eighth and early ninth centuries. The iconoclasts, driven by the hot winds of emergent Islam (a chronicler of the image-smashing emperor Leo III called him "the Saracen-minded"[37]) denounced the veneration of images as idol worship, and sought to strip the church walls bare. For more than eighty years, divided by a brief interval of icon-worship, their writ was law until rescinded by the "restoration of orthodoxy."

Leo's motives for attacking images are as obscure as the history of the movement he led, since the victorious icon-worshippers violently suppressed its works. Some historians speculate that the Emperor, an Easterner himself, wished to accommodate the Jews and the Muslims, the better to convert them; others claim he wished to remove education from the hands of the clergy, attack the entrenched feudal power of the monasteries and so consolidate secular rule—a "progressive" reformer far ahead of his time. His much excoriated successor Constantine V Copronymus ("he whose Name is Excrement") was a model of intolerance who sought to smash not only all depictions of the sacred, but the monastic orders which had perverted and commercialized them. But no religious strictures, no public humiliation of monks could overcome the deep-rooted semi-pagan attachment of the simple folk to the images which depicted, while at the same time they embodied, the saints and holy martyrs, themselves re-embodiments of the ancient cthonic deities of the earth and sky and sea. In 787, the seventh and last ecumenical council of the Eastern Church was convened. At its final meeting, in Constantinople, it reinstated image worship and pronounced anathema on those who refused to accept its fiat. In Salonica, stronghold of a monastic power that would violently reassert itself centuries later in the struggle of the Hesychastes against the Zealots, there was rejoicing.

As the victorious Ottomans consolidated their rule over the second city of Byzantium, the venerated images, the mosaics were once again covered over. But the plaster of the devout conquerors preserved many from destruction. When revealed by cautious restoration, the brilliant reds and golds shone forth in unadulterated glory, as they do to this day in the Church of the Holy Apostles, preserve of the specialists, ignored by the feckless, impious man on the street for whom only the warlike Saint Demetrius holds attraction.

Feeling a touch feckless and impious myself, I sit down in the shade on a low wall as the group hurtles off to its next destination. Salonica's past is mute, but not of its own volition. No, it has been all but reduced to silence. What remains of its voice is obscured by the ambient cacophony of traffic resounding in the narrow streets. So if you think you hear a whisper—perhaps it was only the afternoon breeze off the water humming through the high embrasures of a church wall, or the flutter of women's voices from a neighboring balcony—stop to listen.

A MONTH LATER—it's early December now but the weather is indolent and tepid—I embark on one of my periodic forays into the upper town, crossing the Via Egnatia and Saint Demetrius street. Leaving Kemal's house behind I amble uphill along the cobbled lanes past the compound of the church of Saint Nicholaos Orphanos, a walled, weed-grown garden-oasis, thick with cypresses and orange trees, in the heart of the city. This afternoon my destination is the Acropolis, the walled citadel crowned with its lowering Byzantine-Ottoman fortress, perpetual refuge of the city's defenders, ultimate rampart against invading barbarians. Here, more than anywhere else in Salonica, the two empires converge, dominating the skyline to this day.

Derelict land occupies much of the space within the citadel precinct: A no-man's-land of thistles and wild grass, a neutral zone littered with half-decomposed garbage and discarded plastic water bottles. Along the far borders of this inhospitable ground, as though far enough removed from the shadow of the fortress to avoid its contagion, stands a scattering of modest dwellings, some of them built right into the inner walls of the citadel, survivors of the first wave of refugees which settled in Salonica after being uprooted from Anatolia in 1922. Suddenly there is a rush, more felt than heard, of many small wings. A flight of trained pigeons circles overhead, then homes in on a courtyard. I mosey over to the fence and strike up a conversation with the householder, a stocky, balding man who doubles, he explains, as pigeon trainer. "It's the only hobby we can afford up here," he says, waving his hand about him in a half-circle. "And we can always eat 'em if we have to."

We exchange a few words of regret at the Swiss army's decision to disband its carrier pigeon corps, and I wander upward, scuffing along the weed-clogged footpaths which ring the fortress. Two adolescent boys lounge on a stone wall—surely an early Byzantine relic—puffing cigarettes and talking soccer. The sky has clouded over; dampness rises from the ancient earth. The late afternoon has turned distinctly melancholy. The hour is propitious for my encounter with the Zealots, here on the ground where they made their last, heroic stand.

TOLIS KAZANTZIS, WHO LOVED TO TELL STORIES that cut sharply against the grain of authority, stories that probe like a scalpel for posturing and hypocrisy, first told me of these hard-bitten communalists over a late-night meal in one of the psarotavernas that line the shore. Impossible to remember how we'd gotten onto the subject. The meal had ended, our table was littered with fish bones, bread crumbs and olive pits; bits of spicy cabbage salad floated in watery puddles of oil and lemon dressing, our stubby wine glasses were smudged with finger prints. The naked fluorescent tubes overhead gave the taverna's walls a sepulchral dinginess. In spite of the liver disease that would soon kill him, my host was already into his fifth or sixth cigarette of the evening. Half-obscured behind the cloud of slow-rising smoke, his deep-set eyes gleamed as he leaned forward: "Did you know that the first bourgeois revolution in Europe happened right here in Salonica? 450 years before the French Revolution. If you don't understand the Zealots, you can never understand our city."

Kazantzis' three sentences were enough to set me off on my own quest for the Zealots of Salonica. But, three years later, as I strolled across the grassy slopes of the citadel, I could find not a trace of those mysterious proto-communists, precursors of proletarian revolt who overthrew the ruling nobles and administered the city for nearly five years during the fifth decade of the fourteenth century. No commemorative plaque marks their passing. Like the Iconoclasts five hundred years before, the Zealots have been relegated to the near oblivion of the footnotes by the academic establishment and its hand-maiden, mainstream historiography. As with the Iconoclasts, no primary sources survived their demise and ideological defeat. What little is known of them can be inferred only from the writings of their foes. All the more reason to search out their invisible traces.

Like the Iconoclasts, whose purpose was the suppression of the visible appurtenances of worship, the elimination of dross so that only the pure metal of spirit would remain, the Zealots, whose proclaimed mission was civil equality—a program as radical in 1342 as it is today—left no monuments. Nothing but a vague rejection, as diffuse as it was intense, of injustice; a tradition of popular resistance that would emerge in the last years of Ottoman rule in the form of the *Fédération socialiste*, and find its most recent incarnation in the combative working-class movement of the 1930s. Though my *rendez-vous* would have to be an imaginary one, I was determined to see it through. Its premise was presumptuous of course. Was it an enterprise in futility, like the attempt of the visionary poet Angelos Sikelianos to resuscitate a corpse?[38] Probably. But though the task was impossible, it had to be attempted.

The Byzantine Empire had painstakingly reconstituted itself after being hacked apart by the Crusader hordes more than one hundred years before. Once again the *basileus* reigned, heir to Rome, over the southern Balkans from the Adriatic to the Bosphorus. But the respite was short lived. Civil strife and the rise of a mighty Slav kingdom under the Serbian *kral*, Stefan Dusan, eroded the Byzantine domains, until by the mid-fourteenth century Constantinople's writ extended—politically and militarily—no farther than eastern Thrace and the region surrounding Salonica.

All but abandoned by the capital, the second city of the empire had become, out of cruel necessity, a semi-independent city-state which relied on the acumen of its traders and on the skilled hands of its workmen for its prosperity. Though the Byzantine empire was shrinking rapidly into terminal decline, Salonica remained a commercial powerhouse. Toward it, by land and by sea, flowed the raw materials, agricultural products and finished goods of the Slav-speaking Balkans, Albania and Thessaly. There they would be sold then transshipped to the ports of Western Europe and the Middle East, most of it in Genoese vessels. Venice's chief rival in the bitter competition for Mediterranean trade had won the favor of the ruling Paleologue dynasty. The old Roman Via Egnatia which passed through the city remained the only practicable overland route from the Adriatic to Constantinople, but it was plagued by political instability, and had long been superseded by the sea routes.

Trade, Salonica's lifeblood, reached its peak during the yearly festival of Saint Demetrius. Greek traders who had settled in the farthest-flung corners of the once-great realm of the Eastern Roman Empire—Asia Minor, Syria, Cyprus and the marshy lands of the Danubian delta—congregated at the late-October fair, rubbing elbows with Slav, Spanish, Italian and French merchants. There were to be found, in rich variety, oriental spices, dyestuffs, carpets and aromatic plants; fine silks and rough Bulgarian goat-hair cloth; woven fabric from France, Flanders and Tuscany; silver and gold thread from Lucca, Genoa and Venice; Italian, Cretan and Greek wines; aromatic soaps from Ancona and Puglia; figs from Spain and nutmeats from Naples; olive oil from Sicily and the Morea, laudanum from Cyprus and precious gum mastic from Chios, the orange blossom isle.[39]

The wealth which trade brought to the city created a commercial and industrial bourgeoisie. Artisans, sailors, indentured laborers and slaves made up the bulk of the inhabitants, most of whom were then Greeks and Slavs, along with smaller Jewish and Armenian minorities. Its reputation for cosmopolitan diversity was upheld by a foreign colony of Genoese, Venetians, Spaniards, and perhaps even a few Turks, though the Ottomans had yet to begin their westward thrust which was to redraw the boundaries of the entire region. Salonica's large population and special status within the empire—its official designation was "great city," a title to which only Rome and Constantinople could lay claim—had also assured it virtual administrative autonomy. Unlike the patriarch and the emperor, their absolutist masters in Constantinople, the archbishop and the governor ruled on sufferance of the people. While artistic activity, scientific inquiry, philosophical and theological disputation flourished in the absence of direct imperial control, so also did class conflict, which found expression in bitter political and religious controversy. In the mid-fourteenth century these latent conflicts finally flared up, culminating in the political and religious crisis which sealed the fate of the Byzantine state and the future of Eastern Orthodoxy.

The counterweight to Byzantine Salonica's ostentatious prosperity and cultivated elegance was widespread—extreme poverty, the sort of situation which the dominant class, the landed nobility, was only too happy to perpetuate. This it accomplished by the usual application of force, and through the ideological ministrations of the ecclesiastical elite and the monastic establishment whose land holdings made it an economic power in its own right. The nobles ruled as absolute masters; their pride in the aristocratic lineage which bestowed on them the right to rule was exceeded only by their scorn for the upstart traders, the *nouveaux riches* who had begun to challenge their lordly prerogatives. And all the while, the common folk chafed under a crippling burden of taxation and repression.

Contemporary chronicles speak of public torture of those courageous enough to protest social and economic injustice. Protests against usury were frequent, eloquent and vain. Before the tribunals only the voice of wealth could be heard. All was governed by one of the periodically recurring variants of the inevitability doctrine which counseled passive acceptance of poverty, exclusion, dispossession and social disintegration—exactly as it does today. It was only a matter of time before the ambition of the emerging bourgeoisie and the misery of the impoverished free citizens and slaves would coalesce into an explosive combination of hatred and hope.

The life of a city—of a nation, a people—is infinitely more than the blindly colliding freaks' ballet of market forces, those immutable laws which, intone the high priests of the World Church of Economic Determinism, regulate the universe. So it was with Salonica, where against a background of incipient revolt fueled by mass deprivation, a philosophical and intellectual renaissance was in full flower, nourished, as was its coeval counterpart in the West, by the study of the ancient Greeks in all their subversive, polymorphous humanist perversity. The city considered itself the home and hearth of Hellenism, the Athens of the age, a beacon for philosophers, artists and rhetoricians. Any aspiring philosopher, be he native Salonician or visitor, Greek or non-Greek, was free to open schools, to teach, to propound radical interpretations of religious dogma and to challenge the assumptions of the age. Into this atmosphere of intellectual and political ferment strode an itinerant Calabrian monk named Barlaam, ostensibly to study eastern mysticism, but whose real aim was to preach ideas inspired at once by ancient Athens and the West of the early Renaissance. Barlaam's message not only contested the ideological dominance of the monkish conservatives; it implicitly challenged the material prerogatives of the religious establishment. He was a dangerous man with a dangerous message.

To speak today of Byzantine argument is to conjure up images of tortuous complexity, convoluted abstruseness and hairsplitting hyper-subtlety. The Hesychaste controversy which came to a climax with the arrival in Salonica of Barlaam had the makings of all this, and more. Yet the dispute which swirled around the doctrine of monastic quietism contrived to become the vehicle for an intellectual, religious and social debate which engaged the greatest spirits of the age and mobilized the forces of the Empire. Prior to the fourteenth century the term Hesychaste, derived from *hesychia*, the Greek word for silence, had designated those monks who lived a life of devout contemplation, remote from the rough and tumble of the real world. "The highest, most sincere, and most perfect prayer of the perfect Hesychaste," writes a historian, "is an immediate intercourse with God, in which there exist no thoughts, ideas, images of the present or recollection of the past. This is the highest contemplation—the contemplation of God one and alone, the perfect ecstasy of mind and withdrawal from matter."[40]

But in the second quarter of the century the practice abruptly redefined itself, combining the pursuit of punctiliously subtle doctrinal affairs with the adoption of meditative techniques reminiscent of those employed by Oriental mystics or Islamic Sufis, and probably influenced by them. It was only natural that Salonica, a mere day's journey from the powerful monastic enclave of Mount Athos, would early on feel the impact of the newly revived quietist doctrine, which centered on the obscure but contentious question of the Procession of the Holy Spirit and sought to obtain for its followers a momentary vision of the uncreated light which Christ's disciples are said to have beheld on Mount Tabor.[41]

Barlaam the Calabrian would have none of it, and launched an energetic polemical exchange with the chief of the quietists, Gregory Palamas, a native of Constantinople who began his monastic progress on Mount Athos in the early years of the century. Palamas was a rarity: an articulate mystic whose irreproachably saintly behavior and life of personal privation attracted followers as much as did his beliefs. But in Barlaam he met his match. The Calabrian was a master theologian, with supreme oratorical gifts and a biting tongue. He heaped ridicule on the Hesychastes, attacking them in public meetings as parasites. They, he thundered, to the delight of Salonica's pugnaciously free-thinking citizens, were heretics who were attempting to obtain knowledge of God through mystical techniques which contradicted the Greek heritage of rational examination and logical discourse. No, fired back Palamas, reason is powerless to grasp the verity of God. Only by purification of the heart through ascetic contemplation can the believer attain to divine light, source of all truth.[42] Implicitly, of course, and in the interests of his immortal soul, the believer should also deliver himself and his estate over to those masters of contemplation, the monastic orders, a common enough practice at the time, and one of the causes of Byzantium's economic decline.

The battle was thus joined, not only over the theologically charged distinction between divine essence and divine energy, but over the intellectual heritage of Athens. Ultimately, too, the power and prerogatives of the monastic establishment came under scrutiny. Siding with Barlaam were the liberals who sought, in the classical texts of antiquity, a new humanist vision. Palamas, meanwhile, assumed leadership of the religious faction and intimated that the Barlaamites were really unavowed agents of reconciliation with the Roman schismatics. Such was Barlaam's influence, particularly in the charged atmosphere of public debate in the Salonica forum, that a ranking local clergyman was won over to the rationalist side.

As the controversy spread beyond the city and the monastic republic of Athos, the religious authorities in Constantinople took note of the danger. At a synod hastily convened in 1341 Palamas won a partial but tainted triumph. Barlaam and his allies remained too strong to be either dismissed or proscribed. Meanwhile, what had begun as a purely religious dispute had meshed with the politics of class conflict against a background of civil strife. The decade which began with political and spiritual awakening was to end in violent repression, anathema and the reaffirmation of Hesychaste doctrine. The faith and its bedrock of mystic doctrine was preserved, but the cost was high: the integrity of the Church and the future of the Byzantine state itself.

Though it cannot be demonstrated that Barlaam had any direct connection with the growing popular discontent against the nobility, his teaching made criticism of the established order suddenly not only legitimate, but fashionable. If reason could provide man with the means for apprehending God, could it not also allow him to question the structure of society itself? people began to ask. And if the structure of society could be questioned, could it not also be changed? It was but a short step to take up the defense of the poor and the dispossessed against the injustice and cruelty of the nobility. A handful of enlightened nobles, possibly followers of Barlaam, allied with several members of the rising bourgeoisie to form a political party. They named themselves Zealots, after the Jewish revolutionaries who resisted the Romans until the capture of Jerusalem in 70 B.C. Sensing the danger to its vital interests, wealth joined forces with religion, as it has done since time immemorial.

Revolutions are said to occur when the government is unable to rule in the old way. Indeed. While the gentle science of insurrectionism has lost its luster in our age of Restoration, the formula seems apt to describe the events which shook Byzantium in the Year of Our Lord 1341—although we must accept that beneath the veneer of *post facto* rationality lies a seething morass of unspoken desire, fear, envy, greed and hatred: in short, the full compass of human emotion in its individual and collective forms. Meanwhile, conflict over the succession erupted in Constantinople between the pretender to the throne, John Cantacuzene, and the ostensibly legitimate heir, the youthful John V Paleologus, whose interests were represented by the widowed Empress, Anne of Savoy. The traditional king makers—the archons—rallied to their champion Cantacuzene, who was proclaimed emperor. The rising bourgeoisie and the free citizenry supported John V. The struggle between the two factions became a full-blown civil war which pitted two classes against each other throughout the rump empire. Only in Salonica, however, did hostility to the archons take the form of a social and political revolution, of a violent attempt to overthrow the old order.

There can be little doubt that the pugnacious burghers and free citizens of Salonica found inspiration in Genoa, where in 1339, the hereditary nobility had been overthrown, to be replaced by a democratic regime. Communications between the two trading cities were intense and constant. Merchants and seamen carried more than goods; they carried ideas. It was no accident that Salonica's mariners were among the most devoted supporters of the Zealots.

Like any court intrigue worthy of the epithet "Byzantine," the battle between the pretender and the "legitimate" heir was tortuous, vicious, debilitating and ultimately vain. Both sides—to the mortification of subsequent generations of nationalist historians who insist on seeing Byzantium as the forerunner of the Greek national state—entered into treaties and alliances with Hellenism's allegedly most deadly enemies, the Slavs, the Bulgars and the Turks, the better to defeat one another. Both sides purchased, or attempted to purchase, the loyalty of their subjects. When that failed, betrayal, assassination and massacre became the tactics of choice.

In the spring of 1342, news reached Salonica that the pretender Cantacuzene had crowned himself emperor: the reaction was fierce and instantaneous. The Zealots called for resistance and the populace responded, forcing the archons to flee the city or to seek shelter in the monasteries. Cantacuzene, writing as a historian several years later, could barely conceal his disgust, lamenting: "The poor and the insignificant suddenly became rich and important."[43]

Another contemporary, hardly supportive of the revolutionaries, described the situation this way: "As the waves of the sea, made great by the wild winds, sank with all hands the unfortunate vessels, so they (the revolutionaries), uprooting with boundless rage the homes of those who had money, slaughtered the unfortunates without justification. No sooner was word given that those whose wealth was in money, in land or in livestock, thought to open secretly the gates of the citadel, so that Emperor Cantacuzene might enter than the poor who craved wealth and glory, amidst cries and songs in the city center, declared Paleologus and his mother Emperor, and christened themselves Zealots, thus concealing their evil with a noble name."[44]

The slaughter of the innocents was almost certainly metaphorical. The most serious wounds were those suffered by the pride of the archons as the Zealots set about forming a government, striking down the written and unwritten privileges of their erstwhile masters as they went.

Year One of Zealot rule had been a political triumph. It had also been deceptively simple, as the nobility retreated. The counter-attack, however, was not long in coming, in the form of a plot to re-establish noble rule. Like any self-respecting revolutionary regime, the Zealots had developed an enthusiastic secret police, which quickly sniffed out the conspiracy, involving a distant relative of the ruling dynasty. Even the Paleologus name was not enough to rescue the unfortunate from the death verdict of the infuriated populace. The ring-leader was executed, his body hacked into four pieces, one of which was deposited at each of the citadel's four gates, while his severed head was paraded through the streets on spear-point, a stern warning to other would-be plotters. Large-scale arrests and expropriation of nobles followed: disaster had struck the ruling class.

The first outbreak of serious bloodshed came in 1345. The city's military governor, ostensibly loyal to John V, murdered the head of the Zealots, freed the imprisoned archons, declared for the pretender, and even—the height of temerity—offered him the city. The governor did not live long enough to fully regret his treachery, however. Led by the Zealots, the citizens of Salonica took up arms and laid siege to the citadel where he and the nobility had sought shelter.

In the waning light I stand at the foot of the citadel wall from which, 650 years before, the governor's body would have come plummeting to earth from the ramparts a full seven meters above my head. Urged on by a contingent of sailors the armed populace, which must have surged up the steep hill to which my back is now turned, had penetrated the walls and quickly rounded up the terrified archons. The governor had lain at their feet dazed but still alive for a split second, until someone stepped forward from the crowd and severed his head with one sword-stroke. The signal for the massacre had been given: lesser dignitaries were heaved over the walls—the same walls which are today lined with humble dwellings, coffee-houses and an observation terrace looking out over Salonica Bay—there to be cut to pieces by the blood-crazed mob. The stone gutters, perhaps these very paving stones, ran red with noble gore.

I imagine the roars of the Zealots and their adversaries as a violent modern-day political demonstration, its chants and cries overlapping, occasional words snapping into focus then vanishing in the cacophonous swell, the thudding of truncheons and the grunts and panting of the police as they veer through the crowd like the crazed-eyed animals of a Spanish bull run. The growl of a diesel motor breaks the silence. I look around: a tourist bus is laboring up the steep switchbacks of the street that leads through the main citadel gate. Time to leave. Soon a new throng of besiegers, camcorders in hand, will be drawn up before these undefended walls and their bloody legacy.

FOR THE NEXT THREE YEARS, Salonica survived under Zealot rule as an independent republic. And though the historical sources are unanimous—and virulent—in their hostility, we can infer the contours of the revolutionaries' social and political program from the silences, or from the wrathful denunciations of their foes. Had they done nothing else, their most radical measure, the seizure of the assets of the wealthy by force if necessary in order to provide for the poor, would alone have been enough to earn them the undying enmity of the archons and their clerical allies. But the egalitarian passion of its new rulers could not reverse the city's economic decline, precipitated by isolation from the Empire and the encroachment of the Serbs and the Seljuk Turks.

No longer able to play the two warring factions in Constantinople against each other, the Zealots were forced to seek an alliance with Dusan, the Serb. Now, the citizens of Salonica may well have been republicans, but they were Byzantines, heirs of the Romans, to the last. They rejected the gambit and the tide began to turn. In the fall of 1349, a Turkish army captured the city, which it promptly turned over to Cantacuzene, now crowned legitimate emperor, who rode down the Via Egnatia in triumph, as victor and avenger. Saint Demetrius was conspicuous by his absence. Why would the sad-eyed warrior have taken the side of the rough radicals who belittled him? The handful of Zealot leaders who survived the counter-massacre high atop the Citadel were hauled off to Constantinople in chains. Gregory Palamas, leader of the Hesychastes, could finally assume the archbishop's seat which, for nearly a decade, the people of Salonica had refused him. In 1351, a holy synod pronounced his doctrines to be those of the Church and ordered the writings of Barlaam to be destroyed.

The forces of the Empire had destroyed Salonica in order to save it. The last spark of Byzantine civic and political renewal—if we are to assume that the European model is the only road to such renewal, a complex question indeed in our neo-liberal age—had been snuffed out by an unholy coalition of Turks and noble warlords. The supreme interest of the state as protector of its citizens and guarantor of their welfare existed no longer, writes the Romanian historian Tafrali, as though he had been, in 1912 on the eve of the Balkan Wars, speaking presciently of the waning years of the twentieth century. "It was replaced by the narrow, criminal egotism of personal interest."[45]

Poverty, invasion and civil wars had transformed the lives of the peoples of the Empire into a living hell, had delivered a once-civil society over to marauding tribes and strutting petty warlords. Peace and order had to be re-established, strong government rebuilt. The Ottoman Turks—an invincible military machine armed with a revolutionary religious ideology in quest of a state—would see to that. So it was that the Turks, having been invited by the protagonists to dislodge their adversaries, correctly concluded not only that the Empire was a desirable property, but that its current proprietors were weak, vainglorious poltroons who would happily sell their grandmothers to gain advantage over their adversaries.

Saint Demetrius, undoubtedly as disgusted by the decline of his birthplace as were the few prescient voices of the Byzantine twilight, failed to make himself manifest. The city walls were left unguarded; little remained to protect the still-functioning remnants of a finely tuned administrative and legal machine that had long forgotten its *raison d'être*.

After a fleeting occupation by Venice, more a mercantile arrangement than a military yoke, Turkish armies under Sultan Murad II conquered Salonica in 1430, less than a century after the crushing of the Zealots. The Ottomans' encircling tactics had gradually strangled Byzantium: the Slav-speaking hinterland was their dominion. Constantinople fell 23 years later, as the last of the Paleologue dynasty died, sword in hand, on the battlements.

Chapter 3

TO THE SALONICA STATION

In the melancholy light of a late October afternoon I make my way through twisting streets toward Salonica's Old Station. The sky is ochre, the color of Balkan mud. Rain drips from the brim of my hat as I slosh across a square thick with parked international transport trucks. Two guard dogs look up perfunctorily from their slumber as I pass through the main gate. Having determined that I pose no threat, they doze off again. From the depths of the station-master's office rings an inquiring voice, in the third person singular which Greek civil-servants affect to persuade themselves of their importance,

"What does the gentleman want?"

The station master gets up, walks toward me, steps through the door, and notices the dogs lolling unconcerned at my feet: "They didn't go after you?" he asks, surprised.

"They knew I had good intentions," I reply.

"So, what can we do for you?" he asks.

It couldn't be simpler, I lied. I like old stations. I wasn't prepared to tell him why this particular station sent chills down my spine, though perhaps he knew all along, for I was not its first visitor. Lined today with flowering oleander and gardenia bushes, the station platform is a place of unspoken pilgrimage. A place most Salonicians of a certain age know well, and very few visit. From it the Jews of Salonica—all 48,000 of them—were transported to the forced-labor camps and crematoria of the Third Reich in sealed freight cars. As if by sinister coincidence, a train of empty box-cars pulls creaking into the station and stops. "Look around all you like," says the station master. "But mind you don't cross the tracks. Could get hit."

Glinting faintly, the rails stretch toward the northwestern horizon. The yard is almost deserted. Passenger traffic has long been relocated to a new main station, a damp, echoing concrete leviathan built to accommodate the international rail hub that Salonica fancied it would become. Though a handful of passenger trains still link the city with Sofia, Belgrade, Vienna and Budapest, here in the freight yard Greece's embargo of Macedonia, coupled with United Nations sanctions against Serbia, have brought goods traffic to a halt. The solitary line of boxcars groans and clatters as a switch-engine shunts it to a siding.

Across the square, sheltered by one of the city's surviving plane trees—the only living remnant of its recent Ottoman past—stands the Old Station café, a hang-out for the truck-drivers and railway workers who live in the neighborhood. Loosened by the rain, yellow leaves spiral languidly to the ground. Inside, a solitary man in a padded windbreaker slouches in a corner, worrying a glass of wine. Three computer-game machines line the far wall, their lighted graphics digital intruders in the feeble glow from the bare ceiling bulbs. I've come at an ambivalent hour, too late for midday dinner, too early for the evening supper, the hour when heads nod, eyelids droop and attention wanders, when the citizens of these climes are snoring in their beds alongside their wives or mistresses.

I saunter over to the kitchen counter and strike up a conversation with the cook. His brother, the owner, joins us and within a few moments we're seated around one of the tables drinking *retsina*, on the house. Stelios minds the pots and pans. He's a taciturn man with the roundness of stomach that suggests he likes his own food—usually a good sign in a chef, even though the meal may be nothing more than the humblest fried potatoes and bean soup. His brother Aghis is the manager, the talkative one. "See this place," he says, gesticulating from rear to front of the restaurant. "This is exactly where they marched 'em through, the Jews and the commies. Sent 'em off to the camps to make soap out of 'em. Had this uncle, he's dead now, sold 'em water and bread while they were waiting there, on the platform," he adds, waving in the direction of the station, now murderously dim in the failing light.

I try to imagine the hum of horror and anticipation in the lilting Castilian cadences of Ladino, the speech of Salonica's Sephardic Jews. The whine of credulity and disbelief. The acrid stench of fear. What fate, what ineluctable force had brought them to the Salonica station? The answer to this question, I believed, lay hidden in the opaque darkness of the city's past. This too I had come to Salonica to find. In the end, I found more questions. Night has fallen now and the air tastes like rusty metal. From the marshaling yards echoes the plaintive hoot of the diesel switch-engine.

The first transport—2,800 men, women and children forced into a train made up of 40 boxcars—departed the station after midnight, on March 13, 1943, to begin the final act of a tragedy scripted with the manic obsession for detail that gave the German extermination machine its surreal efficiency. When the Nazis marched into the city two years before, they had found a ghetto—actually, several ghettos—awaiting them. It had not come as a surprise. Their sympathizers within the Greek government of the dictator Metaxas, and among the Greek general staff, as well as the German academics and "tourists" who for years had scoured the country acquiring information as their impeccably philhellenic British predecessors had done in previous generations, would have alerted them to their substantial good fortune.

Fifty years before, in the final decade of the nineteenth century, land around the Old Station had been purchased by the Baron de Hirsch, the Viennese industrialist and financier of the Balkan railway whose terminus was Ottoman Salonica. The land was set aside to provide a temporary home for Jewish refugees from the Russian pogroms of the late nineteenth century and later, for the survivors of the great fire of 1917. There it had remained, a warren of winding streets and provisional dwellings, living reminder that scant space had been allotted to the Jews in the social geography of the new, post-Ottoman, European Salonica. It was as though the city had determined that, for the first time in its 2,000 year history, its human fabric would be Greek, purely Greek. The Jews who remained in this place had, overnight almost, ceased to be of it.

The inhabitants of the Balkans, accustomed to the ebb and flow of short-lived and shifting kingdoms, national states, principalities and empires, had learned long ago—had integrated into their skins and souls—the chameleon principle. They had assimilated, as a matter of survival, the art of lying to the priest and the schoolmaster, the gendarme and the ethnographer, the census-taker and the journalist. They had perfected the technique of being Greek, Bulgarian, Macedonian or Serb, Vlach or Albanian, all or none, serially or simultaneously, as necessary to ensure survival. Only the Jews of Salonica had failed to adapt to their surroundings. Had it been for lack of time, for lack of need, for excessive pride, for reasons of doctrine? Had it been because of their dominant economic role, because they carried their fate in their bones and their tragedy in their faith and culture? Not for them the Balkan art of concealment and dissimulation.

But would it have mattered?

Before dawn that brittle March morning, when loudspeakers atop the rough-hewn plank walls of the ghetto thundered "All Jews to their doorways ready for departure," the morale which might have made resistance possible had already been shattered by Nazi ferocity, betrayed by the pusillanimity of the community's own leadership, and buried beneath the willful indifference of the Greek state. The last sight of Salonica they were to see was the platform; the last sound of it they were to hear, the hooting of a whistle in the darkness.

The rain has stopped. Darkness enfolds the Old Station. Lights glimmer faintly in the windows of the café. Shivering, I walk back toward the city.

> *For, brothers, you became imitators of the churches of God being in Judea in Jesus Christ, because you also suffered these things by your own fellow countrymen, as they also by the Jews who both killed the Lord Jesus and their own prophets, also driving them out and not pleasing God, and being contrary to all men; forbidding us to speak to the nations in order that they be saved, to fill up their sins always. But the wrath has come on them to the uttermost.*[46]

IN THE YEAR 53, Saul of Tarsus, who had adopted a new name and the new faith of the Nazarene messiah on the road to Damascus, arrived in Salonica from the east. He found there, huddled around its synagogue, an ancient community whose deep roots were coeval perhaps with founding of the city, Jews, who had migrated there from the cities of the eastern Mediterranean littoral.

The Apostle Paul preached the new doctrine in the Ets-Haim synagogue. Salonica was then a Roman city, a prosperous cog in the huge, multinational machinery of domination which had ground its way across the Mediterranean, crushing, mixing and melding populations and languages as it went. The Jewish converts to his doctrine were, if sources are to be believed, men of slender faith; some were recent converts from paganism. The words of the newcomer fell upon their enthusiastic ears. At the same time, Paul had understandably and profoundly insulted the community's traditionalists who quickly whipped up public protest against the man they regarded as an impious heretic. Two sympathetic brothers managed to spirit the Apostle and his close followers out of the city and to safety in the nearby town of Veria before the authorities, alerted by the mob in the streets crying for his execution, were able to act. Some claim that Paul, sheltered in the verdant hillside watershed overlooking Salonica, cursed the Jews. Certainly his first Epistle falls only slightly short of a curse. Had that curse become flesh in 1943? Could it have been one of the deep causes for the paralysis which gripped the city as the Nazi extermination machine swept up and dispatched tens of thousands of its citizens?

Paul's path took him through Greece, to Corinth, then on to Rome where his martyr's death cracked open the gate to temporal power for the new spiritual dispensation. Christianity took root in Salonica, where its combination of quietism, stubborn refusal to recognize the old gods and passive rebelliousness coalesced around the figure of Saint Demetrius. It burst into the open when the emperor Galerius accorded it imperial tolerance, and flourished when the edict of Constantine granted it official status, gaining sainthood for his efforts.

The Jews, forever generating messiahs and new faiths which were to negate and calumniate their own, lived on in their compact, inward-turning community, faithful to the Law. Under the worldly, cynical Romans, with whom they had reached a *modus vivendi*, the Jews flourished. Under the Christians, who had sprung from a bitter and violent schism in Judaism, their status as citizens declined from privileged minority to that of outsiders within.

When the peripatetic Benjamin of Tudela visited Salonica in 1169, during the reign of Byzantine emperor Manuel Comnenus, he found a community of 500 souls. Many were involved in the lucrative silk industry, a vital component in the economic and social life of a waning empire whose taste for luxury was exceeded only by the duplicity and incompetence of its ruling caste.

Two hundred years later, only 20 years after the crushing of the Zealot commune and the triumph of the Hesychastes, a group of Hungarian Ashkenazi Jews was settled in the city by imperial decree. They were followed, at the end of the fourteenth century, by Sephardic Jews from Provence, who quickly founded their own synagogue, Provenzia. Life for the Jews in the twilight years of the rigorously Orthodox yet worldly Christian empire was complicated indeed. Each group followed its own distinct traditions, the Greek-speaking Romaniotes hewing to the Palestinian Talmud, while the European Jews generally followed the Babylonian Talmud. Cultural differences exacerbated their divergent religious traditions: the Ashkenazis spoke German, and the Jews from Provence spoke French.[47] Less than one century later, the face of Jewish Salonica—and of Salonica itself—

would be transformed by the arrival of thousands of Spanish-speaking Sephardim expelled from Spain.

As they marched south toward Granada their Catholic Majesties Ferdinand and Isabella, proud liquidators of the Muslim multicultural civilization of Iberia, founded a new European Order which has endured, in a kaleidoscopic multiformity, as a single central, ever-recurring theme, down to our day. When the European Order, in the full cry of maturity, swept across the Balkans during World War II, it was to ring up still another, mournful reordering of the same elements.

Primavera en Salonico
hallí al café Maslum
una niña de ojos pretos
que canta y sona sud.[48]

AS I WANDER THE BACK-STREETS of Salonica my ears are alert for the sound of Ladino which, with its admixture of Greek and Turkish, was the dominant language of the city for more than four hundred years. My eyes scan the sidewalks, the building façades for signs of the community which lived, prospered and was destroyed here. But the language—that of Cervantes, of the wealthy traders of the Sepharade and of the poorest dockers and porters too—has vanished, expunged from public life. Its only speakers are the handful of survivors living out their years in the community's old people's home. All visible signs of Jewish Salonica have vanished, obliterated by the great eraser of willed collective amnesia. Little more than a handful of place names remain in quotidian common usage to suggest that the commerce, the political, intellectual and spiritual life of these streets had once been more Jewish than Turkish or Greek; that commercial activity came to a halt on the Sabbath and on every Jewish holiday. Not a monument nor commemorative plaque, not a public square, not a crossroads nor an alley bears witness to the deported and exterminated, less to the crime and the indifference which combined to cause the deportation and the extermination. At the center of Salonica, where its heart should be, a void of four centuries gapes. From this void radiate the fissures of memory, like cracks in the marble tombstones wrenched from a desecrated graveyard.

When the Ottoman troops of Fatih Mehmet II took Constantinople in 1453, the Byzantine empire was little more than an empty shell. Not as barbarian conquerors but as restorers of imperial dignity, the Turks took rapid steps to bring order and prosperity to cities which for decades had known nothing but turmoil and upheaval. The Byzantines, in their final desperation, had privatized; sold off their economic survival and their defense to the rapacious free-market globalists of Venice and Genoa who, like all entrepreneurial swashbucklers, showed little enthusiasm for defending the civic culture they had come to supplant.

"The Conqueror"—the name which had inevitably devolved to Mehmet for his capture of the metropolis of the age—was a man of culture and refinement, a fluent Greek-speaker who had seriously considered, claims Elias Petropoulos, proclaiming himself emperor of Byzantium until dissuaded by the court muftis and the Muslim men of religion, the *ulema*. In the event, the revitalized empire was to be Oriental, Turkish and Muslim. But it was also to be as European and Occidental as had been its Byzantine predecessor, hewing with an accuracy too uncanny for the work of mere fortuitousness, to the imaginary civilizational fault line, legacy of the Eastern and Western Roman schism, which even to this day zigzags crazily across the Balkans.

The work of revitalization began immediately. A system of conscription and recruitment was set up. Jews, Greeks and Armenians were forcibly relocated or induced to move to Salonica, Smyrna and to Istanbul itself, still a smoldering, blood-stained ruin. Mehmet's policy was one of enlightenment and self-interest. The Armenians, Greeks and Jews—particularly the Jews—would rebuild the trade routes, breath new life into the market-places, resuscitate manufacturing: their destiny was to provide the economic sinew for the new world empire.

More than brilliant soldiers and capable administrators, the Ottomans were also the spear-point of a revivified Islam. In the Islamic world-view, social identity is determined not by nationality but by religion. Though ranking below Muslims, the former empire's Christians and Jews, as people of the Book, were protected minorities. As such they were entrusted with full administration of the internal affairs of their own communities. The empire would collect such taxes and tithes as it required; it would leave day to day affairs of religion and public life to the subordinate yet respected religious authorities who were its mandatees.

Greek historiography, like that of the Christian West, frames the Turkish conquerors as bloodthirsty barbarians, cruel infidels, implacable tormentors and oppressors. Ottoman rule in the Balkans is described as a "yoke" beneath which the Christian populations groaned. Possibly so, perhaps not. The Ottomans were stern and capricious masters, as had been their Byzantine predecessors. But their policy gave Christians, under the spiritual leadership of the Orthodox Ecumenical Patriarchate, full scope to organize schools, to protect and promote the language of the Holy Liturgy (which happened to be Greek) throughout the Balkans, and to thrive economically. Mehmet decreed Greek to be the second language of his empire, and in Thrace and Macedonia it was used in all official communication, alongside Ottoman Turkish.

In the cities this same policy recreated a vibrant, rich and socially diverse Jewish community from the ruins of Spanish Jewry, a community that was rapidly to rebuild Smyrna, Istanbul and most of all, Salonica, into major centers of trade and culture, as well as strongholds of Jewish erudition and mysticism. Between 1493, the year of the expulsion, and 1536, more than 20,000 Jews and Marranos—crypto-Jewish converts to Christianity—established themselves in the city at the invitation of Sultan Bayazid II. The new arrivals adjusted with little difficulty, so the sources claim, to the Italian and Provençal Jews they encountered: they shared customs, a similar ritual, and their languages were related.[49]

Within a century of the arrival of the Spanish Jews, Ladino had become the common tongue of Salonica and had penetrated along Balkan trade routes into the Macedonian hinterland as far north as Sarajevo. "Madre de Israel" they proudly called their city. The silk industry, to which Benjamin of Tudela had attested, was flourishing. The wool dying and weaving industry which was to bring the community its greatest prosperity—and link its fate to its Ottoman protectors—was modeled on that which had flourished since the early Middle Ages in Barcelona, Toledo and Segovia. Within three generations, the Iberian refugees had established an integrated society which encompassed poverty-stricken families and wealthy merchants; porters, small craftsmen and manufacturers; talmudic scholars, kabbalists and bankers. In the half century since their arrival, Salonica's Jews accumulated significant economic power. The harbor came once again to life. Traders secured mercantile contacts with trading cities like Venice, Ragusa, and Ancona, and soon thereafter with Antwerp and London.

Wool cloth from the looms of Salonica produced by the corporations of the *traperos*, the *manteros* and the *pañeros* enjoyed a surge of popularity throughout the Balkans, and as far afield as Alexandria, Smyrna and Istanbul. When, in mid-sixteenth century, the sultan ordained that the workshops of Salonica would manufacture the warm, waterproof wool garments which were to clothe the Janissary corps, the production of wool became more than a community matter: it became a state enterprise. Assured of a stable market for their wool, the shepherds of Macedonia and Bulgaria prospered; even more so the dyers and weavers of the city. In 1568, the Turkish authorities and a delegation headed by the Rabbi Almosnino agreed that the Jewish community's yearly tribute to the imperial exchequer be paid in kind. Each congregation was obliged to furnish a specific quantity of stuffs, in proportion to its wealth.[50]

The Jews of Salonica had taken only a short time to replicate their doomed Iberian homeland. Nowhere was the historical reconstruction so striking in its fidelity than in the presence—palpable, dominating—of a spirit of mystical piety which wove its way through the life of the community like a red thread. In the ascendancy were the kabbalist doctrines which had been developed in the Galilean town of Safed during the sixteenth century and which, for more than one hundred years thereafter, were to dominate Jewish religious life.[51]

Kabbala, which Umberto Eco suggests should be translated as "tradition," is a technique for the reading and interpretation of the sacred text of the Torah. Beneath the letter of the written Torah the kabbalist seeks the eternal Torah, which pre-exists creation and which God had bestowed upon the angels. He approaches the sacred text as a symbolic system which speaks of mystical and metaphysical realities. The technique of *temura*, the art of the permutation of letters and of the anagram, is more than a reading method: it is the very process by which God created the world.[52]

In the hands of Isaac Luria and his disciple Haïm Vital, kabbalism represented far more than a numerological reading scheme, it established itself as a social and historical force within Judaism. "Kabbalism triumphed because it provided a valid answer to the great problems of the time... the kabbalist answer illuminated the significance of exile and redemption and accounted for the unique historical situation of Israel within the wider, in fact cosmic, context of creation itself."[53]

The expulsion from Spain had, a century before the triumph of Luria's doctrines, once again posed the wrenching question of exile. The Salonica community, the largest and most prosperous of the Diaspora, functioned as an incubator for metaphysical inquiry. Small wonder that it took kabbalism to its bosom. In telling the story of divine acts and events, Luria's teachings accounted for the mystery of the world by an inner, mystical process which took place within the Godhead and, in so doing, ultimately produced the "outer" material creation.[54] The doctrine "implied that there had been no defect, let alone disaster and catastrophe, in the divine process, but rather, an organic unfolding of certain fixed laws inherent in the creative activity of God." These ideas were significant in that they gave an "immediate answer to the most pressing question of the time—Israel's existence in exile."[55]

A materialist might argue that the question of Israel's existence in exile—what better expressed it than the Jewish community of Salonica in its near-perfect, reduced-scale version of Iberian Judaism?—could be begged while the community prospered. But the extraordinary first flowering of Jewish Salonica became a slide into decline as European trade gradually shifted away from the Muslim Mediterranean and toward the transatlantic New World over the course of the long sixteenth century. Into a social, economic and religious climate dominated by discouragement, loss of economic vitality, and the vibrant mystical yearning triggered by the kabbalists, strode a false messiah whose ascent and apostasy shook the house of Israel to its foundations, and shaped Salonica in ways which were, paradoxically, to give form and contour to the modern city.

ON A DAY WHEN THE SOUTH WIND is blowing, and high clouds veil the autumn sun, I'm hurrying up one of Salonica's narrow concrete canyons, a street of shoe stores, sweet shops and sidewalk vegetable stalls, as if late for an appointment with the past. Suddenly, I emerge into a clearing under a patch of sky. In a city whose Islamic heritage has been demolished, built over or left to sprout weeds, the sight of an intact mosque takes the breath away. My expedition into the concealed historical labyrinth has brought me to the gates of the last Muslim house of worship built in Salonica.

Straight from the bastard lineage of the late Ottoman neo-baroque, Vitaliano Poselli's effusively eccentric Yeni Cami ("new mosque") enjoyed only twenty years of service, from 1902 until 1923, when its proprietors vacated Salonica. Greece, at the behest of its Great Power allies, had invaded Turkey. In the ensuing, inevitable and catastrophic defeat, Hellenism was swept from Anatolia. Muslim and Christian populations were exchanged.

Though the Yeni Cami appears to be a mosque it was not a mosque. The filigreed frieze which snakes across its façade draws the eyes, focusing them on a decorative medallion in arabesque form above the main entrance. What seems at first glance to be a stylized rendering of Qur'anic verse suddenly snaps into focus as the Star of David. The "Muslims" who worshipped here were not Muslims. They were Jews, members of a secretive sect that occupied the shifting ground between the city's two dominant religions, Judaism and Islam, a sect whose followers lived a lifetime of rigorous double identity in emulation of the man whose intensity and charisma were exceeded only by his gifts of dissimulation. The man whose career revealed "not only the vitality of the Jewish people, but also the deep, dangerous and destructive dialectics inherent in the messianic idea."[56]

That man was Sabbatai Sevi, the flamboyant, self-proclaimed King of Kings, whose life arched across the skies of the mid-seventeenth century like a rainbow of hope and redemption. At one end of the rainbow—which stretched from Smyrna, where the Holy Sinner received his calling—stood Salonica, city of kabbalistic piety and messianic fervor, whence Sabbatai Sevi's faithful followed him on the perilous journey into pseudo-Islam.

If history marched to the drummer of cause and effect, Sabbatai Sevi could be dismissed as little more than a symptom of the economic decline of the Ottoman empire. For such vulgar *a posteriori* determinism we can, following Gershom Scholem, point the finger of blame at the rationalist world outlook, "which narrows the historical perspective and prevents an unbiased understanding of phenomena such as the mystical movement in Judaism."[57] Or, one might add, in Islam or Christianity.

Seventeenth century Salonica was a city gripped tightly in God's embrace, a multiethnic polity over which revealed Truth ruled through mosque, church and synagogue, regulating all but the crowing of the cock at dawn. In the interstices of ruling Ottoman Islam, Sufi sects flourished. Christ was worshipped in low-lying, humble stone churches. The Jews, masters of the urban and regional economy, flocked piously to dozens of synagogues, each one a reflection of the original community of its congregationists. Into this richness of converging and conflicting heavenly vision strode the great messianic catalyst, creator of a new heavenly dispensation; wrecker, dream builder—and reminder that no society can long escape the epileptic seizure of the unexpected, the violent, unpredictable reordering of certainty that is the sole certainty.

THE SABBATIAN MOVEMENT emerged in the specific conditions of the Ottoman empire, but it quickly embraced the entire Jewish world, cutting radically across class and linguistic boundaries. It appealed to the yearnings of the destitute, as does every utopian vision. It also embraced the millionaire bankers and traders of arch-liberal Amsterdam, who put their fortunes at the messiah's disposal, sight unseen. "If there was one general factor underlying the patent unity of the Sabbatian movement everywhere, then this factor was essentially religious in character and as such obeyed its own autonomous laws, even if today these are often obscured behind smoke screens of sociological verbiage."[58]

Sabbatai Sevi, the man whose movement left a greater imprint here in Salonica than anywhere else in the Jewish—or the Islamic—world, was born in Smyrna in 1626, possibly of parents from Patras, in the Peloponese. Among his fellow Smyrniotes he quickly acquired the reputation of a man inspired, as much for his brilliance as a student as for his robust appearance, his luminously ruddy cheeks and mellifluous singing voice. Young scholars of his age gathered around him; together they studied Talmudic and mystical lore, and took ritual purifying baths in the sea. In early adulthood, too, first appeared the symptoms of Sabbatai's affliction—which amplified his gifts as it did his weaknesses. But unlike crippling schizophrenia, his condition of manic-depressive psychosis coupled with paranoid traits not only left his mental facilities intact, but enabled his manic personality to perform extraordinary acts.[59]

(But Scholem's medical reductionism is only a short remove from his own critique of the rationalist world outlook. Sabbatai may have been a manic-depressive psychotic. He may also have been a portent, a divine meteor, a speeding mass of fire and ice whose origins must remain embedded in the ever-receding boundaries of celestial chaos. Or order. I prefer to take the messiah's grandeur at face value, untainted by the projections of a faithless age onto a religious past.)

One such extraordinary act, neither the first nor the last, took place in Salonica, where Sabbatai migrated after leaving, or being driven from, Smyrna in 1651. Here he concluded, in one of his states of illuminated, shining-faced exaltation, a scandalous, blasphemous public marriage to the Torah, which brought about his expulsion from the city. He wandered thence through the Greek provinces of the empire, and on to Constantinople, where the rabbis realized that "some new sect was fermenting in his brain."[60]

In the following years, Sabbatai's peregrinations brought him to Palestine. It was there that he encountered the man who was to transform the antinomian extremism that had won him adulation and enmity in every community he visited, into a full-fledged and fulgurant messianic upsurge. This man was a certain Nathan of Gaza who was at once the new messiah's John the Baptist and Saint Paul.[61] His character combined unflagging activism, original theological thought grounded in the Safed kabbalist movement, and a clear-headed, single-minded perseverance: the mirror opposite of the impulsive, mercurial, charismatic Sabbatai Sevi. Most crucially, Nathan recognized him, in an ecstatic vision, as the messiah: "Thus saith the Lord, behold your savior commeth, Sabbatai Sevi is his name..."[62]

These events took place in the spring of 1665, a time of high eschatological expectation. 1666 would see the advent of Divine Judgment. The kingdom of God was at hand. The political messianism of the downtrodden masses and the mystical messianism of the kabbalists were on a converging course. The voices of reason and caution, the warnings of pinch-mouthed nay-sayers were of no avail. On May 31, 1665, Sabbatai publicly proclaimed himself as savior. Both a king and a prophet had arisen in Israel; now the people accepted their ruler because Nathan his prophet had confirmed his kingship. Shortly after the proclamation, he decreed an end to ritual fasting, and announced that "nothing but joy and triumph" should dwell in the habitations of the believers.[63]

From its earliest moments the movement veered, mirroring Sabbatai's extremes of mood, between severe penitence and exuberant outbursts of rejoicing. This was the pattern in Palestine, and it was to be the pattern when the messiah returned to his birthplace, where he remained hidden for two months before revealing himself. This he did, finally, on the Sabbath, December 16, 1665, when he broke down the doors of Smyrna's Portuguese synagogue with an ax, rushed in at the head of crowd of true believers, as his followers now called themselves, and preached a blasphemous sermon at the end of which he anointed his elder brother Elijah king of Turkey and his second brother emperor of Rome, then forced all present to speak the ineffable name. At the end of this extraordinary ceremony, he sang the "Meliselda," a Ladino *romanza* which was popular among the Spanish exiles, and which symbolized his own mystical marriage to the Torah in Salonica, years before.[64]

The powerful appeal of the Sabbatian message, and its scandalous nature in the eyes of the conservative rabbis, derived, too, from the paradoxical nature of its treatment of women. The false messiah, who had entered into two unconsummated marriages in his youth, married a woman, named Sarah, in Cairo in 1664. Though she was known as "the messiah's consort," her deportment was far from saintly, and rumors of licentious behavior—probably true—accompanied her as would the scent of heavy perfume. Perhaps because his beautiful wife demanded freedom to pursue and satisfy her sensual desires, perhaps for loftier spiritual reasons, Sabbatai seems to have contemplated a radical reform in the status of women; a new, utopian vision of the equality of the sexes articulated in the sole, inimitable manner available to his age. Freedom from divine law as manifested in transgression became transmuted into liberation from the constraints of a law that posited women as lesser beings.

"Is he the Lord's anointed, or a traitor, a wicked sinner and a fornicator?" wondered the doubters.[65] But they were now a minority in Smyrna. Sabbatai's followers controlled the febrile Jewish masses, wielding the potent weapon of faith and the terrorism of a majority possessed, to thrust the messiah into a position of unchallenged authority. The transition from mere factual reality to the transfigured reality of the heart, that is, to legend, had been swift and decisive. The believers beheld miracles and heard prophecies made manifest. This force now bore the unalloyed truth of Sabbatai's messianic powers to every corner of the Jewish world, splitting communities and setting souls to reverberate in heavenly cadence.

Twelve days after the events in the Portuguese synagogue the newly acclaimed messiah departed for Istanbul. The Turkish authorities were prepared to countenance much strange behavior on the part of their Jewish subjects. They may well have been persuaded to ignore the would-be messiah's claims—blasphemous in Islam, where Mohammad is the Seal of prophecy—by Sabbatai's wealthy followers. But a movement which proclaimed itself a kingdom of this world, and appointed a king of Turkey to rule over the empire of the Sultan could only be in rebellion against the state, a capital charge. The disruption of commerce, which was controlled almost completely by the Jews, may also have dismayed the authorities.

On arrival in Istanbul, Sabbatai was arrested and cast into confinement. After seven months of imprisonment in the fortress at Gallipoli, his "Tower of Strength," the anointed one was transferred to Adrianople in September, 1666, and brought at last before the Sultan where two alternatives were laid before him. Sabbatai would be offered as a target to the imperial archers. If he survived the ordeal he would be certified as the true Messiah. Refusal would result in impalement. The alternative was immediate conversion to Islam. He chose conversion, renounced his followers and reviled his faith.[66]

In normal times and circumstances, the shock of the messiah's apostasy should have been enough to shatter the structure of faith and hope that had been built up around him. But throughout the Jewish world, and most of all in Salonica, these were not normal times and circumstances. The Sabbatian movement had struck its deepest roots here, where the Jews, according to eyewitnesses, surpassed all others in their messianic faith and penitential fervor. Salvation was not merely imminent; it had begun. Believers, certain that the messianic message of penitence and joy had liberated them from the strictures of the Law itself, were no longer easily misled by the illusions of the material world. The new forces that had arisen could not be suppressed; people, once convinced, refused to accept the verdict of history, refused to admit that their faith had been but illusion.[67]

Sabbatai Sevi died, almost ten years to the day after his apostasy, in the Albanian-Montenegrin town of Ulcinj, on the Adriatic, to where he had been exiled by the Ottoman authorities who remained skeptical of the sincerity of his conversion. In Salonica, where his illuminated feats of antinomian audacity had deeply imprinted themselves on the consciousness of the community, he was not forgotten. Orthodox rabbinical sources hastened to attack the fallen messiah's followers. "The sinfulness of the world, they claimed, could be only overcome by a superabundance of sin, by the most extreme degree of licentiousness. Among these Salonica Sabbatians, then, shameless profligacy, even incest, were openly practiced—so their enemies declared. In spite, perhaps on account of these excesses, they continually found fresh supporters, who clung to the delusion with pertinacity..."[68]

Unable to suppress Sabbatai's believers by theological persuasion or by excommunication, the Salonica rabbis turned to the secular authorities. The "converts", they submitted, were fair-weather Muslims intent on undermining not only Judaism, but the religion of Mohammad as well. To appease the Ottomans, who were sensitive both to the doctrinal argument and to the power of money, the elders of the dissident community led by the charismatic Jacob Sevi Querido ("the Dear One") undertook, in 1687, a dramatic mass pilgrimage to Mecca, adopted the white turban and proclaimed their fealty to Islam. Three hundred of the city's leading families joined the sect which the Turks promptly labeled "renegades"—*Dönme*—and which they themselves called *Maminim*—"believers"—as they always had.

The Maminim made no attempts to hew to the strict laws of rabbinical Judaism. Nor were they, despite the pilgrimages and the turbans, conventional Muslims. Perhaps their secretive nature reflected the strategies which, centuries earlier in Spain, the Marranos had adopted to conceal their Jewishness beneath a Christian veneer.[69] While the Marrano "infection" thesis cannot be ruled out, the movement, now codified as doctrine, surely drew its inspiration from the duplicitous, yet powerful personality of the false messiah, and its strength from the outpouring of devout solidarity that outlived the man who called himself, to his dying day, the Anointed of the God of Israel.

The Dönme, or Maminim, strictly forbade marriage outside the faith, to Muslims most of all. Their ceremonies incorporated many of Sabbatai's most daring departures from rabbinical law. Their commandments, a parallel version of the Biblical Ten, were distinguished by an extraordinarily ambiguous formulation of the injunction against adultery.[70] As religious free-thinkers who sought for essence beneath appearance, the Dönme were on friendly terms with the Bektashi dervishes, a Sufi order which had attached itself to the Janissaries, and which I was to encounter, in the course of my journey, in Albania. In this they followed the example of their founder. Had not Sabbatai Sevi himself, on one of this visits to Istanbul, stayed at the *teke* of the Turkish dervish Mehmet Nyazi, the author of mystical poems with a pantheistic flavor?[71]

As a stone dropped into still water sends concentric rings rippling across the surface, so the reverberations of the Sabbatian movement were felt throughout the Jewish world in ways that seem at first glance curious, yet on second examination consistent with the power of legend and with the intensity of messianic yearning that legend revealed. "All this shame and disappointment that dreamers and impostors inflicted upon Jewry throughout nearly a whole century, all these wretched occurrences, the work of Sabbatai Sevi and his band of prophets, and the excommunications fulminated against them, were powerless to suppress the kabbalistic Messianic vagary once and for all."[72]

In Poland, heartland of Ashkenazi Jewry, the aftershocks of the Sabbatian movement spawned the brief messianic outburst of Jacob Frank, who declared himself the heir of Sabbatai Sevi, only to convert first to Islam, then to Catholicism, then Orthodox Christianity. Another sect believed, as did the false messiah, that penitence and rejoicing would hasten the advent of the kingdom of heaven. Its members called themselves Hassidim, after their founder Judah Hassid ("the pious"), and today live in happy expectation of deliverance, backs turned on what they regard as the sacrilegious doctrine of Zionism and, not unattractively, most aspects of modernity.

Between 1750 and 1850, precisely the years when orthodox Jewry in Salonica was struggling to recover from the disaster of the Sabbatian movement, the Dönme thrived, drawing new recruits and splitting into three sub-sects. Experts in dissimulation, all three concealed their internal affairs from both Turks and Jews so successfully that rumor was the only source of information about them. Masters of double identity, they used Turkish names for their relations with the Ottomans, Hebrew names for their dealings with the Jews. While both, they were neither.

The close-knit, secretive Dönme acquired influence in public affairs in Salonica. Their economic power was one of the driving forces in the city's emergence as second city of the empire, and as the Ottoman gateway to

Europe. Several ministers of the Young Turk government, aggressive Westernizers all, were Dönme, including the finance minister Djavid Bey. As a vector for the European ideals of nationalism and constitutionalism, they uncannily resembled the Bektashis, who had also rallied enthusiastically to the Young Turk cause and became the heralds of the Albanian national idea. Mustafa Kemal, the Salonica native who, as Atatürk, delivered the final blow to the moribund Ottoman state, was a member of the Dönme. So claimed his Islamist opponents, whom he later hanged for their temerity. And though the assertion cannot be proved, its persistence reveals how fertile was the soil of Salonica for theories of conspiracy, for clandestine brotherhoods, for confraternities of the illuminated.

From antinomian profligates and voluptuaries, the Dönme eventually transformed themselves into a disciplined body whose members flourished in commerce and politics, and eventually wielded power and influence far beyond their numbers. They could only have existed in Ottoman Salonica, which for four centuries provided the Jews with a social and spiritual environment unique in their historical experience. To assert this is not to argue for Ottoman benevolence, for the Turks could be cruel and capricious masters, but to underline the relatively enlightened application by the state authorities of Islamic law which allowed the city to flourish as a Jewish metropolis. The result was a climate of tolerance which the fine Western invention of tribal nationalism was to shatter irreparably.

ONCE THE HEARTBEAT OF THE CITY, Jewish Salonica today is so discreet and self-effacing as to be invisible. On the second floor of the Hirsch building, on bustling Tsimiski Street, guarded by a semi-somnolent Greek policeman who spends his day watching game shows on a small television set, the Community's offices have the musty smell of forgotten dossiers. It is here, in a boardroom the walls of which are hung with the official portraits of the city's chief rabbis, that Albert Nar, the soft-spoken, burly man who functions as resident archivist, historian and poet, has arranged for me to meet the president, a businessman named Andreas Setifah. Both men are the sons of survivors who owed their lives to the Greek families which sheltered them. Both speak with the infinite caution of officials who weigh each word lest they be misinterpreted, lest their fidelity to the Greek state be impugned.

Both assure me, repeatedly and emphatically, that the Jews today are fully integrated into civil life and encounter no discrimination.

Not surprisingly, they tell me, the first result of Sabbatai Sevi's apostasy was a hardening of the heart among those members of the Salonica Jewish community who had not been caught up in the fire-storm of messianic fervor. Doctrinal chill set in; rabbinical orthodoxy reasserted itself; suspicion of mysticism, let alone heterodoxy in any form, was endemic. The advent of the false redeemer triggered an economic collapse from which recovery was slow, painful. The Jews drew back into quietism, became more conservative in their language and thought. Where once 32 separate micro-communities had flourished, each clustered around its own synagogue, a united religious leadership took shape under a rabbinical triumvirate which preached radical conservatism and punctilious legalism. Around them, as the Ottoman empire withered, the Balkans seethed with the first stirrings of Serbian, Bulgarian, Greek and Romanian national awakening. Lacking a national homeland, the Jews withdrew into their Iberian past, asserting their Spanish roots.[73]

So deep had become Salonica Jewry's intellectual poverty, so tattered its social structures, so intransigent and absolute the rule of the traditionalist rabbinate, that renewal could come, it seemed, only from without. This it did, in the person of Moïse Allatini, son of a wealthy Tuscan family which had established itself in Salonica at the end of the eighteenth century. Almost single-handedly, Allatini created a modern industrial structure, the remains of which are still visible today: a brickworks, a brewery, a printing house, a textile mill, an agricultural machinery manufacture, shoe making and tobacco processing works, and ultimately, the Bank of Salonica, founded in 1888.

By the end of the nineteenth century, Salonica had once again become a vigorous, vital community with conflicting political and ideological movements, explains Mr. Setifah. For Salonica, it is understood, read Jewish Salonica. "No Jewish community anywhere else in the world could demonstrate the same degree of maturity: the full social pyramid. By 1885, Salonica was the only place in the world where a Jew could walk with his head held high."

A combination of inner regeneration and Ottoman economic reform, coupled with extreme fertility and the beginnings of modern public hygiene, had transformed a disease-ridden, impoverished Levantine backwater into an emerging industrial metropolis with a Jewish identity which had an immediate impact on travelers. One such visitor wrote in 1914: "Salonica was never Serb; it never became Bulgar despite the unrelenting, persistent efforts of the Tsars; it was only ever so slightly Roman; Turkish it remained, but only superficially. It had been Greek and Byzantine, intensely so. But today it is Jewish, Spanish, Sephardic. In our times it is to the modern era what Toledo was to the dawn of the modern age."[74]

By 1902, there were 62,000 Jews in the city, out of a total population of 126,000. Muslims, including the Maminim, made up the second largest group; while the remainder were Greeks, Bulgars, Serbs, Armenians, Albanians and Levantines.[75]

The 1908 Young Turk revolution was a watershed for the community, continues Mr. Setifah. "They transformed the Ottoman empire into a national state, with obligatory military service, and taught Turkish in the schools. Of course, in the early days of the revolution the Young Turks were hailed as saviors. But their leaders were not only pro-Turkish; they were Turkish agents." As the true nature of the self-proclaimed reformers revealed itself, enthusiasm for their program waned. Few could have mistaken the signs of imminent collapse. When economic crisis hit Salonica in 1911, bringing down many of the city's Jewish institutions, the sense of insecurity took on epidemic proportions.

At the outbreak of the Balkan Wars in 1912, Salonica was home to 70,000 Jews, of whom 55,000 were Ottoman subjects, as loyal to the Sultan and to Istanbul as the Jews of Austria-Hungary were to the Kaiser and to Vienna. In repayment for their devotion to the *ancien regime* under which they had prospered, they were soon to be metamorphosed into foreigners in their own city, a neoplasm to be excised from the national body. That the catastrophe in Greece came about not through a virulent anti-Semitic movement with local roots but from without, through an apparently random act of fate, changed not by one micron the community's destiny.

As befitted the empire's most cosmopolitan city, its gateway to the West, political activity before, during and after its capture by the Greek army was intense. The Jewish community moved with extraordinary caution, Mr. Nar reminds me. The Alliance Israelite, the French-speaking, westernizing elite faction supported, or at least acquiesced in the Greek takeover. They viewed the new masters as Europeans much like the French whom they idealized, people who would safeguard their acquired rights and accelerate the onrush of modernity to which the Alliance was committed. Salonica would be Greek, they correctly reasoned, not Bulgarian. But among the poor, uneducated, Ladino-speaking masses—and those who considered themselves Ottoman subjects—feelings of suspicion prevailed and apprehension was high.

Only the naive could have failed to see the hand of Great Power politics at work in Salonica, operating, as it does today in Bosnia, in a multiplicity of disguises through willing local agencies. In fact, the collapse of the Ottoman empire's Balkan dominions after its defeat in 1913 threw the floodgates open wide, and, quickly, proxy war was to be replaced by the real thing, precipitated by the events of 1914 in Sarajevo. Austro-Hungary still caressed the megalomaniac vision of the *Drang nach Osten* which was to destroy it. The fall of Salonica would have seemed, in the gilded baroque salons of the Ringstrasse or in the cafés where the fate of peoples was settled over *Sachertorte* and coffee *mit schlag*, a Godsend. The city was already the terminus of the Balkan railway, the work of Baron de Hirsch's Austrian consortium. Why not, went the argument, transform the great harbor into a free zone, a Jewish national enclave under Vienna's protection, a semi-Zionist Balkan Israel before the fact. Emperor Franz Joseph's credentials as protector of the Jews were, after all, impeccable.

Did the Austrian gambit have support among the Jews of Salonica? Did it ever graduate from dream to plan? There were 'autonomist' leanings, admits Mr. Nar, who then hastens to add that these leanings were surely the work of individuals. Still, in the climate of intrigue and treachery of the Balkan wars, the Serbs and the Bulgars could ill conceal their claims to Salonica and its Macedonian hinterland; the Jews—some of them—could ill disguise their desire to see their city remain an international metropolis. The Greek conquerors acted in two ways: they arrested the leadership of the community soon after the victory of November 1912, and they moved rapidly to guarantee the rights and property of the Jewish population. Events, as is their wont, quickly swept aside the question of Salonica's political status. The outbreak of hostilities across the Balkans transformed the city into the headquarters of the Entente allies. Business boomed, cafés were jammed, the whorehouses of Vardar Square operated round-the-clock; society became more diverse, colorful and multinational than it had ever been before—a final fierce flare-up before the dying of the light.

The power and fascination of tragedy, as the ancients well knew, lies not in our ignorance of the dénouement, for in the raw glare of hindsight we know full well what must happen. It lies in the majestic rumbling of the machinery of fate—like a Handel aria—as it grinds between its cosmic teeth the unwitting protagonists who have committed *hubris*, eradicates noble families, seals the doom of cities. The great fire which struck Salonica at the height of its war-time effervescence destroyed—tragically—the physical infrastructures, the armature, the brick and wood and mortar that made up the sinews of the Jewish community. In its aftermath the Jews, though they received compensation, were not permitted to recover their property or rebuild on their land. Overnight they had been uprooted, expropriated, dispossessed. The poorest, the dockers and porters and small tradesmen who once lived in the fetid, dark lanes, were consigned to former military barracks and to the Baron de Hirsch ghetto at the railway station. One was called "Campbell," the other two were known only by their numbers: 6 and 155.

Two narratives of the Salonica Jews exist, side by side. Or are they two aspects of the same narrative? As I listen to Albert Nar and Andreas Setifah, I hear a story of official tolerance, of governmental near-benevolence. Greece, which in the years following the Great War set about pursuing its own aggressive nationalist agenda at the expense of the ruined Ottoman state and at the behest of its British and French protectors, rallied enthusiastically to the Balfour Declaration. The hand of the Zionists in Salonica was strengthened, at the expense of the Jewish-led Socialists, who for decades had preached working-class unity in a Balkan federation. But I catch the echo of a subtext, the almost imperceptible vibration which, in retrospect, foreshadows disaster as it advances, imperceptibly, from one tiny isolated incident—which seemed so convenient to ignore at the time—to another, slightly larger incident.

The violent expulsion of the Greek expeditionary force from Asia Minor in 1922—Greece had now been at war for a full decade—brought with it the collapse of Hellenism on the eastern shore of the Aegean. Suddenly Salonica became home to hundreds of thousands of bitter, hungry refugees, many of whom spoke only Turkish and who had little experience of a sophisticated, cosmopolitan urban environment. This bitterness, this hunger were channeled by the Greek Communist Party, which had honorably opposed the Asia Minor folly, into a vigorous, revolutionary trade-union movement. It was also rapidly converted by the disenchanted into suspicion and enmity toward the city's indigenous working population: the Jews.

A proto-fascist organization which labeled itself EEE (Hellenic National Union) in 1932 attacked the Campbell ghetto and burned it to the ground. The pogrom, a Mediterranean version of what had been the normal course of events in Poland, Russia and the Ukraine for centuries, had not occurred in an ideological vacuum. The daily newspaper *Makedonia*, which continues to publish today in Salonica under the same family ownership, had created a climate in which anti-semitism could enjoy a certain respectability. In this respect it was no different from established newspapers throughout Europe, where admiration for the Hitlerian ideal overweighed moral scruples. And when the homeless refugees from the pogrom departed for Israel, the Greek government of the day did nothing to hold them.

Paradoxically, explain my hosts, the success of the Salonica Jewish community had convinced Zionists that a Jewish state could not only survive, but flourish, in Palestine. David Ben Gurion himself had spent several years in the city, and later returned to recruit dock workers for the port of Haifa in 1928. That the rising curve of the Zionist project intersected the descending curve of the viability of Salonica's Jewish community may be only another quirk of fate. The Jews themselves could not have been blind to the accumulating iciness that underlay their superficially cordial relations with their newfound Greek masters. Could they have acted differently? In Greece, the ideas of working-class solidarity and Balkan unity had been long proscribed as subversive. Building an ethnic-based national security state was the task of the hour. On the northern frontier, the Slav-speaking Macedonians were being violently reduced to silence. How, except through a course of voluntary, full-scale assimilation, could the Jews have found a political home? And had they assimilated into the emerging Greek national state, would they have been any more protected from the coming fury than were their perfectly assimilated German correligionists?

THE ARISTOTELIAN UNIVERSITY of Thessaloniki is the city's pride and secular counterweight to the Saint Demetrius cult. At any hour of the day or night the downtown core throbs with clusters of students who laugh, chat, argue and buzz endlessly to and fro on their motor-bikes. The bare-bones apartments which once housed refugees from Asia Minor now provide low-rent accommodation for young men and women from provincial towns and working-class suburbs. Fast-food joints, cheap bars, bookstores and photocopy shops line the streets. Customers spill over onto the sidewalks and plazas which overlook the city's exposed Roman ruins, where the young, with insouciant laughter, perch on the lip of the past. The university is also one of Salonica's largest employers. Its teaching corps enjoys the respect accorded citizens of substance and accomplishment, its professors are regular participants in a lively intellectual whirl of symposia, academic conferences and public lectures. Its title invokes the name of the philosopher who served temporal power as tutor of Alexander the Great, an unintended and rather ironic parallel to the University's modern role as handmaiden to the State.

The campus occupies several hectares of prime land just beyond the ancient eastern wall. On the gentle gradient sloping towards the bay, eucalyptus trees surround a sprawling quadrangle of reinforced concrete blockhouses. At first glance, these buildings seem solidly constructed, typical of modern Greek brutalism in all its numbing banality. Examined at closer hand they betray an unseemly haste. Pathways have crumbled to expose the sandy aggregate, windows are broken, plywood doors are splintered, plaster peels, elevators do not function, anarchist graffiti deface all vertical surfaces. Beneath the superficial solidity lurks corner-cutting, inferior materials, slapdash improvisation, and the scornful disregard of the users for the object used.

The haste revealed in its construction betrays an equal haste to conceal: the University, too, has a story to hide. How many of the students—and the professors—who file up and down these pathways hurrying to class know that precisely beneath their feet lies the ground that once contained the city's great Jewish cemetery? I meander across the campus on a late-fall morning, as the northwesterly breeze strips trees of their dead leaves. Nowhere is there the slightest indication, no sign however discreet, no small tasteful commemorative plaque: nothing suggests that in this place, in earth once consecrated, rested the bones and memories of close onto five centuries.

With Salonica's forcible amalgamation into the Greek state, with the cleansing inferno of the Great Fire of 1917 and the city plan which it spawned, the Jewish cemetery underwent a rapid mutation, its status slipping rapidly from that of hallowed ground to coveted real estate. The city was expanding, and its envious gaze came quickly to rest on the vast expanse of marble gravestones, tombs and vaults. In the years following the Campbell pogrom, the cemetery had been desecrated on several occasions. Such fine land should become a public park, influential voices were heard to say. Relocate the graves. Others had identified the city of the dead as the site for future expansion of the University. The military regime of general Ioannis Metaxas, the pro-British fascist, began negotiations with the Jewish community. Finally, an agreement was reached: the community would cede a portion of the cemetery to the University, and the displaced remains would be relocated. The plan was never implemented. But, Elias Petropoulos told me when we met in Paris, the authorities had already begun to nibble at its edges, slyly setting in motion a process only the Nazis would dare to complete.

Could the land-hungry city fathers have imagined how great was to be their windfall? Could they have dreamed, could they have known? "In Salonica alone, nowhere else in Greece nor in any of the occupied lands, did the insolent Nazis sack a Jewish cemetery with such frenzy," recounts *In Memoriam*, the massive, chilling account of the extermination of the city's Jewish community. "Had it not been for the instigation of their local agents, the sacrilegious idea of destroying the ancient Jewish necropolis of Salonica would never have occurred to them. (...) Certainly one cannot accuse those who proposed that it be transformed into a park, bringing health to the city and making it more attractive, of maliciousness, impiety or vandalism. Nor can we hold as blameworthy the desire of certain persons to hasten the development of the University. What is scandalous is that public figures so bereft of tact and dignity actually profited from the state of terror into which the Nazis had cast the Jewish element, that they sought the diabolical intervention of the Teutons to carry out such a design...

"The protestations of the Jewish community fell on deaf ears. On December 6, 1942, a throng of workers invaded the cemetery. (...) The bones of thousands of the dead were cast about with no respect, thrown onto rubbish heaps. The Jewish necropolis, almost five centuries old, became a huge marble quarry, thrown open to all comers. Builders, marble-cutters and men on the street could take from it whatever they wished, without restriction."[76]

The precious marble gravestones were quickly recycled on order of Dr. Max Merten, the German administrator with responsibility for civilian affairs, as paving stones for the city's downtown sidewalks. Countless fragments found new life in the courtyards of humble refugee homes in Salonica's working-class districts.[77] But not only the houses of the poor reaped the benefits of the immense windfall; Saint Demetrius basilica itself conceals remains of those same memorials.

Today, even as the University's concrete-cast presence endures as a monument to the occlusion of history, a small group of academics have begun the task of speaking—and writing—of the unspeakable. On the courageous initiative of Frangiski Abatzoupoulou, a professor in the Modern Greek Studies faculty, historical fragments, oral and written memoirs of the Holocaust have been unearthed and published, glinting like a small burnished bronze plaque set in those reversed marble paving blocks.

Who better than the Greeks could understand the endurance and the living plasticity of marble? As it writhes beneath the eternal curse of the Acropolis, modern Athens is daily reminded that it cannot escape its past. Salonica, its half-Greek sister, walks—and worships her soldier saint—on the inverted shards of a vanished city of the dead which housed the holy remains of nearly one half million souls. Marble, flesh-like in its veinous translucence, has a life of its own, and it speaks with a sepulchral voice that resonates through time. Dig below the surface in Athens and your shovel strikes sparks as it hits the relics of ancient civilization. Turn over a paving stone in

Salonica and your hands have laid bare an unhealed scar whose cry is the scream of silence.

SILENCE, BROKEN ONLY BY THE SHUFFLING of ill-shod feet and the wailing of infants, accompanied the cortege of Jewish families as they were quick-marched in their hundreds down the Via Egnatia, in full view of all Salonica, to the concentration camp of the Baron de Hirsch ghetto at the Old Station. It was *primavera en Salonico*, of the plangent Sephardic love-song; the mortal spring of 1943. At Stalingrad the onrush of the German war machine had been blunted; the tide of war had already turned. But even as military defeat became a probability, throughout Nazi-occupied Europe the machinery of the Final Solution not only continued to grind, but accelerated its cadence. While the eradication of a people may be apprehended as frenzy and paroxysm, its workings and its mechanism can only be understood as the application of rationality to evil. The strategy for genocide had been established over coffee and Cognac at the Wannsee conference of January, 1942. All that remained for the punctilious bureaucrats of the juggernaut was the matter of tactics, of implementation, of process.

German armored columns entered Salonica on the morning of April 9, 1941, easily overwhelming demoralized Greek forces whose commanding officers yearned only to fraternize with their Wehrmacht counterparts. Two days later the occupation authorities suspended publication of *El Messagero*, the city's remaining Ladino newspaper. The edict was trumpeted on the front page of *Nea Evropi* (New Europe), the Nazis' faithful Greek-language mouthpiece.

But it was not until nearly two years later that the master-builders of the Shoah were ready to go ahead. The plan was limpid in its simplicity. First the Jews would be reduced to less-than-human status. Then, isolated from their fellow citizens, they would be redefined as a "problem" calling out for solution. Until mid-1942, they had been treated with the same diffident, thoroughgoing brutality as their Greek neighbors. Then, on the Sabbath, July 11, all Jewish males between 18 and 45 were ordered to assemble in Liberty Square, where in 1908 the Young Turk revolutionaries, many of them Salonica Jews, had proclaimed the Ottoman constitutional movement and hailed the reborn multinational state. Was the square chosen because the liberty it commemorated was not that of Greece? The Germans, masters of the inversion of meaning, had selected their venue expertly. Here, as at the gate of Auschwitz, the message would be *Arbeit macht frei*.

Before a dense crowd of onlookers, more than 9,000 men were forced to stand at attention in the midsummer Mediterranean sun. Machine guns had been set up atop the buildings which ringed the square, and police strutted up and down the close-drawn ranks. Any Jew who stepped out of line, faltered, fainted, attempted to smoke or to find shelter from the heat was immediately hauled before a panel of officers and forced to execute exhausting gymnastics. Before the sun had set, what had begun as whispered rumor was now known as fact. The occupation authorities intended to conscript able-bodied Jews as forced labor to carry out military works.

Two days later, on July 13, another gathering was ordered. Each conscript was given a pass-book and, as he left the registration office, was rolled like a barrel along the cobblestones by the German gendarmes. The citizens of Salonica looked on in consternation but there was nothing they could do to stop the carefully plotted *mise en scène* of humiliation in the heat and dust. The city's professional, cultural and intellectual elite might have spoken out, but it remained silent.[78]

Working conditions for the press-ganged laborers were predictably brutal; the weakest quickly perished from heat-stroke, hunger and exhaustion. Within weeks, more than twelve percent were dead. Attempts by the Community to send food and clothing encountered insurmountable bureaucratic and logistic obstacles. After long and anguished representations from the Community's leadership, Dr. Merten proposed a bargain: those forcibly enrolled in the labor battalions could be ransomed for the sum of 3.5 billion drachmas. That, Community officials replied, was quite beyond the capacity of even the still-wealthy Jews to raise. The German counterproposal was as brilliant in its deviousness as it was devastating in its simplicity: the ransom payment would be reduced to 2.5 billion drachmas, and the cemetery would be granted as an indemnity worth the remaining one billion. The offer, it was understood, could not be refused.

Within a period of six months the occupation authorities had tested the solidarity of Christian Salonica toward its Jewish fellow-citizens and found it wanting. They had publicly humiliated the Jews, then used the ransom scheme to break them financially. The Community, which refused to place a monetary value on the ancient burial ground, was forced to surrender it free of title. In their hands the Nazis now held the fate of a terrorized, isolated, bankrupted collective of nearly 50,000 souls. Yet here, as at every step toward the precipice, the assent, the acquiescence, or at least the passivity of the victims was as essential to the success of the Plan as was the impotent sympathy or the indifference of their fellow-citizens.

In Salonica the key to this, the most delicate phase of the "operations," was Zvi Koretz, the Grand Rabbi, a highly-educated Ashkenazi from Central Europe fluent in German. Koretz also possessed a talent for organization, a tragic, near-total lack of understanding of the ways and traditions of his Sephardic flock and a taste for unchallenged authority within the community which the Nazis rapidly moved to exploit. "In the final period of its existence, the great Jewish community of Salonica had the misfortune of being headed by an evil master imposed by the dictator."[79]

In fact, Rabbi Koretz had been recruited earlier by the Community itself in the hope that his knowledge of European ways and institutions would hasten the necessary task of overcoming their "Oriental" past, of expunging its lingering Ottoman heritage, itself the fruit of long and harmonious cohabitation with Islam. There were two phases to Koretz's tenure as Grand Rabbi, community president Andreas Setifah told me. Prior to the occupation his organizational skills had helped stabilize finances and streamline the administration. But the Chief Rabbi, believing he had the ear of the Nazis, had protested the bombing by Italian warplanes of Salonica's Saint Sofia cathedral in May, 1941, and for his temerity had been arrested and imprisoned for nine months in Vienna. When he returned, chastened, to Salonica in August, 1942, the Germans reappointed him Grand Rabbi; in December he was named head of the Judenrat. "No one knows what they told him. The method they applied was typically German: first they would humiliate you, then at the last minute they would 'save' you if you agreed to collaborate," says Mr. Setifah.

"As soon as the Nazis placed all power in his hands," adds Mr. Nar, "Koretz took no counsel. Nothing can be proved, but promises must have been made to the members of the Judenrat." How else could his single-minded fixation on pleasing his masters be explained; how else the haste with which the Community acquiesced in the draconian application of the Nuremberg racial laws in February, 1943? That decision was taken shortly after two high-ranking SS officers, Dieter Wisliceny and Aloïs Brunner arrived in Salonica. Their arrival completed the triumvirate which was to oversee local implementation of the Wannsee decision: Dr. Merten, responsible for civilian matters; Wisliceny, an expert in Jewish affairs, whose sole task was to see that Jews were deported as quickly as possible; and Koretz, their foil, a willing tool in the hands of the German bureaucrats.[80]

Henceforth all Jews, with the exception of those holding the citizenship of one of the neutral countries, were to be assigned numbers and required to wear the yellow star. Those who were not already residents of one of Salonica's ghettos were to be concentrated there. All happened with the rapidity of a whirlwind: Dr. Koretz himself was given the number One. The Jews would now, assured the Nazi functionaries of doom, constitute an entirely autonomous community, with its own chamber of commerce, its police force, its municipal officials and economic life. Non-Jews would be expelled from the ghetto, and would be lodged in the homes vacated by the Jews.

Wild rumors began to sweep through the community: Deportation was imminent; Poland was to be the destination. As early as November, 1942, the truth about the Nazi extermination machine had become known in Jewish communities as far apart as New York and Jerusalem. When it was broadcast in Greece on the BBC, those Jews of Salonica who understood Greek could not believe what they had heard. Rabbi Koretz's response was to enjoin submission, discipline and resignation as the only way of purchasing the indulgence of the Nazis. On March 5, 1943, this notice was posted throughout the ghetto: "We invite our coreligionists to remain calm and disciplined, to not yield to panic, to pay no heed to unfounded, alarmist rumors. Each and every one must continue to go about his business and place his fullest confidence in the leadership of the Community."[81]

The history of the Jews of Salonica had been one of mass uprooting and dispersal. Could they have imagined the forced migration to Poland as simply a continuation of their dolorous history, another episode in an unending tale of woe, another uprooting? From the vantage point of hindsight we can, with some dispassion, argue that the Germans were the supremely rationalist heirs of their Catholic Majesties who, as they liquidated the multicultural heritage of Muslim Spain, restored the law of blood purity. But hindsight gives us no easy insight into the power of disbelief, the force of resignation, the double-headed beast of hope and despair that savaged the city's now besieged, isolated, dispossessed, seemingly rudderless Jewish community.

The community may have had been dispossessed, but it was not entirely rudderless. The Judenrat, headed by Koretz, functioned almost until the end. Having entered into a pact with the exterminators, an agreement for which their heads, as Dr. Merten succinctly put it, were the ultimate guarantee, they were bound by duty and cowardice to carry it out to the letter. More than self-deception was at work. Throughout occupied Europe the Judenrate had cooperated with the Nazis, and accepted their initial assurances that only Communists would be deported. In both Vienna and Warsaw, until it was too late, the philosophy had been 'to sacrifice the few to save the many.'[82] The measures that flowed from this philosophy were imposed by the Jewish police force, which did not hesitate to use violence against fellow Jews.

The first deportees from the Baron de Hirsch ghetto were poor and working-class Jews. Among them, the Germans claimed, were Communists who posed a threat to the security of their armed forces. Koretz and his minions acquiesced.[83] The following day, the working-class Jewish neighborhood of Aghia Paraskevi was uprooted and paraded through downtown Salonica to the staging camp, whence its entire population was transported north several days later. Again Koretz and the Judenrat kept silent. Sacrifice the few—Communists at that, the most non-human of all Jews—to save the many. Left unanswered was the question of who identified the politically suspect to the Nazis. Had the state authorities, who in 1936 had shown their readiness to shoot Communists dead in the street, passed on such information to the Judenrat and its police? To the SS itself? Or had the information come from within the community?

It was only when the Germans turned to the middle classes in the days to come that Koretz dared raise his voice in faint protest. But by then the core of the survival philosophy had become its opposite (or what it had really been all along): sacrifice thousands to save a handful. In the first week of April, Greek Prime Minister Rallis, a man described as "persona grata" of the Germans[84], flew to Salonica at the insistence of the Jewish Community of Athens which, in sharp contrast to the studied silence which prevailed in Salonica, had received public support from Archbishop Damaskinos and from a wide cross-section of Athenian business, professional and academic organizations. Koretz, at the urging of the Community leadership, tearfully called on the Prime Minister to do everything in his power to halt the deportations. Rallis' reply was as glacial as it was summary: nothing could be done. Yet even Koretz's tardy, pathetic display of license was more than the Germans could tolerate. The Rabbi was relieved of his responsibilities and placed under arrest, before being transported to Bergen-Belsen where he contrived to survive the war, only to die of typhus three months after the end of hostilities.

The transports of Jews to the death camps closely paralleled efforts by the occupying forces to ship Greek workers off to work in German war industries. In early April, mass demonstrations, organized by the Communist-led National Liberation Front, broke out in Athens, protesting the round-up. On April 16, a similar demonstration was held in Salonica. Throughout the country strikes by civil servants halted the dispatch of 80,000 workers. At no time did the demonstrators call for a halt to or condemn the deportations of the Jews which were already underway, although in February *Eleftheria* (Liberty), the clandestine newspaper of the resistance called on Greeks, Macedonians, Jews, and Vlachs to unite against "mobilization, captivity, extermination."[85]

"THE FACT IS that Koretz did exactly what the Germans asked of him. That was his responsibility. It was he and no-one else who allowed his flock to be led to the slaughter." The man telling me this story, this climactic and apocalyptic tale from which I flee and toward which I am inexorably drawn, is named Heinz Salvator Cugno. He is seated across from me, hands folded on the table in the boardroom of the Jewish Community offices, the same table in the same room where, weeks before, I had met with Mr. Setifah and Mr. Nar. At that first meeting my interlocutors had been two officials mindful of the delicacy of their position, cautious to offer no possible offense, to ignite no controversy. Today, I am listening to the voice of a man who has returned to tell of what he has seen and experienced. To speak the unspeakable. As he spoke, I remembered Primo Levi's haunting evocation of the Salonica Jews, marooned in a man-made universe of absolute arbitrariness:

> *These few survivors from the Jewish colony of Salonica, with their two languages, Spanish and Greek, and their numerous activities, are the repositories of the concrete, mundane, conscious wisdom, in which the traditions of all the Mediterranean civilizations blend together. That this wisdom was transformed in the camp into the systematic and scientific practice of theft and seizure of positions of monopoly of the bargaining Market, should not let one forget that their aversion to gratuitous brutality, their amazing consciousness of the survival of at least a potential human dignity made of the Greeks the most coherent national nucleus in the Lager, and in this respect, the most civilized.* [86]

Heinz Salvator Cugno—Number 109565—is one of the remaining handful of Salonica Jews to have survived. During my three-month stay in Salonica, I had encountered him at several public events, and had been struck by his courtliness and his proud, upright carriage. The dignity of his bearing was that of a man who understands that neither life nor history can ever provide an accounting, yet persists in expecting both. Now, as he speaks in a carefully modulated tenor, free of the whine of self-pity, he reveals himself as both articulate and impassioned, indignant yet resigned to dispassion as the only possible mode for the examination of horror.

For him, Rabbi Koretz remains the aching tooth to which the tongue returns, the focal point of cosmic incomprehension and the personification of disaster: "The Germans were as methodical as they were clever. Why was he held in prison for nearly a year, then released and handed sole responsibility as leader of our Community? What did they do to him? Somehow they broke the man; he had become passive, he made no effort to save his people. Our community was close-knit, and isolated. Where could we have gone? Besides, when your leaders tell you what you want to hear, you'll behave accordingly."

Of course, he quickly adds, one must be cautious in characterizing Koretz too rapidly. "We had not only a military occupation here, we had a dictatorship. It cannot be compared with anything else. The Germans would beat you if you got too close to them on the street. If you attempted to resist, they killed you." A moment of silence. Then, with a sudden hardening in his voice: "I believe Koretz was a coward; he hoped he would survive, even if everyone else died."

Paradoxically, the same Sudeten-Jewish background that in the end assured the survival of the Cugno family, had made it impossible, at first, for them to believe that the Germans could perpetrate a crime of such enormity. "My grandfather," he says, "had been an officer in the Imperial German army. When persecution of the Jews began, as I learned later, he put on his dress uniform, presented himself at city hall, saluted and returned his medals. Here in Salonica, when the first rumors of the death camps began to circulate, none of us believed it. By the time we did, it was too late."

Mr. Cugno was a rangy, bright-faced adolescent of 13 when he and his family were rounded up on two hours' notice and deposited in an improvised holding pen at the café across from the railway station where our story begins. The next morning, at 2:00 a.m., they were loaded into the first transport to depart the Baron de Hirsch ghetto. His father, a well-established businessman, had signed over his affairs to a Greek. The practice was illegal and the penalties draconian: death in Auschwitz for the Jews, five years in prison for the Greeks. "But that death sentence saved us. Our family knew German. When we arrived at our destination, someone had to translate the orders for all those poor Jews. 'Who knows Deutsch?' the Germans asked. Only the four members of our family!"

"For three months we interpreted death orders. But we found food in the railway cars, and that kept us alive. We knew our parents were alive, and we could resist disease. We learned how to live in the camps, to survive. That was all you could think about, survival. You had to believe it. If you had the mark of the victim on you, you were a dead man."

"The Germans were refined sadists," he exclaims. "Monsters. We cannot blame all of them, yet Hitler had widespread support. The worst thing is that the more you search for an answer, the more you learn about those who did the evil. They understood nothing. How can you ever forgive them?"

And the Greeks? Can the Greeks be faulted for their inaction, for looking on passively? Ah, but they were far from passive, Mr. Cugno assures me, stiffening involuntarily. "Remember, any act of resistance was punishable by death. If you sheltered a Jew and they found you out, you were dead. What could you do? And yet the Greeks did what they could to help. Look at Athens, where there were protests, even demonstrations, though not so much here in Salonica."

"Of course there were some who wanted to take our place. Yes, there was some passivity," he says. "But not a lack of solidarity. They begged us to leave town, to join the resistance. But most of us didn't, only a handful and even they came back. The danger of taking in Jews was enormous. Anyone who did this was a hero, acting in the face of deadly, mortal danger. You have to understand: the Germans were unrelenting. If I had been in the shoes of the Greeks, would I have had the guts to do it?"

Thus the final, tragic fate of one of the world's greatest Jewish communities could not have been avoided. In this chilling conclusion Mr. Cugno concurs with the authors of *In Memoriam*. No means existed to save 40,000 people out of a population of 200,000. Most of the Jews still spoke Ladino; only the younger generation had mastered Greek, and even then spoke it with an accent. Only the wealthy could afford to pay the price of being smuggled out of the city, and a mere handful joined the Communist-led National Resistance in the mountains, a hostile environment for a people accustomed to centuries of urban life. The combination of Nazi terror, family solidarity and the treacherous reassurances of Rabbi Koretz quenched whatever spark of collective resistance remained, while personal denunciations, settling of old scores and class hatred did the rest.

"I would never criticize the Greeks as a group, not for anti-semitism nor for racial hatred," he says in a firm voice. This clearly is a matter of pride, born of a powerful sense of Greekness which, though it was denied by the

Quisling occupation government, manifested itself in the camps in extraordinary national solidarity, culminating in organized sabotage against the executioners.

"Here in Salonica there were cases of people being pulled out of the crowd by their lovers as the Germans marched us through the town. We had not realized what would happen to us. And we were led like lambs." Then, fainter still, firmer still: "Somewhere in the city of Salonica a memorial must be established, a plaque, something to mark what happened. Maybe in the Baron de Hirsch camp. But there must be a place."

In this city, designated Cultural Capital of Europe for 1997, Heinz Salvator Cugno's solitary petition has not been answered. Yet only public acknowledgment of the darkness at the heart of European civilization can arm us, its creators, heirs and creations, against the mortal arrogance of its fulfillment. "Now, at least, they are talking about it," he says. "They say time heals wounds. But we must also remember. If we do not, someone will come, someone who will exploit humanity's fears and hopes again. The only answer is to learn to live side by side."

Chapter 4

A DIVORCE IN ALBANIA

> *Poverty in Albania is not the result of climatic conditions, crop failures or desert encroachment, but of the imposition of a social and economic system which in the end could distribute equitably only poverty and finally collapsed.*[87]

ON A NOVEMBER MORNING in 1991 beneath a pelting rain I crossed the border from Greece into Shqiperia, desolate, destitute Land of the Eagles. Emaciated men clad in ill-fitting clothes were winding their way up the hill toward the gates at the Kakavi border post to join the silent crowd gathered there in the downpour, waiting for the gates to creak open. At the foot of the hill, beside a rusted sign-post, stood a lone figure bent beneath the weight of the television set he carried on one shoulder. Rising from both sides of the valley floor, stony mountainsides disappeared into the mist. A rain-swollen river the color of chocolate tumbled north through a wide, gravel-clogged channel.

Panos, the driver, was grumbling. The car, a veteran of dozens of trips into southern Albania, had begun to ping. In the back seat, the sociologist from Athens was wringing his hands in dismay. What will we do if we're stranded here? he moaned aloud. "The plugs are damp, that's all," Panos snapped, as he looked up into the rear-view mirror to check the road behind us for the trucks. I shifted in my seat and glanced over my shoulder, peering past the sociologist's head. There they were, lumbering along behind us: two freezer-trucks carrying frozen chickens from a Greek poultry cooperative for distribution to Albanian villages.

What had been the world's most secretive, most rigorous, most autarkic command economy had entered the terminal phase of its disintegration. Few reporters had visited the country during its glorious days as the hermetically-sealed Beacon of Socialism in Europe, fewer still had come to chronicle the fall of a caricatural dwarf whose fate both resonated with the greater, tragic fall of applied Marxism, and remained, in its obtuse and paranoid pride, resolutely *sui generis*.

Early that morning I had joined the expedition in Ioannina, the capital of the Greek province of Epirus. My flight the previous day from my base in Salonica over the snowcapped Pindus mountains, jagged spine of the southern Balkans, had been brief but turbulent, and as the airport taxi entered the city, rain had begun to fall, cascading down the narrow streets and glistening on the gray, moss-grown walls of old stone buildings. Until 1913, Ioannina had been a Turkish, Greek but primarily Albanian city with a lively Jewish minority. It had thrived, under the reign of the cruel but enlightened despot Ali Pasha, as the center of a semi-autonomous multi-ethnic but primarily Albanian principality covering much of which is now north-west Greece and southern Albania in the first decades of the nineteenth century.

After checking into my hotel, I had walked through the waning light in search of the place I had stayed on my first visit to Ioannina, thirty years before: a two-floored *caravansarai* built in the Ottoman manner around a stone-cobbled courtyard beneath a venerable plane tree. At a bend of the street I found it, entrance boarded up, courtyard now occupied by automobile repair shops and used parts dealers. It had been November then, as well, and I had spent the night hungry and shivering, curled up upon myself under a heap of dirty, frayed blankets. Come dawn I had stepped out into the streets, breath frosting, and before my eyes the minarets and the high stone walls of Ali's fortress loomed against the morning light. The hour was electric. Down a transverse lane I caught a glimpse of the lake reflecting its mountain back-drop. This was the city which Byron visited in 1809, the inspiration for a canto of *Childe Harold.*

He passed the sacred harem's silent tower
And underneath the wide o'er arching gates
Surveyed the dwelling of this chief of power
Where all around proclaimed his high estate.
Amidst no common pomp the despot sat
While busy preparations shook the court
Slaves, eunuchs, soldiers guests and santans wait
Within a palace and without a fort.
Here men of every clime appeared to make resort
Richly caparaisoned a ready row of armed horse

And many a war-like store circled
The wide extending port below.
Above, strange groups adorned the corridor
And oft times through the area's echoing door
Some high-capped Tartar spurred his steed away.
The Turk, the Greek, the Albanian and the Moor
Here mingled in their many-hued array
While the deep drum's sound announced the close of day.

My current visit to Ioannina had a less Byronic cast. Tartars, Turks, Albanians and Moors had long since decamped, driven away by the frenzy of national purification of which the Greeks, *primus inter pares* among their Balkan neighbors, had become perpetrators and theoreticians. Ali Pasha, suitably defanged and pasteurized, had been transformed into a tourist marketing gimmick emptied of his statesman's substance, deprived of his diplomatic genius, stripped of his religious idiosyncrasy, voided of his dark power. Once a city of stone, Ioannina had been overwhelmed by the Hellenic urban blight of cookie-cutter apartment buildings. It was also the staging point for the thrice-weekly relief missions into Albania run by the Greek Foundation for National Repatriation, an NGO with intimate political and financial connections to the conservative government then in power in Athens.

As its will to govern slipped away, loathed by its own citizens who sought only to flee, the disintegrating Communist regime in Tirana had turned its back, as if to taunt them: 'So it's democracy you want, ingrates? Well, take it then.' Whether the remnants of the Party did so willfully, at the bidding of shadowy forces, or whether they were overtaken by events may never be known. Overwhelming Greece's rapidly improvised network of processing camps and holding centers as they came, tens of thousands of hungry refugees streamed south across the now-unguarded border. The Foundation, originally created to integrate ethnic Greeks from the collapsing former Soviet Union, soon found its meager capacity stretched to the breaking point. Prevention became the policy. Better to distribute food to the villages of southern Albania than have their inhabitants cross the border *en masse*. The generosity of Greece, once a land of hunger and rural emigration, was being tested; food distribution was part of its response. In the accompany of a sociologist and two truckloads of frozen chickens, was to accompany one such mission.

Instead of heading due north toward Tirana by way of Gjirokaster, our small convoy turned west and began to climb, laboriously, through abrupt switchbacks and around hairpin turns. This was the main highway to the coast, the military road built by the Italians when they had occupied Albania before World War II, Panos explained. Through stony gullies and along rock-strewn mountainsides we crawled, the hard earth suddenly giving way to hollows lush with olives, citrus, cypresses, beechwood.

On mist-shrouded outcroppings, or like sentinels on watch outside abandoned villages, squatted the hemispheric concrete pillboxes that disfigure the Albanian landscape like a pox. Enver Hoxha, the late dictator and founder of the ruling Albanian Party of Labor, had cast his country into an iron mold of absolute self-reliance. Albania would pursue its own course, Hoxha proclaimed, and demonstrate its proud self-sufficiency to the world. One by one its fair-weather friends—Yugoslavia, the Soviet Union, China—fell by the wayside, accused of tampering with national interests and offending hair-trigger national pride.

In a land ringed by foes, eternal vigilance was the price of security. To the south, Greece had not yet ended the state of war which began when Mussolini invaded the country through Albania in 1940. The revanchists of the Tito clique, as the lingo would have it, were waiting to swallow their upstart more-Marxist-than-thou neighbor. The Italians, who had, in living memory, turned the country into a colony in all but name, were itching to do so again. And in the background lurked those two perfidious superpowers, the Soviet Union and the United States. Safety came at a high price, in the form of hundreds of thousands of reinforced concrete bunkers which were to be the country's first line of defense, manned by peasant militiamen who tilled their fields with a pick in one hand and a rifle in the other, ever vigilant.

Panos, who had been here often, volunteered some details gleaned from Greek-speaking refugees. Albania's largest national minority, ethnic Greeks—whatever that means in a region where ethnicity can be defined by language or religion—inhabit primarily the southern part of the country and in some area, form a local majority. The bunkers, they told him, had been built by voluntary, but not optional, labor. The impromptu construction crews were handed the materials, shown the location, and set to work. When the concrete had hardened, the building team would be led inside while a heavy army vehicle, a truck or a tank, would test the structure by driving over it. Cutting corners in construction would thus be punished by live burial. Like most Albanian stories told by Greeks, this one may have been apocryphal. But it sounded consistent with the haywire punctiliousness of the ultra-Marxist mindset.

The villages through which we passed were like stone excrescences of the landscape. In its collectivist zeal, the regime constructed rural apartment blocks, three-storey structures which mimicked their urban cousins and would bring the benefits of urban living to the countryside. Only the ethnic Greeks, Panos explained, managed to maintain their small stone houses. These were the houses, I surmised, which their families had lived in before Hoxha and the partisans fought the occupying Germans and Italians, and eliminated all opposition to set up socialist Albanian in 1945.

At the center of each village stood what remained of a public building, a school, perhaps a rudimentary medical clinic. All were now devastated, wide smudges of black above gaping windows where no glass remained. In village squares, Party and patriotic monuments had been demolished, the huge exhortatory posters which once praised labor and patriotism defaced, smeared with what looked from a distance like excrement but was probably only the rich mud that abounds in this land of rain.

After nearly fifty years of enforced solidarity the workers, the tillers and the herdsmen—backbone of the regime—had, it seemed, turned on their masters. Violently. With their picks they demolished everything that lay before them on their flight toward the illusion of freedom. The evidence which met my eyes was inescapable. At the first opportunity, the masses in whose name the regime had spoken and acted, from whom it had claimed to draw its legitimacy, had struck out in rage or frustration. The break with the past, I read in the scorched ruins, was to be utter and irrevocable. There could be no going back. Only later was I to learn that the break with the past may itself have been planned and executed by the same cynical authorities who, by the timely expedient of a change of hats, had transformed themselves into democrats by wrapping themselves in the American flag.

The emaciated shadow-like figures were the proud, independent Sons of Eagles, as the Albanians call themselves. They would not suffer the dictates of capitalism, would never be seduced by the blandishments of consumerism. Such fierce assertiveness came at a price, of course. Crimes of opinion were punishable by draconian penalties, and the example came from the top. Disagreement? Had not the dictator himself allegedly shot his prime minister dead in the midst of a particularly acrimonious Central Committee meeting? Internal passports restricted people to their villages of residence. A rigid collectivist system kept track of each sheep, each olive tree. Punishments were collective: the disgrace of the father was visited upon the sons, the wife, all near and distant relatives. Only divorce could cleanse spouses of ideological contamination.

As the car sputtered down a pine-lined boulevard into the coastal town of Himarë, collapse now surrounded us. The municipal infirmary had been vandalized, every window-pane shattered. "No sheets, no anesthetic, no alcohol, no medicine," Panos rattled off the dismal catalogue. We pulled up in front of the town hall. Rain mixed with wind-blown mist from the waves breaking against the jetty slanted, stinging, against our faces as we dashed for the entrance. Drawn by an emaciated mule, a cart mounted on automobile tires creaked by. A man with a canvas bag slung over his shoulder hurried up the quay, leaning into the gale. By now Panos had become my accomplice, my journalist's alter ego: "If the mayor's here you can talk to him."

The mayor was here, of course. The regime had crumbled. Yet still it seemed present, like the humidity that oozed from the walls of the city hall. Eduard Rexho awaited us, seated behind a large desk, the surface of which was bare except for a mechanical typewriter. Behind him I noticed a rectangle of lighter paint against the grimy ochre of the wall. Surely this was the place where the obligatory portrait of first Enver, then of his successor, the lamentably lesser Ramiz Alia, had once hung. To Mr. Rexho's left a hard-faced man, whose functions were never explained, monitored the conversation. Speaking in halting Greek, the mayor chose his words cautiously, and when the man got up to show the sociologist to the toilet, he leaned forward and offered this apology: "We are not able to speak exactly as we feel. Here, in Albania, they wanted to eliminate God entirely. But we had our own little god called Enver Hoxha," and as he said this he shifted his body ever so slightly toward the empty space on the wall. "We believed in him even if we didn't, if you understand what I'm saying. Of course, no one dared say what he really thought. If you disagreed with the Party, automatically you went to prison."

The sociologist and his guide returned. Nature called; now it was my turn. Mr. Rexho whipped out a sheet of foolscap from his drawer and handed it to me. As I followed the assistant along the dank hallway and downstairs, it occurred to me that leading visitors to the loo was probably not the sort of thing that the *Sigurimi* had been best at. The country's dreaded secret police, ultimate bulwark of the regime, had just been disbanded, to be replaced by a shadowy National Information Service, known as SHIK in its Albanian acronym. If the force still existed, however, foreigners must be watched. At the end of the corridor lay the facility, a tiny, unlighted room with a lone window and plumbing which consisted of a hole in the middle of the floor. There was no water. I cautiously lay the precious sheet of paper on the window-ledge while attempting to secure the door, but a sudden gust of wind sent it crashing open and swept the paper out through the window. I clapped my hand over my nose and mouth and backed out.

As I returned, with grim resolve, to the mayor's office I heard him explain that here, in the southern region, there was none of the hunger which stalked the country's impoverished northern mountains. "We have bread, we have olives; soon the orange harvest will begin."

The interview ended, Mr. Rexho invited us for coffee. A few doors along the waterfront from the mayor's office stood Himarë's sole public house, a fetid room already thronged with middle-aged Albanians drinking *raki* from glass tumblers. The village dispensary might well have had no alcohol, but there was no lack of the stuff here, and the men were knocking it back as they stared straight ahead, smoking.

Soon after leaving Himarë, the convoy made its first stop, in a mixed Greek-Albanian village called Qeparo nestled in a narrow valley. The chicken distribution was orderly: the truck drivers read names out from a list prepared by local authorities whose presence indicated that social breakdown was not total. One by one the villagers came forward to receive their frozen fowl. The Greeks hand out the food directly to the people, Panos explained, while the Germans and Italians, with their huge aid budgets, channeled everything through the government, whose poverty-stricken officials promptly diverted the supplies for sale on the black market and pocketed the profits. "That's why they like us here," he said.

The aroma of fresh-baking bread led us down a muddy lane to the village bakery. Beneath a dim electric bulb, the baker was toiling in the steamy heat, extracting loaves from the oven with a paddle and dumping them on a greasy wooden counter. "Bukë" said the baker, wiping his hands on his apron. Bread: my first word of Albanian, a language which, though part of the common Indo-European trunk, and despite a profusion of loan-words from Latin, Turkish and Greek, is—like those who speak it—profoundly unlike any other. Coarse and dark and granular with the grit of cornmeal and the texture of chaff, the loaf was as far removed from the glaucous industrial substance which masquerades as bread in our latitudes as the tongue which spoke its name was impenetrable, opaque.

Back at the truck, a short, bespectacled man was waiting. Yano Koçi was the village school-master and he had a story to tell, a story I was to hear many times over, wherever I traveled in God-forsaken Albania. "They told us that our country was surrounded by enemies; they turned us into an armed camp. 'If we have to eat grass, we'll eat grass in order to protect our independence,' they said. So you can imagine what a shock it was for us to learn that all this time, Enver and his family and his pals were living high, while we were eating the grass."

Mr. Koçi's voice was rising in pitch as he continued. A small crowd had gathered around, nodding gravely at the end of every impassioned sentence. The school-master had not spoken in his native tongue—Greek—for years, and though the words came hard, they came with intensity. "They told us we were the beacon of socialism in Europe. Look at us! Nothing but a bottomless pit."

"But worst of all, we believed him. Enver was a brilliant man, a perfect liar. A democrat in words, a dictator in deeds. We were supposed to be so far ahead, and instead we are the most backward." The nods had become more emphatic. On the fringe of the crowd I spotted Panos beckoning.

We climbed back into the car and set off toward Saranda, the largest town on the coast. The rain had abated and, for the first time, we saw men and women working in the tangerine groves. Boxes full of fresh-picked fruit lined the roadway, lustrous orange in the velvet gray light. Was this the last gasp of the collectivist agricultural system or the first faint murmur of the onrushing market economy? Of course these industrious people are Greeks, observed the sociologist, intent on demonstrating that the miserable Albanians were the authors of their own misfortune. The remark drew a grimace from Panos as he flicked a glance into the rear-view mirror. Then fired back over his shoulder: "Greeks or Albanians, what's the difference? If you can't understand what these people have been through, keep your mouth shut."

Panos' lack of reverence for Academe was exhilarating. The sociologist, a professor at the arch-conservative University of Athens, seemed to have come to Albania to certify the superiority of Greeks over Albanians against a background of human disorientation so complete that it defied anything but mute compassion. Panos was having none of it. The man shrank into his seat and stared morosely out the side window.

To the west, patches of blue sky appeared between the cloud massifs rushing overhead. Suddenly, through a cleft in the hills, we caught a glimpse of steel-blue shimmer. "Thalassa!" cried Panos. "The sea!" As we rounded a curve, the Ionian Sea stretched out beneath us; cloud-shrouded cliffs marched off in close rank to the south, their flanks mottled by a fast-moving chiaroscuro streaked by flashes of lightning. To the southwest lay Corfu, dark green against the fading light of day. We had reached Acroceraunia—the Coast of Thunderbolts—legendary repair of the *pallicars*, the shaven-headed, mustachioed Albanian clansmen *cum* brigands who stank of garlic and improvised rhymed epics in fifteen syllable couplets. These were the men whom Byron recruited as his personal body-guards, prizing their fearlessness, brutality, and loyalty; men whose only religion was absolute devotion to their given word, the *besa*.

But far from the exotic image of a mysterious Orient which once began here, on the eastern littoral of the Adriatic at the westernmost extremity of the Ottoman empire, the landscape that day reeked of fear and hunger and revenge. On the outskirts of Saranda we encountered the charred hulk of a burned-out bus abandoned by the roadside. Around it, punctuated by an occasional horse-drawn cart, pedestrian traffic flowed sluggishly, with the grim-faced, vacant-eyed indolence of people with nowhere to go, nothing to do, no hope and no future prospects.

As we entered the town, built on a crescent bay overlooking the blue-green waters of the Ionian Sea across the channel from Corfu, night was falling. It had taken us five hours to cover 70 kilometers. Panos drove along the sea-front, past kiosks whose windows lay in shards on the pavement, and up a sweeping palm-lined driveway to the main entrance of the Turizëm Hotel, Saranda's former glory and crown jewel of the Albanian Riviera. Bare flickering bulbs cast a crepuscular glow over the lobby. In the overstuffed chairs, complete with greasy antimascars, sat swarthy, ill-shaven men—perhaps they were Party operatives who hadn't yet taken the measure of their disaster—who turned to stare at us as we walked in. A curtain of cigarette smoke hung in the air. We moved rapidly through the lobby and down a corridor. There, in an empty dining room, a delegation was waiting for us: members of the Greek political movement called Omonia ("Concord"), which held a handful of seats in the Albanian parliament.

According to Athenian officialdom, the ethnic Greek minority in southern Albania had always lived here, had always been Greek in body and soul, and had always been an inalienable part of the greater national body. To my surprise, as I sat down to talk with the movement's local leader, a man named Petros Beretis, I heard not a word about Greek claims. Mr. Beretis' message was more subtle, or more desperate: a pro-forma plea for investment from a sad-eyed booster who knows no foreigner will soon risk a dollar—let alone a drachma—in his God-forsaken town.

"Everywhere there's crisis," he said, wringing his hands. "We've lost confidence in everything. Political parties, leaders, everything. For years we built on sand, and now the time of collapse has come. How are we supposed to build a free-market system? Our economists can't even imagine such a system. After 50 years of Marxism, what do you expect? Can you just wipe all that away overnight, pretend it never existed? We have to start all over again, from the very beginning." When Mr. Beretis had finished, the only sound in the room was the rattle of coffee-cups on saucers.

Panos broke the silence: it was time for a decision. The choice was simple: either we stayed the night in Saranda, right here at the Turizëm where there was no lack of room, or headed back to Greece. We had heard that the roads were dangerous after dark. Bands of demobilized soldiers and hungry peasants were roaming the hills, preying on passing automobiles. This information made the sociologist cringe. Let's not take a chance, he whined. But the truck drivers were chafing with impatience. The fleshpots of Ioannina beckoned. What would Albanian highwaymen possibly want from two empty chicken trucks? Not to worry, added Panos. By supplying the local police with what remained of the chicken shipment (mission policy on all trips) we would enjoy zealous protection right up to the border. As for me, the prospect of a night in Saranda was unutterably gloomy.

Ten minutes later we were grinding up the road out of town. As the headlights swept the roadway ahead, their beams fell upon figures, groups of men and women slogging doggedly, almost mechanically forward. The night landscape had suddenly come alive with shadowy, rag-clad phantoms whose bare ankles shone pale in the glare. The night roads teemed with ghostly migrants, once-socialist citizens who had been abandoned by their government to their own devices. Or encouraged to leave by an insidious whispering campaign as a matter of unavowed, but official policy, the human counterpart of the wave of destruction that accompanied the fall.

Four hours later, still sputtering, the car crawled through the crowd waiting in the darkness on the Albanian side of the border crossing. Once through the gate, Panos accelerated across the short stretch of no-man's-land and braked to a stop at Greek customs. The officials waved us past. Suddenly the road ahead was clear; no living specters loomed before us in the glare of the headlight beams. The Albanians who stole clandestinely across the border kept to the hill-tops and ravines.

Paris had never seemed as luminous, never had New York throbbed with such manic energy as staid, provincial Ioannina did that night. The sidewalks teemed with plump, prosperous, well-dressed citizens; automobiles clogged the streets; shop-windows glittered with the brightly-lit accouterments of modernity—computers, household appliances, leather jackets, cars, video dreams in blister-packs; international brands clamored from advertising hoardings. For this Albania slogged south along the highroads, barefoot, to join the world of free-market democracy, smashing every artifact of its collectivist past as it went. The Global Civilization beckoned. Benetton and Coca Cola, Philip Morris and R. J. Reynolds, Sony and Kodak, Ford and Toyota: these would be the Central Committee of the future, the benevolent managers of the inevitable convergence of all things.

TIRANA, IN YEAR FOUR of the capitalist restoration, is Enver Hoxha's worst nightmare come true. Private enterprise, once reviled, is stirring; consumer culture has swept through the city like a hurricane. Rruga Qemal Stafa, along which I'm steering a course between puddles and refuse overflowing concrete bins, boasts several cafés where young men are even now, at 9:30 a.m., sipping espresso on outdoor terraces, hairdressing salons, several microscopic food markets hastily thrown together from concrete blocks, a Chinese restaurant and a discothèque called "Galaxy" which appears to be open for business. Across the street is "Partizani" high school. The boys loll about on the sidewalk smoking and doing their best to look threatening, while the girls sashay back and forth in the schoolyard, arm in arm, rolling hips ill-concealed in body-hugging jeans.

Albanian hospitality has always been legendary. When, despite my telephone reservation from Salonica, no room was available at the Dajti, then Tirana's only functioning hotel, Loreta and Ilir were delighted with my misfortune: "Well, you'll just have to stay with us," they grinned, as their friend Benny, the free-lance driver, drove us through the dusty streets to the head of their narrow alley. The small living-dining room containing the television set, the family's sole source of entertainment, doubles as my bedroom. The couple and their twelve year-old son Anni share the single bedroom. Between the two is a large closet. A minuscule kitchen opens off the living room. The bathroom is an outbuilding, part of the outside wall. Still, it was a home with a tiny garden and a grapevine snaking across a trellis, not an apartment in one of Tirana's thousands of decaying walk-ups.

I had met Loreta and Ilir the year before, on my first trip to Tirana (and second excursion into poverty-stricken Shqiperia). Then she was eking out subsistence wages as a dentist in a village clinic three hours by bus and foot from the capital. Ilir, a precision machinist in the old regime, had turned his finely-honed manual skills to ice-cream making. In the yard of their home I'd noticed the tool of his trade, an ice-cream push-cart which had somehow found its way here from a Greek provincial town. Today, Loreta is without work: her clinic has been vandalized, her equipment stolen. The couple are surviving on state welfare payments equivalent to $30 (US) per month.

For dinner Loreta has prepared roast chicken—a feast for the vast majority of Albanians with no access to hard currency—and potatoes, salads, and cheese, all washed down with a bottle of raspy local red wine. We're lucky, she laughs. Loreta finds humor in the direst of circumstances, and when she laughs her face lights up the entire room. Today the electricity has stayed on long enough to cook the meal. Blackouts are endemic; the obsolete electric power grid cannot meet demand, and private-enterprise pirates are constantly siphoning off power with illegal hook-ups.

I'm not the only guest at this festive table. Sokol, Loreta's brother in law, has returned to Tirana from New York, where he's completing his post-graduate studies in anthropology. On a six-month contract with the United Nations Development Program, Sokol is working as a special coordinator for the agency's report on Albania.

A tall, slender man in his early thirties with deep-set eyes, he radiates the emotional tension and impatience of an adopted American, grown accustomed to efficiency. Over the remains of the meal he speaks his disappointment. Three years after the fall of the regime should have brought improvement, he says. "I'm used to getting things done, you know. I feel frustrated and angry. I cannot accept the fatalism of my people."

But our talk is cut short. It's time for television, and in this image-starved country the flickering picture of the screen mesmerizes viewers, although it has by no means blunted my hosts' critical capacities. The evening's news bulletin leads off with the results—after a curious five-day delay—of President Sali Berisha's referendum on the new constitution. Everyone knows the constitution, which the vocal opposition claims would have given the president near-dictatorial powers, is a dead duck; no one knows precisely how stunning is the president's defeat. My hosts show some sympathy for Mr. Berisha, whom they regard as a man of relative integrity in a sea of slime, but they've developed a healthy disrespect for the "political process." Corruption is everywhere, Sokol tells me. But particularly in government. Members of parliament make the equivalent of less than $100 per month. "How could they possibly save enough money to build themselves villas or buy fancy cars. But they do."

Referendum results behind us, we settle in for the evening's block-buster: the first-ever Miss Albania beauty pageant. The super-production—titled in

English—has been staged in a packed hall in front of a panel of the country's new "beautiful people" acting as judges. Each is seated in front of a computer console, ready to enter data—but what kind of data?—as if to underline the arrival of high-tech virtual sex even in this frontier outpost of the New World Order.

The panel is headed by a generic American actor whose name I cannot pick up from the Albanian commentary. He trots down a flight of stairs dressed in a powder-blue tuxedo, strides across the stage, and addresses the audience in an unctuous baritone voice which oozes hypocrisy like the rancid grease from a cheap *byrek*. But he has the crowd eating out of his hand when he quotes a couplet by the Albanian national poet, Naïm Frasheri, in praise of brotherhood. And now, he intones with the sincerity of a casket salesman in a funeral home, let the competition begin.

Though it is understood, even in this far-distant outpost, that the transition to capitalism means the inevitable commodification of their youthful charm (and by extension their sexuality) still the girls contrive to look spontaneous, and refreshingly uncomfortable, perhaps even embarrassed, in their revealing costumes and their high-heeled shoes. They parade back and forth across the stage in scanty gowns and ersatz "folk" outfits of their own fabrication and design, the latter to reassure viewers—for Albania remains a country of strict morality and rigorous respect for the family—that they are all good-hearted girls who crave nothing more than to become dedicated homemakers. Finally, in a video-clip climax, the contestants are disposed like rag dolls atop concrete bunkers, crowns of barbed wire atop their impeccably coifed heads. Slowly rising to their feet, they strip to swimsuits and cavort in slow motion down to the beach, where they cast their thorny diadems into the Adriatic. A hang-glider on whose wings are written the words "MISS ALBANIA" swoops overhead as the music wells up, throbbing in Wagnerian French horn crescendos.

Throughout the performance my hosts chortle and guffaw. Can this be Albania? The country where the electricity may fail at any hour of the day or night; the capital city whose water runs only three to four hours daily and is unfit to drink?

ON MY WAY TO THE MARKET that bright November morning I pass groups of women rummaging through heaps of used clothing strewn on plastic sheeting. Behind the piles men squat, impassive. From tiny tables, from the bottoms of cardboard boxes, from holes in walls, in the mud of vacant lots, people are selling small objects and trinkets. In the food section peasants hawk bruised, tired-looking fruits: bananas, once unobtainable in Albania and now sold at every street corner, emblem of the world market; and second-grade kiwi-fruit and grapes from Greece. A few steps beyond the produce section, the mobile grilled sausage and chicken stands lie in wait, steaming and sizzling; other carts offer omelets and bread. In another part of the market *kadaïf*—a preparation resembling shredded wheat used in the fabrication of syrupy, nut-filled sweets—is displayed in bulk from a plastic bag lashed precariously to the pillion of a battered motorbike, ready for a rapid get-away. (Albanians have a well-established reputation as confectioners of the syrup-drenched Turkish-style sweets that still excite palates from here through Constantinople to Isfahan and beyond.)

Leaving the market, I emerge onto the busy thoroughfare which leads out of the city toward Elbasan, past the open-air electric market where everything from flashlights to refrigerators is on sale. Across from me is the Parliament building, but it is almost totally obscured by the random confusion of jerry-built, box-like aluminum and glass "palaces," the overnight structures that, for Albanians, express the brash mercantile spirit. In addition to the usual coffee-bars I spot a one-chair barbershop in a lean-to no bigger than a walk-in closet, sidewalk vendors hawking Marlboros by the piece, folding tables buckling beneath the weight of plumbing supplies, Romanian-made kitchenware, used coats, jeans, shoes. No manufacturer's cast-offs, no recycled clothing, no Asian tin toys are too shoddy, too threadbare to compete on the Albanian market. Underfoot, the streets and the sidewalk are coated by a layer of slimy, red-ochre mud.

The streets, crowded during the daylight hours, are all but deserted by 9:00 p.m. Tirana, once a quiet Ottoman administrative center praised by travelers for its greenery and streams, its fine Friday mosque and clock tower, was transformed by the communist regime into a factory town designed for industrious workers whose only dream—for it was the only dream allowed them—was production. The city's urban structure reflects Enver Hoxha's vision of industrial self-sufficiency: neighborhoods consisting of five or six floor walk-up apartment blocks organized around factories and machine shops.

On my way back to my host's home under a steady rain, I take a shortcut through a small park in the city center. To my left is a gaping hole in the earth nicknamed "the Grave." The hole is all that remains of a luxury hotel boondoggle floated by an entrepreneur from Kosova with connections to the former communist leadership. The entrepreneur, having secured start-up funding from the government via a shadowy Swiss-based investment firm called Iliria Holdings, absconded, leaving Albania $40 million poorer. Kosovars, understandably, were not the most popular people in town, despite the obligations of solidarity toward blood brothers languishing under the Serbian yoke. Suddenly, at ground level, a movement catches my eye: two plump rats scamper across the path-way before vanishing into an open sewer. Nearby, the stink of underground public toilets rises like an invisible mist.

From the minaret of the Haxhi Ethem Bey mosque, a jewel of late-Ottoman religious architecture which commands Skanderbeg Square, the dusk call to prayer rings out. On my first trip to the capital I had climbed to the top of the minaret accompanied by the mosque's resident caretaker who encouraged me along with grunts of "hajde, hajde." From behind the chiseled stone parapet the city spread out at my feet: the bronze statue of the square's eponymous hero in winged helmet, sword in hand; the national museum, façade given over to a huge mosaic depicting Albanian patriots in national costume; an empty pedestal upon which had rested the monumental statue of Enver Hoxha until its destruction by an infuriated mob in February of 1991 as police looked on. Clouds obscured the mountainous horizon, and in middle distance plumes of thick brown smoke from burning lignite rose from a thousand stove-pipes.

Now, on the corner across from Rat Park men huddle under umbrellas, waiting for work. They were there this morning, and they will be there tomorrow, stoic, patient, enduring, as if the act of being without work were, in itself, an occupation. Across the square, sheltered under the huge pines that still overhang Deshmoret e Kombit boulevard, congregate Tirana's sidewalk bankers, the money changers armed with umbrellas, pocket calculators and wads of bills. Their approach is casual: a few quick words, and the crucial dollar, mark or drachma exchange rate is flashed on a calculator. Grimy bills then change hands. The exchange rate improves the farther I stray from the hotel. A former teacher describes how much more profitable than teaching is foreign exchange dealing. "Now I can support my family," he tells me in Italian, the dominant second language of many Albanians now that Russian, the tongue of Albania's erstwhile socialist benefactors, has tumbled into disrepute, as useless as the Soviet-built industrial facilities whose rusting hulks litter the countryside.

That evening Sokol and I meet for dinner in a private restaurant, one of several that have sprung up to cater to the exquisite tastes of foreign businessmen and their Albanian emulators. The place has a pleasant, intimate feel; there are fresh flowers on the tables, and the food imitates generic "continental" fare. When the old regime collapsed, Sokol dreamed of a new way for his country. He remains unconvinced that the Western model is right for Albania as it emerges from half a century of dictatorship. People are slow to change; they seem paralyzed. "Look, I want to have kids, raise a family. But I can't do it here, in my homeland. I don't want my children to inherit what I've inherited. The legacy of dictatorship."

Well, I counter tentatively, it's simple enough to remove people from the old regime, but not so simple to get the old regime out of the people. An entire generation may be sacrificed. This I volunteer with an embarrassment I attempt to conceal. "Right," he fires back, fork poised in mid-air. "But we cannot wait a whole generation. Things have to change. We cannot go on like this."

SUNDAY MORNING. Tirana's Orthodox Cathedral is bustling with excitement. An Albanian television crew lurks just inside the church entrance. The sky is bright, cloudless. The air is fresh and light after a full day and night of rain. The controversial and outspoken prelate of the autocephalous Albanian Orthodox Church, Greek Archbishop Anthanassios Yannoulatos, is presiding over the liturgy.

Who says there is no heavenly dispensation? A mere city block away from the church, which the communists had transformed into a gymnasium, looms the former state printing works, one of the largest buildings in the country. In it were published the multi-volume complete works of Enver Hoxha which topped the Albanian best-seller lists month in, month out, for decades. Nothing today marks the building, whose broken windows stare blindly over the entrance to the once-forbidden diplomatic quarter. The existing volumes, in their millions, have since been pulped and made into egg-crates.

Archbishop Yannoulatos, the man I have come to see, has acquired the reputation of an outspoken partisan of the rights of Albania's Greek minority which, after decades of surviving in obscurity, wields an influence well beyond its size, natural enough, since the motherland is a purveyor of precious visas, as well as potential investments. The archbishop is a hero among the Greeks, and well respected by many of the Albanian political figures, particularly in the Socialist Party, which may have partisan reasons for supporting his worship against their foe, Mr. Berisha, who happens to be a Muslim.

Some Albanians see him as a demagogue in clerical collar, whose long-term design is to bring about the amputation of "Northern Epirus" (as the

Greeks term the southern part of Albania) and its eventual attachment, after the requisite period of "autonomy," to Greece. That would not be Greece's first temptation by southern Albania, home of so many unredeemed ethnic brethren. Under the 1914 Protocol of Corfu, later annulled by the Paris Conference of 1921, almost all of the disputed region was to have become Greek territory. During World War II, following their defeat of Italy, the Greeks again established a temporary administration over the area.[88]

As the liturgy ends, the faithful press forward to kiss the Archbishop's hand and take consecrated bread in communion. The throng is a mix of the elderly and the adolescent. Suddenly, a small flurry of excitement at the rear of the church. Miss Albania 1994, an unemployed Orthodox lass, has come to take communion, and to sign autographs for a flock of admiring teenage girls. Now it's clear why the TV crews are on hand.

I wait until the beauty queen has discharged her religious duty for the benefit of the camera, then join the line along with the remaining communicants. After a brief, whispered introduction to the Archbishop, who agrees to meet me the following day, I step outside into the brilliant sunlight. Knots of older men have gathered in the small, muddy open space, which cannot be called a square or a plaza. They are speaking Greek. "We're unredeemed Greeks here," says a white-haired man with a few missing front teeth, using words I thought existed only in the pages of diplomatic history books. "The Albanians," he continues, gesticulating scornfully with his hand as if to dismiss a bothersome fly, "they are nothing but Turks, savages."

Then, from the corner of my eye, I notice a young man wearing a leather jacket edging toward me through the group. After listening for a few moments, he joins in with some slightly acidic remarks about the way the Greeks treat their long-lost brothers from Albania. The young man's name is Theo, he informs me; he's a Greek-Albanian born and raised in Tirana who has studied mechanical engineering for two years at a technical institute in Greece. And now he's come to the church to solicit the assistance of the archbishop in arranging another visa. Tensions along the frontier between the two countries, and the arrest, trial and condemnation of five members of the Greek minority rights movement have made it difficult for Albanian citizens who wish to travel to Greece legitimately to obtain visas. Hundreds of illegals sneak across the mountainous border daily, but many are rounded up and returned.

Theo is angry, convinced that the Greek embassy is passing him over. Perhaps someone's friends are moving to the head of the line, leaving those without connections or corruption money to twiddle their thumbs? he suggests. Rumor sets the going rate for a Greek visa obtained via the back door at between $300 and $350. Later I raised the matter discretely with an embassy official, who reacted sharply. "Look, we issue 12,000 visas per year from one tiny office. Just what do they expect us to do?"

Unlike his elders, for whom Greece is a remote, unreachable dream, visible only on television, Theo is less than sanguine about life there. "Whenever I meet people my age, I'm shocked at their ignorance," he says.

"What do you mean? "

"They haven't even read their own classics. You know, Socrates, Aristotle. Don't have a clue who Shakespeare was. Jack London? Forget it. All they're interested in is clothes and discos and money."

The older men begin to drift away. This is not the Greece they would like to hear about, dream about. But Theo, a product of the last decade of the Hoxha regime, is proud of his education, if not his country, and leaving is less an affair of the heart than a matter of economic necessity. "Back then, reading was all we had," he says. As I stroll back to the hotel for lunch and a quick nap, it occurs to me that Theo may also have been in the employ of SHIK, many of whose operatives are young men who affect leather jackets. The dispersal of the older Greeks may well have been the ancient survival reflex drummed into every living Albanian. When in doubt, clam up and move on.

LATER THAT SUNDAY AFTERNOON Frok Çupi and I are wedged into a red Volkswagen driven by his friend Nujé (every Albanian seems to have a friend who drives a car), rattling along the two-lane highway to Durrës, Albania's second city and main port. Çupi, a powerful, compact man from the rugged Catholic highlands of the north, is one of the pillars of Albania's fledgling democratic movement, and an editor at *Koha e Jonë*, "Our Times," perhaps Tirana's most outspoken newspaper. Which is, alas, saying little in a country where in less than five years, the print media have swung from total government monopoly through a brief crusade against the evils of the old regime, before evolving into sordid, ad-ridden sex and scandal sheets whose reporters are often ill-disguised flacks for competing political and business interests. Much like their western counterparts, in fact. Beside me in the back seat is his son Mihi, a pallid, freckled lad of eleven whose face only brightens when, at the end of the day, we stop off at the Hotel Adriatiku on Durrës beach for refreshments.

As we leave Tirana, passing primitive road-side car washes and tire-repair stands, the mid-afternoon train from Durrës clatters slowly into town. The railway, once the pride of Albania's hyper-socialist regime and key to its hurry-up industrialization policy, has become a public laughing stock, its carriages vandalized, windows broken, precious diesel fuel siphoned from parked engines in broad daylight. Only the horse-drawn carts still widely used in the countryside move more slowly. The 40 kilometer run from the port to the capital takes more than an hour and is not to be undertaken in rainy weather, or, say the untrusting, at night in any weather.

After driving past hectares of greenhouses whose glass roofs and walls have been smashed, past the Iranian model farm and tractor station set up by the *Jihad-e Sazandegui*, the Khomeinite reconstruction crusade, we crest a hill: before us lies the city. It is here at Durrës port, Frok explains, that Albania's share of the flourishing contraband trade in diesel fuel and weapons for the Bosnian war originates.

A ring, patriotically called the "Eagles," operating under the protection of the ruling Democratic Party, controls the contraband trade in fuel oil to Montenegro, and thence to Serbian Bosnia. "They've appropriated the harbor for themselves. Every day a ship discharges its cargo into tank trucks for shipment up to the border. The cheap oil comes from Egypt and Libya, and is resold at eight times the spot market price. twenty percent of the profit goes straight into the coffers of the Democratic Party. Where does the other eighty percent go? Into president Berisha's pocket? I've printed the story time and time again, but people don't care any more," he says, leaning back over the front seat.

Along with oil, guns and ammunition are the essential lubricants of the Balkans. And, alleges Frok, Albanian arms smugglers with links in neighboring Kosova and Macedonia are supplying the Bosnian Muslims at the same time the "Eagles" are providing the lubricant for the Serbian war machine.

On our left as we enter the city is the railway station from which another train is pulling out; we continue past the port installations and finally reach land's end. A westerly breeze is blowing, a gentle swell laps against the quay. The air smells of rotting seaweed. From a seaside café we hear music, with the Oriental wail typical, Frok tells me, of the Durrës region, paradoxically Albania's westward looking window.

Known as Durazzo when it was ruled by Venice, and before that as Dyrrachium under the Romans and the Byzantines, Durrës was the western terminus of the Via Egnatia. In the architecture of its few surviving pre-communist public buildings, the old town evokes Italy, while above the red tiled roofs the minaret of the central mosque thrusts skyward. In Durrës the world of Islam stares defiantly toward Europe, its feet bathed by the Adriatic which, instead of joining Albania to the West, became an impermeable barrier. The paving stones of the Via Egnatia, the Egnatian way which linked Rome to Constantinople via Durrës, thus linking the western and eastern capitals of the Empire, are buried nearby, not far from the ancient ruins of Epidamus. Centuries later, the Ottomans marched westward on this road, on the way to their hostile takeover of the Byzantine empire.

Atop a pine-clad hill at the westernmost extremity of the town, the summer villa built by former King Zog, the Italian puppet who ruled Albania during the years preceding the Second World War, overlooks the Adriatic. In the orange light of dusk the villa, seen from the road below, has a preposterous, Fellinian air; a grandiose, chin-jutting pomposity. But it is patrolled by wide-eyed young men with machine guns who warn us away. The place is a military communications center, Frok explains. As we stare upward at the creamy pink structure with its porthole-like windows, a car roars up the hill through the trees and screeches to a stop. Two young men climb out and arrange a boom box on the hood; rock music blasts from the radio. From the parapet we watch the sun slip beneath the horizon.

A few kilometers down the coast lies the Hotel Adriatiku, the place to which the *nomenklatura* would repair to escape Tirana's searing summer heat. The harbor cranes and minarets of Durrës are silhouetted against the red glow of the dusk-darkening sky. In the high-ceilinged, echoing lounge, which one almost expects to see crowded with Party dignitaries, a small group of men is tippling quietly in one corner while in a wall alcove a young couple nurses a round of espresso. We sink into the overstuffed armchairs and sip luke-warm tea as Frok's son gambols down to the water's edge. The bar-woman, a tight-featured blond whose mouth seems fixed in a permanent pucker, pretends to be busy behind her espresso machine. But no amount of bustle can mask the lifelessness, the funereal emptiness of this vast space.

The melancholy of the bar has gotten under Frok's skin. Leaning forward in his easy-chair with its frayed, stained arm rests, he unburdens himself of some plain truths about his country. The information is unlikely to appear in government releases, or in World Bank analyses which continue to broadcast pre-Chiapas Mexico-style optimism in circumstances which warrant only the gravest pessimism. "The educational system has been destroyed, especially in the countryside" he says. "Children now must work for their families to survive, till the land or mind the livestock."

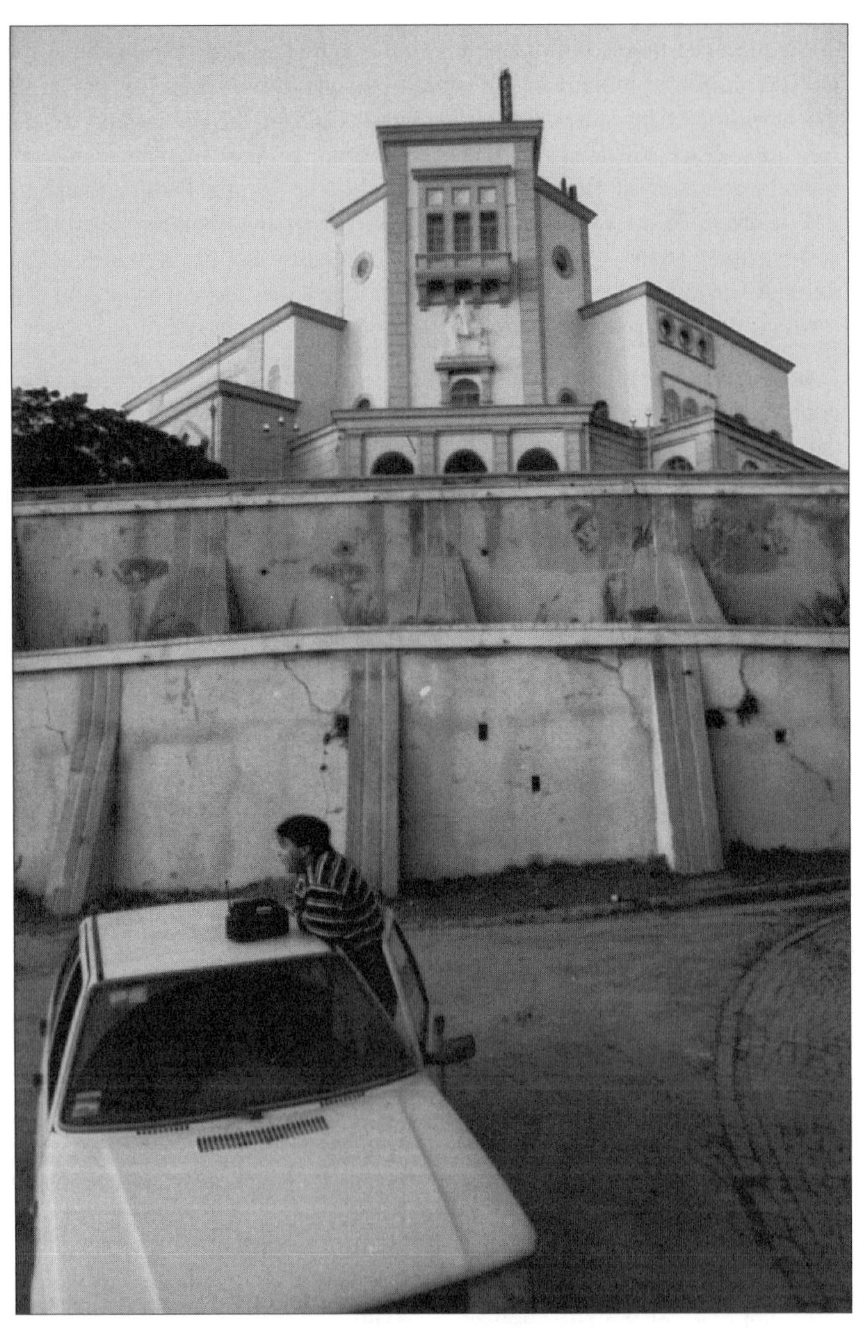

Rock 'n' roll at King Zog's villa, Durrës, Albania.
(Photo by Fred A. Reed.)

"Culture, human rights, everything is a mess. Spoiled food. They're dumping spoiled food on the Albanian market. Nobody is working productively here. There's Coca Cola, a few clothing manufacturers, and hundreds of sidewalk cafés, bars, money changers and smuggling rackets. Before, the factories were operating, at least. We produced our own food, our own milk, the bricks we needed to build. We could supply our market. Sure we all had to work hard to live, but everything was safe."

"My duty is to tell you that what we have now is not democracy; it's like some kind of anarchy! We never imagined this. We were always dreaming of the rule of law. That we would have a constitution, state institutions. The intellectuals, the writers, all of us are bitterly disappointed."

But Frok's inherent optimism slowly rises to the surface, touching off a slow, but perceptible modulation away from the minor key of despair. Things may not be entirely tragic after all. "We were afraid that with all the money he had to spend, Berisha's constitution was going to pass. But the people voted 'no' anyway. And that was a victory for democracy. What you have in Albania is this: the people created a clear field for political parties. And because they did, they have the right to know where we are going."

Night has come, and with it the reality of newspaper deadlines. At his father's call the boy quickly reappears; time to be off. We loop back into Tirana along the Kavajë road, dodging bicycles, donkeys piled high with straw, and peasant families herding their cows along the roadside in the humid darkness of the Albanian night.

MAP IN HAND I set out the next morning along Deshmoret e Kombit boulevard toward the National University, formerly named, as was much else in the land, for the dictator. I cross the Lana, the fast-flowing stream which runs through the city center, gathering raw sewage as it goes, and on whose grassy banks cattle are grazing. To the left stands the former Enver Hoxha Technology Museum, now known as "The Pyramid", in close proximity to the massive bulk of what had been Party headquarters. To the right lies "The Block," a warren of tree-shaded streets and prosperous villas that would not be out of place in any middle-class Greek, French or Italian coastal town. Though ordinary citizens knew of its existence, they had never seen it. The common socialist folk ate grass or went hungry while Enver and his family ate meat, drank imported wine and used real olive oil (which Albania produced but of which people had none) to dress their salads. As a monument to craven decadence, it pales before the Carpathian gothic horrors of Nicolae

Ceaucescu in Bucharest, the forest dachas of the Soviet *nomenklatura*, or the fortified residences of the Chinese communist gerontocracy in Beijing. What hurt most may have been the blow to the people's pride. When Albanians learned that their utter deprivation had been the price of their leaders' life of ease, nothing could assuage their stunned hurt, wipe away the mockery of betrayal.

Today I stroll briskly, straight through the Block. My destination is the diplomatic residential quarter across from Dynamo soccer stadium, Tirana residence of Archbishop Yannoulatos who has agreed to receive me. What map could reveal the ground-level chaos? Street names are not indicated, unmarked alleyways veer off between buildings only to broaden unexpectedly into streets. Finally I locate the stadium, a squat concrete bowl surrounded by a windbreak of eucalyptus trees, and, nearby, the diplomatic "palace," a structure only marginally less desolate than the endemic workers' flats.

One of the Archbishop's Greek-speaking assistants is waiting at the gate; he leads me up a narrow flight of stairs and through a low doorway into the prelate's flat. In one corner a television set is blaring a Greek sitcom dubbed into Albanian. Sunlight streams through the windows. While I wait the assistant brings me a glass of Greek orange juice. A few moments later Athanassios Yannoulatos enters, clad in a black clerical robe with no ornament but a large silver cross hanging from a chain around his neck. The Archbishop seems frail, even fragile. Before the interview begins we must take coffee, he insists. It will be Greek coffee, that is, Turkish coffee, the beverage with the ideal ethnic ambiguity and the just-wrong touch of anachronism in a land where espresso is now the wake-me-up of choice, the Western beverage.

At the Archbishop's bidding I take my appointed place on an upholstered settee, while he settles into an armchair opposite me. Turning his head toward the television, he explains in pantomime that the room is certainly bugged and that we shall be speaking softly to the blaring accompaniment of emotional crisis.

"What happened here in Albania is perhaps unique in history," he begins, leaning forward to address me in a near-whisper. "Starting in 1967, they tried to uproot religion from people's hearts, to destroy religious consciousness completely. With us Orthodox, they not only destroyed our cathedral in the center of town, they built the Tirana Hotel right where it once stood."

Two generations were born and grew to maturity without even the suspicion of religion as a part of public life, he explains. "Hoxha wanted uniformity, domination. He claimed he was an internationalist, but what he really did was build up 'Albanicity.' But now that the old system has collapsed and capitalism has rushed in so violently, there is a terrible crisis."

The damage to the infrastructure of the Orthodox Church—which, according to the regime's last, pre-atheism census, accounted for 20 percent of all Albanians, as against 10 percent Catholics and 70 percent Muslims—was catastrophic, continues his Reverence. Precisely 1,618 Orthodox religious sites, including churches and country shrines and chapels, were destroyed. The destruction was spiritual as well as physical. "When I arrived, I counted eleven surviving priests, who had been treated like galley-slaves. In July 1991 that's what I found. That was our point of departure."

The appointment of Mr. Yannoulatos by the Patriarch of Constantinople set tongues wagging. As in every Balkan country, the Church in Albania had assumed autocephalous (semi-independent) status. And although the Patriarch had granted the Albanian Church this status in 1937, the first Albanian Orthodox service had been held in Boston, in 1908. In fact, the enduring Greekness of the Constantinople Patriarchate was viewed by the rising nationalist movements throughout the Balkans as the sharp edge of a wedge of Greek imperial ambition. Thus, into a fiercely national church whose worshippers include Albanian, Greek, Vlach and Slav-speaking faithful, stepped a Greek theological scholar plucked from a missionary posting in Kenya. "I was as surprised as everybody else," he confides, raising one eyebrow. "I had no previous connection with Albania."

But the Archbishop, clearly a quick study, acted rapidly to appraise himself of the situation, aided perhaps (so his detractors hint) by reports from Greek intelligence. In turn, resistance began to form, particularly within Islamic circles who were dismayed, he tells me, at the Church's success. "In less than two years we've ordained 60 new popes and consecrated 30 churches."

The problem, his Reverence hints darkly, lowering his voice further still, to a whisper, as the television cackles in the background, is that key agencies of the Albanian government are in the hands of what he terms "Muslim fundamentalists" who see the Orthodox community as a tough nut which must be cracked. "There are powerful anti-Orthodox forces who want to strengthen Muslim communities. They want to establish the first Islamic republic in Europe right here, a Greater Albania which would include Kosova and a part of Macedonia. Clearly there is Turkish influence at work here as well. People in the West have to understand that Islam is essentially a political religion."

President Berisha's proposed constitution was to be the means to this end, he argues. The Archbishop, who remains a Greek national, was to have been expelled the day after its approval by referendum. "When I came and saw the situation here, I realized that this was far from an abstract issue. I could put my body on the line, or stay in Athens at the Theological Faculty and write books about Divine love."

Lo and behold, the president's referendum has just gone down to a crushing defeat. No one, sighs the Archbishop, suddenly looking frail as the late-morning sunlight filters through his wispy white beard, expected this outcome. "But the impasses we mortals encounter are but a doorway for God."

NATURALLY I WANTED TO FIND OUT how Albania's Muslim men of religion felt about the future, and about the Archbishop's allegations of a Pan-Islamic anti-Western conspiracy targeting this poor, destitute country. Several days later I made my way to the offices of the Grand Mufti of Albania, Sabri Koçi, in a turn-of-the century building overlooking Avni Rustemi square north-east of the city center not far from the public market. Offering a "salaam" at the gate, I am shown up to the Mr. Koçi's office, a damp room illuminated by one faint bulb. The Mufti, who spent twenty years in prison, seems permanently dazzled by the light, even if it's the gloom of a rainy, late-fall day. Like the Orthodox Archbishop, his beard is sparse and white, but unlike the Archbishop, he is a man who has felt the pain of hardship on his body and has known confinement of the soul.

"Islam in Albania?" he asks, restating my question through a smiling, intense but ineffectual interpreter. "Islam is doing very well, but we are very poor because of the communist regime. We cannot even retrieve what is rightfully ours from the government. Now we are rebuilding. Before, there were more than 1,600 mosques throughout the country; now there are fewer than 200. We've opened Qur'anic schools in ten districts. These schools are approved by the Education Ministry. At last we're free to practice our religion as we please."

"Do you want to transform Albania into an Islamic republic?" I ask him. The Mufti seems torn between indignation and amusement. "Please mister, you must understand," he says in faint protestation. "Albania never Islamic country like in Middle East, or Pakistan. Muslims here include Sunnis,

Bektashis also. Everyone reads the Qur'an, which is for all Muslims, but no can be Islamic regime in this country."

If we are to judge by the extreme modesty, not to say the threadbareness of the Grand Mufti's headquarters, financial aid from the alleged fundamentalist international is flowing into someone else's coffers. In this, the nerve-center of Albanian Islam, I saw not a photo-copier, not a computer, not a fax machine, and only one typewriter, a venerable mechanical survivor from a bygone era. As for the rampant Islamization of Albania, outside on the streets of Tirana a few isolated women wearing *hijab* can be seen, and small knots of young men congregate in mosques. Funds from Saudi Arabia, Kuwait, Egypt and Libya have poured into Albania, it is whispered darkly. But the money has been used to import Albanian translations of the Qur'an, to rebuild mosques, and to found a commercial bank. In fact, the lineup of Albania's Islamic supporters reads, with the exception of Libya, suspiciously like that of the United States' most faithful Mideast clients; a catalogue of their actions reads like the usual list of junior partner obligations. The visible leadership of the country's mainstream Sunnis is made up of old men with missing teeth who are happy to have survived.

ARBEN PUTO HAS MOST OF HIS TEETH, all his wits, walks with a slight limp, and like the Grand Mufti, is also a survivor—of a nightmare of a different kind. In his mid-sixties now, Mr. Puto has enjoyed the kind of career which allowed him to function under the protection of the ancien régime while maintaining a certain critical distance from it. But unlike the novelist Ismaïl Kadaré, who contrived to be absent from the capital, and thus out of earshot of the critical voices of his lesser colleagues, when the communists fell, Mr. Puto remained in Tirana throughout the bitter days of 1991. Author of a standard text on Albanian diplomatic history, he stepped into a high-profile role as founder and first president of the country's Human Rights Forum, which was set up in the waning months of the dictatorship.

To speak of human rights in Albania requires a certain delicacy. During the half-century of single party rule, it was understood that the socialist regime was itself the solution to abuses, that it alone provided the remedy to social inequality. To question this self-evident truth was to court disaster. When, in the last days, Mr. Puto and his colleagues came to the fore, they must have known that they themselves might be perceived as having enjoyed, if not the sympathy, at least the tolerance of the communist masters. But in Albania nothing is so clear-cut. To survive, it was essential to adopt the manner, customs and tics of the ruler, to speak in the convoluted aesopian language of revealed Marxism as distilled through the filter of Enver Hoxha's obtuse genius.

Mr. Puto is as pugnaciously unapologetic as he is intensely pessimistic. "We'll need all the patience we can find for a long, long time," he tells me over coffee in the shade of the canvas awning at one of Tirana's ever-expanding multitude of free-market sidewalk cafés, just around the corner from the Pyramid. On the lawn several sheep are grazing, indifferent to the rock music. "There's no political debate in Albania today; nothing but conflict, a result of the total absence of rules. People have the idea that democracy means 'do whatever you want, whichever way you want'."

When the communist monolith fell, out-of-work Kremlinologists and their Balkan counterparts quickly reconverted to transitionology, the study of rapid social deterioration accompanied by violent enrichment of an unscrupulous handful of former party hacks, local Mafiosi and a raggedy array of international rip-off artists and financial advisers. "Transition" is to be understood as a process, to be interpreted as the pauperization of millions of once-productive working people.

The transition period in Albania is proving particularly difficult, even in comparison with the other countries of the region, Mr. Puto explains. "We have moved from a state of almost hermetic isolation to one of total openness to the outside world. The new reality is one of criminality and corruption."

Worse still, he adds, the medieval Albanian code of honor, the Canon of Lekë has reappeared. The Canon, named for a semi-mythical mountaineer chieftain called Lekë Dukagjini, sets out a strict code of moral conduct—including the sanctity of hospitality, the inviolability of the *besa*, and the obligation of vengeance and blood debt—to guide the lives of the tribesmen of the northern Albanian highlands. "The communists banned the Canon, but now the old ways are coming back. The vacuum of power is reaching to every corner of the country."

Over my dialogue with Mr. Puto hangs a thinly veiled nostalgia for the past, as might well become a graduate of Korcë's Lycée français whose French instructor was its most illustrious graduate: Enver Hoxha. I attempt to draw him out, with immediate results: "Of course I participated in the national liberation struggle against the Nazis and the Italians. Our ideal was to have our own country, a developed country, with real social equality. We were looking for a remedy. I'm certainly not going to deny that the Communist Party dominated our movement, and I'm never going to apologize for having joined the resistance."

What began as zealous idealism began to slide into foreboding after the twentieth congress of the Communist Party of the Soviet Union, in 1956, when Nikita Krushchev famously assailed the Stalinist personality cult in his secret speech. In Albania, the revelations touched off sharp internal struggle which led to a consolidation of Enver Hoxha's power. "It was really a *coup d'État* inside the Party, and it was the end of our illusions."

Now, new illusions are springing up to replace the old, he says. During the Second World War, when Albania was occupied by the Italians, "a large number" of Albanians collaborated with the fascists, who had set up a colonial "Greater Albania" which included the long-lost Yugoslavian province of Kosova. The same ultra-nationalist collaborators later took sides against the resistance. "But today, people politically connected to those collaborators are being called to the summit of power in our country."

I later checked Mr. Puto's assertion. In 1993, I learned, nearly half the Democratic Party deputies in the Albanian People's Assembly owed political allegiance to the right-wing nationalist *Balli Kombëtar* faction, which had fought bitterly against the Albanian communists during and after the war.[89] But the vigilant Sokol was quick to remind me that the Ballists were still highly unpopular among most Albanians.

ACROSS FROM THE SQUARE from the Grand Mufti's office stands a restaurant. Bright and cheery, it looks like one of the millions of franchise outlets that infest every strip mall in North America. The place is staffed by pert teenagers sporting down-home U.S. twangs and "have a nice day" grins. Only alcohol is missing. No imported beer, no whiskey, no Greek ouzo. No normal Tirana free-enterprise café, the restaurant is a gaudy lure attached to a hook trolling in the murky waters of the Albanian spiritual void, attached to a high-test line held by a couple of Christian fundamentalists from Massachusetts.

Dozens of such sects have homed in, with the accuracy of a smart bomb, on Albania after the fall of the communists: Italian Baptists, Jehovah's Witnesses, Seventh Day Adventists, Baha'is, Mormons and mainstream Evangelicals from places like Oklahoma and South Carolina. They have come to test the free-market of ideas and beliefs with solid budgets, quasi-military logistics, sophisticated equipment and enough fundamentalist zeal to shame a *hezbollah* militant. One evening, while exploring the depths of the Pyramid, I caught the faraway echo of music. Following my ears through the labyrinth, I came to a large meeting hall through whose half-open doors I saw a circle of plainly destitute men and women, hands joined, singing a hymn. Though the language was Albanian, the hymn was American. But the voices were off-key and the singing lacked the crispness of true inspiration. In the center of the circle, a stout no-nonsense woman with a mid-south American accent was gently chiding her flock through an interpreter. The hymn-sing was the prelude to a meal, and God who would, through His emissaries shower upon these unfortunate souls His bounty, would be better pleased with a more heartfelt, tuneful rendition. In mid-sentence she caught sight of me standing there, and a few seconds of silence followed. I turned and left. In the distance I heard the singing start up again.

At the restaurant, I meet Debbie Dakas. She and her husband Chris are, she explains with the simplicity born of absolute assurance, here to do God's work amongst the Albanians. She guides me through the spotless building, which contains a small second-floor dormitory for visiting students, and a computer work-shop which doubles as a meeting room for young people wishing to join the Information Age. The basement houses a sophisticated printing and book-binding facility powered by an unmetered direct (and therefore illegal) connection to the main Tirana grid.

Debbie, a plumpish, compulsively pleasant woman who can't stop wringing her hands, is pre-emptively apologetic about the idea of ensnaring Albanian recruits through lessons in computer basics. "Mind you," she says, "this is not some way of proselytizing people, All we're doing is letting the Bible speak. What they do with the message is up to them."

As we chat a young woman comes up to Debbie and asks her a question. Debbie replies in Albanian with an expeditious tone that belies her aw shucks folksiness. Nodding her head, the young woman hurries off.

She's already developed a working knowledge of Albanian, she says. Not like those Mormons in their white shirts and dark business suits who arrive with a sophisticated grasp of Shqip they claim to have learned in Albania. But it's not so sophisticated that the Albanians, who pride themselves on the difficulty of their tongue, cannot spot them as fakes from a mile away. "Me, I make plenty of mistakes," she laughs. "At least they know I'm real."

On the stairway down to the printing shop we encounter her husband Chris, a lean, tense man with a New England twang. The brains of the operation to Debbie's heart. In the course of small talk it quickly emerges that Chris Dakas is of Greco-Albanian origin, and describes himself as a close friend of Nicholas Gage, the Greek-American journalist, author of *Eleni* and latterly, special advisor on Albanian affairs to former Greek Prime Minister Constantine Mitsotakis.

"When my father emigrated to the United States he converted and became a Greek," Chris confides. "We're here for the long haul," he laughs after we've toured the printing room. Debbie nods approvingly. "Besides, I've got a Greek passport. Can't throw me out. I'm part of a protected minority."

As I leave the restaurant, alarm bells start ringing in my head: there has been too much coincidence for one afternoon. The organization, a trans-denominational group called the International Christian Assembly, has the look of a cold-war relic. Are Chris and Debbie simple Yankee soul-fishers tempted by the murky waters of formerly atheist Albania? Is their connection with the politically influential and spooky Nick Gage mere happenstance, a fluke of geography? Or does their polished and well-equipped headquarters with its state-of-the-art publishing plant, conceal something else, something sinister? In the spiritual and political swamp of post-communist Albania, as throughout the Balkans, prudence dictates that we seek the sinister.

Che sembianze! Che vestiti!
Che figure! Che mustachi!
Io non so se son Vallachi
O se Turchi con costor,
—**Lorenzo Da Ponte**, *Cosí fan tutte*

In mock amazement, the ebulliently cynical serving wench Despina marvels *sotto voce* at the extravagant costumes and mustaches of the two Neapolitan lovers who have returned, disguised, to test the fidelity of their ladies. You can't tell whether they 're Vlachs or Turks, she puzzles. In the event they are neither, though maybe a little of each. They are "Albanians," the pinnacle of late eighteenth century exoticism. In the Sextet that ends Act I of *Cosí fan tutte*, Mozart and his librettist, the defrocked Jewish-convert priest Lorenzo Da Ponte, express in their own ineffable way one of the most enduring enigmas of the imaginary frontier which separates Europe from the Byzantine and Islamic Orient: who are the Albanians?

Official historiography, which the democratic regime has seen fit to tamper with as little as possible, traces a direct line back to the ancient Illyrians, an autochthonous population (unlike the late-arriving Hellenes, for instance) which enjoyed a high level of civilization and even, in the fifth century, created a powerful state which aroused the concern of its Greek and Roman neighbors. After more than fifty years of warfare, Rome finally defeated these proud, intractable people, inaugurating more than five centuries of what is termed Roman bondage. As was their custom, the conquerors attempted to Romanize the newly occupied lands, with mixed success.

Most of the Illyrians stood firm, holding stubbornly to their identity and language. But some adopted the language of the conqueror, which, in modified form, continues to be spoken in up-country villages to this day. The people who speak it are the Vlachs, another part of the Mozart-Da Ponte conundrum. Their continued existence—and persistence in their nomadic, Latin-speaking ways—casts a strange light on the discourse of national consciousness in Greece, Albania, and Macedonia, and makes discussion of ethnic minorities a perilous exercise.

The non-Latinized Illyrians remained a majority, and when the empire split into two parts in 395 of the modern era, stayed within the eastern section which was ruled from Constantinople. Wherever Rome had been, Christianity soon followed, and with the great schism of 1054, Christian Albanian lands were fractured into a Catholic north and an Orthodox south, a division which was to endure down to the present day, but not before undergoing two significant, not to say overwhelming geo-social upheavals. The first of these was the mass migration of Slavic tribes south into the Balkans in the seventh century, an event which profoundly and irrevocably altered the "ethnic" composition of the region. The second was the Ottoman conquest, which brought with it not so much the Turks themselves, for the empire relied little on colonization, but their religion, Islam, which anchored Albania firmly to the Orient.

The Western stereotype of Islam is that of a religion driven by conversion at sword point. But when the Turks launched their conquest of the Balkans, their aims were primarily strategic and economic. In the first 35 years following the conquest of Albania, less than three percent of the population had adopted the conquerors' faith. It was not until the seventeenth century that the pace of conversion accelerated, as the benefits of lower taxation and opportunities for social advancement became more apparent.[90] When Sultan Mehmet II, the Conqueror, captured Constantinople in 1453, he promptly extended special dispensations to the Patriarchate and proclaimed himself protector of the Orthodox Christians of the Balkans.[91] Far from conversion, the Sultan's strategic intention was to transform the Orthodox Christians into allies. In this, the Ottomans might have succeeded had it not been for the rise, in the eighteenth century, of a new doctrine more powerful than revealed religion: secular nationalism.

Where they did occur, early conversions to Islam, especially among the Albanian nobility, often had a curiously opportunistic quality which, seen in hindsight, seems to reveal an underlying trait in the national character. Nowhere is the paradox of patriotic apostasy, or of opportunistic hat-changing if you prefer, better exemplified than in the career of the man revered by Albanians of whatever denomination: Gjergj Kastrioti Skanderbeg, whose black double-headed eagle emblem on a red field is perpetuated today in the country's flag. Son of a wealthy land-owning clan from Krujë, a hill town in central Albania, Gjergj adopted the unmistakably Turkish name of Skanderbeg, became a Muslim and rose rapidly in the Ottoman military hierarchy. But after a crushing defeat at the battle of Nish, in 1443, at the hands of the crusading Hungarian armies led by Janos Hunyadi, Skanderbeg abandoned his correligionists and returned to the ancestral estate along with 300 Albanian warriors. There he repudiated Islam and launched a holy war against the Ottomans which was to endure for 25 years before sputtering out after the great leader's death.[92]

On a fine early spring day in 1995, I stand on the parapet of the Skanderbeg museum, a full-scale, tawny stone reconstruction of the illustrious rebel's castle at Krujë, looking west toward the Adriatic, gleaming silver in the distance. Towering behind the castle, itself perched atop an unassailable rocky outcropping above the town, are the flanks of jagged mountains striated with the remains of winter snow. I've come here with Thomas Haxhi, my guide and confidant for the day. Mr. Haxhi, a former cultural attaché at the Albanian embassy in Paris, speaks flawless French, and has the cultivated tastes of a man at ease in the world of ideas. He is also, despite his obvious polish and intellectual qualities—or, more likely, because of his political past—unemployed and no longer able to enjoy those tastes.

Mr. Haxhi has graciously agreed to accompany me on the expedition to Krujë. He has also arranged, at nominal cost, for a silver-gray Mercedes driven by a distinguished white-haired chauffeur wearing a blue serge suit and dark glasses. We are the only visitors to the museum, once an obligatory stop on the carefully stage-managed tourist itineraries laid on for the handful of ideologically acceptable visitors to Albania. Its displays, running to monumental sculpted pieces and heroic murals depicting Skanderbeg's military exploits and political sagacity, were designed by Pranvera, Enver Hoxha's daughter, whispers my guide. "In fact, she designed the whole museum."

The museum does indeed set the patriotic chords vibrating, but it respects the rocky landscape too, and reflects fairly—once you peel away the first layer of patriotic silver-plating—the brutal climate of shifting alliances, desperate resistance, betrayal, fierce battle and political maneuvering that marked Skanderbeg's career—and the entire medieval and modern history of Albania. It also has little of the pompous monumentalism that afflicts a generation of public buildings throughout the defunct socialist universe. If Pranvera's objective was to recreate the rarefied atmosphere of Skanderbeg's stony aerie, she succeeded.

Mr. Haxhi leads me through the vaulted hall where a replica of Skanderbeg's winged helmet lies at the head of a massive carved table, and into a portrait gallery where he shows me a late fifteenth century engraving of the hero. "I discovered it in Paris in a bookseller's stall along the Seine. So I bought it and brought it back to Albania," he says proudly.

On leaving the museum we wander through the ruins of the Krujë citadel. Some of the rough-hewn stone houses are still occupied, the stone-paved lanes are thick with goat and sheep droppings. At the lip of the precipice stands a domed Islamic structure surrounded by the gravestones of Bektashi dervishes, each topped with a stone replica of the order's ceremonial hat. From far below we catch the throb of drums and the squeal of shawms. A marriage must be in progress, says my guide. As we make our way down the cobbled pathway we are suddenly besieged by a group of raggedy urchins offering us postcards, and jewelry that looks like it's been stamped from electroplated bottle caps. "Hey, mister!" they shout. "Rare coins. Gold, best gold!" Mr. Haxhi shakes his head as he shoos them away. Before, this would have been unthinkable.

At the foot of the legendary Turk-fighter's castle and the walled town lies the Krujë bazaar, a relic of pure Ottoman architecture, whose graceful carved wooden façades and overhanging eaves shelter a series of handicraft shops and traditional cafés, all empty. The perfect place, and the ideal hour, for a Turkish coffee, in which Mr. Haxhi, the driver and I gladly indulge. As Greek music clangs away in the background my guide, his pride perhaps piqued by our incursion into the past, unburdens himself.

"Sure we made mistakes, terrible mistakes," he says. "But these men, Berisha and his people, are worse than Enver Hoxha." What's more, he tells me, pausing to translate into Albanian for the benefit of the driver who nods gravely, the tragic events that followed the collapse of the last communist government in late 1991 and early 1992, were the work of paid thugs working for Berisha's Democratic Party. Suddenly my ears perk up. I remember the desolation of the Albania I had encountered in November, 1991, and which I had assumed to be the work of the vengeance-bent "masses."

"The whole thing was remote-controlled from Washington, let me assure you," he continues, indignation flickering around the corners of his mouth. "A man called Gramoz Pashko, who was at the time Berisha's economic mouthpiece and today is the darling of you Western journalists, promised the Albanians he had a blank cheque signed by George Bush. Ryerson, the US. ambassador, appeared on the rostrum with Berisha. There were American flags everywhere, and only a handful of Albanian ones. And while he was boasting, DP toughs systematically attacked and destroyed all the state property they could get their hands on, not to mention Party offices and even our industrial plants. They wanted to convince Albanians that there could be no going back. It wasn't enough for them to destroy the old order. They had to destroy everything we built."

The destruction had been more than material. A few hours later, Mr. Haxhi, his wife, and I attend a concert of orchestral and choral music at the national Opera House on Skanderbeg square. On the stage I count more musicians than there are spectators in the hall. The orchestra and soloist, a barely post-adolescent Italian who gives a sensitive, slightly diffident reading of Beethoven's first piano concerto, pretend to ignore the obvious: that they have been deserted by the public. Prices cannot be a factor: anyone but the absolutely indigent could afford a ticket. "People just don't feel like going out any more," admits Mr. Haxhi sadly. "If you hadn't invited us, we wouldn't have come ourselves."

I test the planned destruction hypothesis that evening on Sokol, Ilir and Loreta. Sokol disagrees vehemently with Mr. Haxhi. The destroyers of Albania's industrial base, the people who ruined state property and Party offices were the communists themselves, he insists. But Loreta, basking in the glow of a successfully performed root-canal in the private clinic she has just opened in her father's apartment, joins the debate with her customary good-humored verve. Reminding Sokol of the US blank cheque gambit she slaps her forehead with her fingertips: "And we believed them!" Ilir nods gravely: Yes, we believed them.

Baba Reshad, head of the Bektashi Dervish Order, Tirana, Albania.
(Photo by Fred A. Reed.)

TO THE EAST, at the foot of Mount Dajti, urban Tirana comes to an abrupt end. A jagged rank of apartment blocks and rusting factories gives way, within the space of a few hundred meters, to fields where, atop a rounded hill, stands a tree-shaded complex of unmistakably Islamic domed buildings. As the taxi carrying me, Marc Clark, a Canadian journalist, and a university student named Ilir—not to be confused with Loreta's husband—who has come along as interpreter, pulls up the curving driveway an elderly man with a flowing white beard dressed in white robes rises laboriously from the bench upon which he has been resting in the late afternoon sun, and walks slowly forward to greet us. On his head he wears a cylindrical, pleated white hat with a band of dark green. The head piece, I was to learn later, is twelve sided, symbolizing the twelve holy Imams, and is called a *Hüseyini Tac*. We step from the car and the man grasps our hands in a firm, cordial grip, welcoming us to the world headquarters of the Bektashi Order of Dervishes, end point of a spiritual journey that began in the thirteenth century in the eastern Persian province of Khorassan.

"Salaam," I say, putting my hand to my heart in the Islamic manner. "Salaam," he replies. Baba Reshad is the senior surviving elder of a sect that expresses in convoluted and mysterious ways the ambiguous nature of Islam in Albania. How convoluted and mysterious becomes apparent as we remove our shoes and follow him into the ceremonial hall of the teké. The walls are decorated with Qur'anic sayings in Arabic script, and with paintings depicting the Shi'ite holy family: Imam Ali, son-in-law of the Prophet, his wife Fatima, and their sons Hassan and Hossein. Another painting shows the battle at the oasis of Karbala, where the forces of the Ommayad tyrant Yazid annihilated the forces of virtue and duty led by Imam Hossein. The imagery is familiar from my travels in Iran: the noble, bearded face of Ali, the dolorous eyes of Hossein, the Prince of Martyrs.

Like his Sunni counterpart, the Grand Mufti, Baba Reshad seems unaccustomed to the bright light of day and to the unbearable lightness of freedom. His blue eyes are clear and bright, his beard thick, luxuriant; his answers come slowly, he searches for words, attempts to please us, his unexpected guests. The encounter begins badly. Clark insists on grilling the Baba in an adversarial manner on contemporary events, of which he clearly knows nothing and cares less. (Later Ilir confesses that Baba Reshad had pleaded with him to "please tell him something, I don't know what he wants to hear.")

Things pick up when the conversation moves to matters of the spirit. The Baba is not a politician but a man of God who does not inhabit this world as much as he resides in a rich and complex past that happens to overlap the present. As an adolescent in 1947, he joined the Order in spite of the proscriptions of the communist regime. Twenty years later, when Albania staged its own version of the Maoist cultural revolution, the Bektashis were outlawed along with every other religious denomination in the land. "I was imprisoned," he says, crossing his wrists. "Thrown into the gulag, transferred from one labor camp to another. We were not allowed to wear our traditional dress, all our property was confiscated. 38 of our leaders were executed."

The faith for which Baba Reshad endured 24 years of captivity, and for which many more perished, had been founded seven centuries before, by a saint named Hajji Bektash Veli, from Nishapour, the town in Khorassan which also gave birth to Omar Khayyam. Hajji Bektash's descent could be traced, claimed his supporters, through a complex process of numerological explication, back to the Prophet Mohammad, making him what Shi'ite Iranians call a *seyyed*. The saint quickly earned a reputation for miracles. One day a disciple breathlessly informed him that the leader of another dervish sect, Ahmed Saïd Rufai, was on his way to meet him, mounted on a lion whose mane was made of serpents. When he learned of this apparent prodigy, Hajji Bektash threw a many-colored blanket over a rock wall, saddled and mounted it, and ordered the wall to march off briskly. The bizarre steed promptly obeyed and carried the saint to his meeting with Ahmed Saïd Rufai, who asked, astounded: "And what does this signify, my lord?" To which Hajji Bektash replied: "To ride a lion is child's play; to cause a stone wall to walk is no simple matter."[93]

Some sources claim that Hajji Bektash was a Turk, and that his crypto-Shi'ite doctrine was a form of Turkish resistance to the dominant Sunni orthodoxy of the Seljuq Islamic empire.[94] Others suggest that the saint was in fact a Persian, and that to this day the songs and chants of the order are recited in the language of Ferdowsi and Ha'fez, even though they may not be understood by the Turkish or Albanian faithful. Whether Turkish or Persian, the Bektashi dervishes were religious subversives in a regime of strict orthodoxy. They adopted Sunni Islam as a cloak to cover the Shi'ite veil which in turn concealed an essentially pantheistic belief system which integrated elements of Nestorian Christianity, and Siberian shamanism harking back to the most distant antecedents of the Turkic tribes that migrated out of north-central Asia.[95] And possibly elements of the ancient Iranian Zoroastrian faith and Indian mysticism.

At one time Bektashiism was the dominant dervish confraternity in the Islamic world, with as many as seven million adherents in the old Ottoman state. One of the reasons may have been the close connection between the Order and the Janissary corps, the elite Ottoman troops recruited from among the first born of non-Muslim households in the empire, and submitted to rigorous physical and spiritual training. The Janissaries gradually evolved into praetorian guards notorious for their arrogance, much given to toppling Sultans who dared displease them. The Bektashi influence "does not seem to have accomplished much in the way of spiritualizing the Janissary way of life."[96] The Order's doctrinal flexibility and predilection for mysticism may, however, have made it attractive to men drawn from non-Muslim backgrounds.

The Bektashis probably arrived in Albania with the troops of Murad II at the beginning of the fifteenth century. Four centuries later, under the reign of Ali Pasha of Ioannina, himself an initiate, Bektashis made up an estimated 20 percent of the population. Perhaps because of Ali Pasha, perhaps for other, more obscure reasons—the truth of legend over the false veracity of historical materialism—the Bektashis became fervent nationalists, and the prime movers of the Albanian national awakening.

Among the most illustrious among them was Naïm Frasheri, a poet who incarnated the combination of religious mysticism and hard-headed practicality which ultimately allowed the Albanian national movement to survive and thrive. Frasheri's poetry ranges from the devotional—his *Querbelja* describes the martyrdom of Imam Hossein at Karbala—to the heroic, as in the national epic *Skanderbeg*. But Frasheri was Albanian to the bone: the subject matter might well be Islamic, the tone and the language were firmly Shqiptar.[97]

In 1908 the Ottoman state entered its final phase of disintegration as the Young Turk revolution raced like wildfire through the Imperial Army in Macedonia and Albania. While orthodox Albanian Sunnis, faithful to the empire, abominated the rebels and their westernizing ways, the Bektashis supported them. In fact, they may even have hoped to establish a Bektashi state in Albania. The first public speech made in Albanian under Ottoman rule was given from the balcony overlooking Liberty Square in Salonica during the heady days of July, when a representative proclaimed: "...now is the day for us also to say freely that we are Albanians. Until today we could not say this, because our tongue would be cut off, we would be thrown into prison."[98]

When the infant Albanian state re-emerged from the wreckage of World War I, the country's Muslims moved to break their religious ties with Turkey. In early 1922, the Bektashis voted to abolish the tutelage of the anti-religious fanatics who now ruled in Ankara, and when, three years later, the Atatürk regime suppressed the dervish orders and closed the Turkish *tekes*, Bektashi headquarters were transferred to Tirana, to the very building in which we now sit conversing with Baba Reshad.

"All religions are one," he confides, at ease now. "We cannot put aside the Qur'an or the Bible. People should be united by love. Do we not all worship one God? The forces of division are not important. The only real power is God's. Look what happened to the communists."

As we are leaving, the Baba spies the silver-mounted agate ring I acquired years ago from a venerable Sufi in Isfahan. "Iran," I say, pointing to it. Baba Reshad embraces me. "Ya Ali," he says, smiling beatifically. "Praise Ali." The old man who is hugging me may be the last of a strange and noble line. Earlier he assured us that young people in Albania were thirsty for religion. But Ilir, the student interpreter, volunteers that he finds the Baba anachronistic and faintly ridiculous. Finding novices to rebuild the Order may prove more difficult than riding off astride a stone wall, or than for a camel to pass through the eye of a needle.

SKANDERBEG MAY HAVE RENOUNCED Islam and fought the Turks, but the faith of Mohammad gradually gained ground among the Albanians. Christian historians, who exhibit a certain, dare we say anti-Islamic bias, explain what they see as a "lapse," by the desire to avoid taxes, by a lack of trained, intelligent clergy to minister to the spiritual needs of the population, and by the attraction of social and material improvement.[99]

The Ottoman empire had begun life as a military and administrative machine in search of a state. Having happened upon that state in the form of the moribund Byzantine empire, they first resuscitated, then expanded it by conquest. This approach created opportunities for the warlike Albanian clansmen. The Turkish rulers, orthodox Sunnis who frowned on the crypto-heretical Bektashis, used religion to differentiate themselves from the ruled; once the Albanians adopted Islam, for whatever motives, they could automatically join forces with the rulers. Suddenly, a vast field lay before them, in which they could hone their martial skills and perfect their administrative talents. This they did, with eminent success. The Köprülü family, whose rise to power in the latter half of the seventeenth century saved the empire from early decline, was of Albanian origin. At least thirty grand viziers, the empire's highest ranking civil authority, were Albanian.[100]

Shqiperia's most glorious contribution to the empire, and at the same time one of the architects of its demise, came not from Albania proper. Mohammad Ali, warrior, administrator, political adventurer extraordinary, and founder of the Egyptian dynasty which ended with the overthrow of king Farouk in 1953, was born in the seventh decade of the eighteenth century in the northern Aegean port city of Kavalla, 600 kilometers along the Egnatian Way from the Adriatic shore at Durrës.

For most of its length the Egnatian Way is like a dream trail, invisible, buried deep beneath fields, covered by shifting riverbeds, overlaid by newer roads or simply forgotten. A memory, not a highway or a name tag for competing multinational pipeline and highway projects; as virtual as the Internet; a concealed vector of history. Yet here, on the outskirts of a Greek provincial town, it suddenly surfaces, winding upward through scrub brush and pine trees like the petrified artery of an ancient imperial mammoth, seeming to echo still with the clang of Roman armor, the screech and rattle of chariot wheels, the panting of men and horses.

When I arrived in Kavalla from Salonica one Sunday morning Thanassis Daskalakis was waiting for me at the bus station, primed for a day of intensive exploration of the city he has called home for the last eleven years. Thanassis, a native of Salonica marooned by the Greek bureaucracy in a town of 60,000 souls, is a rebel at heart, a man with an un-Greek eye for the ironies of the past and the present. After a cup of tea and a slab of hot *bougatsa* dusted with sugar and cinnamon, we set out toward the Kavalla citadel, birthplace of its most illustrious son who, to the chagrin of the good burghers and the self-righteous boosters, was not a Greek Orthodox Christian but an Albanian Muslim.

Mohammad Ali was born in 1769, into a wealthy tobacco growing family whose *chiftlik* holdings extended throughout the region, as far as the island of Thasos, which we can see, looming on the horizon, as the cloud-diffused December sunlight glitters on the water. After his father's untimely death, he was brought up by the military governor of Kavalla and at age 18, was married to one of the governor's daughters who bore five of his 95 children. The marriage not only brought the bright young man into the governor's extended household; it drew his natural political and military gifts to the attention of the Ottoman administration. For what they may have lacked in moral scruples—never the fibre of empire in the best of times—the Ottomans more than compensated for in their esteem for the martial virtues. A young man with a quick mind and a fast hand on the scimitar could go far indeed.

At the governor's urging Mohammad Ali joined the Ottoman expeditionary force to Egypt in 1798 to oppose Napoleon's expedition, the opening salvo in the West's military and cultural assault, fueled by the Enlightenment, on the Islamic world. Though it lasted a mere three years, the French occupation touched off an accelerated breakdown of traditional Egyptian society. Meanwhile, the Turkish-Albanian contingent from Macedonia had quickly established itself as the most effective arm of the Ottoman forces, giving a good account of themselves against the better equipped but overextended French. Turning his political skills to rapid advantage, Mohammad Ali seized leadership of the detachment when its commander was assassinated. In May of that same year, 1805, the people of Cairo rose up in revolt against the Ottoman viceroy and the ulema appointed Mohammad Ali as his replacement. The Sultan quickly invested him with the title of Pasha.

Within a few years the new Pasha had eliminated the Mamluks, the former ruling military oligarchy; expropriated the landowning class; transformed the religious establishment into government pensioners; neutralized the Bedouins; and put down several peasant rebellions.

Mohammad Ali's house, Thanassis explains as we work our way up the cobbled street past the concrete matchboxes that pass for modern Greek urban architecture even in a supposedly historical district, has survived, thanks not to some enlightened policy on the part of the Greek state, but to the back-handed support of the Egyptian government. Were it not for the Egyptians, Mohammad Ali's existence would probably be unknown to most citizens of Kavalla. If we are to judge by the huge concrete excrescence of an Orthodox Church that stands across the square, dwarfing the brass statue of the Vice Regent astride his horse, scimitar drawn, the Greeks would probably have preferred ignorance to recognition of the achievements of their brilliant Muslim-Albanian countryman. Greek denial of its Islamic heritage is deeply rooted and omnipresent: a semi-official history of the town makes no mention whatsoever of Mohammad Ali and his family, nor of the existence of its former Albanian population. That which is not Greek, that is to say, Christian and Hellenic, is deemed never to have existed.

The family home was built in 1760, using the traditional Turkish construction method of plaster on lath over a wood frame protected from the elements by an overhanging tile roof. Following behind a short, stout woman called Maria who acts as house and gate-keeper, we enter. With a little prompting from Thanassis, Maria confesses with quiet confidence: "This place means more to me than my own home."

In the main room stands Mohammad Ali's desk, the house's only remaining piece of furniture. It is a massive, rough-hewn affair atop which leans a framed display of yellowed, curling photographs depicting the last dynasty to rule Egypt: Mohammad Ali, with his white beard and alert, inquiring eyes; his sons Ibrahim and Ismaïl (who later became Khedive); and Farouk, their ultimate and unfortunate heir.

The royal family has long been extinct, for Farouk left no progeniture. But it still owns title to substantial properties in the Kavalla. Eventual disposal of these properties, explains Maria, could provide the funds to carry out badly needed repairs. But, although she cannot explain why, it is clear that the Sadat-Moubarak regime has more important things on which to spend its money. The Greek government, despite its oft-declared good intentions, has done nothing either to procure the house and the adjoining Imaret, or to underwrite its upkeep.

The Imaret, our next stop, is a multiple-domed complex which hugs the contours of the hillside overlooking the harbor instead of fighting them, creating a series of enclosed spaces open to the sky and to the sea, which capture sunlight in winter and create shade in summer. In the Ottoman Empire, Imarets functioned in a multiplicity of roles as semi-public charitable institutions. The poor could find shelter and food, public kitchens were operated, religious instruction was given (a mosque was an intimate part of the complex) and alms dispensed to the indigent. Today, the Kavalla Imaret doubles as a coffee-house during the tourist season. On this cool, damp December morning, the tables and chairs are stacked in the arched gallery one level below the main entrance, birds are flitting through the palms, cypresses and plane trees in the courtyard. The resident cats—well fed and sociable—saunter over to rub themselves against our ankles.

When the dream of Greater Greece collapsed in Asia Minor in 1922, the refugees who ended up in Kavalla made their homes in the Imaret. "This is where I was born and grew up," Maria tells us, with a mixture of pride and sadness. Moving down a flight of graceful marble steps we visit the public kitchens where the starving poor of Kavalla were provided emergency food supplies funded by the Egyptian government during the bitterest days of World War II. In this utilitarian section adjoining the mosque (long since rented out as a warehouse) artifacts are on display, including Greek and English translations of the Ottoman script displayed over the Imaret's entrance, praising Mohammad Ali's character and accomplishments in the service of the Sultan and the faith, particularly his victory over the heretics.

The heretics were the founders of Saudi Arabia. In the early years of his vice-regal reign, at the invitation of Sultan Mahmud II, Mohammad Ali's son Ibrahim expelled the hyper-fundamentalist Arab Wahhabi sect—seen as dangerous renegades by the moderate Ottomans—from the Hejaz, that part of Arabia holiest to Islam, where Mecca and Medina are located. Even as Lawrence of Arabia was rousing the desert Arabs to revolt against Istanbul on the promise of independence for Arabia, the infamous Sykes-Picot accords of 1916 had covertly restored the Hejaz to the Wahhabis of the Al Saoud clan who now rule the Peninsula as a family fiefdom.

The sign says little of the viceroy's subsequent career, particularly his defeat of the Ottoman army in Syria in 1839. The debacle, combined with the desertion of the entire Ottoman fleet to Egypt, touched off European intervention, ostensibly to protect the Empire. The Eastern Question—diplomatic jargon for the dismemberment of the Ottoman state—had begun. Unable to defeat his unruly vassal, Sultan Abdulmecid I in 1841 appointed Mohammad Ali's family hereditary rulers of Egypt. In 1849 the son of an Albanian tobacco grower from Kavalla who had shaken an empire died in Cairo of natural causes.

BETWEEN NOVEMBER 1991 AND FEBRUARY 1992, 600 tonnes of chemical fertilizers and herbicides including lindan and other organo-chlorides containing high concentrations of toxic dioxins, were shipped clandestinely from Germany to Albania. The compounds had been manufactured in the former East Germany and were now either outdated or banned. (European Union regulations allow member-states to refuse toxic wastes from another member country, but leave them free to dump outside Community borders.) For more than a year boxcars carrying barrels of the substances—an environmental disaster in the waiting—stood on railway sidings or under alleged supervision at Albanian army facilities. However, individuals contrived to seize some of the barrels, emptied them and used them for food and water storage. Two years later, under international pressure, the German government assumed responsibility for the deadly cargo and arranged for its repatriation. But the incident had come to typify the role of the new Balkans as toxic waste disposal dump for the developed West.

And, in an apparently unrelated incident:

"What happened to Albanian music?" I asked Loreta one evening over supper. In public places in Tirana the only music to be heard now was American rock, rap, hip-hop and its multiple sub-genres. She laughed bitterly, tossing her head. "Enver Hoxha tells us we must love Albanian music. All we hear is Albanian music. Now Enver Hoxha is dead, and Albanian music is dead along with him. People, they want only American music."

Après moi, le déluge. Hoxha and his successors, who planned to rule forever, certainly never considered the consequences of a policy that made the regime the sole purveyor of national culture. They fostered the country's rich and complex musical tradition as an integral part of the state doctrine of Albanicity. Today, abandoned by the state and shivering in the chill of popular disdain, Albanian musicians must survive by playing weddings, or emigrate to places like the Athens flea market where they can be encountered of a Saturday evening playing for money in the streets.

The toxic waste incident and the departure of the musicians—like children departing a city where they are no longer wanted—express, as reality and as metaphor, the dumping of the West's cultural effluent into the immuno-depressed ruins of a system which, for all its opposition to the capitalist order, shared the same productivist assumptions. The trash music which spews from the hundreds of Tirana cafés, the recycled television series sold cut-rate to once-proud national television, possess all the social utility of a trainload of dioxins. They are, however, American; products of the World Power which laid low the socialist beast. As such they are not merely tolerable, but desirable. More important, they are the breech through which now pour city slickers, fast-buck artists, Mafiosi, and frauds masquerading as international assistance experts, financial advisors, investment counselors, industrialists, developers, bond fund touts, bankers, lawyers, tourist industry promoters, communicators, evangelists, show-biz personalities, along with the other miscellaneous riffraff of the new world disorder. (Yes, there would be some honorable men and women, devoted, underpaid international civil servants and NGO volunteers. whose presence in Tirana was the exception that confirms the rule.)

On my last trip to Albania, a voyage on the overnight bus from Athens to Tirana, one of my fellow passengers was a young woman who spoke Greek with a sharp, acid, low-life snap and a thick Albanian accent. Undaunted by the discomfort of 20 hours on a slow-moving vehicle, she sported tight black pants, a ruffled black blouse and a broad-shouldered suede jacket. It was not long before she had cajoled the driver into playing her personal cassettes:

languorous, twanging music of the kind favored in Greek roadside dives. At one of our many rest stops I asked her about her musical tastes. "Goes with my work in the bars," she replied.

Later, as I dozed fitfully, I overheard snippets of conversation between her and the driver:

"So if a guy wants to go with a girl like you, what's it going to cost him?"

"You want me for the night, for instance, it'll cost you 100,000 drachmas," she fired back. The price, more than $400, reflected her estimate of her desirability to the bus driver more than it did cold market reality. Just how cold was the reality became apparent when she got off the bus in the muddy flat outside the town of Lushnjë. Prostitution in the mean bars of the Athens red light district had become the only escape from the morass of unemployment and idleness.

But young ladies—and young men—will soon have less need to go south to find employment. As drug smugglers, embargo-busters, white-slave traders and Euro-confidence men hover above Albania in ever-narrowing circles, a domestic market is emerging, drawing sex tourists eager to sample its previously forbidden delights. From as far afield as Canada, itinerant pederasts—chickenhawks in trade jargon—variously disguised as writers and philosophers, ever sensitive to the purchasing power of their dollars in the new economy of devastation, have already begun to alight.

A CHAUFFEURED CAR, the same red rattletrap Volkswagen that had driven Frok Çupi and me to Durrës the year before, awaits early on Easter morning of 1995 outside the Dajti. Today it will be carrying me to Korçë, penultimate stop on my ultimate trip to Albania. Although the buses are said to be safer now, no foreigner traveling alone enjoys complete security, Frok had warned me the day before. Behind the wheel is Frok's friend and chauffeur Nujé; beside him in the passenger's seat sits Esmeralda, a voluble, compact woman who will be riding with us as far as Elbasan. Drowsy from lack of sleep, I lounge in the back.

Less than eight hours before, I had attended midnight services held, for the first time in living memory, in the street in front of the former Enver Hoxha publishing house, around the corner from the Orthodox church. As

Archbishop Yannoulatos, looking more frail yet more determined than a year before, intoned the paschal liturgy, alternating between Greek and Albanian, the crowd suddenly came alight with thousands of flickering candles. Christ was not only resurrected from the dead; His grace had manifestly consigned official atheism to that tenebrous realm. But amongst the devout householders and their children were many curious, idle young men who stood by gulping beer and smoking cigarettes. For them, the concept of Easter must have been ineluctably, endlessly strange, perhaps ironic. What was this matter of resurrection? What did it have to do with free-market democracy, the fresh new deity of the hour?

Two hours out of Tirana, as the car whines down the denuded mountains overlooking Elbasan, Esmeralda describes how heavy industry came to, and destroyed, her home town. For centuries an Ottoman garrison and administrative center, Elbasan is known throughout Albania as the "city of the winds," for its location at the point where the Shkumbin valley narrows, funneling Adriatic breezes into the mountainous interior. It was here, in proximity to ore deposits, that the country's master planners decided to locate the monstrous metallurgical complex which was to lift Albania up by its bootstraps into the industrial age and guarantee its prosperity.

The Elbasan metallurgical works was begun in the early sixties by the Chinese, then Albania's eternal brothers and benefactors. And when the Chinese turned out to be too heavy-handed for the dictator's easily bruised sense of self-reliance, they abandoned it, unfinished, to their erstwhile ideological partners. Rumor has it that one still-functioning corner of the derelict complex currently produces AK-47s for domestic use and export to disenfranchised countrymen in the neighboring Balkan hotspots of Kosova and western Macedonia. But this, like much of the information tendered in Albania, is apocryphal and unverifiable.

From a distance, the Elbasan works seem a gigantic parody of Mao Tzedong's infamous back-yard smelters: the scale is different, the concept the same. In its brief lifetime, the complex turned out poor quality iron, steel, coke, ferro-chrome, nickel, cobalt, brick and oxygen at immense cost. Its primitive technology, copied by the Chinese from already obsolete Soviet models, created an ecological horror, Esmeralda explains as we drive slowly past red-rusted smokestacks, yawning coking ovens, and overhead ore buckets dangling immobile from frayed cables. When the plant was operating, tonnes of unfiltered emissions were wafted across the town fouling laundry, gritting between the teeth, and creating a generation of asthmatics.

"Will you stop in at my uncle's house for coffee?" she asks. No question of declining, for this is Albania where hospitality must be respected as a matter of sacred trust. The house, in the old quarter, opens onto a white-washed courtyard planted with orange trees. It was here that she and her brother Ferdinand, both Muslim despite the names, grew up, climbing the trees and chasing the household cats. Today Esmeralda works in Tirana teaching English, earning just enough to look after her son in the wake of her divorce. The coffee arrives, and with it the typical Balkan indulgence: a tiny plate of thick, syrupy preserved fruit. As I let the fruit melt in my mouth, she says: "We're giving up the best of ourselves. Everything that we've worked to build—forget the state—they have thrown it away, like so much rubbish."

A beep of the car horn echoes from the laneway where Nujé has remained to guard the Volkswagen. Time to be off: distances are short in Albania, but the road to Korçë is long.

Four hours later, after cresting the Albanian Alps at Qaf-e Thanes and twisting along the western shore of Lake Ohrid, we reach our destination. I check in at the only hotel in town, a dour blockhouse called the Iliria, noting that I am the only registered guest. As I complete the formalities, Nujé realizes he's forgotten Frok's note with the name and address of my contact, a local painter. Not to worry, he tells me over a lunch of lukewarm spaghetti and dense Albanian bread. It's all arranged. Our man will come to the hotel at 2:00 p.m. The appointed hour comes and goes; I grow restive. "Why not telephone?" I ask. "Is no telephone," responds the clerk, in Greek. Off go Nujé and the clerk to find him. How many painters can there be in Korçë?

I step outside onto the public square where a traffic policeman directs the very occasional automobile or horse-drawn cart, beginning to feel misgivings about this place. The steps of the hotel are crowded with raggedy, dour-faced men and women hanging about like the pariah dogs which prefigure the Consul's doom in Malcolm Lowry's *Under the Volcano*. Brooding and sinister. Under a gauze of high cloud, the biting late-April wind is whipping dust across the broad plaza; the coal-fired power station that looms a half-kilometer away spews brown smoke and cinders into the sky. As I pace up and down, an emaciated man carrying a briefcase approaches: "Dollars, marks, drachmas?" he enquires.

Suddenly Nujé's Volkswagen comes streaking diagonally across the square, and squeals to a halt in front of the hotel. The painter has been found and is awaiting me. Quickly I bundle into the car and in three minutes am swept into the courtyard of an Old Korcë home complete with a hand-pump and a bed of effusively flowering tulips. At the door stands Koço Ristani, the town's preeminent artist and assistant curator of the national museum of medieval art, specialist in the restoration of Byzantine icons, and a man who radiates a magnetic sincerity. Within seconds Koço has taken charge of everything. My belongings are to be removed from the Iliria as rapidly as possible. I am to be lodged with his neighbor, a man called Ylli Mustafa, for half the price. "You cannot trust the hotel," Koço tells me in halting but serviceable self-taught French. "Just a few days ago a visiting foreigner was robbed by thieves who climbed up the wall and broke through the window."

Amid long faces (does the clerk regret the loss of custom or the loss of commission?) I countersign the register and we expeditiously remove my two bags. As we leave, the same people who have been lounging on the steps for the last two hours barely move aside to let us pass. Beneath their carefully composed indifference, coals of resentment seem to smolder. If I were in their shoes, in their dusty, beaten-down, torn-soled sockless shoes, I know how I would feel.

Now that I've been safely established at Ylli's place, Nujé the driver takes leave of us for the long haul back to Tirana. I settle onto Koço's living room sofa as he flips through portfolio after portfolio of his work: oils, pastels, watercolors and pencil studies. Most depict his home town with a singing passion for its beauty, a droning threnody for its tragic plight. He shows me darkened streetscapes beneath tortured cloud constellations, sinister leaning peaked roofs, and defiant self-portraits of a man determined to preserve his integrity in a world gone mad.

Some of Koço's paintings have an abstract impressionist flavor, which I remark on. He bursts into laughter. In the early 1970s, he tells me, shaking his head as if still unable to believe the story he is telling, he was forced to destroy, personally, more than 250 paintings which someone—a friend, a neighbor, a colleague?—had denounced to the authorities as decadent. "What could he do?" he continues, smiling sadly. "If you didn't report on the conversations you overheard they would put you away for twenty-five years. That's how they broke us, destroyed our spirit. Here in Albania there was only one head, and that head belonged to Enver Hoxha. Perhaps it wouldn't have been so bad if he'd had a mind."

As he speaks I recall other conversations with Albanians. The regime's outlook was unambiguous: every foreigner was a spy. Paradoxically, almost the only visitors to Albania were the most trusted, tried and true fellow travelers, ultra-leftists, Marxist-Leninists and their Albania Friendship Society hangers-on. Surely the state, as it welcomed them with hand-wringing hypocrisy, viewed them with the same cynical whimsy that Stalin

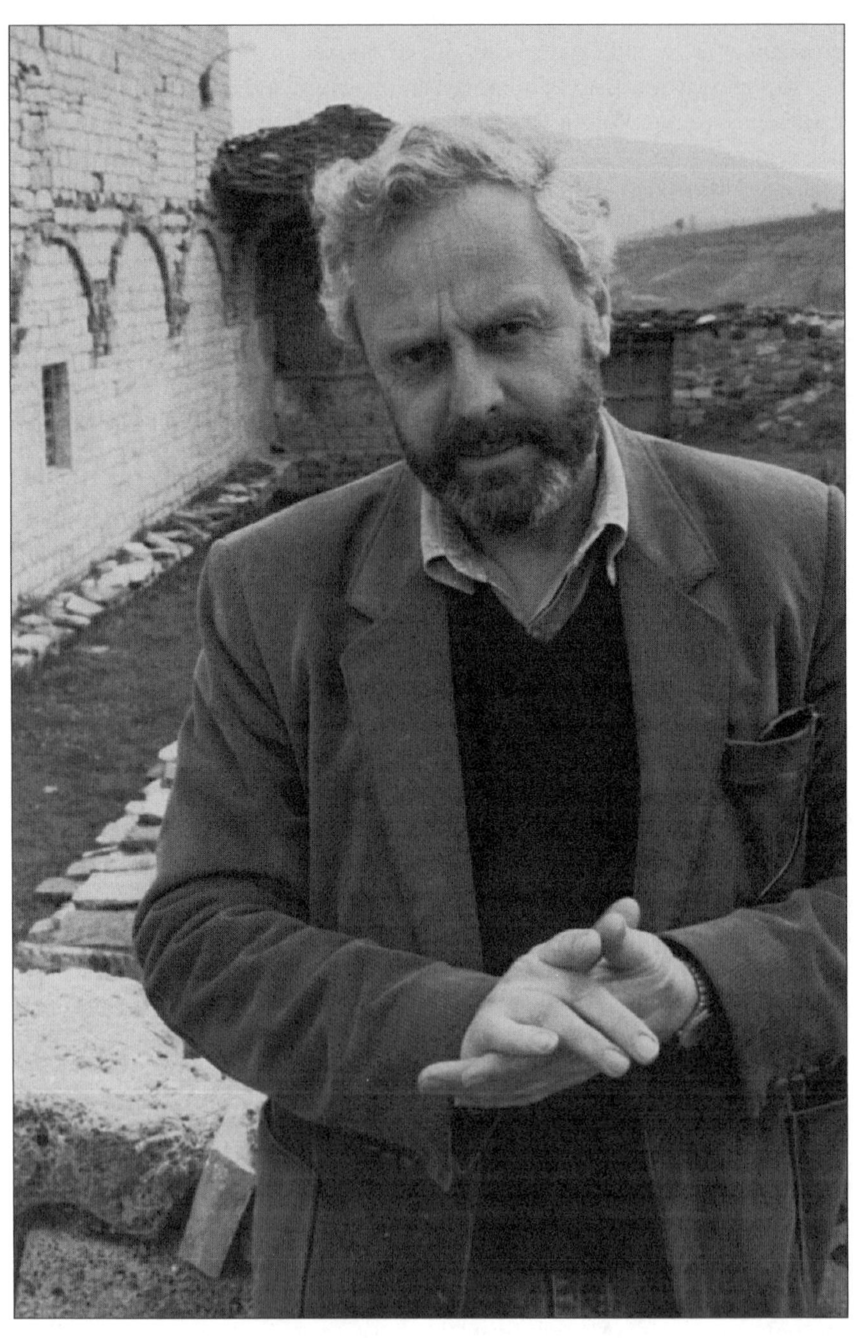

Koço Ristani in Voskopojë, Albania.
(Photo by Fred A. Reed.)

looked upon the sincere Westerners who spied for the Soviet Union: as dupes and fools. They may have had a point. Given the uniquely paranoid mindset of these little fathers of the people (whose dogmas I had spent many years accepting, honesty bids me to add) their well-wishing Western visitors were indeed agents of the capitalist devil, without even knowing it. Unwittingly, on their clothing, on their shoes, they bore the deadly microbe of innocence.

While I sit back and enjoy the paintings, Madame Ristani serves us Turkish coffee in tiny cups filled to the brim, its surface covered with frothy bubbles: coffee precisely as it should be prepared and served. Suddenly, it is as if the hour, the light, and the company have conspired to create a moment of perfectly contained bliss. From the cup sitting at arm's length on a low table I can catch the bittersweet pungency of the freshly brewed coffee. To prolong the pleasure I do not reach for it immediately, watching instead as tendrils of steam curl upward from the cup. Then and only then do I take a first sip, and feel the quickening pulse of a friendly encounter rouse me from mid-afternoon lassitude, prelude to a leisurely stroll down the tree-lined sidewalks of poor, desolate Korçë magically transformed into a city whose true and human contours have reappeared, visible still, amidst the rubble.

Koço guides me through the cobble-stoned back streets of the old town, pointing out the shabby elegance of wealthy villas, the dignified residences of absentee proprietors whose abandoned residences have been taken over by bands of Gypsy squatters. Most of these old Korçë mansions reflect the singular character and personality of their owners. One is an absurdist amalgam of gables, domed roofs, jutting turrets and elaborate plaster work, an unlikely collusion of baroque, rococo and neo-classical detail reminiscent of the castles of the mad prince Ludwig of Bavaria. Around a corner we pause in front of a house built by a wealthy medical family, which features a cupola resting atop grimy, vine-choked Corinthian columns. Yet another would not seem out of place in an Albrecht Dürer woodcut: this is the fetish house that appears in several of Koço's tormented nightscapes.

At the foot of the hills that ring the town to the east, a long flight of steps leads to an immense patriotic partisan monument, of the kind which could be found in every Albanian town or village. In almost every urban area I visited, these massive memorials had been destroyed or defaced, but Korçë's stands unmolested, staring in empty triumph out over the dormant industrial plants, the power station, the unfinished concrete clock tower, and the valley beyond, fists raised in a salute suddenly become incomprehensible and anachronistic.

Night is falling now and Korçë's dim streetlights flicker on. The smoke from the power station boils up, brick red, against the darkening sky. We wander back down into town, stroll along the twilight boulevards beneath leafless trees, for spring comes late to this cold, dry plateau sheltered from the humid breezes of the Adriatic by the surrounding mountains. The sidewalks teem with citizens out for the evening stroll; the glare of tiny convenience store lamps punctuate the gathering dim. From crude impromptu cafés we hear now the thudding of rock and roll, now the whine of a gypsy clarinet, now the sweetly sentimental music of Korçë, voices singing in close harmony over a strumming background of mandolins. Koço leads me to Korçë's only private restaurant, a minuscule six-table establishment squeezed into a half-basement below the owner's home. "It's small; better than the hotel," he says. Rather an understatement. A flawless host, Koço will keep me company though he will not eat, especially not as my guest. No amount of cajoling can separate him from his Albanian pride. Besides, a family gathering is in progress, he tells me; he will eat then. I am torn between *qofte korçë*, Korçë-style meatballs, and a fish called *korani*, a trout-like denizen of Lake Ohrid which is said to be a throwback to another age, and can only be found here, and in the icy depths of Lake Baikal, in Siberia. Finally, I choose the fish. When, in a few moments, it arrives, it is beautifully presented and perfectly cooked.

By now I'm exhausted: from Easter services in Tirana, the long haul to Korçë and my stroll through town with Koço. But my hosts for the evening have other plans. Mr. Mustafa, a municipal official and former party operative ("He's a decent man," Koço had assured me as we crossed the street) with a telephone to prove it, insists that I meet his daughter Ilda, a pert, 19-year old blond who is in her second year at the Korçë teachers' college, and who speaks English with a mixture of textbook precision and impulsive innocence. These are still the provinces, the last refuge of dreams. "My friends, they want just to leave," she assures me, as her father looks on with a proud, if uncomprehending, smile. "But I am wanting to finish my school and be teacher in Albania."

Ilda is charming, her parents cordial and hospitable, the living room is warm and spotless and a German film with Albanian subtitles is playing on television. But I am battling to suppress ever more insistent yawns. Tomorrow morning we must get an early start for Voskopojë, I submit. Mr. Mustafa had assured me that he and his family are not religious, but in the bedroom, which the family has vacated to make room for their paying guest, a new copy of the Qur'an holds pride of place beneath a tiny candle.

Rejuvenated after a sound sleep in the utter stillness of the Korçë night, I awaken to the crowing of a cock and prepare for the rigors of the day ahead with a cup of herbal tea and thick slices of Albanian bread. My destination is the semi-mythical Vlach metropolis of Moskopol, known today as Voskopojë, which the Greeks called Moschopolis ("the city of fragrance"), nestled in the mountains 25 kilometers west of Korçë. Koço, who will be accompanying me, and Mr. Mustafa have located a car and driver. The car is a venerable Mercedes diesel; its driver, a no-less venerable man named Guri who operates a taxi service between Korçë and the Greek border, and speaks a smattering of highly idiomatic Greek. Don't attempt the road to Voskopojë in anything less than a four-wheel drive vehicle, people in Tirana had warned me, adding that there was probably no such thing in Korçë. "Nonsense," laughed Koço. "I make the trip several times a month. No problem; the snow has melted." Guri seems to catch the drift of the conversation, and nods emphatically.

We rattle off down the cobblestone lane, across the square, and through the outskirts of town, a wasteland of derelict textile factories, open-air automobile repair shops, stagnant mud holes the size of small lakes, and barbed wire fences fluttering with torn plastic. Not more than fifteen minutes outside of Korçë the roar of the car becomes deafening; then, in a clangor of metal, the muffler snaps off, dragging along beneath us, striking sparks on the dusty stones. Cursing, Guri brakes to a halt, yanks a wrench and a coil of wire from under the driver's seat and slides beneath the car to make repairs. We wait by the roadside—the quintessential Albanian pastime—as horse carts, minibuses and peasants riding three to a bicycle straggle across the windswept plateau and Guri grunts and puffs. A half-hour later the muffler is back in place, tenuously held by a length of wire.

The road to Voskopojë climbs through sparse groves of cedar, deforested by timber smugglers after the fall of the regime. The half-muffled Mercedes labors upward, swerving around the largest rocks in the roadway, pitching and yawing like an overloaded barge in the ruts. Then as we top a rise, a green valley bisected by a meandering stream spreads out before us. Koço points to heaps of stone, cyclopean ruins strewn on the hillsides: these used to be churches. Further off lay the remains of the great sheep farms that brought the region its prosperity when, at the end of the seventeenth and the beginning of the eighteenth century, Voskopojë flourished as the intellectual, commercial and cultural capital of the southern Balkans.

At its pinnacle, the city boasted Greek schools—for Greek was the language of the Orthodox Church that itself enjoyed protected status and exclusive privilege in the Ottoman *millet* system—printing presses that produced great numbers of books, and a library.[101] But though it also contained an admixture of Albanians and southern Slavs (were they Bulgars or Slavo-Macedonians?) who contrived to live in multi-ethnic harmony for the better part of a century, Voskopojë was, above all, a Vlach city.

This may have been because, in Voskopojë, the collusion between the Ottoman authorities and their Orthodox vassals was both particularly acute and fecund. Voskopojë's Vlachs, those Latinized Ilirians—or were they Latinized Greeks and Albanians, or were they southern Dacians perhaps, which would make them distant relatives of the Romanians?—whose vast flocks produced much of the empire's wool and cheese, enjoyed the direct protection of the Validé Sultan, the sultan's mother, and later of a *firman* issued by the Sublime Porte granting the city mercantile and religious prerogatives unique in the Ottoman state. Vlach caravans made up of hundreds of pack-horses traveled the length and breadth of the peninsula, Vlach traders established wealthy mercantile houses in Budapest and Vienna. Come the end of the eighteenth century, they all but controlled Balkan trade.

Early that same century the city's population had soared to between 40,000 and 60,000 souls. Their largesse notwithstanding, the Ottomans refused to recognize or permit the use of the Vlach and Albanian tongues. Greek was the language of the *Rum Millet*—and the Orthodox Patriarchy willingly complied.[102] Pupils in the Church-run schools of Voskopojë were, as a Greek source delicately puts it, "allophones"—that is, non-Greek speakers who were to be assimilated, via the Greek language, into the emergent Greek national body. "So it was that eminent men of letters concluded that grammars must be established for these languages, that is to say that there should be devised, for each among them, an Alphabet and its utilization for the composition of pedagogical, and ecclesiastical books, and most importantly, dictionaries. It was their belief that their charges, upon realization of the imperfections and incapacity of their respective dialects to plumb the lofty concepts which Greek alone was capable of expressing, and having been drawn to the profundity of these concepts, would henceforth become fervent defenders and advocates of the Hellenic tongue, and thence become as one, in body and in soul, with their Greek-speaking brethren."[103]

At its zenith Voskopojë counted 28 churches, Koço tells me as we saunter down a manure-clogged cobblestone street between stone walls topped by barbed-wire fences. On our left lies the shell of the town's House of Culture, now occupied by a gaggle of free-range geese. A man is mending the fence separating his property from the road. I address him in Greek and he responds, warily, to my questions about his place of residence. "I go back and forth," he says, rather vaguely, with the unmistakable thick vowels of the Vlach accent.

"In Voskopojë you cannot tell for sure who is Albanian, who is Vlach and who is Greek," Koço volunteers. Had he only added 'Macedonian,' who also inhabit these parts, he would have encapsulated the entire south Balkan identitarian enigma. We turn into the courtyard of Saint Nicholas's church, the largest of the five which still stand in Voskopojë. Beneath a wooden gallery, the outside wall of the church is adorned with frescos defaced not by the Turks, but by a generation of Albanian atheists. Inside, far from the wan spring sunlight, the cold is bone-chilling. From the darkness a pope materializes, and lights several large tapers. Then, leading us over to the wall, he shows us the secret cache where the faithful concealed the accouterments—the chalices and the chasubles—of the divine liturgy during the 25 years of atheist repression.

"Look here," whispers Koço with a note of urgent excitement in his voice as he snaps on a cigarette lighter. The flickering flame casts an unsteady light on a darkly luminous wall painting. "This is the fresco I restored; it was painted by master Onufri, in the seventeenth century. There is nothing like it in the whole Balkans. Here, in the corner, you can see a peasant tilling the fields. And over here, look, the benefactor standing in front of the church he built."

We walk back through the village, fording a brook, toward the Church of the Holy Virgin, where Koço has also done restoration work. Along the way a man hoeing a field stops to greet us with a wave of the hand. We stop, and he comes over. "Bonjour!" he says, in halting, though grammatically impeccable French. The man's name is Theodor Falo, he is 70 years old, and a graduate of the Lycée français in Korçë. "They destroyed our city seven times over," he relates, leaning his chin on his hoe handle, a cloth cap shading his small, blue eyes. The first time was in 1769, by Albanians loyal to the local Turkish pasha. Then came Ali Pasha's men. The Turks had granted Voskopojë royal protection; they couldn't very well destroy it, so they set their local vassals to the task. What disturbed them most was that the city might demand political autonomy to match its economic and cultural autonomy." What Monsieur Falo, bright-eyed and alert, avoids saying is who would have sought political autonomy? The Albanians, the Greeks, or perhaps those elusive half-persons who seem destined to remain forever a nomadic minority, the Vlachs?

Even in its ruined state, Voskopojë is rich with its invisible but almost palpable legacy. In this high, remote corner of the southern Balkans where ethnic projects and national consciousness intersect and overlap, often bloodily, and where definitions snap into focus and just as quickly blur, attempting to set out the contours of the nation-state seems an exercise as futile as sowing the desert and plowing the sea.

A few hundred families inhabit the once-flourishing Voskopojë plateau, descendants of survivors of the last sack of the town, at the hands of a band of Albanian irregulars in 1916. The French Army of the Orient, billeted a few dozen kilometers away in Korçë, looked on impassively as the defenders perished and its churches burned. We shall find nowhere to eat here, Koço informs me.

One hour later, muffler repairs still holding, we are back in Korçë, hunched over steaming plates of *qofte* redolent with onions and lemon in the basement restaurant. Then Koço leads me to the *pièce de résistance*, his pride and joy, the national museum of medieval art which occupies a former church. Down a narrow lane lies the former Greek consulate where, in the months leading up to World War II, the Nobel Prize winning poet George Seferis lived and worked.

"Now we can say it out loud: medieval really means Byzantine," Koço laughs, as he walks me along walls of icons, many of them rescued *in extremis* from churches scheduled for demolition, then restored by his loving hand. In their clarity, brilliance and power, in the radiant glow of vermilion against burnished gold leaf, they rival the collection in the museum of Kastoria, a Greek city only 80 kilometers southeast, but a world away. "These are the work of master Onufri, and here, here is an icon by the Zografi brothers, the founders of the Korçë school of icon painting."

As we leave the museum, a boisterous wedding party rushes in. Is it my imagination, or do I hear the distant strumming of mandolins?

The hour is late. I hope to reach Ohrid in time to catch the late bus for Skopje, the Macedonian capital. Guri's car waits outside the museum, to carry me to the frontier. Unexpectedly, Koço leaps in beside me and we rattle northeast out of Korçë. My last glimpse of the city is the towering plume of coal smoke from the power plant. Two hours later, on the narrow road carved out of the cliff face between Enver Hoxha's Lake Ohrid summer quarters and the Macedonian monastery of Sveti Naum, we part. I strike a poor bargain with an Albanian taxi driver to take me to Ohrid, and we pass into Macedonia. Albania was behind me, but not the Albanians.

Chapter 5

THE KOSOVA FLYER

One hour north of Skopje, in a valley between scrub-splotched hills, the bus grinds to a halt at the border crossing that separates the Republic of Macedonia (which the oxymoronical international community calls FYROM) from the truncated state known euphemistically as New Yugoslavia. From 1945 until 1991, no frontier existed in this forsaken place. Nothing but a dotted line on a map delineated the northern limits of the once-autonomous Federal Republic of Macedonia. Today, four years into the bright era of the New World Order, the UN embargo surveillance post at the border bristles with razor wire. The token American military force which patrols the Macedonian side of the border, under UN colors, but really free-lancing, as is Washington's custom in these and other parts, is well out of sight, though not out of mind.

On this gray, windy morning of Saint George's eve, the Orthodox festival that signals the end of winter, no UN observers appear to be observing. Perhaps they are checking for contraband cargo through x-ray binoculars from their sandbagged positions on the hillside? Perhaps they are sleeping off their latest R&R leave in sinful Salonica? Dozens of TIR trucks are backed up waiting for clearance to enter Europe's pariah state. The drivers slouch in their cabs, doing what trans-Balkan truck drivers do much of the time. They wait, inching ahead by one or two truck-lengths, then stop again, sometimes for days on end, before clearing the border and heading north fully loaded (with illicit cargo, guns or motor fuel?) or south, empty.

The twice-daily bus trip from Skopje to Prishtina reminds me, as does my own constantly refocusing Balkan mission of inquiry and fascination, of Zeno's second paradox. In it I, like swift-footed Achilles, race against the tortoise of history. For every ten meters Achilles runs, the beast plods one; for every meter, the tortoise crawls a decimeter; for every decimeter, a centimeter and so on into infinity.[104] This is not a bad thing, and a salutary antidote to the contemporary myth of constant acceleration. Finally, only those who make haste with ever diminishing speed, never overtaking their prey and never reaching the finish line, can appreciate the minutest fissures and blisters of the human landscape, can fall happily through the interstices in the surface of things and into the crevasses of the particular.

The Kosova Flyer crawls between two "countries" (here the word cannot be written without the irony of quotation marks) which are ostensibly Slavic, two societies deeply divided against themselves over the rights—and the place—of a substantial minority which would feel more at home in a state of its own. One of them, the putative Former Yugoslav Republic of Macedonia, is the homeland of those southernmost, and most ethnically ambiguous of the Slavs, the Macedonians. Its northern neighbor Serbia has become the dominant component of the third-time (first as tragedy, second as farce...) new New Yugoslavia following on the premeditated internal demolition of its Titoite predecessor ably assisted by the usual coalition of Western cold warriors metamorphosed into gigantic free-market cockroaches. On the bus the paradox is enveloped, as things often are in these parts, in Balkan irony: with the exception of the driver, there are no Slavs, only Albanians, those prickly minoritarians, those odd men out of the southern Balkans.

Formalities on the Macedonian side are cursory. The travelers are Macedonian citizens whose failure to return would not cause Skopje to grieve. But as the bus churns across the no-man's-land, the atmosphere suddenly becomes one of nervous anticipation. Serbian border guards wearing blue berets and armed with pistols, cartridge belts and automatic rifles bark out a series of peremptory commands; we climb down from the bus and line up, nervously, at curbside in the customs' shed. While two militiamen search the bus—including the engine compartment—others go through the passengers' meager luggage, their cheap suitcases, plastic bags, and cardboard boxes. One man, who had clambered aboard the bus at the last minute in Skopje with a load of two voluminous plastic sacks which appeared to contain empty cans, is summarily pulled aside. Later, relieved of his cargo, he boards the bus with a doleful look on his face.

The universal rule of travel in areas where armed uncertainty prevails is a simple one: always smile at the men with the guns. This group of passengers, and I along with them, are as good-natured a lot as you could hope to find, grinning and shuffling. The Serbian officer who checks our documents is manifestly bored with yet another cargo of obsequious Albanians, each one with an unlikely story and possibly a counterfeit visa. Why are these people coming north? I imagine him saying to himself. To subvert the fragile stability of Kosova? To alter the already tragic demographic imbalance between Serbs and Shqiptars which has transformed us Serbs into a minority in our historic lands? Of course, the officer may simply be bored with the numbing sameness of his lot: to check face after face against picture after picture, to scrutinize passport upon passport, to keep a gruff upper lip. Ah for a seat the office beside the stove, for a flask of plum brandy, for the little cottage in Bukovina or for the Belgrade apartment.

He raises his eyebrows at the sight of my passport. Canada, as an ardent supporter of the UN and its—the word catches in my craw—peacekeeping mission in ex-Yugoslavia, is no longer the great and good friend of Serbian officialdom it may once have been. I had been told brusquely at the Yugoslav embassy in Athens that it would be impossible to visit Kosova for whatever purpose. Diplomatic strings had been pulled. Authorization had finally been granted, as a personal favor to a Greek diplomat friend for services rendered. But by that time I had left the city for Tirana. My visa, I hoped, would be waiting for me there. This is the visa, issued in the Albanian capital, which the officer is now inspecting, intent on discovering some telltale flaw. Everything, however, is in perfect order, and most important, I am clearly not Albanian. "Dobro!" he grunts, snaps my passport closed and hands it back to me.

Hours later the bus discharges its passengers on the weed-grown fringe of the expressway on the outskirts of Prishtina, just short of the finish line. Soon I am gazing from the grimy window of my room in the Grand Hotel over a deserted, weed-grown commercial concourse of broken windows, dark shops and warped public lighting standards. In middle-distance I can see the soccer stadium where the violent Albanian demonstrations of 1989 erupted, then spilled over into the city center leaving damage which has not yet, six years later, been repaired. The hotel is clammy, dank; the taps run only cold water. The UN embargo against rump Yugoslavia has bitten hard into dreary Prishtina in this cold spring of 1995. The room is to be settled on a daily basis, in hard currency, the grim-faced desk clerk informs me when I check in. Deutschmarks preferably, despite Germany's support for the Ustashes—shorthand in these parts for Croatian president Franjo Tudjman's U.S.-armed and trained regulars and his soldier of fortune irregular forces—in their assault on the Serbian nation. US dollars will also do, despite Washington's leadership of the anti-Serb Holy Alliance. What will most certainly not do is New Yugoslav dinars, freshly printed with a fistful of zeros knocked off in an attempt to check runaway hyper inflation.

A single phone call, the mention of a name given in Tirana or Tetovo, is enough to plunge me into the hidden Albanian universe of Kosova. Within an hour I have been met at the hotel entrance by a young woman named Shukrije Gashi. A journalist by trade, Shukrije now works, she tells me as we stroll off, as a teacher in the semi-clandestine parallel school system set up by the Kosovars. It happened in 1991, when Serbian and Albanian schools were segregated on order from Belgrade and 6,000 Albanian teachers were summarily cashiered. The previous year, the police, local government, hotels, all media and state-owned factories had been handed over to Serbs. And by autumn of 1992 at least 100,000 Albanians had lost their public-sector jobs (in a still-socialist economy), including 800 of Prishtina University's 900 academics.[105]

She is also—though she never admits this to be the case—to be my "minder" for the duration of my stay, setting up meetings, coordinating interviews and steering me away, with the appropriate dire warnings, from the clear and present danger of the Serbian police. Shukrije's employer is the shadowy government-in-waiting of the quite real but officially non-existent Republic of Kosova to which she, like most of the nearly two million Albanian-speaking Kosovars, owe their true allegiance.

We make our way rapidly through downtown Prishtina, where massive concrete structures have all but overwhelmed the few graceful late-Ottoman buildings that remain, cross a boulevard, and climb a flight of uneven steps into a half-completed concrete commercial gallery that looks and feels more like a bunker. On the second floor stretches a succession of cafés and restaurants, all of which are thronged with customers and roaring with voices. Cigarette smoke hangs in the air. The Kosovars smoke even more than the Greeks, that nation of sot weed fiends. We take a table in the corridor, where the din of rock music is slightly less ear-shattering, and as we wait for my first encounter, Shukrije gives me an encapsulated introduction to contemporary Kosovar reality. "Here in Kosova there are Serbs, Turks, Montenegrins and Gypsies, but we Albanians are 90 percent of the population."

Only a handful of Kosovars are regularly employed, she continues, as I glance around me at the customers in the café. Many are well-dressed, and seem, if not prosperous, at least comfortable. Amidst the glitter of glass and chrome, the hiss of espresso machines and the clink of cups, these people (are they the nucleus of an emergent Albanian middle class?) lack the downtrodden indigence that stalks the streets outside. We are Europeans, affirms their appearance. But they are marooned in a place which, while geographically European, is not seen by Europe as a part of itself, a place like Muslim Bosnia. In fact, Kosova may well be seen in Paris and London as Muslim Bosnia surely is: an unwanted excrescence, a trouble maker, an undesirable long-alienated relative, an embarrassment, an intruder, an Other. Shukrije, intense almost to a fault, has been following my eyes, attempting to read my thoughts. "Most people cannot work in offices or in government job," she says. "So they open shops, operate pirate taxis, or sell cigarettes on the street and in the cafés. But our main source of money is remittances from workers in Europe."

While we chat and sip our cappuccino—Turkish coffee, once the national beverage, has become as passé here as it has in Tirana—a constant stream of cigarette sellers and newspaper vendors work the tables, moving silently from one group of customers to another. Some are pre-adolescents, girls and boys; others are gray-haired men wearing the round-peaked Albanian skull-cap. "Wages in our parallel system are $35 a month for high-school teachers like me, $65 for university professors. But we are losing our hopes for the future. Most of our young people try to get out. Every day, busloads of workers leave for Switzerland and Germany and Austria, and God knows where."

"We Albanians are a hunted species," she says, advancing an argument I was to hear repeatedly, like an operatic prefiguring, a leitmotif which was to recur again and again, a distant murmur of tragedy both foreshadowed and present. "As far as the Serbs are concerned, we're a foreign body, a cancer. You won't find a single Albanian who believes the people killed by the police were victims of 'accidents.' Me, I spent two years in prison for the crime of supporting the autonomist movement here. The police, they killed my fiancé. There's nothing between us and the Serbs but hatred."

As she speaks, dark eyes sparking, a fastidiously-dressed, gray-haired gentleman carrying a large envelope takes a seat at our table. He is Azem Shkreli, a former chairman of the Yugoslavia Writers' League, the national poet of Kosova, and the first of the Kosovar Albanian intellectuals I was to meet. In happier days, such an encounter would have taken place in an office at the university, or perhaps at the newspaper *Rilindja* ("Rebirth"), the Prishtina daily shut down by the Serb authorities and now published in Switzerland and distributed clandestinely, or at the Kosova Film studios which he used to head. No longer. Mr. Shkreli's office, like that of most of his colleagues, is now a chair in a noisy coffee-house. His receptionist, the waiter. His secretary, a stubby pencil.

Poetry in the West has long since slipped into the silent folds of hyperindividualism or the hermetic obscurity of postmodernist discourses, I observe. Is such the case here? Not in Kosova, Mr. Shkreli assures me, as Shukrije translates. "Our role is a national one, because of the situation we find ourselves in. A poet cannot live apart from the disintegration of the social life all around him. We cannot be as writers in other countries. Maybe we will be more lyrical, more modern when we no longer must bear the burden of our historical circumstances."

Should I venture that lyricism and modernity were no better guarantee of poetic eloquence than free-market democracy? Suggest that repression invests the word with power enough to make the dictator cringe? Of course not. This was the territory cultivated by Philip Roth in his discussions with the Eastern European writers and poets who had suffered the cruelest humiliations even as their work eroded the foundations of the totalitarian state. All things being equal, many told Roth, they preferred their freedom and its concomitant insignificance.

As Mr. Shkreli explains, language, the poet's raw material, is also the unbending backbone of Albanian national consciousness. To Shukrije's approving nods, he tells me: "Our language is perhaps the most important part of our struggle; it keeps us from being assimilated. We are under fierce repression in all aspects of our national life. Our language is what keeps us alive." I thought of Québec, its hair-trigger sensibilities, its devotion to and shame at its language.

But removal from Albanian national life continues to be Kosova's angry, festering wound. To the south-west, in the city of Prizren, following the 1878 Congress of Berlin—the first massive redivision of the Balkans by the European powers—was held the conference that launched the Albanian national movement, discretely supported by the Sublime Porte which saw it as a counterweight to the onrushing European juggernaut. Such was the complexity of religious, tribal and regional loyalties in the disintegrating empire, that the Young Turk revolution was welcomed in the Vilayet of Ioannina, to the south, while in the north the Kosova and Shkoder vilayets, known for their Islamic orthodoxy, remained cool to the new regime. As late as June, 1911, when Young Turk puppet Sultan Mehmed V arrived in Prishtina by way of Salonica for the anniversary of the battle of Kosovo Polje, he was given a chilly reception.[106]

The nascent national movement had limited its demands to the amalgamation of the four Albanian vilayets into one autonomous pashalik within the empire. But revolt, this time against the ultra-nationalist Young Turks, had already broken out in the region. It was fueled by the realization that the great powers were intent on carving up and distributing precisely these four vilayets, and that Istanbul was powerless to halt the onslaught. The movement, whipped along by the outbreak of war against Turkey in the Balkans, spread like wildfire through tinder-dry woods. It culminated in the declaration of Albanian statehood in the southern coastal city of Vlorë, in November, 1912. In May, 1913, the London Conference, attempting to reconcile Austrian and Italian demands for a greater ethnic Albania with Serbian military occupation of what it insisted were its historical lands, drew a border-line which would forever exclude Kosova from the new national entity.

Kosova's—and Albania's—tortuous relations with Turkey are a pale reflection of its long and ambivalent encounter with Islam, the religion of the conqueror. When the Ottoman tide began to recede, slowly at first before the ideological thrust of Enlightenment Europe, then more rapidly as the combined forces of nationalism and imperialism began to formulate ideological propositions in political and military terms, it left behind Islamic islands on the land. Such were the Muslims of Bosnia, the Turks of Bulgaria, Macedonia and Greece, and the Muslim Albanians.

Several weeks earlier, in Tirana, an official at the Foreign Ministry had told me (a strictly personal opinion, he emphasized) that Islam had been instrumental in preserving Albanian national identity, particularly in the border region of Kosova. How did Mr. Shkreli, a self-convinced European, feel about this? "Our history is a paradox," he admits. "To resist the Turks, we Albanians accepted their religion. Islam protected our language and culture, because of our ongoing struggle against the conqueror."

I cannot escape the suspicion that Mr. Shkreli has been asked by some higher authority—who? where? Here in Prishtina, or perhaps in Tirana?—to make sure I understand that Albanians, Muslims or not, intend to stride resolutely into the new European dawn leaving their cumbersome cultural and religious heritage at the door like a pair of muddy mountaineer's clogs.

"We feel some shame at having accepted Islam," confesses the poet. "But this element is not so important to us. Today, our generation takes Albanian, not Islamic names. This is proof that Islam is foreign to us."

Still, no patriotic Albanian would dream of denying that his countrymen distinguished themselves at the highest levels of the Ottoman state, as soldiers and statesmen. Mr. Shkreli's embarrassment is mixed with pride, as in a complex dance of attraction and repulsion. "But they never forgot they were Albanians. In fact, they became the creators of Albanian culture. Cases of assimilation were very few."

Today a specter is haunting Kosova, a harbinger of that which tomorrow will surely haunt Albania as it reconstitutes its shattered religious past. In Prishtina, in Prizren, in Urosevac, in Pec and in Mitrovica, and in hundreds of villages, Albanians continue to attend Friday prayers at the mosque, and to observe the proscriptions of their faith even as their intellectual leadership rushes to redefine them as incipient secularists. A man I had encountered earlier in the café, a well-dressed local merchant whom I shall call Mahmoud, assured me with a sardonic grin: "Why should we Muslims forget our religion? I keep the fasts and don't drink alcohol, and I try to raise my family according to Islam. Does that mean I cannot be a European?"

Mr. Shkreli must now leave for his nightly classes in the parallel school system. As we part with a handshake he hands me the envelope. It contains a book of his poems in English translation. I open it:

Who are you, black owl, crying to me in the night
waking me, lovely, crazy, who are you,
black owl, sheltering my thoughts under
your left wing, proclaiming my sin, and
burning me on the pyre, and creating me anew
from ash and spittle, who are you
black owl...[107]

Darkness has fallen over Prishtina. On the central boulevard the shapes of evening strollers emerge from the mist beneath the bare branches of the trees that line the broad sidewalk. The acrid mist of coal smoke hangs in the air, wafted over the city from the huge thermal generating plant to the northwest. Armed Serbian militiamen stride purposefully along, and in the shadows huddle hot chestnut vendors, faces ruddy from the glowing embers of their braziers. On a light standard I notice a poster depicting a man jauntily attired in a bemedalled dress uniform with a gold-embroidered kepi. We go closer for a look. The foppish individual in the photograph is the infamous Zeljko Raznjatovic, the Montenegrin gangster better known as Arkan, best known in Serbia as a dashing womanizer. The Belgrade gutter press recently devoted multi-page spreads to his latest marriage with a popular singer, whispers Shukrije with a mixture of disgust and amusement. Arkan's Serbian reputation is surpassed only by his international notoriety as war criminal in the Bosnian theater.

Prominently displayed on the poster is the emblem I've seen crudely stenciled on walls throughout the city, the coat-of-arms of the Serb ultranationalists known as the four Cs—Cyrillic "S's" standing for Samo Sloga Srbina Spasava (Only United can the Serbs Survive)—surrounding a

Greek (sorry, make that Orthodox) cross. Prishtina, she adds with an ironic chuckle, is Arkan's electoral stronghold. As the Albanians have boycotted every Serbian election, the handful of Serbs in the city have returned their comic opera colonel with his Muslim blood thirst unopposed to parliament in Belgrade.

One hundred meters up the street from the Grand Hotel we part. As I cross the lobby, I catch a glimpse of a statuesque blond woman wearing a crimson dress and stiletto heels as she disappears down the staircase leading to the bar, enveloped by the raucous laughter and Serbian music pouring upward like Balkan bean soup overflowing a vat. Two fully-armed commandos in battle-dress are clanking back and forth in front of the elevators. Veering quickly to the left, I take the stairs. From my window the dim lights of Prishtina flicker in the darkness. Later, after midnight, I hear the unmistakable crack of automatic rifle fire before falling off to a fitful sleep.

Was that shooting I heard last night? I ask Shukrije the next morning at the café. "Probably," she shrugs. But the look on her face tells me that in Prishtina it's open season on Albanians. The Council for the Defense of Human Rights and Freedoms in Prishtina claims the "individual and collective rights of the Albanians are systematically and brutally violated in Kosova in all fields of life and work." The itemized bill of indictment makes scary reading. In 1994, 17 Albanian citizens died at the hands of the police, while more than 2000 were physically abused, most of them during police searches for clandestine weapons. In Kosova, Serbian police and paramilitary groups possess overwhelming firepower. And, like ruling minorities everywhere, they live in terror that the Albanians one day might take up arms.

Abdullah Karjagdiu, the slight, graying gentleman I had come to the café-bunker to meet on this sunny Saturday morning, is a continuously erupting volcano of nationalist excitement and anti-Serb vehemence. My hosts' perspicacity in selecting this place as a venue is slowly sinking in. The bunker is a tacit no-go zone for the Serbian authority. Shops here are run by Albanians sympathetic to the movement; the customers are all Albanians constantly table hopping or moving about in unpredictable ways; an office could be easily bugged, but not this place, where the noise and confusion would confound the most sophisticated listening or surveillance system; the cigarette resellers and newspaper hawkers function as eyes and ears, bringing news of incipient police and militia movements from the street. Here we may speak frankly, protected by a thick, resilient human blanket.

From the instant he sits down and orders the first of a string of espressos, until we part more than two hours later, Mr. Karjagdiu bombards me with salvo upon salvo of historical anecdote, couched in the uplifting, resonant prose of a skilled rhetorician. A former professor of English literature at Prishtina University, when it operated equally in Albanian and Serbian during the golden years of the autonomy devised by Tito to keep Yugoslavia's dominant Serbs under on a short leash, Abdullah Karjagdiu was a founding member of the Yugoslavia-Canada friendship association, translated Faulkner, Shaw and Saroyan, lectured on Norththrop Frye, specialized in Byron and the Albanians, and even—*mirabili dictu*—visited Montréal several decades ago and remembers the city fondly.

Horizons have shrunk. Four years after the mass dismissal of Albanian faculty members from the University of Prishtina by the Serbian authorities, Mr. Karjagdiu, deprived of his passport like his colleagues, has nowhere to go. Enough to explain any man's rancor. But at the same time, in this microcosm of national yearning set against a wider world where the mighty now strive to cast nationalist movements as tribal throwbacks, echoes of a primitive, bloody past resound. An uncomfortable note of anachronism persists, like the involuntary dissonance of badly tuned violins. Didn't these people know that nationalism was passé, that the global marketplace was tomorrow's paradigm, that the refinements of cosmopolitanism (against which Sarajevo, like its forerunner Salonica 80 years earlier, is only an unfortunate exception which confirms the rule) far outweighed the moody, bloody-minded fixations of ethnic identity? Well, didn't they?

But don't the Serbs, I venture cautiously, claim Kosova as their historic homeland, the cradle of Serbia? "Ah!" he bursts out, primed for the question. "If that's so, then where are the kids? You know what? We're victims of the use of history by a more powerful neighbor. They characterize us as savages, devils. But we are descendants of the Illyrians, the oldest race in Europe."

When the Albanian uprisings of 1912 shook the pillars of the Ottoman state, the Serbs marched southwest, claiming that they were liberating their own lands. But these same lands, argues Mr. Karjagdiu, had been part of Turkey since the fateful engagement at Kosovo Polje in 1389, more than 500 years before, and had been inhabited by Albanians for much longer. "In 1913, we were delivered from the Turks and handed over to a much more vicious oppressor. Half of our population and our lands were left outside the national borders. Millions of Albanians were expelled to Turkey, 60,000 were executed by the Serbian army whose job was to liberate their Slav brethren by mass murder of our people. The Serbs were worse than the Turks. But still our numbers grew. It was a miracle which makes me believe in God."

Rule of thumb: whatever is true of Albania proper is doubly, triply true of Kosova, focal point of the historical contradictions that have shaped the Albanians' self-perception, or to use the more fashionable but equally vain encapsulation, their sense of imagined community. Sensibilities on the periphery have always been hypertrophied; vulnerability exacerbated by the proximity of the Other, self-definition shaped by the certainty, painful and indelible, of what one is not. Yes, thunders Mr. Karjagdiu, whose gesticulation and stentorian tones hardly disturb the matinal torpor of the café, we Albanians were the best warriors in the Ottoman empire, but we also staged 35 or 40 uprisings against Turkey. "No other nation both led the state and fought against it as an occupying power. Was there any comparable example of resistance among the Greeks, the Bulgarians? But Europe abandoned us to the Turks, just like they abandoned the Poles to the Russians. That's why we are very cautious about things today."

"The Turks made the greatest efforts to assimilate the people who fought hardest against them," he continues, the words flowing from his tongue with the eloquence of the outraged and the abused. "And where was the staunchest resistance? In Albania, of course. Which is why the Turks were determined to have such fighters in their ranks. But at the end, when their empire was collapsing, they used Albania, then left us at the mercy of our enemies. They were happy to concede our lands to the Serbs in order to protect Istanbul!"

My talk with Abdullah Karjagdiu cannot properly be described as an interview. How dull the standard journalistic question and answer compared with the vigor and the sweep of his arguments—which we both understand to be dramatized, schematic versions of historical fact, exemplary narratives in which the magnitude and the horror of oppression aggrandize and ennoble its victims. Here, in the verbal flux, the secondary themes can be heard, oddly enough, in their absence: it is as if the bright colors and hard-edged lines of the painting held up for contemplation have at the same time secreted a counter-image, like the shadowy outline on the shroud of Turin. But let me not plummet down the slippery slope into post-modernism.

So it was that the Bucharest Conference of August 1913 endorsed an Albanian frontier which assigned Kosova, and the Albanian territories in Macedonia, to Serbia. Mutual frustration and decades of conflict were the result. Serbia, fresh from victories in the Balkan Wars first against Turkey, then Bulgaria, found its access to the Adriatic blocked by the new Albanian state, which enjoyed the support of the Austro-Hungarian Empire and Italy.

Further north, Austrian annexation of Bosnia-Herzegovina in 1908 had lit the slow-burning Balkan fuse which led straight to the European powder keg. The events of Sarajevo in August, 1914, were but an epiphenomenon, a tragic denouement of an infernal process set in motion decades earlier. One that seems strikingly familiar today, in the last decade of the twentieth century as capitalism triumphant, determined to play out the logic of competition to its customary ultimate conclusion, slouches toward its rendezvous with fate.

Throughout the Balkans, the great powers of Western Europe had become objects of emulation. The national model they had created spread like a flesh-eating bacteria, attacking the tissues and the sinews of the multi-ethnic empires of the nineteenth century and reducing them to pulp. As the Hapsburg and the Ottoman states were swept away they left behind jagged fragments, racial or linguistic states intent on realizing national manifest destinies in a region where such destinies intersected, overlapped and conflicted. In Kosova, the Serbian authorities closed Albanian schools and sent settlers to people the newly liberated lands. When the Austro-Hungarians occupied Albania between 1916 and 1918, they promptly reopened the Albanian schools and allowed the Albanian flag to fly, establishing a precedent for Germanic sympathy toward the Kosovars—and Kosovar sympathy for Germany.[108]

The Paris Peace Conference which opened in January, 1919, laid down boundaries between the Kingdom of the South Slavs (the Serbs, the Croats and the Slovenes)—the first Yugoslavia—and the countries surrounding it. While Albania now existed, albeit as an impoverished semi-satellite of Italy, Kosova languished under a doctrine of assimilation which denied outright the existence of its Albanian population, reclassified as "Turk" or "Muslim." "The Serbs purified our lands, under the benevolent supervision of Europe," growls Mr. Karjagdiu. "Hundreds of thousands were sent into exile to Turkey, where their descendants are still living. They know their forefathers were expelled by the Yugoslavs between the two World Wars."

When Italy invaded Albania in 1939, officializing a de facto occupation that had begun several years before, the Kosovars looked on with fascinated anticipation. Relief was not long in coming. Mussolini's hapless troops may have been mauled by Greece in the bitter Albanian campaign of 1940, but they were soon rescued by their German allies, and handed Albania—including Kosova and western Macedonia—as a consolation prize. The Italians reopened Albanian schools in the region, for the first time since 1918. For the unredeemed nationalists of Prishtina, chafing under Serbian domination, it was a dream come true, and like all dreams delivered by a conqueror, soon would become its opposite.

"The Italians allowed our national consciousness to re-emerge. Finally, the Kosovars could visit their families in Albania. There was confusion among the youth, and the intellectuals. The invaders acted almost like liberators. The Serbs, they pleaded with the Albanians to help them, and protect them. But they had never done the same for us. It's a fact; there was large-scale collaboration in Kosova. Our schools were opened, our customs were respected. It's easy to understand why people went over to the 'wrong' side."

Mr. Karjagdiu does not tell me that the Germans, repeating their success in Croatia, organized an SS Division named for the national hero Skanderbeg which campaigned for the extermination of the Serbian population.[109] In fact, Nazi tactics throughout the Balkans played on the fear of Serb domination—from which acceptance of the doctrine of the sub-human nature of the Slavic peoples was but a small step—among the Croats, the Bosnians, the Albanians and the Bulgarians. These tactics played as well, of course, on the obsession with national aggrandizement, and found eager ears and willing allies.

Curiously, the Albanian communists never lifted a finger to link Kosova with Albania proper. Perhaps Enver Hoxha's partisans believed that a Balkan federation led by Tito would somehow join Kosova in a fraternal embrace with the motherland. Perhaps Hoxha and Tito had made a deal: the Albanians would drop their claims to the province in return for Yugoslav assistance against the Nazis and their local collaborators. "You see, back then internationalism made all talk of borders superfluous," he says. "But the fascists and the communists had one thing in common: neither were for our interests as Albanians."

When the second Yugoslavia was founded under Tito's ironclad leadership, the promised plebiscite to decide the future of Kosova was indefinitely postponed. "In fact, they granted us autonomy to avoid the plebiscite. But their attempts to make us Albanians hate each other failed. The second Yugoslavia was destroyed right here where you're sitting, in Kosova. A third Yugoslavia is impossible," he rasps, in a voice grown hoarse from two hours of impassioned exposition. "The mothers of Albania have saved our country by bearing more sons and daughters. Under the Turks they did it; under the Slavs; under the communists. Ninety percent of our people are under 27. And they're ready to fight; ready to die for their country."

We push back our chairs from the table, rise to our feet to say good-bye. Abdullah Karjagdiu holds no official position in the parallel government that governs Kosova's Albanians. His views are probably extreme enough to set the teeth of Dr. Ibrahim Rugova, president of the semi-clandestine Republic of Kosova, on edge. But he speaks from a heart heavy with grievance, bitterness, resentment and wounded pride. It was a voice I was to hear again and again before I departed Prishtina. Not so much the voice of resignation as the voice of anger.

I yearn for fresh air. My nerves are buzzing, my lungs burning, my ears ringing from the smoke, the incessant coffee, and the loud conversation of the bunker. Let's take a stroll, and find some *byrek* for lunch, I suggest to Shukrije. Anything would be better than the Grand Hotel Prishtina, where I had paid more than $40 (US) for a plate of spaghetti with a greasy, insipid sauce the night before. "I know just the place," she says. "The best Albanian *byrek* in town, and afterward, we can go to my house. I want you to meet my family."

Prishtina is built on a series of hills overlooking the valley of Kosovo Polje—the field of the blackbirds—where the fateful battle took place. The town center is all late Yugoslav brutalism: empty concrete façades, too much aluminum and glass, a few brightly painted modern apartment buildings. It has the look and feel of a garrison: pairs of militiamen patrol the streets, arms at the ready. Armories are crammed with tanks and heavy artillery ready for rapid deployment. From the open windows of the officers' club comes the whistling and infectious throb of Serbian music and above it, shouting and raucous laughter.

But once past the Friday mosque, we enter into the Albanian donut that surrounds the Serbian hole. Here the buildings are ramshackle, built in the classic Turkish manner. Chewing our savory, steaming *byreks* we work our way downhill through the market place, and into the winding streets of old Prishtina. The high-rises and administrative buildings have vanished; only minarets puncture the skyline, and lead-clad mosque domes gleam in the cool, bleached sunlight.

Shukrije's family lives above the furniture shop operated by her father and an uncle. Through a half-open door I catch the spicy fragrance of fresh-turned wood, and spot a stack of cradles, as if to prove—had I ever doubted his word?—Mr. Karjagdiu's assurances about the heroic mothers of Albania. As we step into the house, the Gashi family, mother wearing *hijab*, is just sitting down on the floor to its midday meal, served in a large round platter on a low table in the oriental manner. I decline an invitation to join them, and sip tea. Shukrije's brother Mehti, an dark-eyed young man whose intensity matches that of his sister, rises from the family circle and plops down beside me on the sofa. He is 24 years old, a third-year medical student, he tells me in slow but precise English.

"There are about 200 of us studying medicine in the 'parallel' system. Our courses are given in the basement of a private home. Our professors are all graduates of European or North American universities, but as students we feel much frustration. With our diplomas, we will only be able to work in Kosova, or in Albania."

How much longer can the Kosovars go on studying in basements, living in the shadows? I ask Mehti. "How much longer? That depends on Europe, not on us," he responds with a frown of resignation. "But we need more than United Nations resolutions. You can see what good they did in Bosnia. If Europe and the U.S. don't help us, all we can do is wait. The Serbs are too strong. Maybe something will happen. We are not satisfied with the leadership of the parallel government. Our dream is to live in one Albanian state."

Here, in the politically naive formulation of an earnest young medical student dreaming of the future, lay the crux of the Kosova dilemma: the clash of illegitimate power against the unarmed force of moral legitimacy fueled by an incendiary sense of righteousness, sustained by an argument of historical necessity. And necessity, as the ancient Greeks knew well, alone could overrule the will of the gods.

Nationhood denied, as apprehended in the dusty streets and smoke-clogged cafés of Prishtina, and in the clandestine schools and medical clinics of hundreds of villages, is the aching tooth to which the tongue constantly returns, the unchanging bass drone that underlies a fleeting melody, an unseen force field that envelops and energizes, at once perceptible yet immaterial.

No visit to Kosova would be complete without an audience with Dr. Ibrahim Rugova, president of the putative Republic of Kosova. The diminutive leader, with his thick horn-rimmed glasses, high forehead and silk scarf knotted jauntily around his neck, was the living embodiment of the Kosovar personality: an affable yet hard-headed blend of caution and audacity, a gift for carefully calculated provocation and soothing reassurance. And, as befits the non-head of a non-state, a diplomatic tightrope walker of the first order.

The meeting, however, was not to be. Dr. Rugova had arrived in Tirana the day after I left, on his way to a tour of the Scandinavian countries where support for the Kosova cause is strong. Not the least striking aspect of this non-country is the effectiveness of its non-diplomacy. In the shack which houses the offices of the Kosova Information Center, I am handed a book on the Albanian democratic movement, replete with photographs of Dr. Rugova shaking hands with luminaries as diverse as Pope John Paul II (calculated to make the ferociously anti-popish Serbs gnash their teeth), the Swedish foreign minister and former United States Senator Robert Dole, would-be president and great friend of the Balkan peoples.

Encounters with the president, like breakfast with the ambassador, are the main course of mainstream journalism. They flatter our vanity, console us in our illusion that in perceiving the burnished surface as set before us by men of monstrous ego and even more monstrous desire, we can somehow grasp the inner mechanism of events and extract their secrets. We confuse the living press-release, the prevarication served over brioche and coffee, with the hard-bitten world of secret treaty and of international double-cross performed in subterranean situation rooms with red pencils, of which we will only become aware when armies begin to march or guided missiles begin to impact their targets. We are too often the foolish virgins, the faintly protesting handmaidens of deception, the naive purveyors of tainted messages.

These judgments may be too harsh, unfair to the handful of hardworking correspondents who do not live by the hidden motto: "When in doubt, make it up." And in speaking the issue, I am aware that suddenly I may have wandered too close to the deadly precincts of self-referentiality, as a careless climber, driven by curiosity and the rapture of danger, ventures too close to the lip of a live volcano. And still, the account of breakfast with the ambassador may be better than no account at all, particularly if one's media reading strategy is to believe the opposite of the broadcast account.

Of course Dr. Ibrahim Rugova, an accomplished poet, former student of French semiotician Roland Barthes, a man of modesty and a non-president to boot, would have spoken his heart to me, revealed what promises he has obtained from Senator Dole; explained the price of his policy of passive resistance and the source of the funding that keeps his movement afloat. You bet your silk neck-scarf he would. In the event, I never met the non-president, and so side-stepped the moral dilemma. As consolation, though, the faithful Shukrije has arranged for me to meet one of Dr. Rugova's adjutants, a man named Hydajet Hyseni, vice-president of the Democratic League of Kosova.

I was glad I did. Like his mentor Dr. Rugova, Mr. Hyseni is member of the Kosova Writer's Association. Unlike the president, Mr. Hyseni, around whose eyes I detect a mantle of sadness (or is it the disabused remoteness of the realist), has spent several years in the revolutionary schools of the Yugoslav prison system. His first crimes, he relates in measured French, pausing to sip his coffee (for we are back in the bunker café, which is also the Democratic League's public relations office), were those of the written word. "In 1978, the year I went to work as a journalist at 'Rilindja,' the secret police grabbed me in the middle of the market place, took me to a hideaway in the mountains, and tried to make me admit I was the author of seditious poems. What they really wanted to do was to turn me into a collaborator. Of course I refused."

Marshall Tito was still alive then, and Kosova enjoyed relative autonomy. Back in Prishtina, Mr. Hyseni eluded his escorts and went underground for the next four years. "It was clear to us that when Tito died, everything would change in Yugoslavia. Sure enough, within a year of his death Belgrade restored an openly anti-Albanian policy."

In March, 1981, Albanian students at the University of Prishtina demonstrated over social issues. The authorities denounced the protest as hooliganism and began arresting student organizers. The students reacted with a second demonstration, challenging the arrests. "They beat Albanian students, and violated university asylum; for us, it was as if they were attacking our cultural aspirations. Two weeks later came the great demonstration of 1 April, with more than 100,000 participants. It was the largest protest ever held in the so-called socialist bloc. This time we called openly for independence. It was a peaceful demonstration, but without warning the police and the militia opened fire. They claimed twelve died. But the real figure was more than 100."

As Mr. Hyseni's tale becomes more heartrending, his tone becomes calmer, more measured. "I was one of the organizers of the April 1 demonstration; they arrested me, put me on trial, sentenced me to 15 years. I spent four months in solitary. They tried everything: sleep deprivation, beatings, psychological torture. Then they sent me to a psychiatric clinic. All the time I kept telling them, 'just leave me alone.'"

Kosova was finally stripped of its autonomy in 1989, its status downgraded to that of a province of Serbia. In December of the same year, the Democratic League was founded. Less than a year later, in September 1990, the parliament of Kosova, meeting in the small town of Kaçanik, near the Macedonian border, proclaimed the republic. In 1991 Yugoslavia finally collapsed, hard on the heels of UN recognition of the independence of Slovenia, Croatia and Bosnia-Herzegovina. But it was too late for Kosova. The same international community which had demonstrated such flagrant disregard for internal borders when it drove the former federation into disintegration suddenly showed punctilious respect for Serbian claims to the once-autonomous region.

Meanwhile, Mr. Hyseni languished in prison in Belgrade. When he was set free, in 1991, the republic for which he had labored and suffered was now a virtual reality. Not the thing itself, but the image of the thing, a structure of imagination and potential, an ever-receding mirage and a government-in-waiting, rolled into one.

How much longer can the Kosovars keep faith in a passive strategy which appears to be playing into the hands of the Serbs? "Every day it becomes harder for us to keep up our non-violent policy. The Serbian government is taking advantage of our patience and our peaceful spirit. And we would feel more secure if the world community appreciated our approach as an alternative to the Bosnian or Chechen models."

Bosnia and Chechnya cast a long shadow across the southern Balkans, and nowhere is the shadow deeper than in Kosova. "It's true, our people are losing patience," admits Mr. Hyseni. "But what we've seen in Bosnia has made everyone think twice. You can have all the principles in the world, but they don't count for much against brute force. There are people in our movement who say we should abandon our passive strategy. What I fear is that if we begin violent resistance, it will touch off a catastrophe. This isn't Bosnia; it would be impossible to isolate a conflict within our frontiers."

"Wouldn't your ethnic brethren in Albania come to your assistance if trouble breaks out?"

"The Albanian people would never let the Kosovars down," comes the swift reply from a man who has never been to Albania, from a prisoner in his own house who cannot even obtain a passport, let alone an exit visa. "We're all from the same national body. But we are our own masters. We don't intend to insist on reunification, no matter how dear it is to us. What we want is independence for Kosova, within its historic borders."

Our meeting ends on a note of melancholy tinged with iron: "I don't know how much longer we can hold out. If the outside world doesn't help us, we won't be able to control the situation. Beware of the sudden anger of the quiet man."

On a Prishtina side-street, just around the corner from the mosque which has given space in its Qur'anic school to the Kosova Human Rights Defense Council, is the office of an angry man who is more than happy to speak his mind. Well-fed, effusive, the antithesis of the lean, self-effacing Mr. Hyseni, Bajram Kelmendi emanates the solidity and self-assurance of the successful lawyer (and the relative prosperity to prove it).

Mr. Kelmendi, Shukrije had informed me, enjoys a reputation as Prishtina's most skilled legal counsel, a fearless defender of his countrymen before the Serbian courts where every case involving a Kosovar becomes a political trial. The most frequent charge is "separatism," of working to reunite Kosova with Albania by force. "My courtroom strategy is to insist that no such crime exists. No force is being used to separate Kosova from Serbia. Opinions are being expressed, which is not a criminal offense. The defendants are not armed. They are simply Kosovars who don't want to live under Serb occupation. It's as simple as that."

The accused are always found guilty, he shrugs. The reason? Because they are Albanian. "Still, I defend them because these are political trials, and in them I can work to discredit the Serb state. If we are not present, international opinion would accept the Serb pretension that the trials are legitimate."

The lawyer, whose broad, polished desk is decorated with the red, double-headed eagle flag of Albania, offers the most outspoken criticism I've yet heard of non-president Rugova's policies. "Our movement has become passive," he blurts out. "The Albanian parties believe that the national question can be solved by dialogue. What they've done is to pacify our own population, hoping that the international community would support us. This is an illusion for which we will pay a high price. We are giving weapons to our opponents. The democratic movement is losing strength. We must find another way. More inventive people must take the leadership."

Instead of passive resistance, goes his prescription, the Kosovars should begin defending their integrity when attacked. "It's right and natural to defend yourself, isn't it? Look, if the Serbs intend to provoke a war in Kosova, I say let them come. An armed conflict here cannot be localized like in Bosnia. The international community couldn't sit on the sidelines; their interests would be directly involved. If there is going to be such a war, it would involve Albania, Macedonia, Greece and Turkey."

"Today Serbia can disguise the situation here as peace. But listen," he says, the pitch of his voice rising and his cadence accelerating, "if there's war in Kosova, even though Albania is weak, the Serbs aren't strong enough to crush us. How much longer can the international community justify aggression as an 'internal question?' They've totally compromised themselves in Bosnia, in Chechnya, in Kurdistan. But in the end, they'll have to fight."

"We may not have our own Skanderbeg," he says, and suddenly his voice softens, as he folds his hands on his desk. "But our people will find a way. Our generation is a sacrificed one. But our children will never accept to live under the Serbs. Either we free ourselves, or face elimination as a people."

As dusk falls, Shukrije and I retrace our steps back to the Qur'anic school in the courtyard of the neighborhood mosque. There, behind a door bearing an Arabic inscription, under a bare light-bulb, Sami Kurteshi is hunched over a computer, setting up, as he later explained, a Kosova e-mail service. Mr. Kurteshi, the Secretary General of the Council on Human Rights, is an "eighty-oner," the Kosovar equivalent of France's *soixantehuitards*, a member of the generation which, as students, staged the heroic and bloody Prishtina demonstrations of 1981 in support of Kosova autonomy. His eyes have the same sadness, the same darkness and pain I'd noticed in those of Hydajet Hyseni, and his smile—like a mark of Cain—is that of a man who mistrusts hope. Like Mr. Hyseni, Mr. Kurteshi is a graduate of the Yugoslav prison system and its graduate school, the solitary confinement cells of Belgrade. "I still can't really understand how I survived," he tells me. "They deprived me of sleep, but I kept exercising, to build up my strength. Finally, in late 1990 they released me, as part of a general amnesty for political prisoners."

Having experienced it on his own skin, Mr. Kurteshi shares with his fellow alumnus a healthy disrespect for violence as a solution to the woes of Kosova. "Whatever might happen," he assures me, with the quiet conviction of the righteous, "we'll have to live together with the Serbs. If there is a war, there will be winners and losers, and the losers will always be making ready for the next war, for new killings." The never-ending story of the Balkans.

Kosova's hope is also its incipient tragedy. "There is no dialogue, no communication between Serbs and Albanians," he explains. "The regime would like nothing better than for us to fight our Serb neighbors. But there is no inter-ethnic conflict, not for the moment. Of course, the politicians are always talking, but not the people whose lives and livelihoods are at stake. We live side by side, but we never meet. In our country we live on myths, and myths are more dangerous than guns."

> *We must not cherish illusions as to future developments of relations in Europe. This horrendous war will hardly be the last. We will still remain at the crossroads and be exposed once again to the first stroke of some new war."*
>
> —**Dr. Vasa Cubrilovic**, 1944[110]

MYTH, DISINGENUOUS AND DEADLY, thrusts into the sky above Kosovo Polje—the Field of the Blackbirds—in the shape of a roughhewn rectangular stone tower. On plaques embedded in the parapet, the armies of Prince Lazar Hrebeljanovic and of Sultan Mural I clash, their mortal trajectories frozen forever in bronze and polished by the caress of countless fingertips. On the treeless plain below, a mammoth cement works and the Kosova coal-fired power plant pump billowing yellow smoke into the cool spring air.

The morning of June 28, 1389, had dawned warm and clear. The Serbian knights and their European allies knelt as bearded popes intoned the liturgy of Saint Vitus, the fourth-century martyr whose feast is celebrated on this date. On Saint Vitus' eve, goes the legend, the angel Elijah had appeared to Prince Lazar, and offered him a choice. Military victory could be his, and with it an earthly realm; perhaps the restoration of Stefan Dusan's glorious yet short-lived Serbian kingdom which had collapsed 40 years earlier with Dusan's death. Or, announced the angel, he could chose martyrdom on the field of combat and gain the heavenly kingdom for eternity. Some say the prince chose; others claim that the angel chose for him.

To the southeast, the forces of Ottoman Sultan Murad I were drawn up in full battle array, under the green crescent flag. The Commander of the Faithful led one of the most formidable itinerant fighting machines ever to tread the bloody soil of the Balkan peninsula. We do not know if the Sultan had also been visited by an angel on the eve of battle, but in Islam, he who dies as a martyr for the faith will surely achieve paradise. That the conflict pitted one rapacious imperial host, bent on expansion, against another in defense of its lands and wealth, has faded into the insignificance of time past, into that curious warp where the base metal of greed, treachery and cowardice is transformed into the purest gold of legend to become—because fervently believed—the deepest truth. A cynic might argue that this is so partly due to the efforts of nationalist myth-makers. However constructed, the new truth possesses a transfiguring power that inhabits this site.

By day's end the field lay strewn with corpses. Prince Lazar's men had fought valiantly against impossible odds. Early in the day they appeared to have gained a tactical advantage until, inexplicably and tragically, one wing of their army under Vuk Brancovic, retired from the field. Legend also tells of a Serbian nobleman who, feigning surrender, made his way to Murad's tent there to assassinate the sultan with a poisoned dagger. From the summit of the monument, I can make out the small, domed Islamic shrine atop a lesser hill where Murad is said to be buried, and to which no visible path leads.

But the Turkish armies, made up of battle-hardened Anatolians and zealous new converts picked up along the way, outnumbered their Christian foes by two to one, and the slain sultan's son Bayazid proved an energetic and capable tactician. Urged on by the throb of drums and cymbals, the Muslim combatants sliced their way through the Serbian lines, their arrows a whispering torrent of death. Prince Lazar was captured and killed. While both leaders ascended to the promised heavenly kingdom, blackbirds in their millions picked clean the bodies of the dead. The road to conquest of the Balkans, a road that was eventually to lead to the outskirts of Vienna 200 years later, now lay open to the Ottoman juggernaut. The dream of a Greater Serbia which perished with Prince Lazar was to be resuscitated only when the ideology of nationalism swept across the peninsula like a flood tide half a millennium later.

600 years after the event—on June 28, 1989—the irresistible rise of Serbian president Slobodan Milosevic brought him here to Kosovo Polje. The collapse of Yugoslavia was, for its former leaders become feuding national warlords, all but an accomplished fact. Serbian grievances over under-representation in the life of the Titoist state had emerged as a powerful nationalist movement in a region where no slight is too small, no imagined humiliation too insignificant, where memory of the past is the memory of blood. So goes the doctrine of the nation as sacred repository of collective identity. To a cheering crowd of nearly two million Serbs come from every corner of crumbling Yugoslavia and from the Diaspora, Milosevic promised: "Serbian people, never again will you be humiliated."

Mitja, a tall, broad-shouldered young Serb I'd encountered at the Grand Hotel Prishtina, had agreed to drive me to the battlefield monument. Six years before, he had been one of those two million. "Milosevic?!" he snorts, dismissing the Serbian leader with a scornful wave of the hand, as if swatting away a bothersome insect. "Just another politician. We didn't come here because of Milosevic. We came here because this is our ancient Serbian homeland. No one can ever take it away from us."

Since the founding of Yugoslavia, first in its monarchical form, then as a socialist federation following World War II, the central authority had embraced the chimera of a South Slav state free of the embarrassing presence of non-Slav national minorities. The main obstacle was the Albanians, whose insistence on their prior ownership of the land, and prior cultural presence—they were, after all, the descendants of the Ilyrians, who had inhabited the region for three thousand years—made Belgrade's claims to Kosova look suspect, perhaps even hollow. In a 1937 memorandum entitled "The Expulsion of the Albanians" (for whom the Turkish word 'Arnaut' was used) Dr. Vasa Cubrilovic, then a political advisor to the monarchy and who was later to become a member of the *nomenklatura* and of the Academy of Arts and Sciences of Serbia, laid out an ambitious plan for the forced resettlement of the Kosova Albanians to Turkey and Albania proper, and for their replacement by Slav colonists. The plan, a master blueprint for ethnic cleansing before the term had become fashionable, was promptly put into operation, only to be forestalled by the onset of war.[111]

Tito had structured post-war Yugoslavia as an elaborate system of counterweights designed to restrict Serbian power. When Kosova's autonomous status was abolished after his death, claim the Kosovars, the Cubrilovic plan was silently resurrected, with emigration to Western Europe replacing forced relocation to Turkey. Mitja, born in a small village near Belgrade, now lives in Prishtina, perched forlornly atop a lonely Serbian islet surrounded by a hostile Albanian sea. He and his fellow colonists will soon be joined by Serb refugees fleeing the Croatian army's blitzkrieg in Krajina and from the NATO-imposed partition of Bosnia-Herzegovina.

Let us be blunt. The colonists are living in a fool's paradise. No more than the Palestinians will politely agree to vanish, leaving their lands to swaggering, gun-happy self-styled settlers from Brooklyn, no more than the French-speaking Québécois will obligingly dissolve themselves in a pluriethnic English-speaking sea, the Kosovars cannot be relied upon to pack their bags and slink away, leaving behind their prickly Albanicity. Whatever the forces that shape national consciousness—the sense of imaginary community, the Marxist trio of common geographical, cultural and economic space, or Michael Ignatieff's alliterative formula of blood and belonging—they have, in Kosova, bred a stern, unbending attachment to the need for a distinct Albanian political entity. Ultimately, this entity would be a single national homeland for all the Albanians: a Greater Albania of seven million, a new, potentially explosive radical in the complex, unstable Balkan molecule.

No Albanian I encountered, in Tirana, in Prishtina or in Tetovo, would ever admit to such a thing...for the record. In the name of stability, existing borders cannot be changed, agree the politicians and ministers and spokesmen I met, ever anxious to please their new European or North American mentors. But, they quickly add with a gleam in their eye, the Albanian question is the last unresolved national dilemma in the region. Few Kosovars can believe, in their heart of hearts, that the semi-independent Kosova promised by Dr. Ibrahim Rugova's Democratic League would not eventually vote, in the most free and democratic way, to attach itself to Albania. Likewise, a breakup of fragile Macedonia would certainly send its numerically powerful and well-organized Albanian minority hurtling into the embrace of Tirana for protection. Happy to oblige its unredeemed brethren, the Albanian government promptly recognized the phantom Kosova republic. In 1992, Albanian president Sali Berisha's Democratic Party reiterated its commitment to an eventual democratic union with Kosova.[112]

In the Balkans the geopolitical equivalent of continental drift is still underway. Old fault-lines have re-opened, social and political aspirations and illusions grate against one another. Albania, or more properly, the intense desire of the three Albanias to become one, is as likely an epicenter as a historical seismologist could hope to find. But, just as the cracking and sliding of the earth's crust defies prognostication, so the time and nature of the coming upheaval in the Balkans cannot be predicted. The only certainty is that it will come.

In *Blood and Belonging*, a TV spin-off masquerading as a book, Michael Ignatieff seems surprised to certify that "the key narrative of the new world order is the disintegration of nation-states into ethnic civil war; the key architects of that order are warlords; and the key language of our age is ethnic nationalism. (...) We assumed that the world was moving irrevocably beyond nationalism, beyond tribalism, beyond the provincial confines of the identities inscribed in our passports. (...) In retrospect, we were whistling in the dark. The repressed has returned, and its name is nationalism."[113]

Perhaps because he had grown up in the genteel world of diplomatic breakfasts and international stuffed shirts, this had previously eluded Ignatieff, who acknowledges that "globalism in a post-imperialist age permits a post-nationalist consciousness only for those cosmopolitans who are lucky enough to live in the wealthy West."[114] With the collapse of the Soviet Empire and its satellite regimes, he argues, the nation-state structures of the region collapsed as well. This left hundreds of ethnic groups at one another's throats, while the globalists looked on in shock and dismay.

In the Balkans, which partook of the late and unlamented "socialist" vision of globalism, the return of the repressed looks more and more like the return of an updated model of the status quo ante. No need to be a Marxist to note the post-modern irony of the expression 'post-imperialist', with its eerie resonance of the 'end of ideology.'

Free market capitalism, competition be thy name, runs the prayer of the 'post imperialist' cosmopolitan. And in the untrammeled Hobbesian conflict of all against all, the ultimate logic of economic competition is its continuation by other means. Whether in the name of renascent nations, trading groups, supra-federal blocs, or as punitive actions by the *Weltmeister* of the age assisted by the usual allies, the scrubby underbrush, forests and mountains of the Balkans can expect to resonate with the clash of arms.

In fact, the globalists have secreted the very identitarian crises whose virulence so startles them, whose re-emergence they dismiss in psychobabble as the return of the repressed. In Kosova, where repression—social, political, racial—has been the daily diet for decades, the Albanian-speaking minority looked on helplessly as the autonomy it once enjoyed in a federalist structure evaporated. Grievances are real. Community is neither virtual nor imaginary.

The idea of community has been manipulated by the very cosmopolitans who now stand, disingenuously shocked, their aristocratic hands aflutter, above the fray. Europe, hearth of tribal nationalism, the Jacobin state and the Prussian bureaucracy, heartland of colonialism and inventor of imperialism, now presumes to lecture its acolytes. Do as we say, not as we do, rings their hypocrite chorus. The Kosovars may well be forgiven for playing their part with such exemplary fidelity. It has been scripted by the masters.

CHAPTER 6

THE BALKAN QUAGMIRE

THE MAN IN THE COMPARTMENT huddles in the corner, hands thrust into his pockets, wool cap pulled down to meet the upturned collar of his coat. A feathery tracery of frost coats the window. Shifting in his seat he growls with the certainty of experience: "That's the Greek Railways for you. Cheap. Won't turn on the heat till we're moving." With a shiver which I intend as a sign of agreement I sit down across from him.

Right on schedule, the morning local for Edessa and points northwest, lurches out of the Salonica station in the oblique light of a December dawn. As it gathers speed it sways and rattles across switches, past rows of derelict carriages and the hulks of rusted steam locomotives. I glance at the man in the wool cap. He is short, gray-haired, and gray-eyed, with high cheekbones and a ruddy complexion. We strike up a conversation. In similar compartments, in earlier days, I had encountered a pebbly-voiced mezzo who regaled me with the operetta arias she would sing in provincial towns to the accompaniment of brass bands or accordions, and a wild-eyed Gypsy with slicked-back hair and a white ersatz leather jacket, who only claimed to be a singer.

But artists rarely depart at dawn. My compartment mate is a former railway worker and this morning he's heading home to Edessa, my destination, after a day of shopping in Salonica. Frozen meat and chicken, he tells me, pointing to the bulging white plastic shopping bags at his feet. His Greek is curiously accented. "Makes sense to shop in town when you've got a pass," he says. "Got enough here to feed the missus and me for a month. This here's chicken legs; that's lamb. The minced meat's in that bag there. Look. Fifteen kilos. You know what I'd have to pay for that at home? Twice as much."

"Well, today it won't thaw out," I note.

Now the wheels are clicking in syncopated rhythm as the ranks of leafless poplars drawn up along the track like a disconsolate honor guard flash by. Finally, with a percolating sound the heater begins to pump, less warmth than the idea of warmth, into our traveling refrigerator. I pull out my multilingual Swiss map of the southern Balkans. Our train will be following the main line to Athens for a few kilometers more before veering off, at the Plati junction where homeless Albanian migrants huddle in small groups around open campfires, and from there into the Salonica hinterland.

Maps are useful conversation-starters, especially in these parts. People enjoy pointing to their town or village, tracing the red line of the road, the thick, once-impenetrable delineation of national boundaries which, for all their print-frozen permanence indicate not an immutable state of ethnic or linguistic fact but a fluid, more subjective state of collective mind. My traveling companion leans forward and peers, upside down, at the symbolic representation of northern Greece. Here's the railway line, I volunteer, tracing with my forefinger our route along the meandering line linking the chain of cities and towns: Salonica, Naoussa, Veria, Edessa, Florina.

He looks up at me with his small, bright gray eyes. A smile flickers around the corners of his mouth. "All this land used to be ours," he says, matter-of-fact and unassuming. It was an unexpected confidence, of the kind only fellow-travelers who will never meet again entrust to one another.

Nowhere—if we except the heritage of Belgian colonialism in Africa—has the divining of nationality been a more perilous, a more imperious exercise than in the Balkans. The opprobrium which the self-satisfied European world reserves for what it describes as the tribal excesses of ethnic consciousness or national identity is poor preparation for the hard, bitter fact that here little else really matters. Dispassionately perused, the ringing abstractions, the fashionable theories of cosmopolitan poly-identity espoused by the Westernized intellectual/cultural/business elite, that self-referential, self-perpetuating loop which describes itself with breathtaking lack of irony as the world community, have a certain crazed elegance. But these theories are useless in a world where, in order to understand who you are, you must—absolutely and unconditionally—know who you are not. Not, depending on circumstances, the Serb or the Greek, not the Turk or the Vlach, not the Gypsy or the Albanian or the Macedonian. Not, God forbid, the Other. Still nearby is the questioner, not so remote the day when, had your answer been too precise, the price might well have been, if not death, immediate departure. And had your answer been too hesitant, too vague, or your speech wrongly accented, your fate would have been provided for you, no matter what your imagined communitarian connection.

To my fellow voyager I divulge not a word of my internal monologue. "You wouldn't be a 'native', would you?" I ask him, offhandedly. In any other corner of Greece the natives are just that: the men and women from this or the next town or village. But here it means—in the Aesopian language of a repressed culture deemed officially not to exist—a Macedonian of the Slavic persuasion. He cracks a broad smile and nods.

"How do you know about us?" he asks.

Writer, journalist; I tick off the list.

"Figures," he grunts. "Not many tourists around here this time of year."

Outside the train windows frosty fields slip by, giving way to expanses of soft-fruit orchards, the cross-hatching of their bare twigs like brown smudges against the ice-streaked ochre earth. At every small station, knots of men in thick-padded coats stand rubbing their hands, breath frosting. My compartment mate waves to them. Railway workers, he explains. They come down to the station every morning to meet the train. The schedule gets in your blood.

The Macedonian railway line along which we are traveling was built by the Ottomans at the end of the nineteenth century, when the entire area still lay at the heart of the empire's European dominions. It had been designed as a military railroad to follow gentle gradients along the foothills, to curl up mountainsides in sweeping curves, a route designed to haul troops as far as the southern reaches of Albania and Kosova where the rebellious Shqiptars were constantly challenging the Porte's best-laid plans for administrative reform, where grim Bulgaro-Macedonian anarchist insurgents were muttering of autonomy, where Great Power agents were fomenting the collapse of the moribund Ottoman state. It was along this rail line, sinew of empire doubled by its twin telegraph line, that first the news, then the victorious mutineers of the Young Turk rebellion, surged eastward from the Macedonian garrison town of Monastir to Salonica in 1908.

We've left the Naoussa station well behind when my compartment mate speaks up again. By now the horizon has edged closer; ranks of gun-metal gray hills and behind them, snow-capped peaks, crowd around us as the train clatters up a noticeable incline, snaking over viaducts and through short tunnels. "My grandfather used to graze his sheep on these hills," he says. "Now it's all peaches, for export to Germany."

"You see those villages," he continues, pointing to white smudges on the hillside in middle-distance. "They all used to be ours'." Then he launches into a catalogue of place-names whose Slavonic resonance I immediately recognize: Golishani, Negush, Stredno Selo, Vladovo, Orizari, Vrtikop, Voden, this stream-bed, that church-yard, those hillsides. And suddenly beneath the official map, with its irreproachably Greek names, another map unfolds, a hidden map of a concealed land which now exists only in the memories of old men, and, as I was later to learn, in the bitter resentment of their exiled sons and grandsons. A map whose dimension is time, not space

In one of Jorge Luis Borges' fictions, the cartographers of the realm are set the task of preparing a map which must be accurate in every detail, down to the tiniest fold of the land, to the merest rivulet. To accomplish their mission they produce a map that fits precisely, in one-to-one scale, the contours of the land they must describe. Here the cartographers of the modern Greek state have sought—and achieved—nothing less. They have superimposed a full-scale, revised map over a landscape whose details fitted neither the national ideal nor the history reconstructed to justify it.[115]

The train creeps into the station at Edessa, perched atop its green-lipped precipice. From my window I can see the water cascading into the valley below. "This is Voden," the man informs me. "My home town. It means place of the waters. Look!" And he points to the falls and the mist swirling up at its base. We step down from the carriage, shake hands, and he strides briskly off, shoulders stooped from the weight of the frozen meat.

AS THE TRAIN PULLS OUT of the station with a short hoot of its whistle I stride diagonally across the platform. A tall, dark-skinned man heads in my direction, hand extended: Kostas Stalidis, retired teacher and resident historian, greets me with a firm handshake and we walk briskly to his car, shivering in the chill breeze.

The history of Edessa/Voden, for Mr. Stalidis, is the history of Greece: a bright succession of ancient civilizations, five centuries of Ottoman obscurity, and national renaissance which flowered when the Greek army marched in unopposed in 1912. Like most of the inhabitants of Greek Macedonia today he is a "refugee," born of a Greek family which had lived for generations on the Black Sea coast of Bulgaria. Under the Neuilly Treaty, he explains, the Greeks of Bulgaria left because the Bulgarian government decided to close Greek schools. There was no violence; simply the threat of assimilation, and loss of Greek identity. Delicately, he leaves unsaid the *quid pro quo*, the departure of Slavic-speakers for Bulgaria, presumably for similar reasons.

The accelerating onrush of time weaves in exploded, contrapuntal harmony through the sinuous streets of old Edessa, where Mr. Stalidis and I now stroll, sheltered from the wind. Here, on the edge of the precipice, citizens have finally awakened to the extraordinary beauty, and the irreplaceable character of the area's old houses, most dating from Turkish times, by acting to preserve, then restore them. This was the Christian quarter, he explains as we zigzag along the last lane before the drop, where buildings stare out over the abyss. It was not until the late eighteenth century that national identity began to supplant religion as an indicator of social differentiation, he explains. Schools organized by the Patriarchate, in which Greek was the language of instruction, were established throughout the region. A century later, the Exarchate followed suit, opening Bulgarian schools. By 1899, Edessa/Voden could boast four Greek, one Bulgarian and one Serbian educational institutions. What the original language of the students was, remains unclear.

Now we are standing in a small park at the lip of the plateau; beneath our feet rushing water foams out over jagged rocks before cascading down into slippery oblivion in the dusk-darkening valley. Slav-speakers here had Greek consciousness, he confides. Many of those who fought on the Greek side in the 'Macedonian Struggle' were natives, Macedonian-speakers. "Here, people's consciousness has always been Greek." Then, turning to me, voice raised to make himself heard over the churning water: "You've got to be careful with these questions of division. Too dangerous to play around with. I'm a historian. My job is to try and hold back the fanatics on both sides. Whatever it takes, we must keep away from war."

My day in Edessa had begun as a corrective, and had ended in the confusion of ambiguity and uncertainty. Fairness dictated that I listen to the view of the majority which now makes Greek Macedonia its home. Mr. Stalidis proved the ideal interlocutor. His hospitality was irreproachable, his credentials impeccable, his view of history unclouded by overt political considerations, his conclusions deeply felt, sincere. Yet his version of events, his story of the town, the map which he laid before me, contradicted both the particularity and the generality of "native" history. At his disposal were the tools of an ancient, complex cultural tradition which concerned itself little with the ways of the Barbarians, that is, those who did not speak Greek. Nothing else, certainly no racial theory, could explain his reluctance to see Macedonia as the Slav-Macedonians see it. The "natives" possess no written language—some say they have no language at all, only a debased patois—their traditions are oral, their history passed on furtively from the mouths of the elders, their songs and dances proscribed. For even well-intentioned, broad-minded men like Mr. Stalidis, they escape examination, cannot be understood, are not easily inserted into the complex analytical schemata which the Greek mind is capable of devising. They are people of the shadows, these Macedonians; phantoms. Their speech, fleeting whispers spirited away by the wind; their land, clods of anonymous earth wrapped in newly-printed title deeds; their existence, a pang of abstract conscience. And though invisible, yet they do not disappear.

> *Surely the history of Balkania must be the despair of a philosopher bent on reducing the world to an intelligible order, for in Balkania throughout its long agony it is difficult to discover so much as a trace of any evidence that human affairs work out to the ends of reason or morality.*[116]

AROUND THE CORNER from the Salonica Metropolis, where I had naïvely sought the legend of Saint Demetrius, stands a modest, Ottoman-era building, like a stranded survivor of another age, amidst the frantic, traffic-clogged downtown warren of high-rises, fast-food joints and glossy world beat store-fronts. A small brass plaque on the wall, one of the few in the city not disfigured by anarcho-hooligan graffiti, identifies it as the Museum of the Macedonian Struggle. Here, in the building which housed the Greek Consulate during the tumultuous years preceding the capture of Ottoman Salonica in 1912, the Museum is dedicated to the proposition that the sole legitimate Macedonian identity is Greek.

This being so, runs the implicit argument, there can be no other "Macedonian" identity, despite the efforts of Greece's newborn northern neighbor to persuade the world of the contrary. The argument is directed not at the casual foreign visitor, since almost all the museum's exhibits are labeled exclusively in Greek, but at the Greeks themselves, and particularly at the younger generation which, in the country's rush toward Europe, may find itself forgetting that it inhabits the heart of a region which its neighbors may still consider—though they dare not say so—as disputed territory. But the overarching question is this: do the Greeks consider non-Greek

Macedonia to be disputed territory? Aside from a tiny fringe faction of hyper-nationalists, neo-orthodox romantics and demagogues, no respectable Euro-Greek will admit of such designs. And yet, as I peruse the Museum's exhibits, the nagging feeling persists. Ah, if only some fortuitous event were to occur, some avenging angel providentially to intervene, some fragile mini-state to the north to cease to exist, then the Great Idea of the resurrected Byzantine empire might yet be set in motion once more.

Every graphic, every map, every photograph, every piece of archival material has been organized and disposed to prove that Greek Macedonia extended—and extends—well beyond the limits of the modern Greek state. (Reader beware: use of the term "Greek Macedonia" may itself be controversial, for some hot-bloods assert that all Macedonia can, by definition, only be Greek, yesterday, today and tomorrow.) Perhaps unwittingly, perhaps out of deference to unavoidable demographic fact, to the extent that such fact exists in the Balkans, it also tacitly accepts, more by what it does not say, that others than Greeks inhabited the entire area. What did the more than one million who demonstrated in Salonica in March, 1994, shouting "Macedonia is Greek" at the instigation of a coalition of government and religious leaders, really believe?

On prominent display is a large map in French dating from the late nineteenth century, showing the relative size of "national communities" as reflected in school enrollments. The communities shown on the map are "Greek", "Bulgarian" and "Muslim." But the categories are those of the Ottoman administration, which recognized no national identity, and instead categorized its subjects by their religious allegiance. "Greeks" were those who hewed to the Ecumenical Patriarchate in Istanbul; "Bulgarians," those who recognized the Bulgarian Orthodox Exarch, created by the Sultan's *firman* in 1870, as their religious leader. In the event, some "Greeks" spoke Bulgarian, while some "Bulgarians" spoke Greek.

The exhibits, mostly in the form of old photographs, show Greek religious and community institutions in places as far from Salonica as Krushevo, capital of the eponymous and ephemeral "Republic" established during the Ilinden Uprising of 1903 (of which more later). Maps depicting the sites of clashes between Greek bands and their Bulgarian rivals for the hearts and minds of Macedonia illustrate the total absence of front lines and controlled territories, a point the map-makers concede. With the touch of a button, tiny bulbs blink on marking military engagements: green indicating "Bulgarian" forces, red showing Turkish. Who attacked whom in collusion with whom is never clarified, the assumption being that the Greek cause is sacred, self-justifying and beyond need of detailed demonstration.

As my Swiss map conceals an older map, the museum obscures an earlier Macedonia. Students of Balkan history, or even the curious perplexed, will not have failed to note that just as history books are written to reflect and promote the national policy of their country of origin, so maps reflect an ideal nation-based geography. As I wander from one exhibit to another, from one map to another, a sense of *déjà vu* overtakes me. Reverse *déjà vu* to be exact. Here I am looking at the model for Bosnia: a territory populated by inextricably mingled ethnic groups broken down into spheres of influence, national zones, districts marked out for ethnic cleansing. Map wars. The pursuit of conflict by other means. A quaint old Balkan custom. A Procrustean bed for the ultimate rationality of national purity. Any one, or all, of the above are at our disposal.

At the heart of the museum is the semi-mythical figure of Pavlos Melas, an ambiguous national hero who might equally well be described as a terrorist, except that terrorists for the winning side are statesmen or heroes. Like several other complex Balkan personalities, Melas is better known for his death than for his life. An exhibit consisting of personal effects, correspondence and photographs commemorating the 90th anniversary of his demise in 1904, shows progressively a vain, self-centered young officer sporting a waxed handlebar mustache of the variety much in vogue among members of a certain generic Balkan camarilla, an impeccably attired scion of the privileged class who married the sister of a visionary called Ion Dragoumis, Greece's consul in Monastir (now Bitola) and apostle of the romantic and mystically aggressive Hellenic nationalism which was known as the Great Idea. We see Melas posing with fellow cadets at the Athens military academy; here he is astride his horse as Greek forces march off to humiliation at the hands of the Ottomans in the short, disastrous war of 1897. Once more we see him on horseback, this time bravely leaping a barrier; in another photograph he has a saintly look, as tender father and loving husband and; finally, we see him as avenger, in full Macedonian freedom fighter regalia, gold piping on wide-shouldered black cape, pistols thrust jauntily into cartridge belt. Now, for all the sartorial elegance, his expression is grave, the shadow of death upon him. Still he radiates the iron resolve of the visionary who contemplates the future unafraid. Melas' sword and pistol are displayed below the portrait, as is the tiny religious icon he carried on his person. And later in Skopje, when I visited the offices of the Macedonian VMRO, offspring of the self-same Slavo-Macedonian (or Bulgarian) nationalists Melas fought against, I was struck by how much these Greek sacred relics resembled the crossed pistol and dagger of the shadowy, archetypal Balkan anarchists.

Melas met his end in a skirmish with Turkish troops in a rock-poor village in the Pindus mountains, a likely victim of treachery. Our hero, it seems, harbored "illusions" about cooperation with the Ottoman forces against the common Bulgarian foe. The Ottomans, masters of duplicity, would have been only too happy to provide the gullible would-be liberator with the kind of information that eventually led, not to a successful ambush against the Exarchists, but to his own death. But his violent, militarily insignificant end ignited—as these things have a way of doing in a region prone to ready ignition if not spontaneous combustion—pro-interventionist sentiments in Greece, and stimulated greater Greek involvement in the struggle against Macedono-Bulgarian armed bands, whose impetus had been blunted by the failure of Ilinden. Kostis Palamas, the anti-nationalist poet, dashed off lines of glowing tribute to the national martyr. Public opinion was galvanized. His equally violent—perhaps quixotic— death became the kernel of a much more sophisticated strategy which was to culminate, eight years later, in the Greek capture of Salonica. The Macedonian revolutionaries met their nightmare in the form of Pavlos Melas' mustache. Their ultimate horror was the Balkan Wars of 1912-1913 which carved up their tormented heartland and shared it out amongst Greece, Serbia and Bulgaria, the three most successful Balkan emulators of their Great Power sponsors. The hapless Macedonians (but who were they? did they truly exist?) were abandoned to fester under three generations of triple oppression.

JOURNALIST AND FORMER MEMBER of the Greek parliament for the Eurocommunists, Traïanos Hadjidimitriou, is also the grandson of Slavic-speaking Greeks, and as such, should be uniquely qualified to speak of the delicate workings of national consciousness. In a forceful baritone voice which belies his rumpled plumpness, Mr. Hadjidimitriou is putting the historical pretensions of "Skopje"—such is the Former Yugoslav Republic of Macedonia obligatorily referred to in public—through the wringer in front of a crowd of several hundred Salonica citizens at a public lecture at the Society for Macedonian Studies, the scientific arm of the Macedonian Struggle Museum (there are no formal links between the two institutions, but they share the same resolutely nationalist outlook, and, whisper some marginal voices, the same Cold War roots). A gaggle of dignitaries, headed by the Minister for Macedonia and Thrace, occupies the first row of seats. They beam beatifically as the speaker punctures the illusions of those hyperborean upstarts.

The authorities in Skopje, he tells the audience, claim descent from the ancient Macedonians. But who were the ancient Macedonians? Were they Greeks? Did they later become hellenized? Though historians are not unanimous, Alexander himself—and who dare argue with the man who shook the world?—refers to Macedon, the kingdom his forefathers founded, as part of the Greek world. "The Macedonians saw themselves as part of Greece," argues Mr. Hadjidimitriou, as heads in the audience nod approvingly. "Skopje's contrary claims simply cannot stand in the face of the evidence."

The study of tombal inscriptions clearly indicates, he continues, that Macedonian was a Greek dialect. With only a handful of exceptions, the Macedonian conquerors gave Greek names to the cities they founded. And furthermore, Macedonians took part in the Olympic Games, where participation was restricted to Hellenes. Of course, he admits, not everyone liked the Macedonian dynasty, especially in that hot-bed of democracy, Athens. There, the orator Demosthenes caustically dismissed Alexander's father Philip as having "nothing to do with Greeks", as the "worst kind of barbarian." (And—though this he does not tell the crowd—when democracy was restored to the city beneath the Acropolis after the death of Alexander in faraway Persia, his mentor Aristotle was forced to flee for his life.)

The more serious historians in Skopje don't press the claim of descent from the ancient Macedonians, Mr. Hadjidimitriou tells the crowd. They argue that a "Macedonian" people was formed by Slavic tribes which migrated into the southern Balkans where they successively came under Bulgarian, then Turkish domination. In fact, the sixth and seventh centuries in Europe were marked by the emergence of Slavic tribes throughout the continent. Some of these groups were drawn to the southern Balkans by demographic factors: prime agricultural land was available, as a result of the collapse of the western Roman empire, of epidemics and population movements. These were not nomads, he stresses. They came as immigrants, to stay. But with their primitive political structures they were incapable of creating a state, even in medieval terms, such as the Bulgars, and later the Serbs, were to do. But these people were Slavs, not Bulgars (who were distantly related to the Turkic tribes of high Central Asia). They claim Tsar Samuil, whose empire was centered on the city of Ohrid, was a "Macedonian" but he was a Bulgar. In the long run, the Byzantine system transformed these Slavs into Romaioi, inhabitants of the eastern Roman empire, until, by the middle of the fifteenth century, they had become assimilated. Greeks, that is.

Moving right along to the late Ottoman period, when the "Macedonian" question was at the heart of Great Power competition for markets and spheres of influence, the 1904-1905 Ottoman census shows Greeks as the second population group after the dominant Turks, and well ahead of the Bulgars. Greek school enrollment was four times that of the Bulgars. "Macedonians" were nowhere mentioned. "No such identity existed," he declares, and the crowd sighs its assent. However, Mr. Hadjidimitriou has omitted to tell his audience that the Ottoman census classified individuals by religion, not nationality.

Romanian and Bulgarian propaganda in the area under Ottoman rule was intensive, but nowhere is there any mention of "Macedonia." There were no "Macedonian" candidates to the new Ottoman parliament which was elected in the aftermath of the 1908 Young Turk revolution; only Turks, Greeks, Bulgarians and Jews. "Most Slav-speaking people had Greek national feelings," he says, avoiding with exquisite delicacy describing the speech of such people as a "language." Instead, he calls it an "idiom" or "dialect"—of what, it is not clear.

And, after the Balkan Wars of 1912-1913 and World War I, some 60,000 Bulgars departed, "voluntarily," under the provisions of the Treaty of Neuilly. Those who remained were simply staying on the land they felt was theirs. In fact, asserts Mr. Hadjidimitriou, most of the resistance fighters of the late nineteenth and early twentieth century were native Slavic speakers who "had a Greek national consciousness."

Thus far, Mr. Hadjidimitriou's lecture has been the predictable catalogue of approved arguments. He has defended them with wit, verve and intelligence. But when he reaches the present, I prick up my ears. Skopje, he insists, has created—when it was part of the former Yugoslavia—a Macedonian language, purifying it of Bulgarian elements. When Tito's partisans founded a Macedonian state on the anniversary of the Ilinden uprising in 1944 their aim was to weaken Serb domination in the nascent communist-led federation, and to undercut pro-Bulgarian—and pro-Albanian—feelings.

At this point, the Minister and his major domo exit the hall, eyes fixed purposefully on the floor. Do they have other commitments, or are they signifying to the speaker that his arguments suffer from a patriotic deficiency? I detect the latter. Unflinching and undaunted, Mr. Hadjidimitriou pushes on. "Pay attention, dear friends," he warns. "Nations can be created. Look at Israel. Today, Macedonia, no matter what we call it, is an accomplished fact. For 50 years, we Greeks avoided raising the issue, mostly under pressure from the United States. Today, ladies and gentlemen, we are paying for our own indifference and our lack of foresight."

LUGGAGE SLUNG OVER MY SHOULDER, I'm slogging through no-man's-land along the muddy gravel road carved into a steep, mesquite-covered hillside. It is the fall of 1994, and I am entering tiny, isolated Macedonia for the first time. The Albanian border crossing—a shack perched at the edge of the roadway—slowly disappears behind me. Before we reach the frontier post a uniformed guard waves me and the other passengers of the Tirana-Koumanovo express bus toward a plastic trough containing a disinfectant-saturated sponge. A cholera epidemic is "raging" in Albania. Several dozen deaths have occurred, mostly in institutions following a collapse of hygiene. We dutifully squish through before presenting passports.

A duo of itinerant guitar-strumming young men with long, greasy hair who had boarded the bus at Elbasan and entertained us with their music on the interminable climb over the Albanian Alps, are refused entry, as are several other Shqiptars. As the foot bath protects against the cholera microbe, so the vigilant cross-examination by the Macedonian border authorities is the social equivalent. When I witnessed a similar attitude on the part of Serbian border guards toward Albanians travelling to Prishtina six months later, it became impossible to avoid the feeling that, in this corner of the Balkans, it is the Albanians who are seen as an epidemic. One is continually hearing *sotto voce* asides about their fertility, about demographic pressures, about their eastward advance from the high, barren pastures of Albania into the more fertile lowlands of western Macedonia. These people are Muslims, they breed like rabbits; they are expanding, taking all the best lands, speak the whispers which are sometimes articulated in the columns of newspapers.

Customs formalities finally completed we crowd into a fresh bus, a faster, more comfortable ex-Yugoslav model, for the run past Sveti Naum and along the rocky, pine-grown shore of Lake Ohrid to the eponymous ancient city which today claims the honor of being the historical birthplace of Macedonia. To our left the sun is setting over the Albanian mountains, tinting the still waters of the lake a fluid palette of pink, rose, orange and pale crimson. A Turkish gentleman in the seat across the aisle taps my shoulder and motions with his head. Then he smiles and kisses his closed finger-tips in the Balkan gesture of esthetic appreciation. "Mir," he says in Albanian. Very fine indeed, I nod.

High, feathery clouds veil the sun, and a chilly breeze ruffles the surface of the lake as I walk briskly along the waterfront the next morning, fortified by a breakfast of eggs, bread and cheese. Swans paddle industriously back and forth while, farther offshore, flocks of water birds swoop and dive. The Macedonian landscape is everywhere inhabited by spirits, peopled by legends. Nowhere are they more concentrated, more powerful, more ambivalent in their supra-historical truth than in this busy town of 40,000 souls.

In 1014, the army of Tsar Samuil, an energetic ruler who established his capital at Ohrid, encountered a superior Byzantine force led by Emperor Basil II, a man lionized in Greek history as the "Bulgar slayer." Basil, having defeated Samuil's army in a decisive engagement that was to destroy the Bulgarian (or was it Macedonian?) kingdom, then proceeded to blind the 14,000 soldiers he took captive, leaving one man for each one hundred to guide them back to their homeland. When the Tsar beheld the mournful sight, he was so stricken that he died on the spot. But did he? Another legend has it that he sent his remaining troops out to collect the eyes and place them in a gold casket which he then caused to sink into the deeps of Lake Ohrid—which bequeathed to the lake its shimmering surface.[117]

In a square overlooking the still waters, surrounded by the immaculately preserved Ottoman-Macedonian houses which have brought Ohrid recognition by UNESCO as a monument of world architectural heritage, stands Aghia Sofia, the church of Holy Wisdom—God's, that is. It is the third, and westernmost, on my itinerary of the four Byzantine churches bearing the name, the others being the great mother church at Istanbul, the smaller eighth-century cathedral at Salonica, and the modest brick structure in the shadow of St. Alexandr Nevsky in the heart of Sofia.

A slender, prematurely balding young man called Atanas takes my 100 dinar entrance fee and guides me through the sepulchrally frigid church. Aghia Sofia served as a mosque for 500 years; a massive minbar carved in marble still stands, facing southeast toward Mecca. The Ottomans, recognizing superior devotional architecture when they saw it, converted Byzantine places of worship as their forefathers had converted the immense and overpowering Aghia Sofia of Constantinople. Above it, in the perfection of Balkan syncretism, extends a fresco depicting the Dormition of the Virgin, where deep greens, purples and blues predominate. Though Islam tolerated no representation of the sacred, the Ottomans did not destroy the wall-paintings they encountered, but covered them over in an act of unintentional preservation. Now released from their coating of plaster, the devotional images glow with an almost youthful vigor. Dating from the first half of the eleventh century, they are thought to be the work of master painters from Salonica, which then rivaled Constantinople as a cultural center.[118]

After our tour of the echoing, clammy structure Atanas invites me into his office for a cup of hot chocolate. The "office" turns out to be a tiny, glass-walled cubicle adjacent to the entrance equipped with a hot-plate and two chairs. My host has an arrangement with the municipal authorities: 20% of the gate instead of a salary. It would have been an attractive arrangement in the days before the collapse of Titoite Yugoslavia when people visited Aghia Sofia primarily as a cultural monument and less as a place of devotion. In these days of post-communist uncertainty things are so slow as to be motionless during the winter, only slightly better in summer. Ohrid, once the Riviera of landlocked Macedonia, has been deserted by foreign tourists. Hotels are closed, signs for private accommodation creak in the cold wind. Restaurants remain open but empty. The steamer which toured the lake is tied up at the end of the dock. And Atanas waits, rubbing his hands over a battered electric coil heater and sipping ersatz hot chocolate.

As we sip the steaming beverage Atanas shows me his collection of old photos of the town. Here is Aghia Sofia, there the battlements of Tsar Samuil's fortress, and hovering over the picturesque sepia townscape, the delicate skyward-pointing fingers of minarets. The next exhibit is an envelop of snapshots of his winter vacations in Vietnam and Cambodia, a memento of the days when the tourists flocked to Ohrid and his 20% cut meant regular holidays in exotic places. It was easy, he explains, to make pocket money by taking photographs of villagers, then selling them a copy the next day.

"Here, look at this," he says, moving right along to another subject. Atanas rummages through a stack of papers on a shelf and pulls out a fistful of leaflets, a gift from some recent Bulgarian sightseers. They insist, he explains with a certain reluctance, that Macedonia is really Bulgaria, and that the Ilinden uprising—lodestone of Macedonia's historical consciousness—was organized and led by Bulgarians. The documents bear the imprint of VMRO, the Slavic acronym for the Internal Macedonian Revolutionary Organization, the archetypal anarchist/mad-bomber coalition of exalted patriots who flourished throughout Slav-speaking Macedonia at the turn of the century. The leaflets are published in Sofia, not Skopje. What does Atanas think of all this? He shrugs his shoulders. Guides to historical monuments must be even warier than barbers of the shifting winds of politics, for they wield no straight razor. Surely we will forgive him for being a touch blasé. "We get all kinds here. Personally, if you ask me, I am a Macedonian not a Bulgarian."

Out of delicacy, I would not have asked. For the historians of the reawakening ethno-nationalist Balkans, Ohrid is still contested territory. The frescoes of Aghia Sofia are unmistakably Byzantine, their inscriptions are Greek, their inspiration—and the skilled, anonymous hands that labored to create them—from Byzantine Salonica. But the city on the lake has become the focal point of efforts by modern Macedonian historiography to establish an unbroken link with the past, to create the letters patent of a distinct culture, the lineage of what the Québécois are accustomed to describing, minimally, as a "distinct society."

For the revisionists who dominate a historical discourse as yet unsullied by views excessively divergent from the official line, the Slav-speaking empire of Tsar Samuil, he whose ruined fortress dominates the hills overlooking the town and the lake, was the prototypical Macedonian state, emerging for a fleeting historical moment between the alternating yokes of the Bulgars and the Byzantines. Samuil's empire was, in a sense, the administrative culmination of the work of those two great Orthodox missionaries Cyril and Methodius. They were the inventors, in the ninth century, of the Cyrillic alphabet which is still in use by the Slav peoples from the Adriatic to the Bering Strait, and from the Russian-occupied Caucasus to the Arctic Sea. The two saints, whom Greek sources praise as the greatest sons of Macedonia since Alexander the Great[119] may have been Slavs, though they are claimed by Greece. Whatever its national identity, the saintly duo was imbued with the Orthodox culture of the Byzantine empire whose vector was the Greek language. Crucially, they were followed a half-century later by St. Clement and his acolyte St. Naum, both native Slav-speakers who realized that the fate of Christianity among the Slavs depended upon the creation of a Slavonic-speaking clergy. This they set out to create, training thousands of priests, and overseeing the translation of sacred texts from Greek into Slavonic, the native Macedonian Slavic dialect.

Not so, reply Bulgarian historians with rising intonations of indignation. The language employed by Saints Cyril and Methodius, St. Clement and St. Naum and a host of other medieval writers and teachers is a variant of old Bulgarian. For more than a thousand years, they argue, "the Slavs living in this area have been considered Bulgarians, or to be more precise, Western Bulgarians whose idiom is distinguished by certain dialectical peculiarities."[120]

Bulgaria's rejection of a distinct Macedonian identity was, until recently, far from an abstract academic debate. Ohrid, cradle of Slavic Orthodoxy and of the *ur-sprache* of Old Slavonic, marked the westernmost point of Bulgaria's claim to the territorial entity of Macedonia during the final fifty tormented years of Ottoman rule. In 1878, after victorious Russian armies under the Slavophile Tsar Alexander II had brought the Ottoman empire to its knees, the short-lived treaty of San Stefano awarded Bulgaria not only a new state, but the whole of Macedonia from Ohrid to the Black Sea and from the Serbian border to the outskirts of Salonica.

The treaty proved richer fare than the rachitic new nation could possibly ingest, let alone digest. And it proved far more than Moscow's rival imperialists in London, Paris and Vienna were prepared to countenance. They correctly saw the treaty as the leading edge of messianic Pan-Slavism, itself a veil for Russian ambition in the Balkans. Furious diplomatic activity ensued, and a second, enlarged international conference was convened in Berlin later that same year, at which the frontiers of the infant state were pruned with all the rigor of a stern gardener trimming his hedge-rows. Macedonia was returned to Ottoman rule. The Sultan, ever grateful, promised administrative reforms.[121]

Few in Bulgaria, flushed with the intoxicating grog of national redemption, doubted that the Macedonian Slavs were Bulgarians. The task, as the Bulgarian political class saw it, was to make sure that the Macedonian Christians viewed themselves as Bulgarians. The geopolitical corollary was to liberate the region from Ottoman rule, and ultimately annex it to Bulgaria. Ohrid by the lake became an obsession in Sofia. The course was set for more than a century of Balkan bloodshed.[122]

I continue my peregrinations through the cobblestone lanes of the old town, beneath overhanging enclosed balconies and around sharp corners. The air is fragrant with the smell of wood smoke; leaves have yellowed and are floating to the ground. On the far shore the mountains of Albania loom out of the haze. Opposite the ruins of the fortress, at the crest of a hill, stands the church of St. Clement, pride and patron of Ohrid. Unlike Aghia Sofia, St. Clement's is a working church, its cramped, cruciform interior redolent with beeswax and incense, where hundreds of bright votive candles sparkle in the semi-darkness. Far from a common church, it constitutes a repository of late Byzantine painting probably unequaled in the Orthodox world. The walls of St. Clement's glow with a gem-like phosphorescence: every square centimeter teems with frescoes whose vibrancy contrasts utterly with the flowing brushwork and rather somber tones of Aghia Sofia, less to the detriment of the latter than to the greater glory of the former.

For these wall paintings flow from the hand of a master. Two masters, in fact: Mihail and Eftychios of Salonica, whose work reflects what art historians have called the "Byzantine Renaissance." This resurgence of the pictorial is said to body forth the onrush of humanism, the breath of the emerging European spirit as it penetrated the immutable, tenebrous universe of Eastern Orthodoxy—an esthetic reflection of the challenge of Barlaam and the Zealots to the monkish quietism of Gregory Palamas and the *hesychastes*.

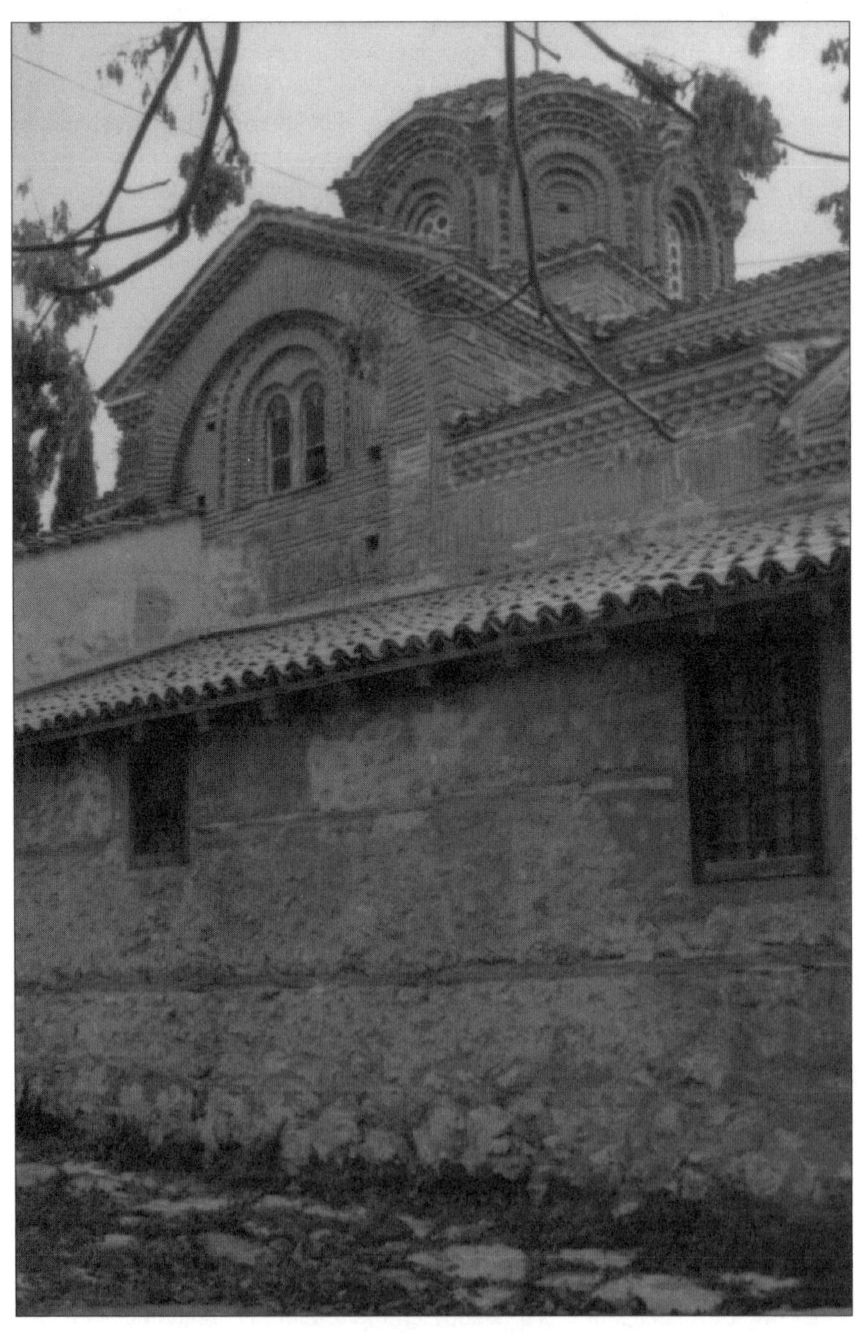

The church of St. Clement, Ohrid, Macedonia.
(Photo by Fred A. Reed.)

The frescoes of St. Clement's are unique not only in their lively palette, unquenched by the centuries, but in their depiction of common folk. Here is a group of professional wailers attending the lamentation of Christ; human emotion is indelibly transcribed in the faces of the true mourners. Daring Byzantine convention, the artists are tempted by vanishing point perspective. They suggest it in the Last Supper, where the disciples are disposed around a circular table seen simultaneously from eye level and from above. But what draws my eye are the near-life-size depictions of the "warrior saints," George, Demetrius and Mercurius, each occupying the front face of the square columns that support the dome. The saints are drawn up at attention in full armor, their rich tunics falling in stylized yet natural folds, muscular legs firmly planted on the earth, alert, relaxed but ready to fight, fists grasping sharp weapons. The kind of men you'd want on your side in the struggle of faith versus impiety.

As Ohrid is a bone of contention for the rival claims of Macedonian and Bulgarian historians, it also marks the place and the moment of transition where the religious art of the Greek-speaking Byzantine empire gave way to a style more characteristic of the South Slavs. The frescoes and icons of Ohrid are best seen in their purity, free of the dross (and the *post facto* self-justification) of modern cultural nationalism, whether of the variety secreted by the Party hacks of the Macedonian academy or by the "objective" scholarly hacks of the Greek establishment who conflate the cultural achievements of the multi-ethnic Byzantine state with Greekness. They are far removed from, and ultimately inaccessible to the modern-day crusade to reduce the spiritual heritage of a people which defined itself as a religious community to some vulgar emanation of national consciousness.

Though Ohrid partakes of both the Greek and the South Slav expressions of Byzantium, it is owned by neither and neither can possess it. Byzantine art—revealed here in one of its epiphanic moments—still stands free of the double-headed pseudo-esthetic of progress/process which would have us see it as anything other than consummate skill wielded in the service of faith at a pinnacle of creative energy. Not a fragment of some putative forward movement whose culminating moment is—should we be surprised?—late twentieth century Western ("universal") civilization.

Slavo-Byzantine, Macedonian or Bulgarian, Ohrid dissimulates another facet of its rich, multiple identity: its Turkish-Albanian Muslim side. Though tourists, including the wealthy Turkish businessmen who swept up the hill to St. Clement's in a Mercedes sedan as I was departing, come here to visit the churches and stroll along the lake front at dusk, they must walk through a living city whose central square lies beneath a majestic plane tree, surrounded by coffee-houses and a mosque. The cobbled main street beyond the tourist district is lined with small shops producing shoes and slippers, with smithies which echo with the ping of brass being painstakingly shaped by ball-peen hammers. The artisans who keep these ancient trades alive claim to be Egyptians, distant descendants of craftsmen who migrated to Macedonia centuries before. They have petitioned the Egyptian government to protect them; no reply has been forthcoming. Locals scoff that they are Gypsies. No one knows, I least of all. Some things must remain, in their profound inscrutability, forever unknowable.

As darkness falls I step into a small restaurant on a back-street; the sort of place that serves the neighborhood trade. My Macedonian is non-existent, and the few words of Russian I dredge up from the bottom-mud of memory are unequal to the task of ordering. The waitress, a brassy gum-chewing young woman, reacts with a sullen upward flick of the head. Something tells me not even to think about Greek. So I try the handful of Albanian words I know. Suddenly her face comes alive: with a mixture of garbled Shqip and crude pantomime I order a plate of spicy grilled sausages, fried potatoes dusted with kashkaval cheese, a tomato salad and bread. The other customers in the café are curious; this is not part of the Ohrid tourist circuit. And, for the time being, the Ohrid tourist circuit is, if not dead, hovering on the edge of catatonia.

Unwittingly, though providentially, I have stumbled through the looking glass and into the duality of Macedonia. This tiny, fragile newborn nation at the southern fringe of the Slav world seems to exist as a state at the sufferance of a substantial, vocal and fractious Albanian minority whose grievances may be strong enough to pull it apart even before the glue hastily applied by its communist-cum-free-market-democrat nation founders has set. The nameless café into which I have wandered functions as an informal clubhouse for local members of the country's Albanian opposition, the Party of Democratic Progress. Before I've finished my meal, several men have joined me at my table, pouring out their grievances as charter members of the league of the disregarded and the downtrodden.

One of them speaks passable English. His name is Safet. He has worked for years in the Netherlands and now he is back in Ohrid on vacation visiting his family. "Us Albanians, we're the blacks of Macedonia," he rasps, leaning across the table to drive home the point. "We do not have, what do you call it, representation? Yes, representation, nowhere in this country. Look at the houses we live in. Have you been to the Albanian quarter here in Ohrid? Yes?

The police, they are all Macedonian. Everywhere there is discrimination against us. If they do not treat to us better, there will be a war."

Grave heads nod around the table. While these men are divided in their support for the more extreme faction of the PDP, led by the fiery Arben Xhaferi in Tetovo, they all share Safet's core view. One of them, a tall, blond-headed man with piercing blue eyes and a deep voice warns: "This is dangerous situation. I have seen before. In Bosnia." "Where are you from exactly?" I ask the man, whose name is Mohammad. "Sarajevo," he says.

WHAT ARE YOU DOING in Macedonia? the teenage girl beside me asks, more incredulous than aggressive, as if my presence here were a curiosity, an anomaly. It is an anomaly, really. Disinterested, curious, diffidently fascinated, scribes and tourists, apostles of the sect of been-there-done-that, wander through landscapes of real or incipient horror in perfectly insulated, transparent capsules, observing, consigning to purgatory or paradise, leaving. We are rarely challenged, more rarely held to account. Who was this girl? Did she know who she was talking to? I could have been an American.

We've been assigned adjoining seats on the Ohrid-Skopje express, and now as the bus lumbers out of Ohrid and up through the pine and maquis covered slopes of the Bistra Planina, Maria, a bright, precocious and ever-so-slightly world weary fifteen year-old lays aside the dog magazine she had been reading and entertains me with a non-stop recitation of her pet peeves and gripes, ranging from her separated parents—her father got the family mastiff in the breakup—to the frustrations of growing up in a society where yesterday's truth has become today's fiction.

"Yugoslavia used to be everywhere, now it's nowhere," she complains, as she describes how school history text-books were suddenly changed to reflect the new, Macedonian perspective. "It's not just the books. Our school used to be called Vladimir Ilich Lenin. Now it's called Gotse Delchev [one of the founders of VMRO, the Macedonian insurrectionist movement]."

Athens, in its single-minded dedication to proving the illegitimacy of Macedonia, brandishes maps drawn from school books published in Skopje which allegedly show territorial claims on northern Greece, known here as Aegean Macedonia. (Other exhibits in the court of public opinion include the label of a locally brewed *raki* which depicts Salonica's White Tower, clear evidence of expansionist designs.) So, I ask Maria during a lull in her monologue, do the maps in her geography and history books show parts of Greece and Bulgaria as a "greater Macedonia?"

Not at all, she replies. "The map shows Aegean and Pirin Macedonia [that section today within the borders of Bulgaria] as what Macedonia used to be, when it was an Ottoman province."

Dogs prove to be Maria's only concession to nationalism. Flipping open her magazine she points to a photograph of a massive, barrel-chested, furry creature poised defiant atop a snowy mountain ridge. "You see this dog? This is a Sharplaninec, our native Macedonian breed. The strongest dog in the world. It can make short work of any pit bull. And now the Serbs are claiming it's Serbian! Can you imagine? They'll never get away with it."

The outburst of canine chauvinism aside, Maria seems as short on national enthusiasm as on optimism. Have you seen "Before the Rain?" she asks. I had indeed, and found its portrayal of the latent intercommunal violence between the Christian, Slav-speaking Macedonians and their Muslim-Albanian countrymen bleak indeed, and striking in its cruel beauty. "If we can't settle our problems soon with the Albanians," she says, echoing what I had heard in the café in Ohrid, "there is going to be big trouble in Macedonia."

Not for lack of effort on her part though. "Next year I am going to enroll in the Albanian high-school in Skopje," she tells me, in the confidential tone of a secret being imparted. Her intention is to learn Albanian—a language few ethnic Macedonians speak—and see how the country's minority, perhaps one third of the population, lives. But, she confides, "my friends all think I'm crazy. 'What do you want to talk their language for?' they are asking me. They cannot understand."

When we reach the capital a light spring rain is falling. Maria darts from the bus and into the waiting arms of her mother. I sling my bag over my shoulder and slog across the Stari Most, the graceful Ottoman foot-bridge which spans the Vardar, into the broad, tree-lined streets of modern Skopje, a cityscape dominated by concrete office and apartment buildings thrown up in the aftermath of the devastating earthquake of June, 1963, which leveled the town and killed thousands.

Several months before, on my first visit to Skopje, I'd been guided across the bridge in the opposite direction by a man I shall call George, a doctor by profession and a dissident by avocation. A sharp north wind was sweeping down the Vardar valley, driving wispy high clouds across the moon. Stocky, dark-skinned, with jet-black hair, George grasped my elbow as he led me through the twisting lanes of the market district, the Bit Pazar, with its of narrow, winding streets, antique mosques, and smoking grilled sausage emporia, keeping up a steady flow of conversation as we went. "According to the Greeks, we don't exist, our language is not a language, our country is a fiction," he laughed. "Did you ever hear anything so crazy? Just look around you, listen. What do you see?"

George belongs to a vocal, influential category of Macedonian citizens: those who, as children, were driven from their homes in Greece (or, as Greek official history asserts, abducted by the retreating communist-led Greek Democratic Army) during the Greek civil war of 1946-1949, and sought refuge in the welcoming arms of Marshall Tito's newly created Socialist Republic of Macedonia. The viscerality of the Greek position on Macedonia pales beside the impassioned intensity of my host. After two years of the Greek-imposed economic embargo, whose aim was to make Skopje amenable to changes in its flag, constitution and even its name, an agreement was in prospect on that blustery fall evening of 1994. But George, like many of his compatriots, was having none of it.

"There's much more to this dispute that the question of a name," he growled, guiding me around a corner and down a narrow, cobbled street. So immersed were we in this sudden, declamatory, one-way conversation that passers-by have faded into flitting, ill-defined shapes, the picturesque store-fronts of the old quarter have metamorphosed into flimsy, one-dimensional stage settings, perhaps from some provincial production of the *Abduction from the Seraglio*. His narrative had expanded to fill all available space. "You know, we cannot visit the place where we were born, where our families had rich, fertile land, where our grandparents are buried. But our lands are just as much a part of Macedonia as this," he said, with a sweep of his hand.

The issue of the name, as it is euphemistically termed in Greece, is a pretext for a wider, more sinister plan, he told me. Macedonia's neighbors, goes this scenario, would like nothing better than to return to the Bucharest Treaty of 1913, which divided the territory among Greece, Bulgaria and Serbia. "And now, now they want us to surrender our name. Never! Abolish our name and you abolish our right to exist. If our government ever accepts this kind of a compromise, it's days are numbered, mark my words."

To describe the ethnogenesis of Macedonia as "complex" is to understate egregiously its tortuous, labyrinthine obscurity. Beneath the forested mountains and fertile plains of this Balkan crossroads where intersect the north-south and east-west corridors of migration, commerce and invasion lies a ramifying, branching network of figurative caverns through which flow the dark currents of identity, a virtual representation of its superficial, symbolic double, the political map.

Balkan historians, like spelunkers, strive to penetrate these nether spaces and from their depths emerge, eyes blinking, with their catch of sightless fish, translucent crustaceans and polished stalactites which are hailed as conclusive proof that the speech of the men and women who reside above is, for instance, a dialect of Bulgarian, that the repressed ethnic consciousness of the sheep-herding Vlach mountaineers is Greek, or that the Macedonian tradition of holding the *slava*, a typically Serbian name's day celebration, makes the inhabitants of the villages and towns Serbs in spite of themselves. Only the Albanians, those shadowy figures on the pages of Balkan history, really know who they are, it seems. But for their Slav neighbors they are dismissed as Turks.

At the heart of the Macedonian enigma lies the story of the Internal Macedonian Revolutionary Organization, known by its Slavic acronym as VMRO. Rarely has a national awakening had the misfortune of being led by a movement of such bumbling brutality, vindictive cruelty, divided loyalty and absolute, burning dedication; a movement which concentrated the best and the worst of pan-Slavism, Bulgarian expansionism, anti-Hellenism, proto-communism, anarcho-syndicalism, Balkan unitarism and post-Romantic pseudo-European nationalism into a wild, unpredictable, incendiary cocktail.

Naturally, no one agrees on the true nature of VMRO. One thing seems certain: the organization was founded, not in Sofia, but in the cosmopolitan heart of Ottoman Macedonia—Salonica—as a conspiracy of six young men, in the Chelebi Bakal Street home of one Ivan Hadzhinikolov, in November, 1893.[123] The city on the bay, not Skopje (Üsküb, as it was then called by the Ottomans), was the political focal point for growing national contradictions in the southern Balkans—and Macedonia, its hinterland, was the prize.

At the Congress of Berlin, in 1878, upstart Serbia had received Austro-Hungarian blessing to expand into Macedonian lands possessed by Serbian monarchs in the fourteenth century and to acquire Salonica as a substitute for a port on the Adriatic. Greek national policy strove to recreate the Byzantine Empire by obtaining Constantinople, Thrace and Macedonia. Bulgaria, reduced by the Great Powers to a modest Balkan principality whose reach exceeded its grasp, now shared a frontier with Macedonia, which a large number of Bulgarians fervently believed was both ethnically and historically theirs.[124]

For the better part of the previous decade, Bulgaria's ambitions had been buoyed by the creation of a distinct Bulgarian Orthodox Church. From the late eighteenth century until 1870, Christians in the Ottoman-ruled Balkans fell under the ecclesiastical jurisdiction of the Ecumenical Patriarch in Istanbul. Irrespective of their language or ethnic background—Bulgarian, Greek, Slavo-Macedonian, Vlach or Albanian—all were lumped together as "Greeks", members of the Rum millet. But in 1870, a *firman* issued by Sultan Abdulhamid created the Bulgarian Exarchate. Gone was simplicity, come was a sticky web of complexity.

Consistent with the Ottoman policy of playing off the empire's subject peoples against one another, the Sultan's decision reflected growing popular resentment with the Patriarch's metamorphosis into a vehicle of Hellenism, the advance guard for the secular aspirations of the Greek state. The creation of the Exarchate shattered the Greek monopoly on education, and stopped the rising tide of Hellenic assimilation among the Slav-speaking peoples. Within five years of the Sultan's decree, most Slav-speakers in the vilayets of Macedonia had departed the Patriarchate for the Exarchate, though not all identified themselves as Bulgarians.[125] Who were they? Greeks or Macedonians?

Meanwhile, the rising tide of Bulgarian national ambition was lapping at the feet of Salonica, where a Bulgarian *Lycée* was founded in 1880 under the nominal administration of the Exarchate, but financed directly by Sofia. The six fiery-eyed conspirators who met at the home of Hadzhinikolov thirteen years later were all teachers at the *Lycée*. More than mathematics, chemistry, physics, Latin and Bulgarian was being taught. In fact, the staff of the institution could best be described as employees of the national cause—as were the thousands of intensely devoted young teachers from Greece, Bulgaria, Serbia and even Romania who flocked into contested Macedonia, less to instill the love of learning, more to release—or to create from the whole cloth of a backward, possibly mystified peasantry—pent-up national sentiments: to win, in the modern idiom, hearts and minds.

Looking on from Constantinople with a mixture of concern, ineptitude, and of the blindness born of overconfidence, the Ottomans worried little whether the Christian inhabitants of Macedonia saw themselves as Bulgarians, Greeks, Serbs or even indigenous Macedonians. They were determined, however, that the status of these people as obedient subjects of the Porte remain unchanged. But the Bulgarians had sharply differing priorities. Their task was to bring the undifferentiated Slav-speaking Christian mass to see itself as Bulgarian, then try to pry the region from the Ottoman grip before the Greeks did. Naturally, they reasoned, these neo-Bulgars would hasten to reunite with the Principality, and thus recreate the Greater Bulgaria of San Stefano denied at the Congress of Berlin.[126]

The next three decades were to leave the Macedonian valleys and mountains with a legacy of intercommunal strife, not only in the footnotes of history books but etched in the consciousness of the Macedonians themselves. In 1887 Bulgaria, under Prime Minister Stambulov, the "Balkan Bismark," adopted a strategy of strengthening Bulgarian culture in Macedonia. Promoting the emergence of a strong, urban Bulgarian propertied class under the nose of the Turkish administration, cheek by jowl with Muslim landowners and Greek and Vlach merchants was the tactic of choice.

But it was a slow process, demanding far more patience than the restive Bulgaro-Macedonians, their aspirations honed to a knife edge by the messianic patriotism of the schoolmasters and by the priests of the Exarchate, were prepared to concede. A powerful, vocal and militant Macedonian lobby had sprung up in the Bulgarian capital. Stambulov responded with police repression to their clamor for direct action against Istanbul to liberate their blood brothers. In 1895, the hard-knuckled Prime Minister was assassinated by Macedonian extremists in the shady streets of Sofia. Before his corpse had fallen to the ground, it was literally torn to pieces by his assailants.[127]

The dismemberment of Stambulov was followed by that of his policy. The emboldened Macedonians, the tail that wagged the Bulgarian government's dog, embarked on a policy of armed provocation. While the six Salonica conspirators who founded VMRO under the nose of the Ottoman secret police could not be directly linked to Sofia, a second, parallel organization for the "liberation" of Macedonia, known as the Supreme Committee, enjoyed close ties with the Bulgarian army and had protectors at the highest levels of government. These "Supremacists" quickly moved to subsume the upstart VMRO, which sought not union with Bulgaria, but autonomy for Macedonia.

Instead, they were outmaneuvered by the conspirators from Salonica, led by two youthful organizational geniuses called Dame Gruev and Gotse Delchev, names still oft encountered in these latitudes.

GEORGE AND I ARE WEDGED behind a rear table in a restaurant in the old quarter, surrounded by chain-smoking, gesticulating students. The people around me are drinking wine, not *raki* or *slivovic*. Is this a part of Macedonian distinctiveness, this preference for the conviviality of wine in a peninsula where fruit brandy consumed in careless quantities is the tough guy's beverage of choice, the lone man's drink, the murderer's pick-me-up? A bottle of locally-produced wine appears on the table, along with a plate of sizzling grilled sausages. The noise is deafening, an unrelenting fortissimo of shouted conversation, wild music, the clatter of utensils on plates and the roar of the exhaust fan. The noisiest Greek taverna would resemble a haven of tranquillity in comparison.

The din of the restaurant provides ideal cover for my host's verbal deconstruction of the Gligorov regime. According to George, not only have Macedonia's current leaders schemed to sell out its national interests in their dealings with the Greeks, they have perpetuated the social and political *status quo* inherited from Yugoslavia. All this he conveys to me in an urgent whisper in which I detect a note of probably well-justified paranoia. "Here in Macedonia we still have the secret police. We must be careful what we say. The government controls the press. Look, we only have one daily newspaper, *Nova Makedonia*. The people who run our country are the communists, the old *nomenklatura*. Not so old, in fact. Nowadays they call themselves democrats, but they are the same people."

The directors of the large, non-profit publicly-owned firms slated for privatization—for such is the will of the IMF and the World Bank, that heavenly duo of Structural Reform—are nothing but former party hacks who will become the new capitalists of tomorrow's free-market Macedonia, he snorts. Meanwhile, unemployment rises and living standards collapse. Only the proverbial stoicism of the Macedonians has averted large-scale social upheaval. "But," he says, looking me in the eye, "our patience is running out."

By now only a few drops of wine remain in the bottle. My host's eyes glisten as he relates the misfortunes of his family which, he suggests, are coterminous with those of Macedonia. His father, an officer in a Macedonian detachment of the Communist-led Greek Democratic Army, lost a leg in combat, then spent two years convalescing in a military hospital in Tirana, before being shipped to Poland. The family was only reunited 16 years later. "What the Greeks really wanted was our land," he mutters through clenched teeth. And then, the lament which I was to hear again and again in the course of my Macedonian peregrinations, on both sides of the border: "Today the people who live there are refugees from Asia Minor or Russia. And we, the original owners, we can't even visit our former homes."

Shouldn't George's political views make him a supporter of VMRO, the sworn opponents of Mr. Gligorov? Not really, comes his tantalizingly ambiguous reply. "I support the Democratic Party." (Which, along with VMRO, boycotted Macedonia's second "democratic" elections in 1994.) But, he confides, "maybe you can meet the VMRO's leaders. I know some people there."

VMRO presidential candidate Ljubisha Georgievski, Skopje, Macedonia.
(Photo by Fred A. Reed.)

Two days and a series of cryptic phone conversations with George later, I am waiting in the antechamber of VMRO headquarters on the top floor of a downtown Skopje office-building. Intense, well-muscled young men with short-cut hair hurry back and forth down the corridors, doors open and close; from down the hall come the urgent tones of a meeting in progress. Cigarette smoke hangs in the fetid air. Then the door to the inner office swings open and a male secretary (I have seen no women) ushers me in to the office of Ljubisha Georgievski, VMRO's defeated candidate in the 1993 presidential elections and the movement's most eloquent spokesman.

On the wall behind his desk hangs a large map of Macedonia. Quick. Is it one of those expansionist maps that so obsess the Greeks? No. This one shows the current boundaries of tiny, landlocked FYROM. But on a low table beneath a window lies an eye-catching installation: a revolver and a knife criss-crossed atop an open Bible, one page of which has been replaced with hand-lettered parchment. "Should I betray my oath, may these arms kill me," translates Mr. Georgievski in a rich baritone voice, modulated ever so slightly with a chuckle. "It was the motto of the original VMRO."

In a region where, for nearly a half-century, politics remained the sole prerogative of the communists, intellectuals have rushed in to fill the vacuum created by the collapse of the *ancien regime*, though the completeness of its collapse may prove to have been, as in Romania, an illusion. Who better illustrates the frustrations of old-style politics than the man with the intense, burning eyes and carefully-trimmed beard who would have been president of Macedonia? Mr. Georgievski comes from far away indeed. An internationally-known theater director, he describes himself rather self-deprecatingly as a dissident, to the extent that dissidence was possible in "soft" communist Yugoslavia.

What leads a man who proudly claims he can get a U.S. green card whenever he wants into the arms of VMRO, the archetypal Balkan insurrectionists? "My reasons were intellectual, and moral. I, and many people like me, were sickened at the spectacle of the former communist *nomenklatura* still in power, sickened at the lawlessness and the criminal activity, at the institutionalized 'kleptocracy,' not only in the form of corruption, but as the outright theft of political power."

Look, he says, eyes boring into me like red-hot embers through old newspaper, "silence is guilt. In our special situation the intellectuals are morally obliged to participate in shaping the new nation. The job is too sensitive to be left to the politicians. Someone had to say something, right? In my presidential campaign against Gligorov, I wasn't expecting victory. I wanted to open new democratic horizons. My program was hard work, and discipline. Kiro Gligorov offered foreign aid and credits."

But, I protest mildly, what about VMRO, what about its reputation for ruthless dedication to the Macedonian cause, what about its predilection for terrorism and violence in the pursuit of its aims? All of that belongs to the past, Mr. Georgievski hastily assures me with a wave of the hand. Today's VMRO resembles not at all its historical namesake except in its commitment to freedom and recognition for the Macedonian nation. "The communists called us terrorists and hard-liners. I told the people my personality is the best guarantee against fanaticism."

Who would run on a war program today, especially in the Balkans? he asks with a certain rhetorical resonance. "The first condition of our political program is peace. It would be unimaginable, and ridiculous too, to stand for violence while living in such a small, deprived country. We have no army, and we're caught up in a deep economic and political crisis. Macedonia is the last country in the world which could nourish dreams of military expansion."

VMRO's pervasive, not to say obsessive anti-communism also won Mr. Georgievski's sympathy. No other party, he explains, was prepared to fight against the corruption of the power elite. Paradoxically, he adds, the entire Western political establishment has thrown its support behind Gligorov, the Party man. There was no Macedonian Lech Walesa. "My appearance as a candidate was totally unexpected. Gligorov would have had 90% support, just like Milosevic and Iliescu; he would have given the Albanians national status; he would have made concessions to the Greeks, maybe even traded away our name. Now he cannot. No true Macedonian will ever accept it."

Indeed. When, in October 1995, the armor-plated Mercedes-Benz limousine carrying president Kiro Gligorov was blown to smithereens by a bomb as it passed in front of the Hotel Bristol, across the street from the remains of the Skopje railway station where the hands of the clock still point to the fateful hour of the quake, I thought back to my meeting with George in the restaurant, to my encounter with the intense, articulate Mr. Georgievski. Gligorov, faithful Titoist, father of his country, supreme and cynical realist, had just returned from Belgrade where he had been briefed—and perhaps had his arm twisted—by Slobodan Milosevic on Macedonia's decision to make concessions to Athens. In return, the crippling embargo was to be lifted. Brokered by Washington, it was to have been the perfect deal, the honorable solution. And the betrayal of decades of sacrifice and struggle by the hard-core Macedonian nationalists. Now the eighty year-old Gligorov lay in a hospital bed deep in coma, crippled by his wounds, never to govern again. Once again the long arm of Macedonian resentment had struck, with all the venomous accuracy of a coiled viper which has just been trodden upon.

THE BLOODY, ASCENDING PATH of Macedonian national aspiration reached a summit in the summer of 1903. In the decade since the Salonica congress, the two competing Macedonian organizations, the VRMO and the Supremacists, had pursued contradictory yet convergent aims. They agreed that the three remaining Ottoman vilayets, the provinces of Salonica, Monastir and Skopje, the administrative arrangement which allowed Istanbul to avoid referring to the area as 'Macedonia', must be wrested from the control of the Porte. They also agreed that this result should be achieved by armed insurrection. They emphatically disagreed on the desired outcome. VMRO favored autonomy for an ill-defined Macedonian entity; the Supremacists, annexation by Bulgaria.

By the turn of the century, the incremental policy of cultural assimilation identified with poor, dismembered Stambulov, had been replaced in Sofia by a strategy of violent aggrandizement. Tsar Ferdinand, like other Balkan rulers, the descendent of a princely German family, in his case the Saxe-Coburgs, had expansionist ambitions. The Greater Bulgaria of San Stefano would, he pledged, be his gift to the restive Bulgarians. With political and logistic support from Sofia, Supremacist activity in Macedonia reached a zenith in 1902 with an abortive uprising. Meanwhile, the indigenous Macedonian VMRO, from its base in Salonica, was consolidating its sophisticated network of arms procurement, agitation, supply and finance, and dreaming of much bigger things.

Action by the two interlocking yet competing organizations grew in intensity and frequency. The Sofia government proved hypocritically powerless to curb Macedonian agitation, even on its own territory. Despite a series of spectacular arrests in Salonica, the Ottoman police could not dismantle the resilient, tentacular VMRO. Trouble was brewing. Rumors multiplied. The acrid stench of insurrection filled the air. Nearly 100,000 Ottoman troops were concentrated in the Monastir region. The Porte believed, correctly in the event, that the VRMO Central Committee was fostering a policy of provincial unrest to provoke intercession by the Powers.[128]

Even at the beginning of a century of terrorism and upheaval, the insurrectionists had understood the power of public opinion to influence

Great Power policy, and to tweak the heartstrings of the populace in the Western democracies. In 1902, a VMRO guerrilla band abducted an American Protestant missionary called Ellen Stone and held her for ransom. In a fit of Reaganesque pique, the United States government declined to spring for its own citizen, whom the Ottoman commissioner in Salonica accused of plotting her own abduction. Ransom was eventually raised from private sources. Gotse Delchev, who had opposed the kidnapping, was said to have been delighted with the outcome, and particularly with the money which was promptly plowed back into the purchase of arms. Mrs. Stone was released and, in an early example of the Stockholm Syndrome, promptly took up a career as a public lecturer on behalf of the Macedonian cause in the United States. But the episode had exacerbated the already hair-trigger tensions between a Christian population irrevocably divided against itself, and its Muslim rulers. These same tensions also reflected, with all the distorted imperfections of an image seen in a deforming mirror, the latent Great Power proxy war for the remains of the Ottoman state.[129]

The first clear indication that the year would not be an ordinary one came in Salonica in late April, 1903 when a group of former students of the Bulgarian *Lycée* who called themselves the "Boatmen" launched a campaign of terror bombing. Poetically, they had abandoned the safety of land, taken to the stormy seas of clandestine illegality. Their strategy, too, was to call the attention of the Great Powers to continuing Ottoman oppression in Macedonia, and force them into action. Their tactics were plotted for maximum effect in a city where intrigue among Macedonia's European suitors was the dominant pastime.

The conspirators rented a storefront opposite the Hotel Colombo, which shared a wall with the Ottoman Bank. From the rear of the shop a small wooden staircase led to a basement, from which they tunneled under the street and up to the foundations of the bank, emptying the sacks of dirt into the water along the quay.[130]

On the morning of April 28, the French mail steamer Guadalquivir was preparing to sail from Salonica Bay. Two days earlier Delchev and Gruev had left town precipitously, warned by the 'Boatmen' that certain events were to occur. Suddenly, a violent explosion ripped through the ship's engine room, transforming it in minutes into a flaming hulk. Fortunately there were no casualties. That afternoon, a bomb blast destroyed a section of track just outside the Salonica-Ville railway station, causing the Istanbul Express to derail. And in the early evening of the following day, a massive explosive charge placed in the carefully prepared tunnel beneath the Ottoman Bank was detonated, reducing the structure to ruins. At the same time, bombs were thrown into several of the busiest cafés of the city's European quarter. Loss of life was miraculously minimal. But the 'Boatmen' had succeeded—superbly—in capturing the attention of the Powers. Cosmopolitan Salonica's poverty-stricken, strife-ridden hinterland was bubbling with an insurrectionary desperation that could not longer be ignored.[131]

Though the 'Boatmen' episode left little doubt about either the intentions of the Macedonian organizations or their ability to take armed action, the Great Powers temporized while Istanbul searched desperately for a link between the Salonica bombers and the shadowy VMRO network. For the Porte, the signs and portents were particularly ominous. In 1902, the organization had changed its name to include the Adrianople Vilayet, which bordered on the capital itself, signifying its intention to "liberate" all of the empire's European dominions. It had also broadened its membership to include non-Slavs. While Greek historians point to the Adrianople connection as evidence that VMRO was a mere tool of Bulgarian expansionism, the active recruitment of Vlachs into the cause in the mountains of western Macedonia indicated a rather more independent policy. In fact, VMRO may never have had the precise strategy which its Macedonian or Bulgarian heirs, or its Greek detractors, have since projected upon it.

The organization's effectiveness was certified by incipient panic in Athens, which dispatched Pavlos Melas, he of the Macedonian Struggle Museum, into Ottoman Macedonia at the head of an armed band. There, with the blessing of Archbishop Karavangelis Germanos of Kostur (Kastoria), he agitated and sometimes fought as titular ally of the Turks. The archbishop, meanwhile, toured southern Macedonia, warning peasants to return to the Patriarchate or face Ottoman reprisals.[132]

Events were careening toward a showdown. Within VMRO, cooler heads suggested that action be postponed until conditions had ripened. Gotse Delchev, the heart and brains of the organization, advocated caution. But he met death in a skirmish with Turkish troops in May. Rumors flew of betrayal by the Supremacists, or possibly by the Greeks. Undeterred, the conspirators pushed ahead. In May, 1903, VMRO confirmed its decision to stage an armed insurrection throughout Macedonia.

The uprising would take place in Monastir Vilayet, an ideal location. Most of the population hewed to the Exarchate; abuses of Christians by the Ottomans and their *bashi-bouzouk* irregulars (often Muslim Albanians) had been worse here than anywhere else; a significant number of Slav and Vlach villagers and townspeople supported VRMO. The mountainous terrain was ideal for guerrilla warfare, and its distance from Bulgaria would avoid any confusion between the organization's efforts and those of its Supremacist rivals in Sofia.[133]

At dawn on August 2, 1903, the day of Ilinden—the feast of St. Elias—Macedonia burst into flame. Haystacks were set fire, signaling the start of the uprising. Rising from the earth like a dawn mist, fast-moving bands of guerrillas cut telegraph wires, dynamited bridges, occupied strategically important buildings and established military control over villages. Four days later, on August 6, Adrianople Vilayet rose up in what soon became known as the *Preobrazhenski* or Resurrection Day Uprising. The goal, said one participant, "is not to defeat Turkey, but only that she not defeat us."[134] Moved by the depredations of the Turks against the defenseless villagers, and by the valor of the rebels, the Great Powers would surely intervene to solve the Macedonian Question once and for all.

VMRO was dreaming, For all its revolutionary romanticism, it was never a popular organization. While many Slavs and Vlachs may have secretly admired its daring opposition to the Sultan, the ambiguity of its aims and the brutality of its methods won it few friends among the God-fearing Macedonian peasantry which insisted on seeing itself in the old Ottoman manner, as Christians languishing under Islamic rule. For most Greeks, of course, VMRO was nothing more than organized banditry, the personification of Pan-Slav expansionism. And the main obstacle to Greek control of Macedonia.

Ilinden flared with brief intensity, then sputtered and flickered out, like a fire in a field of straw lit by boys playing with matches. More than 200 battles and skirmishes took place, most of them lost by the insurrectionists. Provisional governments were established in four localities, all Vlach mountain villages in the south-western quadrant of Monastir Vilayet. And in only one of these, under the flag of free Macedonia, did a miniature, ephemeral state come into existence: the Republic of Krushevo.

MY WELCOMING COMMITTEE consists of a full-figured, pink-cheeked woman wearing white rubber boots and a padded red coat. No sooner have I stepped from the bus than the she strides over, grasps my hand and says: "Welcome to Krushevo, I'm Victoria." I'm taken aback not by the greeting, but the language it which it is given. The lady is speaking to me in Greek, which I assumed had vanished from these parts more than eighty years ago when the Balkan Wars of 1912-1913 divided the last Ottoman province in Europe

Krushevo, Macedonia.
(Photo by Fred A. Reed.)

between Greece, Bulgaria and Serbia, the Serbian section becoming part of Yugoslavia in 1918. In the process, Krushevo's precarious Greek identity had evaporated. Or so I had believed.

As we move rapidly uphill through the cobbled streets, where the fragrance of wood smoke hangs lightly in the mountain air, Victoria quickly sets the record straight. "I'm not even Macedonian, you know," she says. "I'm Vlach, just like half the population here. But some of us still speak Greek. It used to be the language of commerce, and of culture."

According to some Greeks I encountered in Salonica, Krushevo had all along been a Greek town, Hellenism's northernmost penetration into Slav Macedonia. Certainly, it could claim a well-attended secondary school and an Orthodox cathedral, as well as a Hellenic intellectual tradition. But were the Krushevites Greeks?

I could not claim I'd been entirely unprepared for surprises, for the discovery of identities within identities. Several days earlier in Skopje I had encountered a Krushevo-born architect named Niko Boschku. Rapidly, his description of the town's architectural features, the wealthy multi-storied manor houses with their pitched roofs and pediments displaying family coats of arms, had slipped off into a passionate defense and illustration of the Vlach soul—something I was to experience in my every encounter with members of this tenacious, mysterious and, regrettably, vanishing Balkan minority. "You're going to Krushevo, eh? Well, I have a good friend there. I'll call and let her know you're coming. Her name is Victoria. She will look after you."

Mr. Boschku had not told me was that Victoria Peti was director of the Krushevo historical museum, and of the battlefield memorial which commemorates the bloody uprising that engulfed the town in 1903. Naively I had thought I would learn little in Krushevo but the close-up story of an epic, quixotic Balkan battle, that I would touch an ideal as fleeting and intangible as it was hard, glistening and palpable: freedom for a people without a name, for a country without a past. How grotesquely mistaken I was to be. My entire Balkan journey had been a slow emergence from the ingenuousness inculcated by the Universal Culture's great uniformization crusade, a pilgrimage undertaken with all deliberate speed into the realm of complexity, into fertile and danger-ridden chaos, a trip downward into the vortex.

Victoria has drawn up an itinerary that barely gives me time to catch my breath—no easy task in the rarefied mountain air. At 1350 meters, pine-girt Krushevo is the highest town in the Balkans. It is said that all Balkan settlements above 1000 meters are populated by Vlachs. In the event, our town walkabout was to begin not at the battlefield monument which crowns the summit, but with the Vlach connection which suffuses its every fiber.

At her urging, I deposit my luggage behind the counter of the only bank in town. "Don't worry, no one will touch it; this is Krushevo!" she assures me, and leads me upstairs into the manager's office where Toma Kardula is waiting. Over a glass of plum brandy and a cup of Turkish coffee, Mr. Kardula, a lanky deep-voiced man with the hands of a lumberjack, a banker's sharp eye for figures and a barrister's affection for disputation, quickly sketches out the history of the town's inhabitants.

The Vlachs, he explains, speaking Aroumani (the Vlachs' word for their language, in which we easily recognize "Roman") as Victoria translates into Greek, are an industrious nomadic people who live in high country villages throughout the southern Balkans, speak a Latin dialect strikingly similar to Romanian and tend huge flocks of sheep. "300 years ago, we were the largest population group in the region. The Greeks tried to make Greeks out of us, the Romanians claim we're Romanians. But we are who we are, a people without borders. The salt and pepper of the Balkans."

As the bus entered Krushevo I'd noticed that, unlike most Macedonian towns, there were no minarets to be seen. Now, before I could ask why this was so, Mr. Kardula is providing the answer. While most of the Balkan peoples were tied to the land by their Turkish masters the Vlachs enjoyed special status under the Ottoman Empire as purveyors of wool, cheese and mutton, and as organizers of the huge horse caravans that transported goods from one corner of Ottoman Europe to another. Over time this obscure people, this semi-distinct society of semi-nomadic mountaineers had generated the commercial, financial and intellectual elite of a region extending from what is today northern Greece, Macedonia and Albania as far north as Bosnia and beyond, into Croatia, and Austro-Hungary.

But who are the Vlachs? "Well, we are the real, original Macedonians," he asserts with the bluntness that I was later to encounter among Greek Vlachs who claimed, from the ringing heights of conviction, that they were the descendants of the original Greeks. "We are descended from the Thracians, and our language is an ancient member of the Romanian family."

But didn't the Romanians inherit their language from the Roman occupiers of Dacia? "Inherit our language from the Romans!" he bursts out, "Nonsense. How could the Romans have bequeathed their language to an entire people in less than two centuries. Impossible!"

Mr. Kardula's account of the genesis of the Aroumani tongue does not precisely correspond with prevailing scientific wisdom. Such wisdom is often itself torn by the conflicting national theses of Greek and Romanian scholars. The former assert that the Vlachs were Greeks who adopted the Latin idiom as a result of proximity to the Romans, the legionnaires who had arrived in Macedonia in the second century of the pre-Christian era and stayed on to found the Eastern Roman Empire. Not at all, claim the latter: they are descendants of the Romanized Dacians who migrated south, driven by waves of invading Goths, Slavs and Bulgars. The proof? No mention is made of the Vlachs in Byzantine sources until the tenth century of the modern era.[135]

Is Mr. Kardula's impromptu lecture part of a hastily organized semi-official visit staged for my benefit by the shadowy "authorities" to somehow strengthen Skopje's claim to Krushevo's pre-Ilinden heritage, or is it the *cri de coeur* of an ignored and disappearing minority? My demitasse of Turkish coffee has dwindled to the dregs, and still he talks on. The 'official visit' hypothesis begins to look flimsier as the bank manager and Victoria engage in a heated disagreement in Vlach, from which neither seems prepared to back down. This is not the façade of serene harmony, nor the self-assured unanimity, which should be presented to the visitor. Official history, too, is taking a beating. I had come as would a pilgrim to the secular shrine of Ilinden in the semi-devotional spirit of suspended disbelief, only to be confronted with the remnants of a proud people whose sense of identity antedates that of the modern-day Macedonians.

If the Vlachs have committed an original sin, admits Mr. Kardula, it was to have accepted Orthodox Christianity. "If we were Catholics, we would have had our own state. Instead, the Greeks tried to make Greeks out of us, through the Church. Today, we're Orthodox, but we belong to the Macedonian church. We don't want anyone on our heads."

Prevailing dogma in the Balkans, from the stirrings of post-Enlightenment national revival to the post-Communist explosion of national reassertion, posits the Ottoman empire as a uniquely evil and retrograde apparatus of oppression. What I am hearing from Mr. Kardula, in the board room of the Krushevo bank, is not precisely this dogma. As he sees it, the main adversaries of the Vlachs were less the Turks, with whom an accommodation had been reached, than the Phanariot Greeks. These were the wealthy Istanbul aristocrats who had insinuated themselves into the very fabric of the Ottoman state, the better to promote Greco-Byzantine cultural-national aims using the power and influence of the Patriarchate.

In the torrent of argument, I catch the word “Moskopol” flitting from Mr. Kardula’s tongue as does a hummingbird from flower to flower. No possible doubt: the director is talking about the barren rubble heap called Voskopojë which I had visited in the hills above Korçë, in Albania. Moskopol, he asserts as Victoria rushes to catch up, was larger in its heyday than Zagreb, Lubljana, Belgrade, Sofia and Athens combined. The rector of its Academy, which opened in 1760, was a man called Cavalioti, the father of Vlach culture, who published and taught in Aroumani, and even translated the Holy Liturgy. “My theory is that the Phanariotes convinced Ali Pasha of Ioannina to destroy the city because the Patriarchate feared the emergence of a written Vlach language and national identity,” he says.

Whatever the theory, Moskopol was indeed destroyed in 1769 by brigands loyal to Ali. Cavalioti’s disciples were dispersed throughout the Balkans, some seeking refuge in the Hapsburg domains and in Venice. Others came to Krushevo, where the special protection accorded by the Validé Sultan, the Sultan’s mother, to the Vlach people still obtained. Several decades later, in 1813, a grammar of Aroumani was published in Vienna, the work of a certain Mihail Boiagi. But once again the perfidious Phanariotes conspired to keep the offending book out of Vlach communities, he explains, pausing to slip a copy of the original grammar—in Aroumani, German and Greek—across the table. I pick it up: the ancient book crackles with the brittleness of age, a yellowed repository of a language almost forgotten, a kind of linguistic living fossil, a glossal coelacanth dredged from the opaque waters of oral tradition. As I leaf cautiously through its pages, he goes on: “The Greek priests called our language the ‘devil’s tongue’, and ordered parents not to send their children to Vlach schools.”

The priests’ policy failed, as all such policies must. And though Greek influence in Krushevo remained substantial, the town’s Vlach identity survived. At the turn of the century, on Ilinden eve, the prosperous settlement of 15,000 souls—Vlachs, Greeks and Macedonians—awaited the tempest in dread and longing. “All of Macedonia was supposed to rise up,” explains Mr. Kardula, the bitter inflection of his voice communicating his feelings even before Victoria translates his words. “But only in Krushevo did the rising succeed. And that is how our beautiful city was destroyed. What I am telling you I learned from my grandparents. The official history says that the revolutionaries set up a committee of 15 Albanians, 15 Vlachs, 15 Greeks and 15 Macedonians. But official history is a lie. I’m a Vlach and I know how many there were.”

He doesn't say how many, but the answer is as implicit as clear: they were all Vlachs.

"For us, it was a disaster. The Turks recaptured Krushevo and burned down the Vlach part of the town. 60 shops were destroyed. Hundreds of houses. Ilinden? It was one big mistake. Maybe it was a good idea, but it came at the wrong time. Why did they stage the uprising in Vlach cities? Because they were far from the main roads, high up in the mountains."

But where were the Macedonians? I ask, transfixed as the director dismembers the Ilinden myth. "Macedonians? We were the Macedonians," he snorts. "Us Vlachs. We used to fight the Slav kids all the time. As far as we were concerned, they were Bulgars. We always thought the organizers were Bulgars." By now, the approved version is lying in shreds on the table, next to the Aroumani grammar. Victoria, who has translated Mr. Kardula's eruption with good grace and perhaps some slight embarrassment, for she herself has brought me to his office, smiles inscrutably, glances at her watch, then at me.

The Ilinden memorial awaits us.

Krushevo radiates a sturdy, self-assured prosperity even to this day. It reminds me of the Vlachs themselves: tall, open-faced, ruddy and direct, yet secretive and difficult to approach. Many of the town's finest houses, built in a semi-baroque style quite out of keeping with the Turkish manner, are more than a century old. Several of these stolidly bourgeois dwellings still display elaborate semi-heraldic motifs painted in a naïf style above their doors. Like the mercantile houses of Amsterdam's golden age, whose austere stone fronts concealed great wealth, the residences of Krushevo evoke substance, a regard for community and a horror of ostentation.

A few hundred meters further up the hill, we emerge onto the broad plateau which overlooks Krushevo town. The sun has finally cleared the pine-forested crags, and casts its oblique light over the cascade of frost-clad rooftops. Across the Pelagonian plain, on the southern horizon, hidden by a smudge of brown haze from the coal-fired power plant at Bitola, lies Greece.

But the plateau is dominated by the Ilinden memorial, built in the shape of a gigantic hand-bomb, the kind associated with the bearded, wild-eyed, turn-of-the-century Balkan anarchists of caricature. Seen from the outside, the structure is a monument of heavy-handed, heroic symbolism at its mind-numbing worst. Victoria pulls out her keys, unlocks the door and slides it open. Sunlight pours through four stained-glass windows onto the white interior walls while from concealed loudspeakers wafts haunting, ethereal choral music. In the center of the chamber stands a block of white marble engraved with the name of Nicola Karev, president of the Krushevo Republic, the first, short-lived, democracy in the Balkans. Behind it hangs a blood-red flag, its Cyrillic inscription proclaiming "Freedom or Death", motto of so many vain and glorious Balkan insurrections.

The banner, Victoria explains, is a copy. The original is still in Istanbul, despite president Kiro Gligorov's best efforts to retrieve it. It is almost, she tells me, as if the Turks were determined to remind Macedonia that the Ilinden Republic was crushed after ten days of existence, Krushevo—including its cathedral—burned, and most of its 15,000 citizens turned into refugees.

Outside, as we stroll through the landscaped grounds, Victoria points to a series of plaques engraved with the names of the insurrection's heroes. Here is Gotse Delchev, who actually opposed the uprising but was assassinated before he could stop it, perhaps because he wanted to stop it. Here is Pitu Guli, the fierce-eyed, full-bearded Vlach mountain fighter who stood his ground and died in battle against an attacking force of 20,000 Ottoman regular infantry.

Victoria's version of events is, predictably, at odds with Mr. Kardula's. "I'm telling you the real story, not some tall tale. Ilinden wasn't Bulgarian," she explains in her delicious colloquial Greek. Two days after the rising the Turkish garrison left Krushevo. The townspeople formed a revolutionary council made up of Vlachs, Macedonians and Albanians. Within a day, they had drafted a Manifesto which declared the first independent republic in the Balkans, and elected the anarcho-syndicalist Karev, a man who carried a copy of the Communist Manifesto next to his revolver, as its first and only president.

The Krushevo Manifesto is a curious piece of insurrectionist literature, less programmatic document than appeal for solidarity directed towards the region's Turkish Muslim population. "We have not risen to slaughter and plunder, to burn and steal," it proclaimed. "We have not risen to convert your people to Christianity or to dishonor your mothers, sisters, wives and daughters... We took up arms to defend our property, our lives, our religion and our honor."

"We call upon you to join us in this struggle for freedom and human life. Join us, brother Moslems, so that we can attack both your and our enemies. Join us under the flag of 'Autonomous Macedonia!' Macedonia is our mother and she calls on us for help..."[136]

Karev may have been a socialist, but the Vlach shepherds and merchants probably reacted with the solid skepticism of self-sufficient mountaineers to the notion of proletarian dictatorship. Still, they fought hard and bitterly to defend their mountain peaks and their proud town. The members of the 1,200-strong defense force were heroes, says Victoria. "But they didn't know a thing about serious warfare. All they had against the Turkish artillery was muskets, and one cannon made from the trunk of a cherry tree, which blew up with the first shot."

By the time Victoria and I have completed our slow peregrination of the memorial park, afternoon shadows are long on the ground. The wind has dispersed the smudge haze, and to the south the peaks that march across the Greek border loom purple on the horizon. From the pine-covered mountainside below us, through which the Turkish troops made their final assault on Pitu Guli and his remaining handful of defenders, wafts the sweet scent of resin.

Back downhill we stride. Groups of high-school students are dashing headlong for the bus station, shouting boisterously. Men and women moving at a more leisurely pace cross our path; Victoria exchanges greetings with them in Aroumani and Macedonian, with an occasional Greek 'kalispera'—good evening—thrown in for good measure. A besieging force of hunger is now testing my defensive perimeter. When Victoria invites me to share the evening meal with her and her mother, I surrender with what must appear unseemly alacrity.

Viewed from without, the house more resembles a ruin of crumbling plaster and slumping roof than a habitable dwelling place. In front stands a gnarled crabapple tree possibly more ancient than the structure it half conceals. Proudly, Victoria informs me that this is one of the oldest dwellings in Krushevo, a survivor of the fire which destroyed the town after the uprising. Here she lives, custodian of the past in the custody of the past, with her mother Zaharia, a white-haired woman of deep old age whose forehead and wrists are tattooed with the tiny crosses all Vlach women once bore as a protective talisman against forced enrollment into Turkish harems. Unlike her daughter, mother Zaharia has forgotten her Greek. Our conversation is a mix of monosyllables, gestures and smiles. What she has not forgotten is the secret of meals expressly suited for the kind of appetite only a day of trudging up and down cobbled streets in the crisp mountain air can create. Soon the table creaks under a load of dense bread, fresh yogurt, chicken with rice, home-distilled *raki* and a sublime white *kashkaval* which the Vlachs, those master cheese makers, claim as their contribution to the world's culinary heritage.

In Zaharia's kitchen, warmed by the wood stove and the *raki*, the atmosphere is dense with nostalgia. Victoria pulls a shoe-box from the kitchen cupboard. Opening the box as if it were the secret house of her heart, she reveals to me her collection of sentimentally priceless postcards. Printed in Salonica, their inscriptions in Greek, they depict the town before and after the catastrophe. Some picture the leaders of the "Republic." Here is Nicola Karev posing in profile. His jutting goatee reminds me of that of Ivan the Terrible when he receives the delegation of the people in Sergei Eisenstein's eponymous film. Another shows Pitu Guli, bearded and irascible, his heroic chest criss-crossed with bandoleers, the classic Balkan bandit/liberator. "When school kids come to the museum, I tell them that something like this will never happen again. People were starving for liberty. Today, we have our liberty." Then she pauses, looks at me, smiles. "Still, I think Delchev was right. The whole thing was a mistake. You know what we say in Macedonian? History is a whore."

The last bus has long since departed and I am quite happy to have missed it. Krushevo leads a double life as a ski resort, complete with rusting lifts. Accommodation is available in the barn-like hotels that ring the upper perimeter of the town. But the resourceful Victoria finds me a room in a local home for one quarter of the price. My host for the evening is a retired physician called Nicola, who speaks only Macedonian. As the television set hisses, sputters and groans in the background, I venture a question about the 'name question' controversy. Will Macedonia give up its name to please the Greeks? "Anyone who dares to change our name will have to come here and answer to us," he snaps back, as Victoria translates into Greek. "We are Macedonians and nothing else, and we're not going to stop being Macedonians to please anybody." And if there is an attempt to divide the country? The answer is loud and unanimous, as Nicola's wife looks up from her embroidery and states with the calm conviction that means the discussion is closed: "Over our dead bodies."

Sleep, beneath a fluffy eiderdown, is as deep and complex as Macedonian history. My dreams are inconclusive, their resolution just beyond reach, receding like a mirage. Yet I awake refreshed as the light of dawn filters through lace curtains. After a breakfast of bread, cheese and tea with my hosts, Nicola escorts me, slithering down the ice-slick cobblestones, to the depot where the morning local to Bitola waits.

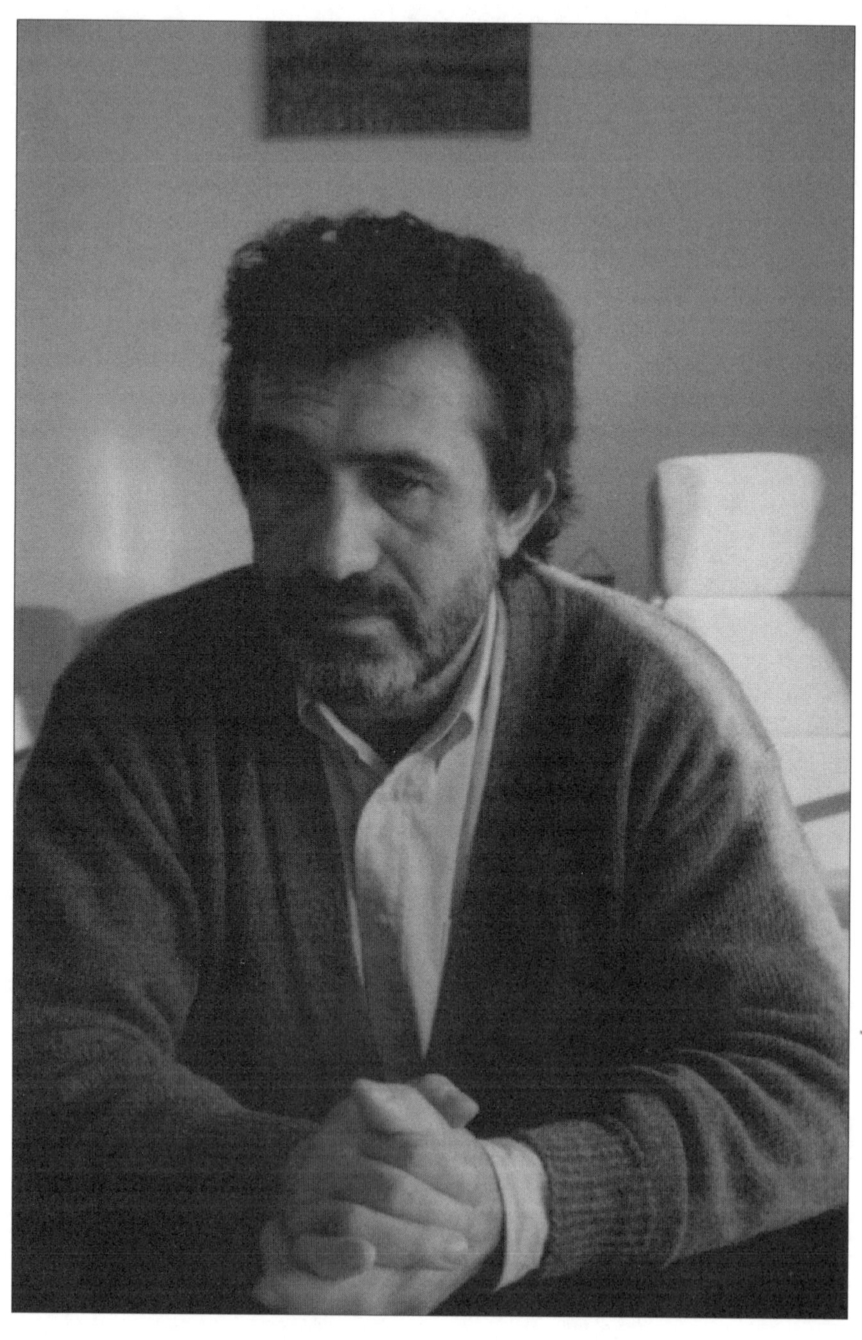

Arben Xhaferi, leader of the Party of Deomcratic Progress, Tetovo, Macedonia.
(Photo by Fred A. Reed.)

NOTHING EMBODIES BETTER the precarious, schizophrenic essence of Macedonia than Tetovo. In this city of 40,000, set hard against the slopes of the Sar Planina a mere 20 kilometers from the Kosova border and only a bit farther from the once hermetic frontier of Shqiperia, throbs the heart of an unredeemed Greater Albania embedded in a body which harks back to Ottoman days when religious affiliation, not nationality, stood as the organizing principle of society. Tetovo's duality is mirrored in the sharp contrast between the Yugo-socialist "downtown," whose concrete administrative buildings and apartment blocks overlook a broad, weed-grown central boulevard, and the sinuous, narrow tree-lined streets of the ancient Albanian-Turkish town where small shops selling agricultural implements open directly onto the beaten-earth sidewalks. Here the air is fragrant with wood smoke, minarets dominate the skyline and a fast-flowing tributary of the Vardar gurgles beneath arched bridges, past mosques and coffee-houses shaded by water-loving plane-trees.

Beware of Tetovo, I had been warned before I left Salonica. "You'll see," volunteered Greek know-it-alls who had never visited the town, much less Macedonia, but believed what they read in the county's colorfully imaginative press, "Albanians selling AK-47s on the street, and women too, as sex slaves for the European market." Perhaps it was my misfortune to visit Tetovo on a cool, sunny Sunday, not on market day. I saw no guns, no women for sale, though I could not vouch that such phenomena did not exist. No perfidy, no debauch, no crime is too ignoble for the shadowy Other who lurks amongst us.

Tetovo's Macedonian downtown looked deserted. Not so the outskirts, populated almost exclusively by Albanians who thronged the streets. These citizens have remained rigorously conservative in their dress: the men wore Islamic skull-caps or the conical Albanian peasants' cap; many, perhaps most, of the women were dressed in various forms of *hijab*. I caught a glimpse of a group of older men dressed in baggy pantaloons disappearing quickly down an alleyway, turbans wrapped around their heads, looking for all the world like Afghani refugees in a Tehran satellite town.

I have stepped from the would-be post-modern Westernism of Skopje, where dreams of Macedonian multiculturalism are debated with an attentive eye to the two uncles—George (Soros) and Sam—into a vibrant Albano-Islamic town. Religious repression in Titoist Macedonia, was never as severe as in atheist Albania. Religious tolerance, even promotion—as in Bosnia—was the price of social cohesion. The Tetovo Muslims I saw wore their faith with a self-assurance which seemed curiously at odds with the assurances of the man I had come here to meet, the Albanian nationalist Arben Xhaferi, leader of the Party of Democratic Progress and uncrowned ruler of the imaginary yet plausible autonomous Republic of Ilyria.

Few in Macedonia are indifferent to Mr. Xhaferi (pronounced Jaferi), a graduate in philosophy of Belgrade University and, for 15 years, the chief editor of cultural programs for Prishtina television. For the hurriedly recycled postcommunists of the *nomenklatura*, he is the devil incarnate; for the hard-boiled Macedonian nationalists of VMRO, a pragmatist with a hard-core constituency like themselves, a man with whom a deal can be struck; for the beleaguered Albanian minority, a savior-in-waiting. What he may be for the long foreign fingers poking, prodding and testing the ruins of former Yugoslavia in their search for proxies, is a source of constant speculation in Skopje. Normal enough. If foreign investment is the only language of salvation, politics can be expressed only as the clashing interests of transnationals and markets.

Most people in Tetovo know the location of Mr. Xhaferi's office, though the shambling structure has no visible street address. "PDP" I tell the cab driver. "PDP!" he fires back with a grin, and within ten minutes I am sipping a cup of espresso while the leader explains, in halting French, how the communists in Skopje who now wear democratic hats drink only Turkish coffee. "When I was still in parliament, we wanted to introduce an espresso machine as our contribution to the battle against communism," he laughs. "They refused. It just shows you how deeply rooted are the old ideas inside the mental structures of the Macedonian leadership."

We are interrupted briefly by the arrival of the interpreter, a precise, courtly gentleman named Mr. Ibrahimi, a former professor of English at Prishtina University, that fertile seed-bed of Albanian national consciousness. The interview will take place in Shqip, not in Macedonian, a language neither man relishes speaking and may even speak poorly. On Mr. Xhaferi's desk are the red and black double-headed eagle flag of Albania and the banner of the PDP. The Macedonian banner, that which bears the sixteen-pointed sun drawn from the royal tombs at Vergina, an emblem the Greeks claim belongs to them, is nowhere to be seen.

The Albanian strategy he sketches out for me would bypass Macedonia altogether and claim for itself a fresh new autonomous identity based on European standards. The appeal to European standards, encountered constantly in the Balkans, seems designed to seduce credulous journalists, wide-eyed investors, foreign NGOs and visiting dignitaries. Speak not your heart to the uninvited guest, runs this quintessentially dissimulative logic; tell him only what he would like to hear. But why am I surprised? The contrary would have been surprising. It is by their stories that we shall know them.

Mr. Xhaferi runs down the catalogue of grievances. Albanians are marginalized, they cannot find work, cannot get an education in their language. While they account for as much as one third of the population, only two percent of the national police force is Albanian. Percentages in the judiciary and the civil service even lower, a scandal. Only two percent of the graduates from the country's two universities are Albanian. "This is because the Macedonian state is based on a dominant/subordinate relationship. We are alienated spiritually and politically as well. If we cannot satisfy our aspirations within the system, we will eventually look outside for spiritual, political and religious answers."

Is this a threat? I ask. Not at all, merely a statement of fact. The essence of Soviet communism was, he argues, a thinly disguised version of Pan-Slavism, an extremist, expansionist policy which originated with Peter the Great, and saw small nations at the early stages of national development, nations like Finland, Romania and Albania, victimized by their proximity to the Russian Slav imperial center. But while the Great Powers of Western Europe were able to discard their colonies outside Europe, the geographically contiguous Slav zone continues to provide a buffer for Slav imperial ambitions which now work not through the multi-ethnic Soviet empire, but through a pleiade of smaller Slav states.

"To destroy the devil, you must first create him," says Mr. Xhaferi as I scribble busily. "The Slavs are attempting to show the West that the devil is Islam, and that the cross is the only defense. This they use as a pretext for their expansionist policy. Look at the Serbs; by attacking the Muslim Bosnians they have created an 'Islamic factor' in the Balkans. There is talk of Islamic penetration, of Turkish influence, of an 'Islamic corridor.' They are creating a devil, as I see it. If they succeed, there will be a continuation of the policy of 'religious cleansing' which has been going on since the Balkan Wars."

Yes, and the Albanians are Muslims, aren't they?

"Listen, we Albanians have sore throats from shouting that we're Europeans. Islam never became part of the structure of Albanian national identity, it never played a dominant part in Albanian history. European cultural codes have always prevailed. Europe entered the Islamic world via Albania, via Albanian Catholics. Did you know that the University of

Istanbul was founded by Albanians, that the first Ottoman encyclopedia was written by an Albanian? We were the catalyst for westernization!"

What really interests Mr. Xhaferi — as it does his brethren in Prishtina — is nationality, not religion. Among the Macedonian majority there are whispered accusations that the Albanians are expanding eastward into Slavic lands, creating a local demographic *fait accompli* through their high birth rate, and stealthily appropriating the land. Not so, he prickles. There have always been Albanians on both sides of the Kosova border, long before an independent Macedonia was anything more than a fantasy. In any event, 'Greater Albania' would correspond to today's ethnic Albania, which is only a shadow of what it once was, when Skopje and Bitola/Monastir (not to mention Ioannina, in Greece) were Albanian cities. "The Albanian ethnic zone is contracting," he says, a tone of wounded indignation creeping into his voice. "What is left is the core, the vital substance of Albania. We are not being persecuted for religious, but for cultural reasons. Not on account of Islam, but on account of our Albanian national culture!"

Rare is the political discussion in the Balkans over which the looming presence of Washington does not cast a long shadow. The Yanks, Mr. Xhaferi tells me, have inserted themselves into the Macedonian imbroglio for long-term geostrategic reasons. Perhaps even as a result of some secret US-Soviet deal cut at the Malta summit between George Bush and Mikhail Gorbachev, itself a source of almost bottomless and not unjustified Balkan paranoia. "We're not hoping the US will side with us, but we hope to gain some advantage from the westernization of Macedonia, from the construction of a new state with a political system based on the West. After all, an American presence means the penetration of American values."

Only with the most extreme self-control do I avoid volunteering my personal assessment of American values. By now the interview has already stretched well beyond the two-hour mark, yet Arben Xhaferi shows no sign of flagging. The same cannot be said for the interviewer. I am growing weary, my note-taking hand is cramped. Yet I am fascinated by his single-minded concentration, unmediated by the falsely indulgent, manipulative cynicism typical of Western politicians. Words, for the man who would perhaps deliver the dream construct of autonomous Ilyria over to tomorrow's Greater Albania, of which he and Ismail Rugova would be revered as founding fathers, still carry the urgency, concreteness and immediacy of action. These same words would give him and his cohorts the power to manipulate the Powers, to appeal to world public opinion, to rally the US and Germany—for instance—against the perfidious Slavs. But who am I to cry 'illusion', to whisper 'deceit,' to pour the icy water of cynicism over the head of a charming, hospitable Balkan mini-demagogue? Especially when history may be on his side.

Taking my leave, I stroll through Tetovo. Near one of the town bridges stands the Serena Dzamija, the Painted Mosque. Every outside surface of the 150-year-old building is covered with bright-hued floral and geometric patterns through which run, like gold thread in a fine carpet, a leitmotif of Qur'anic inscription. I remove my shoes and enter, treading lightly on the footworn carpets. The same decorative scheme has transformed the inner space into a garden of the spirit. A *tasbi*—Islamic prayer beads—and a copy of the Qur'an lie on a window sill where they have been left in perfect repose by a worshipper. The mosque glows soft red, green and gold in the failing autumn light. Soon the dusk call to prayer will ring out from the minaret and the faithful will come to kneel, heads bowed toward Mecca.

Behind the Serena Dzamija and across a rutted street from Tetovo's sprawling Muslim cemetery lies the walled enclosure of the Arabati Baba Teké. Formerly a monastery of the Bektashi Order, the Teké was transformed into a combination hotel-restaurant-casino by the Yugoslav nation builders of Macedonia. Mainstream Islam, they must have reasoned, was too strong—or too inoffensive—to be attacked. The Bektashis, with their combination of mystical pseudo-Shi'ism and Albanian crypto-nationalism, were another matter. Experts in *taquiye*, dissimulation, the Dervishes could be both subversive and dangerous, they must have reasoned. But after years of suppression, the Order has slowly begun the work of reclaiming the place for God and against the forces of Mammon. The back buildings, harmonious peak-roofed structures in dark wood, are now inhabited by a handful of Bektashi brothers who are not on the premises this afternoon, but whose hand is visible: in a small burial shrine adjacent to the main mosque, murals depicting Mecca and Istanbul have been restored, the grounds are swept, the sanctuary breathes with the life of the spirit. On one the gravestones which line the grassy yard, I come upon an inscription in Greek and Latin. The graven letters are timeworn, the message indecipherable, the evidence unmistakable. This place rests squarely atop the jagged cultural frontier that bisects the Balkans, the frontier that cannot be covered over, cannot be eluded. The ancient frontier that divides us still.

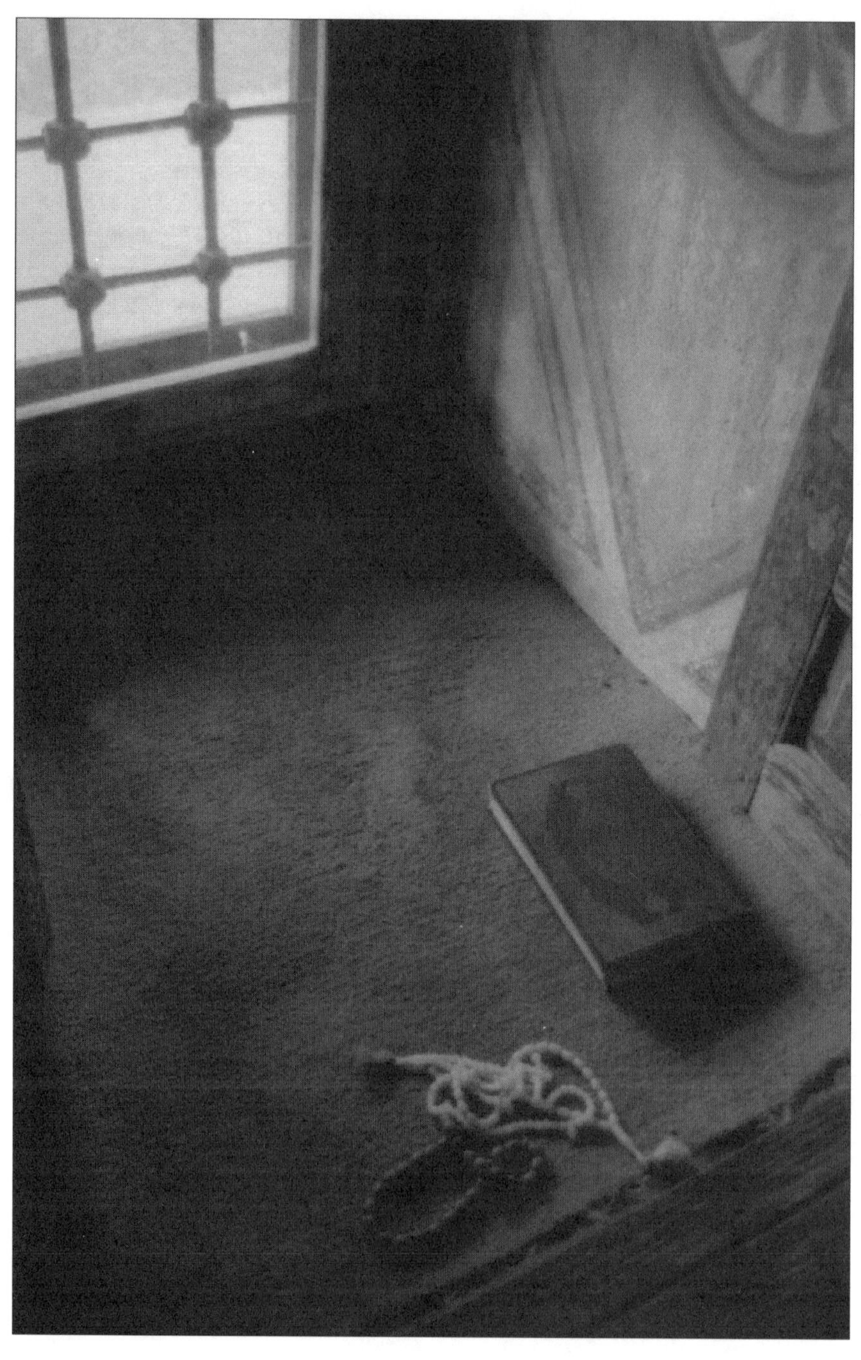

A copy of the Qur'an and a *tasbi* in the "Painted Mosque," Tetovo.
(Photo by Fred A. Reed.)

Seven months later I was back in Tetovo. Armed police posted at the intersection of the main highway to Ohrid were searching private automobiles, but the Skopje bus coasted right through. Waiting for me at the Serena restaurant was Mr. Ibrahimi, the courtly gentleman who had interpreted for Mr. Xhaferi. There was barely have enough time for a quick bite before hurrying off. Excitement was high. The trial of the founder of the self-styled Albanian University, proscribed by the Skopje authorities, had begun earlier that morning. The Albanians of Tetovo were demonstrating in the streets.

The University, the keystone of the Macedonian Albanian strategy of establishing autonomous cultural institutions as a prelude to setting up the autonomous Republic of Ilyria, had become a flash point in early 1995 when State authorities closed the institution's rudimentary campus. The action touched off violent street riots in which an Albanian student was killed, allegedly at the hands of the Macedonian police. Several days later Dr. Fadil Suleimani, the Prishtina-educated "rector" of the University had been arrested and imprisoned on charges of sedition.

Even as we reached the town square, a plaza surrounded by the squat, bunker-like concrete structures which block out the wood and plaster architecture of old Tetovo, the demonstration had begun. The crowd massed in the square beneath the leafless trees was humming with nervous anticipation. Then, from the main street leading from the old town to the square echoed the throb of rhythmic chanting. Within seconds the first ranks of marchers appeared, stretched across the entire width of the avenue, carrying banners written in Shqip and English, with not a Cyrillic letter to be seen. "Dr. Suleimani, we are with you!" said one. A delegation of adolescents several hundred strong brandished placards which read "Keep our teachers in school, not in prison." As each contingent—women's groups, knots of school-children, farmers, teachers—marched into the square they were met with cheering and shouted slogans. The Macedonian police had evaporated; only a few capped heads protruded discretely above the surrounding roof-tops.

By now the atmosphere had begun to crackle with the electricity that thousands of determined, angry people alone can generate. Last in a short slate of speakers, Arben Xhaferi took the stand, a low podium thrown up at the head of the square. As he fired off sentences like machine-gun bursts, the crowd responded with laughter, sighs of indignation or applause. The loudspeakers whined and hummed, but the leader's guttural, urgent voice knifed through the static. I could understand nothing but the essence:

Albania, University, autonomy, resist, fight. Fists were brandished in the air, banners snapped in the wind, the urgency was palpable and yet with it came a sense of stolid, rock-hard endurance.

Unlike the February protests, the march was peaceful and orderly. It unfolded with a near-military precision, control and seriousness that made its pent-up energy all the more threatening. Scores of marshals with red armbands ringed the square, and when the last shouting had died away they channeled the crowd along diverging dispersal routes. Within fifteen minutes the square was empty, with only the remains of torn placards to remind the trees and raw concrete that thousands of people had just massed there. "Come with me," said Mr. Ibrahimi, "Mr. Xhaferi will be happy to see you."

PDP headquarters had, since my last visit to Tetovo, gone upscale. Where before we'd huddled in a cold, dank room with plywood partitions, the party's new office now boasted carpeted floors, glass dividers, three telephones, diverse office machinery, and a well-dressed secretary. In one corner gleamed a late-model Italian espresso machine—emblem of Western modernity, antithesis of fusty, sinister Communist Turkish coffee—as technologically advanced and complex—and more pleasing to look at—as any fax or computer. Mr. Xhaferi, who was now sporting a full beard, was still wild-eyed, his pupils dilated, his nostrils flaring, high from the intoxication of the demonstration. The turnout—10,000, according to an unsympathetic Radio Skopje account—and the discipline of the marchers had established his party as the dominant force among Macedonia's aggrieved Albanians.

Eight months ago Mr. Xhaferi had been clean-shaven, cool-headed, reasonable, European. On this day—though, to be fair, public acclaim is a powerful elixir—he resonated like a rabble-rousing fundamentalist of the kind I'd become familiar with in Tehran. With a full and bristly beard, he even looked the part. The Albanians have made three huge concessions, he told me. They have accepted the existence of the Macedonian state, they have abandoned the idea of 'special status' as proposed by Lord Carrington; they have even swallowed a *fait accompli* and agreed to participate in institutions designed neither for nor by them. What now? "We may withdraw from these institutions, just as we have withdrawn from parliament. There must be dialogue. If there is no dialogue, there will be a fight. There will be war."

"This trial," he said, pointing in the direction of the Tetovo courthouse, "is putting more than Dr. Suleimani on trial. The language of the court, the judges, the prosecutor, the symbols—everything is Slav Macedonian. What is the message? That we Albanians are under occupation. It's not enough for the government to occupy our lands, they want to occupy our minds as well. But I tell them this: you cannot put ideas in prison like you can a man. Thank God, the number of people dedicated to this idea is increasing every day."

A driver from the PDP took me to the bus terminal. "This," he said, the sibilant vowels whistling through his teeth, "is next Bosnia. Look! The bastards!" and he pointed to armed police patrolling the streets. "We're under occupation."

IF TETOVO EXISTS in an exalted and dangerous near future, Skopje, a piddling 40 kilometers to the east, exists in a more prosaic but equally dangerous present. Where Mr. Xhaferi and his fellow advocates of Albanian autonomy seem secure in their own sense of collective selfhood, the Macedonians of Skopje radiate defensiveness, apprehension, insecurity. In a turbulent zone where ethnic identity remains the only social currency, an ambiguous, ill-defined multi-ethnic mini-state cannot easily contain the flagrant diversity, not to mention the conflicting historical narratives, of Albanians and Macedonians. The nub of the problem is this: how can a country which defines itself as the homeland of a people whose existence is denied by its neighbors accommodate within its bosom a powerful Muslim Albanian minority that it doggedly refuses status as co-founder, whose traditions, religion and history are at such utter variance with its own? * Macedonia far too resembles, in microcosm, the former Yugoslavia for the illusion of a harmonious future to survive its projected shelf-life in the supermarket of the New World Order.

Politicians in the post-communist Balkans have today become almost as mindful as their Western counterparts of the constraints imposed by their new democratic personae. From masters of what the French call *la langue du bois*, the opaque, invert jargon of the dear, departed socialist regimes, they have marched eagerly into the former enemy camp, have become fast-learning apprentice manipulators of the equally tendentious lingo of free market democracy, world culture and foreign investment. Unable to beat 'em, they have joined 'em.

(*As an adopted Québécois I was constantly surprising myself in the act of pondering the same question with regard to the Canadian dilemma. Of course, there exists little more than a remote, tenuous similarity between the condition of Macedonia's Albanians and that of the French-speaking citizens of Québec. And yet the underlying malaise, the stiff-necked denial by a self-doubting, ungenerous majority, of the minoritarian Other's assertion that it exists in and of itself and will define that self, has touched off reverberations that I can recognize.)

Better, infinitely better, to talk to poets, creators and renewers of language.

The man sitting opposite me, sipping Turkish coffee in a Spartan café in downtown Skopje, wears a threadbare jacket, shiny-kneed trousers and sandals whose soles have known many sidewalks and paving stones. As we chat, he brushes wisps of long brown hair from his forehead with a bony hand. Gaunt, intense Eftim Kletnikov, now in his early forties, has visibly made no peace with the new secular authorities. His Macedonia is hewn from an ancient massy monolith with the word-sculptor's sharp-edged implements of verse and legend. "Poets are the identity of a country," he says. "Our first poet was Clement of Ohrid. He not only founded the first university in the Slavic world, but a school of literature besides. I belong to that school."

In well established countries, it's normal enough to have a tradition of introspective, personal poetry, he maintains. "But in a small, fragile country like ours, we must sing our identity at the top of our voices. Our language is our homeland. When I write poetry in Macedonian, I speak the distinctness of my country from the Bulgarians, the Greeks and the Serbs. For centuries our language was forbidden. When we created ourselves in 1945, it was only natural that it erupt with such vigor. For centuries it was waiting for the chance to spring out of oral tradition."

But who are the Macedonians? I ask, popping the fateful question. "We are a cosmopolitan people, which may be the root cause of our tragedy. We preserved our identity with our intelligence, our rites, our beliefs, our language. We took scrupulous care of it all. We may not have had a state, but we knew who we were, always."

Macedonia is a rich and beautiful land, muses Mr. Kletnikov, his wistful tone tinged with sadness. And Macedonia's neighbors were always more powerful, more ruthless. "We were open to everyone, and this cost us dearly. I believe that today we are experiencing the greatest threat to Macedonia in all its history. The Albanians just don't want to live with us, and they have shown it from the very first moments of independence."

The most hurtful paradox of contemporary Macedonia, if I understand my poet-interlocutor, is that at the precise moment of its emergence as a fully independent political entity, the precious identity which its poets and intellectuals have struggled to create has abruptly become a devalued currency. The second paradox is that the communist regime, which in Mr. Kletnikov's eyes stands accused of having all but destroyed the human spirit, somehow contrived to foster the sense of national cohesion which the post-communist Macedonian government is speedily abandoning. "The state itself wants nothing to do with culture. But our culture is our identity. How are we supposed to present ourselves to the world? 'Leave it to the market,' they tell us. What market?"

"Our culture is under as serious a threat as our country. Today, the only thing that counts is money. But what good is money if we have no soul?" An argument with which a Denys Arcand could empathize. Several days later, in a sleek office complex on the outskirts of Skopje where sleek, glossy computers and photocopiers whirred and whispered, I encounter comfort and indifference in the person of another poet, a man as glacial and self-assured as Eftim Kletnikov was outgoing, perplexed, and apprehensive. Kim Mehmeti undoubtedly has excellent reasons for his optimistic view of the Macedonian present and future. Not only is he dressed in the kind of relaxed but expensive clothing which would shame no transcultural yuppie in leisure mode, he holds that most coveted of Balkan sinecures, a full-time position with the Open Society Foundation of Macedonia. The Foundation is the agency funded by the Hungarian-born American speculator George Soros to promote his idiosyncratic views of the proper relation between citizens (or should we say consumers?), markets and the state.

Where Mr. Kletnikov had been spontaneous, effusive and generous with his time, and manifestly in the employ of no one, Mr. Mehmeti would clearly rather be in Philadelphia, or wherever Soros' world headquarters may be. Not for him the impertinent questions of an itinerant scribe two notches short of nobody with no monster media calling card. With a diffidence as ill-concealed as a yawn, he consigns my questions to the requisite slots. How does an Albanian poet fit into a Macedonian national state? "Macedonia cannot work as a national state, it must have a multi-national identity." So how can Macedonia survive? "Today, we must talk of world citizenship. Fixation on nationality doesn't contribute to quality of life. And in any case, the disappearance of states and nationalities is not a new thing, historically speaking."

All that's missing here, following the introductory remarks, is the plant tour and the delegation in native costume. Whoah, wrong regime. Make that the in-suite fax, health club, cell phone, business lunch and drinks in the VIP lounge. Blasé, detached, Mr. Mehmeti serves up the current batch of eternal, immutable verities of the powerful as only an obsequious flack can. Stirred well, they form an unctuous, glutinous pap which adheres to the palate and sticks in the craw. And what is the Soros Foundation doing in Macedonia? "Soros is doing what the Western countries should be doing but aren't, helping us emerge from our backwardness. I don't believe Soros wants anything in return." Isn't your relation with Soros a Faustian bargain? I venture, attempting to rattle my imperturbable host. "Soros doesn't even know who works at these foundations. Personally, I really believe in his idea of the open society. And whatever the case, this is a hell of a lot better than what we had before."

I had to admit that the hand of God often moves in strange ways.

George Soros arrived in Skopje from Sofia, capital of neighboring Bulgaria, one afternoon in September, 1992, liked what he saw and heard, and made an on-the-spot decision to invest in Macedonia. An Open Society Foundation office had already been in operation for several years, like its counterparts in places as diversely similar as communist-ruled Hungary, Bulgaria and Ukraine. The Soros strategy in these places had been, as Connie Bruck writes in the New Yorker, "to nurture the weak and subvert the powerful."[137] But in Macedonia, Soros apparently realized that, by inverting the formula, he could help decide who would hold power and thus directly impinge on it, in the interests of an open society to be sure. The decision to throw his weight (read money)—and excellent connections with official Washington—behind Kiro Gligorov, in the form of two twenty-five million dollar loans and public endorsement of the Macedonian government's position in the 'name conflict' with Greece, may have been motivated by altruism, though those who know Soros have expressed doubts that he possesses such qualities. The man who has become one of the largest landowners in Argentina and runs a Sarajevo TV station may have been amused, diverted by the prospect of actually owning a country. Did Soros drop off to sleep with fantasies of Balkan fiefdoms dancing before his eyes; visions of huge ballrooms crowded with beribboned, mustachioed officers whirling across polished floors with countesses in flowing gowns to the tune of Austro-Hungarian waltzes? Given the continuing erosion of national sovereignty under the hammer blows of what the masters of the world are wont to call globalization, Soros' day may come sooner than we expect. Unless his unavowed aim is to resuscitate the Hapsburg empire in a new form.

Curiously, though Soros' Open Society Foundation claims to want to encourage Macedonian multi-ethnicity as a counterweight to the endemic, exclusionary nationalism of the Balkans, by supporting Kiro Gligorov it had thrown its weight behind a policy which has led to discord, violence, the real threat of an Albanian autonomist movement, and perhaps not incidentally, the physical neutralization of the great Stability Figure, without which no right-functioning free-market economy can even contemplate operating.

Fresh from my encounter with the two poets, I met Vladimir Milcin, the Open Society station chief in Skopje, at a low-key party held at the Macedonian Information and Liaison Service. The Service is a privately-owned press-club-cum-cultural-center run by a polished, inquisitive man named Ljupco Naumovski, a former high-ranking member of the now defunct Yugoslavian foreign ministry. Accompanying Mr. Milcin was a hulking, furry Sharplaninec mastiff whose massive, rectangular head readily cleared its master's waist. I had been well prepared for the meeting, and for the dog. Mr. Milcin is the father of Maria, the precocious teenager who had been my seat-mate on the bus from Ohrid several weeks earlier.

The New Yorker depicts Mr. Milcin as an ardent Macedonian nationalist, but in the flesh he comes across as a man of considerably greater subtlety. He may also be wary of what his daughter, in adolescent frankness, may have told me about her father. "Graves are graves," he says, by way of introduction, in the elegiac mode of the stage director, his real-life trade, "and bones are bones; if we truly wish to respect them, we cannot use them as weapons. Still," he adds, a note of bitter irony creeping into his urbanely modulated English, "no one in the Balkans is prepared to respect the will of the people living here. I am sure you can imagine how my daughter reacts to that!"

Under the Yugoslav regime which self-destructed in 1991, Macedonian history was taught from a 'Serb' viewpoint, which laid the country's ills at the feet of Greece and Bulgaria, he explains. Meanwhile, the Bulgarians deny ever having 'occupied' Macedonia during World War II; 'liberation' they call it. "There's no denying our common history with the Serbs. And I cannot ignore the fact that more than one million Macedonians went to Bulgaria as refugees. That, too, is part of our common history."

Macedonia, admits Mr. Milcin, could conceivably collapse from within. But a close reading of Balkan history shows that its neighbors have always taken more than a casual interest in such a collapse. Take 1992. That was when Albanian president Sali Berisha vetoed a secret deal brokered in Athens to divide Macedonia among its four neighbors: Greece, Bulgaria, Serbia and Albania. Berisha promptly alerted his great friends and protectors in Washington and the deal* fell through. But Serbian military intelligence is

(*I had heard of the plan in 1992 in an off-the-record talk with a member of former Greek Prime Minister Andreas Papandreou's staff. The official sketched for me, on the back of a paper napkin, a schematic map of Macedonia, then divided it into four sections. "Some people believe this is the way of the future," he said. "Including the Greek government?" I asked. The official smiled.)

still active in Macedonia, and may have been linked with the profanation of a mosque in Tetovo, and with an outbreak of violence in Skopje's Bit Pazar, in which several Albanians were killed by police. "Who profits from the conflict between Macedonians and Albanians? Slobodan Milosevic, of course, the better to conceal the festering sore of Kosovo."

AS MY STAY IN THE MACEDONIAN CAPITAL drew to a close, weather conditions turned suddenly propitious. The optimism of spring filled the air; warm air from the Aegean had seeped up the Vardar valley, and suddenly trees burst into leaf. I could almost smell the salt tang of Salonica bay. On my last day in Skopje, I met a man who seemed to concentrate, in his eighty four years, all the paradoxes and contradictions, all the headstrong obduracy of his countrymen and their complex, troubled, ambivalent heritage. Had Archbishop Mihail, primate of the Autocephalous Macedonian Orthodox Church and spiritual leader of the world's nearly three million Macedonians, been just a bit shorter on piety, had his white beard been less flowing, he could have passed as a retired professor, or perhaps a sea captain whose salty practicality was now tempered, like the weather-worn planking of a ship's deck, by the sagacity of age.

The circumstances of his Church conspire to encourage modesty while they sustain a fierce pride. In the eyes of its Orthodox brethren, the Macedonian Church is a rogue organization, recognized neither by the Ecumenical Patriarchate of Istanbul, nor by the Serbian Church from which, allege the Serbs, it split. Of such doctrinal adversity are lives of great stubbornness made. Can there any greater Macedonian quality?

The meeting had taken months to arrange. On my first trip to Skopje, the Archbishop had been unable to receive me, though we had spoken briefly on the telephone. When I arrived for my second visit, he was indisposed. But by the end of my stay, he had recovered sufficiently to see visitors. Now I was waiting in an anteroom in the modest two-story structure that houses the head offices of the Macedonian church, in the shadow of Skopje's reconstructed Orthodox cathedral. An inner door swung open and his worship, bareheaded and clad in simple black robes, strode into the chamber in the company of two younger clerical adjutants.

The worst mistake people can make about Macedonia is to believe that it is an artificial creation of the communists, the archbishop assures me. Quite the contrary. The Macedonians form an ancient people whose history began eleven centuries ago at Ohrid, with Saints Clement and Naum, those spiritual

Archbishop Mihail, head of the Macedonian Orthodox Church, Skopje.
(Photo by Fred A. Reed.)

brothers who preached in the native tongue of their compatriots and baptized the population into the Macedonian Church—the same church he leads today.

It was not until the tragic defeat of Tsar Samuil at the hands of Basil II that the Macedonians lost their political freedom to the Byzantines. "We became slaves of the Greeks, but our archbishopric continued to live. Even Greek clerics had to learn Macedonian to communicate with their congregationists. Throughout the centuries of Byzantine, Bulgarian, Serbian and Ottoman enslavement, our church at Ohrid was the source of our spiritual life, our faith and our national being. The great miracle of Macedonia is that it has survived at all. And this survival is due to the religious traditions of our people."

Survival has not been easy. The archbishop's see at Ohrid, lodestone of Macedonian national consciousness, was abolished by the Turkish authorities in 1767. "But our church was not annulled canonically. We continued life as the mother of the Serbian church, which now claims to have jurisdiction over us."

In 1921, when the first Yugoslavia was formed in the wake of the conference at Versailles, the Serbs took possession of Macedonia, calling it South Serbia. "They paid 1.5 million gold francs to the Patriarchate and bought our church from the Greeks. When they came, they did not come as missionaries, but to assimilate us, just as the Greeks and the Bulgarians have done in the past. Praise God, none of them succeeded."

As befits the head of an outcast, oppositionist church, the archbishop's curriculum vitae includes several years as a leader of the Macedonian resistance organization known by the acronym of ASNOM, six years in a Yugoslav prison, and six years as a priest in Melbourne, Australia, where he became a small-aircraft pilot, hopping from one far-flung parish to another. They called me "the flying priest of the Macedonians," he reminisces with a wistful smile, gazing back from the impenetrable complexities of high old age onto the graceful simplicity of a heroic past.

Ah, Archbishop Mihail seems to say, if only it weren't for politics. Alas, however, there are politics. As Macedonia's neighbors have hedged their recognition of the new country, or, like the Greeks, denied it outright, so the Archbishop's sister churches have proven less than charitable in their acceptance of the Autocephalous Macedonian Orthodox Church. So acute has been their rejection, friends in Skopje told me, that the Macedonian church has opened secret negotiations with Rome with a view to becoming

Uniate—Orthodox in rite but who acknowledge the primacy of the Pope, a position which would be anathema to the Serbs, Bulgarians and Greek Churches who see themselves, not the schismatic Popists, as guardians of the True Faith. I test the Uniate hypothesis on the Archbishop. His voice remains even, his demeanor calm: "Of course we travel to Rome as pilgrims, to kneel before the grave of St. Clement. Or course we are in touch with Vatican leaders, who understand us and give us assistance. It is true that some of our intellectuals have pleaded with us to recognize the primacy of Rome. I am sure that our people would oppose unity with Rome. We are thankful for their understanding. But we are not Uniates. We are Orthodox."

"I'M STILL NOSTALGIC for old Skopje" says the white-haired gentleman strolling beside me along the Vardar embankment as the late afternoon light falls obliquely through the fresh-leafed trees, bringing the graceful arch of the Stari Most—the old bridge which links modern, post-earthquake Skopje with the old quarter—into sharp relief. The air is soft, and the birds have begun their evening chorus. "It was a lovely, close-knit town with a compact urban structure."

Mateja Matevski, my companion for the afternoon, is a poet and president of the Macedonian PEN-Club. Where Eftim Kletnikov dressed in the tattered clothes of the social outcast, and Kim Mehmeti in the casual uniform of the World Culture, Mr. Matevski wears the slightly rumpled postcommunist suit and tie with the ease of a man accustomed to poetry festivals and international literary delegations. Where Mr. Kletnikov makes his office in the cafés and public squares, and Mr. Mehmeti in the high-tech-crammed cubicles of the Soros Foundation, Mr. Matevski sits at the heart of the Establishment, the Macedonian Academy of Arts and Sciences, a massive structure on the left bank of the Vardar which speaks authority, solidity, immutability.

In his long and distinguished career as what one might term an apparatchik, although that might be uncharitable, Mr. Matevski worked as both a print and a television journalist before being promoted to director of the state radio and television network. "You had to earn a living, and you couldn't do it as a writer, not in Macedonia," he reminisces, dare I say disingenuously. "For ten years, I was president of the Macedonian Commission for Cultural Contacts with Foreign Writers, and for three years, a member of the collective presidency of Macedonia, just before we left the Yugoslav Federation. But I was always dreaming of the day I could retire, to work full-time as a writer and poet."

The day has arrived, the dream come true. Mr. Matevski is free to meander from his office at the Academy along the tree-lined banks of the Vardar with visiting writers, to compile anthologies of verse, to set the past on a steady course through the present and into a bright global future of interdependency...poetic of course. "Fifteen centuries of domination made this land of ours what it is today," he says, grasping my sleeve as we come to a stop beneath the trees overlooking the Old Bridge. "Our heritage is one of terror, forced assimilation, war. When we see the catastrophe of Bosnia, all we can think about is peace. Pacifism is in our blood. Still, there are forces who don't want stability. But I say a stable, independent Macedonia is the key to stability and peace in the Balkans. You see, we don't belong to anyone but ourselves."

Mr. Matevski and I shake hands and part. I stand for several minutes looking at the bridge. Who does he mean by "ourselves?" Across the bridge, in Old Skopje, lies another self which partakes not at all of the neo-cosmopolitan gloss of the reconverted Macedonian establishment. The Bit Pazar, a warren of open-air stalls and rambling shacks selling everything from individual cigarettes, Korean-made kitchen utensils and farm implements to sophisticated German electric appliances and carpets from Turkey (though once again I find neither AK-47s nor underage girls), could well be a scene from Istanbul or south Tehran; a spirited mix of jostling, shouting crowds, pickpockets, smoke from grilling kebabs and diesel fumes, the chirping of caged birds and the whine of Turkish music. Indelibly "oriental," unmistakably Islamic. At the heart of the bazaar is the mosque, and at the heart of the mosque, groups of earnest, bearded young men from Bosnia, from Debar, from Kicevo, from Tetovo, from Skopje itself, are immersed in the study of the fundamentals of their long-lost, omnipresent faith. The world of Islam not only exists here in proudly Slav Macedonia, it has an autonomy of its own, a contiguity with the social fabric, a tenuous yet indelible system of beliefs and values that reaches as far east as Mindanao.

Balkan nationalism, exalted, vicious and founded on an egregious construct of myth and fantasy—a kind of monstrous, virtual southeastern Euro-Disney before the fact—oversaw the destruction of cosmopolitan Salonica, of "cosmopolitan" Sarajevo. Perfected by the West to help prosecute the crusade against Ottoman Islam, it is at work in sub-cosmopolitan Skopje as well. But now the West, whose contours are as impalpable as the tide, yet as hard-edged as shadows on a wall, cynically conceals its past and cloaks its thirst for domination in the cloth of globalism and supranationality. Simultaneously, surreptitiously, it secretes the most sordid of ethno-racialist aspirations. For ethno-racialist aspirations, following the collapse of

The old bridge over the Vardar, Skopje.
(Photo by Fred A. Reed.)

class-based collectivism, remain the only means by which peoples can express their belonging, their social solidarity; the only credible refuge from the blight of free-market globalism. The Balkan nightmare, from Bosnian actuality to Macedonian potentiality, is the encounter between Masters of boundless cynicism, and acolytes whose greed is exceeded only by their ambition. The Balkan quagmire is our quagmire; a muddy vortex slowly sucking us under.

SLOUCHED IN THE BACK SEAT of a Bulgarian government Mercedes parked behind the House of Parliament in the center of Sofia, I wait. The chauffeur sits, imperturbable, behind the wheel. The limousine's radio is tuned to one of the private radio stations which have infected the airwaves of the Bulgarian capital as an antibiotic-resistant virus invades a weakened body; from it booms "Big Dick Man." Here in Bulgaria, even more than in Albania, the greater had been previous political isolation, the more abject has become the craving to embrace an imaginary American Way, desirable as the absolute antithesis of that which had gone before.

Normal enough. Yet a cynic might note that promised American investment is closely linked with liberty narrowly defined: that of made-in-USA cultural products to "compete" in the Bulgarian market. In fact, American investment in Bulgaria has so far consisted of the takeover of radio and television outlets, those late twentieth century missionaries whose fervor exceeds, while it complements, that of their more modest cousins, the Evangelicals.

I had arrived in Sofia via Prishtina and Nish, following the trail of the Macedonian Question, and discovered a capital city wracked by a violent outbreak of crime and financial collapse, scoured by the coarse abrasives of Western Pop Culture, transformed into an open-air flea-market of communist and religious memorabilia, of ideas and ideals. Sofia's graceful sidewalks teemed with itinerants, with knots of dark-skinned men squatting, in the Oriental manner, beneath newly-erected hoardings which trumpeted the virtues of banks, automobiles, whisky and cigarettes. For several days I had stared out over this human landscape, its bleakness exacerbated by a cold, driving rain, from the window of my hotel room, from the breath-misted windows of creaking, crowded streetcars, from beneath the dripping trees of the city's vast parks. I had completed my tour of the four Balkan churches dedicated to the Aghía Sofia, and had gaped at the grandiloquence of the mammoth St. Alexandr Nevsky cathedral dedicated to the 200,000 Russians who fell in the fight to deliver Bulgaria from its Turkish oppressors in 1878 and into the hands of Pan-Slavism.

In the clammy offices of the Institute for Balkan Studies, on a tree-shaded lane only a few hundred meters from the huge cathedral, I encountered Varban Todorov, a bright, bespectacled academic whose research specialty is the ethnic complexity of the southern Balkans. "I am one of those Bulgarians who believe there is a Macedonian identity, and a Macedonian question," he told me as we sipped tea, facing one another across a polished oak conference table. Books, thousands of books on Balkan affairs, stared benignly down on us from the walls. Outside, rain dripped from the eaves; inside, the dampness had penetrated to the marrow of my bones.

Furthermore, he added, most of Bulgarian opinion remains convinced that the Macedonian issue is a sacred one. When the Bulgarian government recognized Macedonia in 1991, it could have specified that it was recognizing a state, a nation and a language strictly within its present borders. This it did not do. "In recognizing only a Macedonian state but pointedly not a Macedonian people," he added ominously, "president Zhelev may have opened the door to the eventual break-up of Macedonia."

Since the fall of the communist regime in 1989, the Bulgarian scientific and intellectual community has become persuaded that the Macedonians are truly Bulgarians, he went on. The Macedonian autonomist movement led by VMRO was Bulgarian, as was its Salonica section. Historical leaders Gotse Delchev and Jane Sandanski may have been born in geographical Macedonia, but their national consciousness was Bulgarian. The Ilinden uprising, too, was a Bulgarian affair.

But my host was a realist. Macedonia, he said, was here to stay. 50 years are enough to create a state with its own national consciousness. There will always be a dispute with Macedonia over history, of course. But the history of the region has also shown that a direct Greek-Serbian-Bulgarian border is not a good idea. This would come about were Macedonia to disappear, to be partitioned by its neighbors or simply to be swallowed up by a protective Serbia. Better a buffer exist. "If not, there would be danger of a third Balkan war."

The following day, under clearing skies, I returned to the Institute for a meeting with Mr. Todorov's father. Nikolai Todorov is a walking legend, a compact, pugnacious, white-haired former member of the anti-fascist resistance, a survivor of communist prisons and first president of the post-communist Bulgarian National Assembly. A man who speaks gruffly, gestures expansively and smiles a quicksilver smile. The problem in the Balkans, he explained as he paced up and down the room, remains one of reconciling the demands of the region's omnipresent minorities with the principle of the inviolability of borders. European recognition of the mini-states which constituted the former Yugoslavia has been, he insisted, a tragic error. How could they have imagined they could treat the Serbs as a minority in what had been their country? "Personally, I supported the Serbs; they had the courage to oppose the setting up of a Muslim state which would have opened the door to a Muslim axis running from Istanbul to Sarajevo."

Why, wondered Nikolai Todorov aloud, should a Bosnian-Croat "federation" be legitimate, while a federation linking the Serbs of Krajina and Serbia not be? "The effect will be to legitimize a second Albanian state, in Macedonia. The example is likely to spread, and it is a dangerous example."

I quickly understood why Mr. Todorov the elder enjoys a reputation for frankness in an age of mealy-mouthed euphemism. "Macedonia is historically Bulgarian," he insisted, adding with a slightly malicious grin: "And the Greeks know it very well, having assimilated over one million Bulgars. But if Macedonia is not viable today, this is not so because of Greece and Bulgaria. The problem is the Albanians. If the government cannot maintain some kind of domestic equilibrium, what will the Slav element do? If the Albanians manage to break off a part of Macedonia, the rest will revert to Serbia, Greece and Bulgaria. Macedonia is nothing but a geographical name, you know."

THE STOCKY YOUNG MAN in a well-cut brown suit hurries across the parliamentary parking lot towards the Mercedes. The driver quickly lowers the radio volume as Anatoly Velichkov pops into the back seat and shakes my hand. We had met the previous day at a ceremony held in Sofia's sprawling Palace of Culture to commemorate the demise, 92 years ago, of Gotse Delchev, the Macedonian—or was he Bulgarian?—national martyr. Between solemn, polyphonic songs performed by a choir of men and women wearing Macedonian folk costumes, Mr. Velichkov had given an impassioned speech, in which he had praised the memory of the man claimed by Skopje as the founder of independent Macedonia, and by the Macedono-Bulgarians as the supreme personification of their dual identity. I understood not a word, but fully captured the rhetorical intensity of this man, one of the two members of the Bulgarian parliament to openly identify themselves as members of the long-proscribed Macedonian revolutionary organization VMRO (not to be confused with its homonymous mirror image in Skopje). We had chatted briefly in French, still the second language of educated Bulgarians, and he had invited me to accompany him and his colleague Evgeni Etkov to a political meeting being held the following day in a village in the heart of the Pirin, that region of historic Macedonia which today lies within the borders of Bulgaria and whose population is, Mr. Velichkov informed me proudly, almost totally Macedonian. “A member of our party has just been elected mayor; he has invited us to speak. Meet me in the parking lot behind Parliament at two o’clock tomorrow. You will be our guest.”

Today—the ninety-third anniversary of Gotse Delchev’s death in obscure circumstances a scant few months before the Ilinden Uprising—is the day. As the Mercedes pulls out of the driveway, Mr. Etkov comes trotting up the sidewalk and jumps, puffing, into the front seat. He reaches back to shake my hand, and the Mercedes roars out onto the yellow-brick streets of central Sofia, along General Totleben Boulevard and south toward the our destination, a few kilometers short of the Greek border.

Mr. Velichkov’s and Mr. Etkov’s organization shares with its estranged Skopjian twin the same history, the same heroes, the same martyrology and the same unquenchable Macedonian fixation. But where the Skopjian VMROists claim the purest Macedonian and even anti-Bulgarian credentials, my two hosts are intent on convincing me that the real VMRO was, is and always will be Bulgarian. “Ilinden was a purely Bulgarian insurrection,” states Mr. Velichkov, interrupting to translate his own words for Mr. Etkov, who nods emphatically from the front seat. “The participants were all ethnic Bulgars. No matter how great their ideological differences, the leaders of the movement were fighting for the autonomy of Macedonia, Thrace and the Adrianople Vilayet as a stage in the struggle for union with Bulgaria, to recreate the Great Bulgaria of 1878.”

Well, you won’t hear *that* in Skopje.

The creation of the first Yugoslavia frustrated the legitimate ambitions of the Macedonians, he continues, and irredentism was the inevitable result. Come World War II VMRO, which had continued to exist, organized action committees to welcome the Bulgarian troops who marched into Vardar and Aegean Macedonia behind the armies of the Third Reich.

There, alas, was the rub. Along the Aegean littoral, the Bulgarian military was seen by the Greeks as worse than the Nazis. In Vardar Macedonia, the equivalent of today’s new country, the liberators quickly began to swagger about like they owned the place, behaving as liberators often do, like oppressors and assimilators. Still, as the Greek Civil War was soon to show, a Bulgaro-Macedonian self-awareness did exist, and proved a determined foe.

We make a brief stop in Blagoevgrad, the spiritual capital of Pirin. There the two deputies purchase a handful of bananas, the once forbidden fruit which in these parts now symbolizes, along with American cultural trash, the omnipresent world market. Back on the road, the Mercedes rushes south along the fertile banks of the Struma River, one of the great historical corridors of invasion and migration. This is the spot, Mr. Velichkov proudly notes as we speed through a cliff-girt defile, where an inferior retreating Bulgarian force stalemated the Greek offensive during the tragic, short and nasty second Balkan War of 1913.

In 1912 the Balkan states—Greece, Serbia, Bulgaria and Montenegro—aided and abetted by Russia which hoped to use them as a counterweight to Austro-Hungary, had declared war on Ottoman Turkey and, in a three-front campaign, driven it almost entirely from its European possessions. The war left Serbia in control of much of Macedonia, and the Greeks had captured Salonica. Bulgaria coveted both, but its armies had born the brunt of the fight against Turkey, a strategic error. In a poisoned atmosphere of claim and counter-claim, the Bulgarians attacked Greek and Serbian positions in Macedonia in late June, 1913. The action had been intended as a "demonstration" designed to provoke Russian mediation and an adjustment of borders. Instead it provoked war, for, unbeknownst to Sofia, Greece and Serbia had concluded a secret alliance to divide Macedonia among themselves.

The conflict was brief, bloody and, for Bulgaria, a self-inflicted tragedy of Aeschylian dimensions. The victorious Serbs marched into Vardar Macedonia; Greek forces thrust north, burning and destroying Bulgarian towns and villages as they went, until finally they came to grief in the Struma gorge. But the damage had been done.

The sun is setting beyond the rounded summits of the Pirin range as the car turns west off the main north-south highway. A few kilometers more and we reach Novo Delchevo, a dusty farming settlement of 2,000 souls which has been freshly renamed in honor of the national hero. The Mercedes pulls up in the town square, an open space between the municipal building and the schoolhouse, both relics of the socialist era and now in a state of visible deterioration. In the schoolyard a welcoming committee is drawn up, awaiting the delegation. I am portentously introduced as a visiting journalist of significance. The mayor, a stocky, bright-eyed man wearing a cloth cap, pumps my hand vigorously. Off to the side, up against the wall of the schoolhouse, on an impromptu ground-level stage beneath the red and black VMRO banner, a trio is playing. Sinful, sophisticated Sofia is far, far behind us; "Big Dick Man" has yet to reach this forsaken place. For small graces I praise the God of former atheists. The musicians, led by a dark-skinned clarinetist who is almost certainly a Gypsy (though for the occasion he passes muster as a true Macedonian), weave the complex rhythmic and melodic textures of Balkan music, the clarinet sighing, chirping, mocking and weeping. Little boys romp across the schoolyard pursuing one another with squirt guns, while groups of villagers stand off to the side waiting for the official festivities to get underway, noisily crunching and expectorating roasted sunflower seeds. Pre-adolescents on bicycles dart in and out of the crowd, swerving and popping wheelies, and above, swallows flit gleefully against the darkening sky.

Suddenly it is decided that a critical mass has been attained. Let the festivities commence. The mayor strides up to the microphone, the music stops, people step forward to form a wide, ragged semi-circle. The old men who had been kibitzing beneath a sheet-metal roofed gazebo turn their heads in expectation. The children stop playing, the bikes skid to a halt. First Mr. Etkov, then Mr. Velichkov are called to the microphone. I pick out the words "Macedonia", "Bulgaria" and "Gotse Delchev." Heads nod, people applaud dutifully if diffidently. Little girls in frilly frocks look on, wide-eyed. Then Mr. Velichkov turns and beckons to me. "And now" he says, "our honored guest, the eminent journalist..." Rather than risk offending by impoliteness, I walk up to the mike and express my admiration for the life and work of "that outstanding revolutionary Gotse Delchev." I pointedly omit his nationality. These are the Balkans; one cannot be too cautious. Mr. Velichkov translates, there is applause, the band strikes up, and the dancing begins. The dignitaries repair to the village cantina for the ceremonial meal, while I continue my journey south toward the frontier.

An hour later, threading my way between the TIR trucks lined up waiting for customs clearance, I walk across the border into Greece. Two hours later I am perched in the high cab of an empty, unmarked Bulgarian oil tanker as it jolts and rumbles through the darkness toward Salonica. The tanker is probably a blockade buster, heading south to pick up a load of crude, then re-entering Bulgaria before veering northwest into oil-starved rump Yugoslavia. The driver and I exchange few words. He speaks no Greek; I, no Bulgarian. Each of us inhabits a tiny, self-contained world, the contours of which are outlined by the headlight beams on the road ahead. After midnight we crest the hill and begin the long descent into Salonica, starting point of my Balkan journey several months before. Flames from the oil refinery flicker in the night sky; the stink of sulfur mingles with the bite of iodine in the salt-moist air.

Chapter 7

THE SEARCH FOR MACEDONIA

Surrounded on three sides by snow-capped peaks, the valley is a place of fog: the cool, gentle-fingered shrouds of early summer mornings, or the clammy, bone-chilling mists of winter which seem to seep from the marshy ground itself, like the wraiths of ancient Macedonian fighters, muskets in hand, singing mute songs. On the official map the valley is called Almopia, a name resuscitated from ancient Greek. Once it was known by its Slavic name as Moglana, the land of the fogs, and because today fog envelops trees and houses, Moglana is again what I shall call it. A few kilometers north, beyond the mist-shrouded mountains, lies the upstart state of Macedonia. In this remote region, the Greek State is locked in combat with an adversary that is at once everywhere and nowhere, as evanescent and persistent as the fog: the faint voice of a Macedonian identity that increasingly dares to speak its name.

I have come to this valley, a two-hour bus ride from Salonica, to hear the stories of two men who live less than five kilometers apart yet inhabit different worlds. Both I encounter here, in the heart of the Moglana, in a market town called Aridea—S'botsko on the invisible map of greater Macedonia—whose contemporary form seems designed to obscure its past. That there are excellent reasons for this becomes clear as I listen to Kostas Tzanis, the editor-publisher of the regional weekly published here.

Mr. Tzanis, eleven years ago, did something few of his countrymen would even contemplate. He moved north, to this border region of mists and ethnic ambiguity from which emigration, voluntary and involuntary, has always been substantial, and married a local girl, a "native"—that is to say, a Slav-speaking Macedonian. There may have been another, unconsciously symbolic reason for the move. Mr. Tzanis is a Communist, a member of the party which waged a bitter, four-year armed conflict in these very valleys and mountains, a civil war which ripped the social fabric of the land asunder and sounded the death knell for Greece's embattled Slav-speaking minority.

His story, like every story heard in the Macedonian triangle, begins thus, with the dense, multilayered presence of the past: When a detachment of the Greek army marched in during the Balkan Wars, in 1912, the population of the Moglana valley was made up mainly of Greek-speaking Muslims who had converted to Islam in the eighteenth century. Following Greece's crushing Asia Minor defeat at the hands of Kemal Atatürk's Turkish revolutionary forces 10 years later, the two countries exchanged populations. The exchange was based not on ethnic, but religious criteria. Turkish speaking Christians from the depths of Anatolia were settled here; Greek-speaking Muslims were plunked down in new homes along the Aegean littoral of Asia Minor (where, in isolated villages, old men can still be heard speaking the Greek dialects of their birthplaces). The descendants of these transplants, who are still known as "refugees" even today, now form a majority of the region's population. But the Muslim Greek-speakers they supplanted had not been the region's only inhabitants. "Of course," he assures me, as he sips cold Nescafé from a tall glass, "this area was inhabited by Greeks in ancient times. The way I see it, people changed languages and began speaking Slav (he scrupulously avoids the terms 'Bulgarian' or 'Macedonian') when the region came under the authority of the Archbishop of Ohrid, and Slavonic was used in the Holy Liturgy. Later, Bulgarian families settled in the surrounding villages and adopted a Bulgarian identity during the reign of the Bulgar Tsar, Samuil."

When the Muslims—most of whom had been prosperous land-owners or small farmers—departed, those who remained expected to share the prize, the newly vacated land. But title to the land was given to the newcomers instead, Mr. Tzanis tells me. Thus was created the germ of the deep resentment toward the refugees which the "natives" still feel today.

In 1936 a fascist regime, inspired by the Hitlerian model then popular in Europe but supported by the British, was set up by general Metaxas, author of the Liberty Square massacre of 1936. The general took an extremely narrow view of such niceties as minority rights. Both Slav-speakers and Turkish-speakers, who then formed the majority of the valley's population, were mercilessly persecuted, their languages forbidden in public, banned in the school-yard. "The dictatorship was a disaster," sighs Mr. Tzanis, as if all this had happened only a generation ago. Indeed, in the Balkans, such is the recurring nature of disaster that every outrage seems to have happened a mere generation ago—that is to say, an hour ago—so intense is the memory of family, clan and national grievance. "Instead of solving anything, it created new tensions and greater problems. The same people who had welcomed the Greek army as liberators 25 years before began having second thoughts."

The German occupation, resistance to it, and the four-year civil war which followed had a devastating impact on the "natives," and violently deconstructed the Macedonian dream. The Greek Communist Party found itself leading both the resistance struggle and the ill-fated campaign to pry Greece out of the Western sphere of influence to which it had been assigned by Churchill and Stalin at Yalta. "During the civil war, the natives leaned toward autonomy, and they found support with Tito, who had designs on the region. Cooperation between the Greek guerrillas and Tito's Yugoslavia was a fact. But let's go back a bit: during the occupation, if you wanted to fight the Germans, you had to follow the Communist Party. There was no one else. Many in our area who joined were for autonomy for the region, but most of the others were drawn to the Party for ideological reasons. The 'autonomists' were a minority."

"Look, the CP never had a clear position on this issue. There were both autonomists and Greek nationalists in the ranks. Of course, the Comintern claimed that Macedonia was inhabited by a distinct national entity. But the Greek communists later rejected this position, and declared that there is no such national minority in the region, which I agree with. But I can't deny there are racial differences here. If people feel a part of a national minority, I can't stop them from believing it. There's nothing wrong or strange about someone having a national consciousness."

There is a feeling in Greece, a feeling so persuasive that it could be regarded as an obsession, that foreign powers are tinkering with the country's destiny. Such an attitude is convenient in that it diverts attention from the tragic folly of the country's recent career as a regional mini-imperialist. But it is also well founded in sordid fact, which cannot be explained away only by the ease with which outsiders have recruited eager local henchmen to carry out their plans. So, despite the war of words between Greece and the Former Yugoslav Republic of Macedonia, the situation remained relatively calm, explains Mr. Tzanis, until one day in August, 1992, when the United States Consul General in Salonica visited Aridea to meet with the leaders of the autonomist organization known as MAKIVE, the Macedonian Movement for Balkan Prosperity. "One thing's sure," he bristles, showing me the front page of his newspaper with a photograph of the official. "These guys are not interested in minority rights. They were here for other reasons. The Americans are trying to keep old wounds open, trying to create situations they can use later, if they decide to redraw our borders for instance. The U.S. won't hesitate to do this, if for some reason Greece doesn't go along with its long-range plans."

I take my leave of the communist newspaperman and stroll down to the town hall, which overlooks a deserted, weed-grown public square. Within five minutes Dimitris Papadimitriou drives up in a dented blue Volkswagen which, on closer inspection, appears to be held together with wire and ducting tape. As we rattle out of town toward his home in the nearby village of Tsakoni, he apologizes preemptively for his wife's absence. She's off in Athens visiting her family. "My wife's Greek," he continues, casually. "Me, I'm Macedonian." Not the kind of remark I've been accustomed to in my travels in this part of Greece, where the M-word is never used to describe Slav-speakers unless a high degree of mutual confidence has been established and only then in the privacy of whispers. For though Greek political life displays a rough-and-tumble, democratic openness, it has retained more than fragments of an older, authoritarian core, a sacred, jealously guarded latently iron-fisted consensus over what may and what may not be said. This sensitivity is well founded. The names of places, people and events are crucial to understanding not only the history of Macedonia itself but the way in which the protagonists have depicted it: the language of power which defines; the language of powerlessness which struggles toward self-definition.

This is Mr. Papadimitriou's story, which begins as we rattle down a country road through fruit orchards. We are in prime peach country, and my host is president of the local fruit growers' co-op. The car pulls up in front of a handsome neo-Macedonian farmhouse complete with a pair of glossy cats frolicking in the flower bed. Here, explains the robust 61 year-old with the broad face and blue-gray eyes who speaks Greek with a discernible accent, there are the "natives," the Slav-speaking Macedonians, and there are the "refugees," the people who came from Asia Minor in 1923. "Me? I was born right here in Tzakoni and I'm as native as they come. And when we say 'native', we mean someone whose mother tongue is not Greek."

But isn't Macedonia really Greece? I venture, essaying the gambit of false naïveté. He answers with a guffaw. "That one's for the school books! When the Turks left in 1924, maybe ten percent of the people here were Greeks. Us, our nationality is Macedonian. We have our own culture, our own language, both of which are Slavic. Before 1912 Macedonia was a single entity under Turkish rule. National boundaries were only drawn later. But they were the result of war, and of back-room deals. They had nothing to do with natural boundaries. There should have been no borders. Macedonia should have remained a single country."

The deeper I penetrated into the south Balkans, the more the tragically failed Ilinden revolt became a touchstone, a sacred marker, a litmus test marking some furtive yet irreducible national consciousness which predates the conventionally accepted ethnogenesis by the agency of Tito's outstretched finger energizing the amorphous mass. "The uprising was for an independent Macedonian state," he rushes to assure me, pausing to down a mouthful of *raki*, the Balkan social lubricant which can also function as a conscience-dulling incendiary liquid. "The revolutionaries had the same aims and desires we do today..." adding quickly: "Of course, we don't intend to pursue our aims in the same way. So, as I was saying, when the Macedonians revolted, the Greeks and the Bulgars reacted with hostility. Each country really wanted Macedonia for itself. The revolutionaries had to face not only the Turks, but the Greeks and the Bulgars too."

The Greeks—and particularly the militant Archbishop of Kastoria, Karavangelis Germanos—collaborated openly with the Ottomans, says Mr. Papadimitriou, lips curling as if he were uttering the Devil's name. "Some of our Macedonian fighters were betrayed by Greece to the Turks. It was only the beginning. Since then, they've done everything in their power to wipe us out."

Perhaps it's the *raki*, perhaps the painful narrative. Mr. Papadimitriou's voice is crackling with emotion, like the hum produced by high-voltage power lines, more felt than audible. Perhaps my months of Balkan travel had attuned me to these inaudible frequencies. "As a people, we don't even know our own history. What I know I learned from listening to the elders, the ones who never spoke Greek, only the language we still speak today. It was hard to learn. At first, even they didn't want to talk. We had become a second-class people, a people without a history, without a culture. The Greeks! They destroyed our churches and schools, they wiped out every trace of Cyrillic, they stole our holy icons. They wanted to get rid of us because they wanted our land. And they took it. Everything that wasn't Greek, they destroyed."

The charges are grave indeed. But evidence supporting Mr. Papadimitriou exists, buried deep in Greek state archives. Official policy, since the integration into the modern Greek State of the region called Macedonia, has been to deny the existence of the Slav-Macedonians as a distinct people, separate from the Greeks. But lingering just below the bright, hard surface of the discourse of authority is an ill-concealed malaise. In 1925, the country's education ministry prepared a primary school reader in Slav-Macedonian entitled *Abecedar* for submission to the League of Nations. The book was to be held up as proof that the Macedonian Slavic tongue was neither Bulgarian nor Serbian, but a distinct language protected and encouraged by the State. On the delegation's return from Geneva, the *Abecedar* was confiscated and destroyed.[138] Two years later, by government decree, all Slavonic church icons were repainted with Greek names. Why had it become necessary to eradicate that which did not exist?

"They still claim there's no such thing as a Macedonian people," he says, topping up his tumbler with *raki*. "The Bulgarians say we're Bulgars; the Greeks used to claim we're Greeks. And now they call us Skopjians! A few weeks ago I met an old man in a village not far from here. He was 92; he saw what happened as a kid. The Greeks came, and hanged our priests upside down over fires of cattle-dung. That's the reason 66,000 people left as 'Bulgars' after the Treaty of Neuilly between Greece and Bulgaria, right after the First World War."

In the southern Balkans in this, the final decade of a century of identitarian blood, national strife, struggle for supranational domination and the wildest extremes of religious and ethnic politics, no one dare speak for a revision of frontiers, even were such a revision to accommodate better a new reality. Not the aggrieved Albanians of Kosova or western Macedonia, not the frustrated Macedonians, not the Bulgarians who steadfastly refuse to recognize a Macedonian nation, not the Greeks who glaze longingly toward their unredeemed brethren in Northern Epirus. In a chorus of naive and innocent unanimity, they sing their adoration of the status quo, even as that self-same status quo has undergone a wrenching revision a scant few hundred kilometers north. Populations violently shifted, sacrosanct borders ripped up, mass atrocities perpetrated. But, all add in whispers, our adversaries are plotting against us, the Great Powers are scheming, we are being betrayed.

"Even though we accept the situation as it is," says Mr. Papadimitriou, "we're fighting for equal rights for all. We want our former political refugees, most of whom are dispersed throughout the countries of the former Soviet Union, to be free to return. We want to be able to dance our dances and sing our songs without fear of persecution; we want to set up cultural clubs so we can develop our traditions. And we want title to our land. The refugees that came here in 1924 have title, but not us, the natives. Without our title, we have no access to European Union development program funds."

Critics say that the Americans are either supporting or using your movement to destabilize Greece, I counter, remembering my conversation of the morning. Mr. Papadimitriou bristles, and from a tattered manila folder whips out a short letter signed by an official from the US Consulate in Salonica thanking him for information received on his recent visit. "This is US moral support? Look, at least someone is paying attention to us. But the Americans can't solve our problems; that's up to the Greeks."

NOWHERE IS THE LAMENT for lost land, tightly bound up with the hair-trigger issue of political refugees so suffused with longing as in the Macedonian city of Bitola. Here, a few kilometers from the frontier with Greece, in clear view of the mountains whose southern slopes loom over the Moglana valley, and of the forested cliffs of Mount Grammos which ring the Greek provincial town of Florina, a group of angry men gaze south in longing and frustration at the land that once was theirs.

Bitola is another of those south Balkan cities that enjoyed a brief flowering as a cultured, Europeanized enclave during the last years of Ottoman rule: a miniature Paris, a tiny London, a microscopic Vienna. Architectural relics of the fervid decade before the Balkan Wars when the town, then called Monastir, was known as "the city of the Consulates," line the main street. On the outskirts, surrounded by well-manicured parks, stands the former Ottoman military academy whose most illustrious alumnus was Atatürk, and in the city center loom two elegant mosques. Bitola was Salonica *en petit*, where French was the language of diplomacy, Greek the lingua franca of commerce and culture, Aroumani the language of trans-Balkan trade, Turkish the medium of administration and military power, while Albanian and Bulgaro-Macedonian were the half-hidden tongues of national dreams. As garrison of the multinational force set up by the International Community to keep Macedonia's warring factions from each other's throats, its streets, cabarets and whorehouses also echoed with the guttural dipthongs of Austro-Hungarian German and the thick-necked vowels of Russian.

[The Mürzteg reforms, instituted by the Double Empire and Russia in October 1903 in the aftermath of Ilinden provided that Russian and Austrian civil agents accompany the Turkish inspector general on his tours and report on conditions. The Ottoman gendarmerie was to be reorganized, placed under the command of a foreign general and staffed by foreign officers. When order was restored, new administrative districts would be drawn up, along ethnic lines. Predictably, propaganda and violence soared instead as each side redoubled its efforts to improve its position.[139] Of course, any resemblance between the Mürzteg program and a Bosnian peace agreement living or dead is purely coincidental.]

Today Bitola's picturesque past has a somber patina. The warren of alleys and laneways clustered around the fast-flowing brook that bisects the town has been restored, and baptized the Montmartre of the Balkans. But the fine old mosques have fallen into disuse, and to the east the coal-fired power station pumps thick smoke into the atmosphere, giving the air a sulfurous bite. In the drafty, echoing café of the Hotel Epinal, a dank and mournful hulk more reminiscent of a morgue of memory and hope than a place of the living, I listen as a knot of bitter men pour out their grievances. Their names are Alexei, Simon and George. They speak a mixture of broken Greek and Macedonian.

The men are sons of combatants in the Greek Democratic Army, the Communist-led guerrilla force that for four years held the Greek national army and its British and US advisors at bay in the rocky, forested mountains to the south. Today they are full-time soldiers in the great international army of the dispossessed. From 1941 to 1949, their fathers fought alongside Greeks, Turks and Vlachs, driven by the dream of equality within the Greek state. They had the most to lose; and they lost everything.

Acting on orders from the Comintern, whose strategic turnabouts were legendary, the Greek Communist Party recognized a distinct Macedonian national identity in 1935. While it later retreated from a position that proved a political hard sell among Greek workers, it continued to agitate for full rights for the Macedonian minority whose members, say the men, joined the Party for patriotic reasons, and fought for a redress of wrongs. "Since 1913, they've stolen our names, our land, our language." 'They' are the Greeks.

History, like a mosquito in a dark room, has a nagging, whining presence; it unerringly seeks out the patch of exposed flesh where blood flows closest to the surface. In 1904, the first Ottoman census to be carried out according to European standards listed 648,000 Patriarchists and 557,000 Exarchists, which Greek exegetes rush to identify as Greeks and Bulgars. Not so. Many of the Patriarchists were Slav-speakers, probably—though unprovably—Macedonians. The census, devised by the able and intelligent Turkish administrator Hilmi Pasha, revealed that 54.2% of the Macedonian population was Muslim, presumably speakers of Turkish and Albanian, though not necessarily; some Greeks and Macedonians had also converted to Islam. And while 30.8% of the population was in fact Bulgarian-speaking, a mere 10.5% spoke Greek. When the Greeks marched north into Macedonia, their goal was to "liberate" slightly more than ten percent of the population.[140]

"We're not a minority," the men insist, with the anger born of futility, the kind of anger that creates despair—and desperation. "We're the real natives, the sons of the soil. We've always been there. What we would like to know is why we can't return to our home villages, why our kids can't learn Macedonian in Greek schools, why we can't hear our language in church. We fought the Turks in 1821, and in the Balkan Wars, we fought in the Asia Minor campaign, in the Resistance against the Germans, we fought in the Civil War against the monarchy. The men who led us are living comfortably, and we're still waiting," says George Volchevsky in passable Greek, brandishing his open palm in the direction of the peeling walls and the fly-specked windows. And as he speaks his eyes flash with the white heat of indignation. Heads nod around the table.

"When I was 6 years old, in 1948 it was, we were taken away. The National Army was closing in on our village, Bouf is its name—you can almost see it from here... I remember the guns firing. I was in kindergarten, just learning Greek. The Democratic Army ordered families to send their young children north, for their own safety. That was when Queen Frederika, the German, was rounding up Macedonian kids and sending them off to prison camps in the Aegean islands to make Greeks out of them."

Alexei, eldest of the three, was 16 at the time. He, like many of his countrymen, joined the Communists to free Macedonia. The reasons for the Party's initial success, and its ultimate failure, were simple enough: it recruited Macedonians to fight for their national rights. "Repression made communists out of all of us. I remember how the gendarmes used to listen at our front doors to find out what language we were speaking at home. Get this straight. For us it was never a civil war. For us, it was a war of liberation. A fight against Greek fascism."

Bitterness, anger, frustration and resentment have come together here in this quiet, dusty town in southern Macedonia to form a purulent abscess which time, the enemy of reconciliation in the Balkans, will not absorb. Predictably, George, Alexei and Simon curse the Greek government for its draconian policy of national purification. Perhaps not surprisingly, they accuse the ex-USSR and its socialist minions of betrayal. The Yalta agreement sent the Macedonian people into war in full knowledge that their revolution would fail, they insist. "Their intention was to break us, disperse us, to divert attention away from the socialist countries."

Before he died, Markos Vafiadis, the charismatic guerrilla leader of the Democratic Army, admitted that his forces had lost the war, but won Macedonia. Markos, say George, Simon and Alexei, turned over his most faithful, devoted supporters, like Salomé presenting the severed head of Saint

John the Baptist to Herod, to the Greek nationalist cause. "He delivered the Macedonians to the Greek state, to its policy of extermination."

TWO EVENINGS LATER, on the Greek side of the border, in a Florina café which would not have been out of place on Salonica's swish Tsimiski Street, I encounter the younger generation of Macedonian activists, two men in their late-thirties. One, Pavlos, is an architect; the other, Pandelis, is a physician. Both are founding members of MAKIVE; both are well-dressed, relaxed, educated, articulate. Their message is one of realism and accommodation which suggest that the bitterness of Mr. Papadimitriou, and the anger of the three men in Bitola, must be tempered with recognition of brutal fact.

Eighty years of occupation have produced results for Greece, they explain, conceding that a 'Macedonian' consciousness simply did not exist 200 years ago. For those Macedonians who have been assimilated into the Greek majority through the school system, it is too late. Politically, the Macedonian minority is itself heterogeneous in the extreme. A significant portion is conscious of its Macedonian identity but conceals it for reasons of political or economic advancement. Another, smaller group has migrated to the opposite end of the spectrum to become super-Greeks and spies for the Greek secret police. A growing cohort, one which did not even exist as recently as ten years ago, is becoming restive at being defined negatively as Greek citizens who are not Greeks, while others are fully aware of their distinct cultural identity and seek, even at some risk to their professional lives, to affirm it. "As a movement, we avoid using terms like 'ethnic'. Instead of calling ourselves a nation, which leads to nationalism, we prefer to define ourselves as a different culture."

Ultimately, insist Pavlos and Pandelis, the region's past woes and contemporary tensions must be laid squarely at the feet of the greater nationalism: that of Greece. Like every other state in the Balkans, Greece is a new country, their argument runs. A sense of national consciousness where none existed before had to be created to maintain internal cohesion and facilitate control. Alas, throughout the country but particularly in the north, lived national, ethnic or religious groups which had to be either eliminated or incorporated into the national structure, made a part of the new national ideal, made to serve the national myth. The Vlachs and the Arvanites—the Albanian Christians who migrated south after the Ottoman conquest of Albania—both found themselves forcibly absorbed into the modern Greek state where they subsist today as folkloric remnants.

"The heart of the question," they say, "is the need to establish ethnic myths, and to do this, you have to go back in history, to ancient Greek civilization. By now, you would have thought a modern society would find contemporary arguments, would have drawn on the presence of its minorities. But they have done exactly the opposite. When you get right down to it, the Greeks are the ones with the identity problem."

MAKIVE's detractors label the movement as an agent of Skopje, a stalking horse for eventual Macedonian territorial claims on Greece's northernmost provinces, a mask for growling irredentism, a U.S. front. As a result, people like Pavlos and Pandelis are concerned to depict their organization as a strictly cultural one. "There is nationalism in Macedonia, the newly created republic," they admit. But the Yugoslav system, for all its failings, helped overcome the worst excesses, of the kind that did happen in Greece. People there accept, in their majority, the idea of a multi-ethnic community."

Greek rejection of Macedonia's use of the name as usurpation of an identity dating back to Alexander the Great has served as a mask for Greece's refusal to recognize its own Macedonian minority, they believe. "If Greece recognizes Macedonia as such, and normalizes relations, Greek nationalists will lose their grip, and Macedonia will develop. If the nationalists win out, economic relations may resume but discrimination will not end. Our generation can play a decisive role in bringing the two countries together." It all seemed reasonable, a clear-headed assessment by two moderate, well-educated, articulate men. Too reasonable, I find myself thinking as I hurried through the silent, chilly streets back to my hotel. The illusion, in which I had become a willing participant, dissipated when the phone rang the next morning at seven o'clock.

"Kostas here, Kostas Gotsis," rasped the voice. "I'll pick you up in a half hour. Wait for me at the corner. You're coming with me, to visit my village." After a bracing breakfast of the peppery tripe soup called *patsas*, washed down by an abrasive wine that seemed perfectly in tune with Mr. Gotsis' pugnacious mood, we are picking our way through the pot-holed streets of Bouf, our breath misting in the air. Today the village is called Akritas, a Greek word meaning "border guard;" the Macedonian frontier is only a few kilometers distant over the mountain barrier. This is the birthplace of George Volchevsky, the angry man I had met in Bitola two days before.

Call it Bouf or call it Akritas, the place exudes a bleakness and desolation I have never before encountered in Greece. The grand two-story houses of the wealthy Macedonian stock-raising and farming families who once flourished here lie in ruins, exposed to the merciless mountain winter. The school, once an elegant Balkan baroque structure, stands forlorn, windows shattered, weeds sprouting in the yard; a tattered Greek flag droops in the calm of this frosty May morning. Their faces masks of hostility and studied indifference, a knot of old men stare at us as we walk across the square. In front of a half-ruined hovel an old woman clad in black feeds her chickens.

This sad place is also Mr. Gotsis' home town. He has brought me here to certify the obliteration of the Macedonians. Bouf's population was once 3,000; now it has collapsed to just over 100. Where Pavlos and Pandelis spoke of hope, his voice breathes rancor and despair. "Half the people who live here are government agents," he rasps in a guttural voice, looking from side to side, his eyes narrowed to slits. "If we stay here much longer, the police will show up and start asking us questions."

We had driven up through a Macedonian landscape of bare poplars, fresh green pastures with an icing of frost, and rolling hills which give way to rocky slopes and looming crags, and into the scrub-clad hills where, fifty years before, some of the most bitter battles of the Greek Civil War had raged. It had been the classic confrontation of peasants equipped with small arms and mortars waging hit-and-run warfare against an American-trained army using heavy artillery and aircraft. Many Slav-Macedonians had joined the conflict in the belief that they were creating a country. They had suffered the indignity of being transformed over two decades into a minority in their own lands; their language had been forcibly suppressed, mass deportations disguised as voluntary departures had taken place. Cynically, the Communists—argue embittered men like Mr. Gotsis—promised to change all that. Were they entirely cynical? Quickly Macedonian schools were opened, the old tongue re-emerged to be spoken with pride in the high valleys and lowland villages. Some units of the Greek Democratic Army—thus did the Communists rather optimistically describe their ragtag forces—functioned almost entirely in Macedonian. What had given them their strength became their undoing. The Communist leadership, fighting a class war against what it described, not without some accuracy, as Monarcho-fascism and imperialism, had tried to harness the hunger of the Macedonians for national justice to the Great Cause of Proletarian Internationalism. But in the mountains of Macedonia, the formula was quickly stood on its head by the stubborn "natives" who were less concerned with the plight of the Greek working class than with their own collective survival and affirmation as a people.

Such is the tale that Mr. Gotsis relates in rapid-fire bursts, his rough-hewn hands chopping the air like woodworking tools, as we tramp up the steep village lanes. At an open gateway he pauses to engage an elderly resident in conversation. They speak Makedonski, but the man is in no mood to chat. His answers come in snorts and brusque nods. No sign of traditional village hospitality here. "I told you," Mr. Gotsis says, turning to me. "Look what they've done to us. How they've driven us down, made us disappear."

The 50-year old carpenter calls himself a survivor of the bitter conflict that he defines as a war to eliminate the Macedonians. His father, a guerrilla fighter in the Communist forces, was killed in a skirmish with the Greek national army in 1948, then tried and sentenced to death posthumously for treason in 1952; the family's property was seized. "Don't let anyone ever tell you these people left here voluntarily," he rasps, his voice ragged with anger. "They were driven out like animals, robbed of their land."

In 1983, the first socialist government led by Andreas Papandreou brought in legislation granting general amnesty to all participants in the Civil War. Long-exiled Greeks returned from Poland, Romania, from as far away as Tashkent. All except Macedonians, to whom the amnesty law, which referred to 'Greeks by genus', pointedly did not apply. "When I tried to rehabilitate my father's memory, the authorities told me he wasn't a Greek; they couldn't do a thing. Look, they discriminate against us even when we're dead!"

Later that day, as I wait in the Florina—make that Lerin— bus station for the Salonica express, the voices I hear around me are speaking not Greek, but Macedonian. Openly, naturally. This is more than a vanishing handful of non-people who whisper shamefully a degraded sub-language. But the mystery subsists. How many such people live today within Greece's borders? Do they constitute a national minority? The last census figures, dating from 1951, listed 41,000 inhabitants throughout Greece as Slav-speakers. A 1992 US State Department Country Report estimated the number to be between 10,000 and 50,000. At the other end of the scale, the Skopje government suggests that as many as 270,000 inhabitants of Greek, or Aegean, Macedonia are members of the Slav-speaking minority.[141] My unscientific hunch is that the Skopje estimates are closer to what, for want of a better word, we call "the truth."

Nikos Mertzos is a living icon of Greco-Macedonian indefatigability from whose prolific pen flows a steady stream of newspaper and magazine articles, polemics and books on the Macedonian Question. Mr. Mertzos, a brusque, florid man of 58 who sports a handlebar mustache of heroic proportions, edits a Salonica monthly entitled *Macedonian Life*, the influence of which extends well beyond the geographic confines of Greek Macedonia.

One clammy evening in November I make my way to his office, just a few blocks from the Macedonian Struggle Museum. Let no one accuse Mr. Mertzos of lack of directness. Journalists, for him, are clearly a perpetual pain the lower part of the anatomy and of this he hastens to apprise me, adding that he is also suffering from an intestinal disorder. But as he warms to the subject, his diffidence rapidly metamorphoses into the combativeness for which he has won a reputation. For all his pugnaciousness, Mr. Mertzos possesses an inestimable asset. Being himself the son of Greek-speaking Vlachs from the mountain town of Neveska, one of the centers of the Ilinden rising, he has acute, bred in the bone knowledge of the terrain.

Slav-speaking Macedonia has, for nearly two centuries, been an apple of discord, he blusters. And yet, at no time was the existence of such a thing as the "Macedonian nation" ever raised. Between the two wars, the USSR created a new model, that of a Balkan Federation, which would have been a kind of Soviet Union in miniature. It was then that the Slav-Macedonians were first claimed to be a distinct nationality. During World War II, Bulgaria, which had entered the war on the side of the Axis powers, administratively transformed eastern Macedonia and Thrace, as well as a wide strip running from Skopje to the Greek border, into Bulgaria.

When this happened, asserts Mr. Mertzos, the local population welcomed the Bulgarian troops as liberators. Shortly thereafter Tito, as head of the Yugoslav resistance movement, promised to recognize a Macedonian nation and to establish a Macedonian republic. Present at the ceremony was a young officer named Kiro Gligorov. Tito's move, which Mr. Mertzos describes as a master stroke, had three aims: to split the Slav-speaking population away from Bulgaria and at the same time to wipe away the stain of collaboration; to gain a chunk of territory from Serbia; and, most important of all, to use the term 'Macedonia' as a pretext to embrace not only Slav Macedonia, but also Greek Macedonia, including Salonica and Mount Olympus.

Ever the staunch Cold Warrior, Mr. Mertzos, in his devotion to the Greek cause, appears more Orthodox than the Patriarch. Thus is Tito's role in the Greek civil war reduced to a pretext for a takeover of Macedonia. Only Stalin's intervention, he thunders in high indignation, stopped the Greek civil war, and forced Tito to turn to the West. Greece, in return, had no choice but to hold its tongue when the Republic of Macedonia was formed as part of newly liberated Yugoslavia.

"But what does that make us?" he asks, eyebrows arching in the rhetoric of Greek bodily oratory. "I say I'm a Greek Macedonian. Why are they trying to rob me of my identity. Why don't they call themselves Slav Macedonians and be done with it? Why insist on this monopoly?"

To be fair to Mr. Mertzos, he draws his arguments from the present and the recent past, in sharp contrast to the Athenian policy makers who insist on appropriating the less-than-perfectly democratic Alexander the Great in proving their point to the world. "Alexander doesn't mean a thing," he says, waving his hand as if to drive away a stubborn fly. "But if you say I'm not a Macedonian because I'm a Greek, I get angry. Really angry." It was a plea, a *cri de coeur*, a matter of pride and self-respect, I was to hear repeatedly from friends and acquaintances in Salonica. A mephistophelian cocktail of disbelief, innocence, resignation and sudden indignation is what it was.

My host's round face has turned several shades of crimson and his handlebar mustache has begun to quiver. After a few moments of silence, he returns to a calmer mode. "The situation is extremely fluid today," he continues. "You have two or three generations who have grown up having the idea that they are 'Macedonians' drummed into them. Now, if such a person is not a Macedonian, what is he? In Skopje, they've successfully Macedonized the Bulgarian cultural heritage. They want psychological security, they say? Fine, call yourselves Macedonians—we're all related anyway—but don't do it at Greece's expense."

Not the least of Mr. Mertzos' virtues is his insistence on saying aloud what others only dare to whisper. I found a certain cogency in his stridency, a seductive internal ideological cohesiveness where I had believed only chaos reigned. Where former leftists praise accommodation with their Skopjian neighbors, Mr. Mertzos has been ringing alarm bells to which few are disposed to listen. "Today's situation in the Balkans is essentially a replay of what happened before both World Wars," he says. "Today, Germany's zone of influence in central Europe coincides roughly with Hitler's dream of a Great Reich."

Does that mean war in the Balkans? I venture. "It does," he states, with a mixture of finality and resignation. "The criminal ignorance of Greek politicians has isolated us from Europe; today, our leadership is playing the American game. Don't get me wrong, my whole life has been devoted to supporting the United States in its fight against Communism. We owe them our gratitude. But then they come and do this to us! And I predicted all of it four years ago. The Americans have changed their strategy in the Balkans. They want to control a wide corridor running from the Adriatic through to

Kazakhstan: that's their New World Order. But no matter what happens, Hellenism will survive."

Evangelos Kofos, whom I met several days later, is an equally complex figure: a scholar whose job it is to make an emotionally-charged, ambiguous situation understandable in such a way that it lends credence to the government position. Mr. Kofos, a well-read and charming man, is a spin-doctor who has argued that the last vestiges of the Slav minority departed the country en masse with the end of the Civil War.[142] As resident academic in the employ of the Greek Foreign Ministry, he wears the double hat of expert analyst and partisan with a certain uneasy grace and a wry, understated sense of humor.

When he tells me, between bites of a cheese sandwich in a fast-food shop across from the University of Salonica where he's attending an academic symposium, that he doubts the Greek government would allow former Greek refugees to return to their homes, I hear the dulcet voice of the State whispering like a serpent. These refugees, he explains, are mostly the children evacuated in 1948 by the Communists who were then brain-washed to instill in them a new Macedonian sensibility, change their characters and inculcate a sense of revenge. "Not surprisingly, the Greek government has pursued a defensive policy. One part of such a policy is to refuse repatriation to such people."

Well enough. But the evidence of my eyes tells me that the policy stands morally doomed for two reasons. It is inapplicable and it is unjust.

Greece, for all the puissant assimilative apparatus it wields, for all the historical attraction of a dominant language and culture, has not been able to break the resistance of a people whose stubbornness seems of a piece with the gnarled trees and rocks of their mountains. But who will speak for the "native" Macedonians? The Hellenized politicians and functionaries of the official establishment, the Greek-educated moderates who rely on a fine balance of resentment and realism to restore lost cultural pride, or the bitter, hard-bitten men on both sides of the frontier—and tomorrow, their sons and daughters—who dream only of an ideal Macedonia which never existed and probably never will?

AT ALL TIMES AND IN ALL PLACES, nothing is more ephemeral than the status quo, nothing more resembles a sand castle at the edge of a tidal zone than stability, nothing is more elusive of outside definition than human self-awareness, nothing more egregiously fallible and self-serving than the prognostications of the soothsayers, cartomancers, political scientists and economists. In the mountains and valleys of the southern Balkans, the process of constructing national consciousness is still in full operation. Greece, now standing poised at the threshold of a European supra-identity, magnanimously posits its own assertive national identity as the invisible field against which lesser nationalisms wriggle, quaint in their anachronistic simple-mindedness. Our age, Athens argues, the better to divert attention from its own ethno-national claims, is a global one. The national project of the Macedonians is thus no better than a throwback to a bygone era of tribalism and blood feuds. A bright, post-national era beckons.

But the shift has been too rapid, too deceptively simple to disguise the intentions of its promoters. By the act of its own self-identification, the World Culture has attempted to obliterate the past; by sacrificing history on the altar of simultaneity, it has liberated the chthonic power of myth. Surprised once already by what they described as the virulence of nationalism in the Balkans, the cosmopolitanists who drape themselves in the cloak of inevitability are committing that most classic of antique Greek failings: *hubris*. Attributing to others their own worst offenses.

SALONICA IN WINTER is a clammy, gelid place. Sidewalk cafés fold their chairs and umbrellas, people hurry about their business; as Christmas approaches bands of Gypsy musicians take to the streets, drums and tambourines throbbing and rattling, clarinets skirling; and when the Vardari whips down through the mountain passes out of Macedonia, the few hardy strollers along the corniche lean into the wind, clutching hats, eyes watering.

Once more cosmopolitan than Sarajevo, once the economic heart of the entire Balkan peninsula, the city has become an outpost of self-assertive insecurity. Where once Bulgarians, Jews, Turks, and Albanians lived side-by-side with Greeks, they have now vanished utterly, bulldozed into an amorphous past. Salonica's haste to remake itself—better, the haste of its Greek masters to remake it in their image in 1913—has cut it off from the Macedonian hinterland from which it drew its wealth. Faraway sounds and rumors seem to dissolve in the pollution of its traffic-choked streets, the distant clamor of identitarian awakening, the whine of tension on the frontier...little can shake the city from its combination of single-minded commercialism, from the blissful torpor of ignorance and self-congratulation.

Salonica is a city which has given up waiting for the Barbarians who would have been, as Cavafy—who knew history—says, a certain solution. Today's

Barbarians are clever people. Already they are within the walls; it is they who have decreed the banishment of memory, obliterated the past, condemned the citizens to a senseless, connectionless real-time present.

They will, it may confidently be predicted, fail. The memory of things and events inhabits the paving stones, the walls of ruined mosques, the smoke-stained surfaces of ancient frescos, the cobblestones and the place-names of the invisible map, inaccessible to the carbon dating of archeologists, as perennial as marble, as indestructible as DNA. The icon contains within it the saint. Virtuality, for all its efforts, can neither supplant nor suppress the world of the senses. The poet Odysseus Elytis' small, great world. Against the tyranny of images, new iconoclasts plot.

As I depart Salonica Terminus for Athens, at the old station the Balkan Express is always just pulling in; the last train of Jewish deportees is always just pulling out. Barely visible on the horizon, assimilated Vlachs gesticulate, their lips forming the syllables of the ancient Latin tongue; Shqiptars and Kosovars in the garb of Bektashi dervishes dream and whisper of Great Albania. Macedonians with grave faces sing and dance the silent words of a forbidden tongue that waits, yearning for its home, across the mountain frontier. The tourists have decamped. The whores of Vardar Square are sleeping. Steely dawn is creeping across the Balkans.

REFERENCES

Foreword

1. **Chossudovsky, Michel**, *La Bosnie sous administration occidentale*, Le Monde Diplomatique, avril 1996; p. 12
2. **Said, Edward**, *Culture and Imperialism*; New York, Vintage Books, 1994; p. 314

Chapter 1: City of Shadows

3. **Levi, Sami**, *Souvenir du Voyage de S. M. I. le Sultan Mehmet V à Salonique*, Salonique, 1911.
4. **Stavrianos, L. S.**, *The Balkans 1815-1914*, New York, Holt, Rinehart and Winston, 1963; p. 107
5. **Lewis, Bernard**, *The Emergence of Modern Turkey*, London, Oxford University Press, 1961; p. 168
6. **Risal, P.**, *La ville convoitée: Salonique*, Paris, Perrin et Cie., 1914; p. 305-306
7. **Ibid.**, p. 312
8. **Lewis**, p. 203-204
9. **Risal**, p. 315-316
10. **Lewis**, p. 209
11. **Ibid.**
12. Quoted in **Lewis**, p. 214
13. **Autrement**, *Salonique, La "ville des Juifs" et le réveil des Balkans*, Paris, Éditions Autrement, 1992; p. 240-241
14. **Levi, Sami**, *Souvenir du Voyage de S. M. I. le Sultan Mehmet V à Salonique*, Salonique, 1911.
15. **Ibid.**
16. **Savinio, Alberto**, *The Departure of the Argonaut*, New York, Petersburg Press, 1986, n.p.

17. **A. Yerolympos**, *Urban Evolution of Thessaloniki*, Thessaloniki, 1994. (Occasional document)
18. **Autrement**, *Salonique. La "ville des Juifs" et le réveil des Balkans*, p. 240-241
19. **Stavrianos, L. S.**, *The Balkans 1815-1914*, p. 113
20. **Crawford Price, W. H.**, *The Balkan Cockpit. The Political and Military Story of the Balkan Wars in Macedonia*, London, T. Werner Laurie Ltd., n.d.; p. 104
21. **Ibid.**, p. 115
22. **Ibid.**, p. 114
23. **Ibid.**, p. 277
24. **Stavrianos, L. S.**, *The Balkans 1815-1914*, p. 123
25. **Autrement**, *Salonique. La "ville des Juifs" et le réveil des Balkans*, p. 256
26. **Savinio, Alberto**, *The Departure of the Argonaut*, New York, Petersburg Press, 1986
27. **Ibid.**
28. **Autrement**, *Salonique. La "ville des Juifs" et le réveil des Balkans*, p. 262-263

Chapter 2: Saints and Zealots

29. **Calasso, Roberto**, *The Marriage of Cadmus and Harmony*, Toronto, Vintage Canada, 1994; p. 342
30. **Sakellariou, M. B.**, Editor, *Macedonia, 4000 Years of Greek History and Civilization*, Athens, Ekdotiki Athenon, 1983; p. 205
31. **Bakirtzis, Ch.**, *The Basilica of Saint Demetrius*, Thessaloniki, Institute for Balkan Studies, 1988; p. 11-12
32. **Kyriakidis, Stilpon**, *Τρείς Διαλέξεις*, Θεσσαλονίκη, Εταιρεία Μακεδονικων Σπουδων, 1953; p. 17
33. **Kitromilidis, Paschalis M.**, *'Imagined Communities' and the Origins of the National Question in the Balkans*, in Martin Blinkhorn and Thanos Veremis, Editors. *Modern Greece: Nationalism & Nationality*, SAGE-ELIAMEP, Athens, 1990; p. 40
34. **Vasiliev, A. A.**, *History of the Byzantine Empire, 324-1453*, Madison, University of Wisconsin Press, 1958; p. 509

35. **Papadopoulos, Antonios M.**, *Ο Άγιος Δημήτριος εις την Ελληνικην και Βουλγάρικην Παράδοσιν*, Θεσσαλονίκη, Εκδόσεις Πουρνάρα, 1971; p. 78-80
36. **Eustathios of Thessaloniki**, *The Capture of Thessaloniki*. A translation with introduction and commentary by John R. Melville Jones, Canberra, 1988; p. 105, 113
37. **Vasiliev, A. A.**, *History of the Byzantine Empire*, p. 255
38. **Kazantzakis, Nikos**, *Report to Greco*, translated by P. E. Bien, New York, Simon and Schuster, 1965; p. 188
39. **Tafrali, O.**, *Thessalonique au quatorzième siècle siècle*, Paris, Librairie Paul Geuthner, 1913. [Reprint by the Institute for Balkan Studies, Archive of Historical Studies 3, Thessaloniki, 1993]; p. 123
40. **Vasiliev, A. A.**, *History of the Byzantine Empire*, p. 667
41. **Sakellariou, M. B.**, Ed., *Macedonia. 4000 Years of Greek History and Civilization*, p. 336
42. **Tafrali, O.**, *Thessalonique au quatorzième siècle siècle*, p. 185
43. **Kordatos, Yannis**, *Η Κομμούνα της Θεσσαλονίκης 1342-1349*, Αθήνα, 1975; p. 56
44. **Ibid.**, p. 57
45. **Tafrali, O.**, *Thessalonique au quatorzième siècle siècle*, p. 290

Chapter 3: To the Salonica Station

46. **Saint Paul**, *First Epistle to the Thessalonians,* 1:2, 14-16, King James II version, 4th edition; London, Trinitarian Bible Society, 1980
47. **Stavroulakis, Nicholas P.**, *Jewish Sites and Synagogues of Greece*, Athens, Talos Press, 1992; p.162
48. *Primavera en Salonico*, Sephardic folk songs. Lyrics edited and commentary by Xenofon Kokolis. Lyra Records, Athens/Thessaloniki, 1994. *"In spring in Salonica I found at Mazloum's café a dark-eyed lass singing and playing the lute..."*
49. **Stavroulakis**, p.163
50. **Autrement**, *Salonique, La "ville des Juifs" et le réveil des Balkans*, p. 52-53
51. **Scholem, Gershom**, *Sabbatai Sevi, the Mystical Messiah 1626-1676*, Princeton, Princeton University Press, 1973. Bollingen Series XCII; p. 7. Monumental in its erudition, sweeping in its intelligence and compassion, Scholem's biography of Sabbatai Sevi is an extraordi-

nary tale of an extraordinary man on which I have drawn extensively in telling the story of the false messiah.

52. **Eco, Umberto**, *La recherche de la langue parfaite dans la culture européene*, Traduit de l'Italien par Jean-Paul Manganaro, Paris, Édition du Seuil, 1994; p. 41-42, 45
53. **Scholem**, p. 20
54. **Ibid.**, p. 27
55. **Ibid.**, p. 44
56. **Ibid.**, p. xii
57. **Ibid.**, p. xi
58. **Ibid.**, p. 7
59. **Ibid.**, p. 123, 127
60. **Ibid.**, p. 161
61. **Ibid.**, p. 207
62. Quoted in **Scholem**, p. 207
63. **Ibid.**, p. 223, 237
64. **Ibid.**, pp. 397, 400-401
65. **Ibid.**, p. 403
66. **Ibid.**, p. 679
67. **Ibid.**, p. 689, 691
68. **Graetz, H.**, *History of the Jews*, Philadelphia, Jewish Publication Society of America, 1895; Vol. 5, p. 210
69. **Stavroulakis**, p. 168
70. *Encyclopaedia Judaica*, Jerusalem, Macmillan, 1971; Vol. 6, p. 148
71. **Scholem**, p. 836
72. **Graetz, H.**, *Popular History of the Jews*, New York, Hebrew Publishing Company, 1919; Vol. V, p. 231
73. **Stavroulakis**, p. 169
74. **Risal, P.**, *La ville convoitée: Salonique*, Paris, Perrin et Cie., 1914; vii
75. **Autrement**, p. 65
76. **Communauté israélite de Thessalonique**, *In Memoriam. Hommage aux victimes juives des nazis en Grèce*, Publié sous la direction de Michael Molho. Thessalonique, 1973; p. 72-73. My translation.
77. **Zafiris, Christos**, *Θεσσαλονίκης Τοπογραφία, Θεσσαλονίκη*, Παρατηρητης, 1990; p. 71

78. *In Memoriam*, p. 60-61
79. *In Memoriam*, p. 21
80. **Hilberg, Raul**, *The Destruction of the European Jews*, Holmes & Meier, New York, 1985; p. 694
81. *In Memoriam*, p. 86-87. My translation
82. **Hilberg**, p. 1042
83. **Ibid.**, p. 696-697
84. *In Memoriam*, p. 108-109
85. **Yagoel, Yomtov**, *Απομνημονεύματα*, Εισαγωγη-επιμέλεια Φραγκίσκη Αμπατζοπούλου.΄Ιδρυμα Ετς Αχάιμ-Παρατηρητης, Θεσσαλονίκη, 1993; p. 29
86. **Levi, Primo**, *Survival in Auschwitz: the Nazi Assault on Humanity*, Translated from the Italian by Stuart Woolf. New York, Collier, 1961; p. 72.

Chapter 4: A Divorce in Albania

87. **United Nations Development Program**, *Albania 1995*, Human Development Report. Tirana, Albania, 1995; p. 9
88. **Hall, Derek**, *Albania and the Albanians*, London, Pinter Reference, 1994; pp. 11, 191
89. **Ibid.**, p. 184
90. **Ibid.**, p. 42
91. **Skendi, Stavro**, *The Albanian National Awakening*, Princeton, Princeton University Press, 1967; pp. 9-10
92. **Hall**, p. 36
93. **Degrand, A.**, *Souvenirs de la Haute-Albanie*, Paris, Welter éditeur, 1901; p. 229
94. **Birge, John K.**, *The Bektashi Order of Dervishes*, London, 1937, p. 16
95. **Ibid.**, p. 213
96. **Ibid.**, p. 75
97. **Skendi, Stavro**, Ed., *Albania*, London, Atlantic Press, 1957; p. 306
98. Quoted in **Skendi, Stavro**, *The Albanian National Awakening*, p.345
99. **Ibid.**, p. 8
100. **Ibid.**, p. 21

101. **Skendi, Stavro**, *The Albanian National Awakening*, p.17-18
102. **Hall**, p. 43
103. **Gatsopoulos, Stavros Matt.**, *Μοσχόπολις*. Ιωάννινα, Εκδόσεις Ιδρύματος, Βορειοηπειρωτικων Σπουδων, 1979; p. 37

Chapter 5: The Kosova Flyer

104. **Borges, Jorge Luis**, *Labyrinths*, New York, New Directions, 1962; p. 196-197
105. **Hall**, p. 209
106. **Skendi, Stavro**, *The Albanian National Awakening*, p. 418
107. **Azem Shkreli**, *The Call of the Owl*, translated from the Albanian by John Hodgson, Prishtina, 1989; p. 62
108. **Jelavich, Charles and Barbara**, *The Establishment of the Balkan National States, 1804-1920*, Seattle, University of Washington Press, 1977; p. 200-201
109. **Ibid.**, p. 203
110. **Cubrilovic, Vasa**, *The Minority Problem in New Yugoslavia* in *Serbian Colonization and Ethnic Cleansing of Kosova, documents and evidence*, a publication of the Kosova Information Center, Prishtina, 1993; p. 77
111. **Cubrilovic, Vasa**, *The Expulsion of the Arnauts*, reprinted in *Serbian Colonization and Ethnic Cleansing of Kosova, documents and evidence*, a publication of the Kosova Information Center, Prishtina, 1993.
112. **Hall**, p. 211
113. **Ignatieff, Michael**, *Blood and Belonging, Journeys into the New Nationalism*, New York, Farrar, Strauss and Giroux, 1993; p. 5
114. **Ibid.**, p. 13

Chapter 6: The Balkan Quagmire

115. **Poulton, Hugh**, *Who are the Macedonians?,* Bloomington, Indiana University Press, 1995; p. 88. In November, 1926, Greek government decree N° 332 ruled that all Slavonic names of towns, villages, rivers and mountains must be replaced by Greek ones.
116. **Schevill, Ferdinand**, *The History of the Balkan Peninsula*, New York, Arno Press & The New York Times, 1971; p. 159

117. **Poulton**, p. 21
118. *Byzantine Frescoes from Yugoslav Churches*, Introduction by David Talbot Rice. A Mentor-UNESCO Art Book, New York, Mentor, 1963
119. *Macedonia. 4000 Years of Greek History and Civilization*, Athens, Ekdotike Athenon, 1983; p. 263
120. **Stammler, Heinrich**, *What is the National Character of the Macedonian Slavs*, Sofia, Union of the Macedonian Brotherhoods in Bulgaria, 1991; p. 6
121. **Crampton, Richard J.**, *Bulgaria, 1878-1918. A History*, New York, Columbia University Press, East European Monographs, 1983; p. 22
122. **Ibid.**, p. 81
123. **Perry, Duncan M.**, *The Politics of Terror. The Macedonian Liberation Movement 1893-1903*, Duke University Press, Durham and London, 1988; p. 38
124. **Ibid.**, p. 8
125. **Ibid.**, p. 14-15
126. **Crampton**, p. 81
127. **Ibid.**, p. 140, 158
128. **Perry**, p. 112
129. **Sherman, Laura Beth**, *Fires on the Mountain, The Macedonian Revolutionary Movement and the Kidnapping of Ellen Stone*, Columbia University Press, New York, 1980; p. 22
130. **Megas, Yannis**, *Οι Βαρκάρηδες της Θεσσαλονίκης. Η αναρχικη Βουλγάρικη ομάδα και οι βομβιστικες ενεργειες του 1903*, Αθήνα, Τροχαλια, 1994; p. 56
131. **Autrement**, p. 134-135
132. **Perry**, p. 120
133. **Ibid.**, p. 131
134. **Ibid.**, p. 124-135
135. **Poghirc, Cicerone**, *Romanisation linguistique et culturelle dans les Balkans, Survivances et évolution, in Les Aroumains*, Cahier N° 8, Centre d'étude des civilizations de l'Europe centrale et du sud-est; Paris, Publications Langues d'O, 1989; p. 44-45
136. *The Manifesto of Krushevo*, Skopje, Ogledalo, 1983; p. 25-26
137. **Bruck, Connie**, *The World According to George Soros*, in *The New Yorker*, January 23, 1995

Chapter 7: The Search for Macedonia

138. **Poulson**, p. 88

139. **Stavrianos, L. S.**, *The Balkans 1815-1914*, New York, Holt, Rinehart and Winston, 1963; p. 103-104

140. **Lithoxoou, Dimitris**, *Το Μακϵδονικο Ζήτημα και η συγκρότηση του Ελληνικου ϵθνικου μύθου* in *Ελληνικος Εθνικισμος Μακϵδονικο Ζήτημα*, Αθήνα, Κίνηση Αριστϵρων, 1992

141. *Denying Ethnic Identity: the Macedonians of Greece*, Human Rights Watch / Helsinki, New York, 1994; p. 12-13

142. **Kofos, Evangelos**, *National Heritage and National Identity in Nineteenth- and Twentieth Century Macedonia. in Modern Greece: Nationalism & Nationality*. SAGE-ELIAMEP, Athens, 1990; p. 128